A
WORLD
DESTROYED

A
WORLD
DESTROYED

THE ATOMIC BOMB
AND THE
GRAND ALLIANCE

MARTIN J. SHERWIN

ALFRED · A · KNOPF
NEW YORK
1975

THIS IS A BORZOI BOOK
PUBLISHED BY ALFRED A. KNOPF, INC.

Library of Congress Cataloging in Publication Data
Sherwin, Martin J.   A world destroyed.
   Bibliography: p.   Includes index.
   1. World War, 1939–1945–Diplomatic history.
   2. World War, 1939–1945–United States. 3. United
States–Foreign relations–1933–1945. 4. Atomic
bomb–History. I. Title.
D753.S48   1975   940.53′2   75–8213
ISBN 0-394-49794-5

Portions of this book were previously published in
The American Historical Review.
Grateful acknowledgment is made to Yale University Library for material from the Papers and Diaries of Henry L. Stimson; and to Holt, Rinehart & Winston, Inc. and the Estate of Robert Frost for the poems "U.S. 1946 King's X," "The Road Not Taken," "Fire and Ice," and "The Secret Sits" from *The Poetry of Robert Frost*, edited by Edward Connery Lathem. Copyright 1916, 1923, 1947, © 1969 by Holt, Rinehart & Winston, Inc. Copyright 1942, 1944, 1951 by Robert Frost. Copyright © 1970, 1975 by Lesley Frost Ballantine.

Manufactured in the United States of America

First Edition

Sponsored by:
Program on Science, Technology and Society and Peace Studies Program, Cornell University–1971–73

For
Mimi and Harold
Susan, Andrea and Alex

U.S. 1946 KING'S X

Having invented a new Holocaust,
And been the first with it to win a war,
How they make haste to cry with fingers crossed,
King's X—no fairs to use it any more!

—ROBERT FROST

CONTENTS

Foreword by Hans Bethe xi

Acknowledgments xv

INTRODUCTION *3*

I
THE SECRET SITS

1   THE END OF THE BEGINNING   *13*

2   SOLDIERS OUT OF UNIFORM   *40*

II
THE ROAD NOT TAKEN

3   THE ATOMIC BOMB AND THE POSTWAR WORLD   *67*

4   THE TWO POLICEMEN   *90*

5   A QUID PRO QUO   *115*

III
FIRE AND ICE

6   THE NEW PRESIDENT   *143*

7   PERSUADING RUSSIA TO PLAY BALL   *165*

8   THE BOMB, THE WAR, AND THE RUSSIANS   *193*

9   DIPLOMACY—AND DESTRUCTION   *220*

Notes   *241*

*On Primary Sources in the Field:
A Bibliographical Essay*   *273*

Appendices: Selected Documents   *281*

Index   *follows page 318*

FOREWORD

I spent the period from spring 1943 to a few months after the war in Los Alamos. In the spring and summer of 1945, whenever those in-the-know gathered out of earshot of those not-in-the-know, the conversation soon turned to the great and urgent questions: "How should the bomb be used?" and "How can it be used to ensure the peace?" By May 1945 the betting inside the "Tech Area" was no longer on *whether* there would be a nuclear explosion, but on its size. Work pressures eased a bit, and other concerns, suppressed for two years by the need for total concentration on scientific problems, came back with increasing force. Our early qualms—which had been overcome by reports that the Germans were seeking to develop a nuclear bomb—now revived, and we began to debate what and how much influence the bomb would have on national and international policy, and how we ourselves could affect those policies.

Many of us had been influenced directly or indirectly by Niels Bohr, the great Danish physicist. He argued that only international control of nuclear weapons could save the world from a nuclear arms race, and that such a race would imperil, not enhance, the security of the United States and Great Britain. Many other scientists, especially at the University of Chicago Metallurgical Laboratory, at the initiative of Leo Szilard, had come independently to the same conclusion.

In the summer and fall of 1945, U.S. atomic policy left us troubled and perplexed. Roosevelt, we thought, had been committed to a policy of international understanding and conciliation. The culmination of this policy was the formation of the United Nations which was to continue cooperation between the wartime allies (and neutrals) so as to prevent any recurrence of the state of affairs that had led to World War II. Truman's policy, however, appeared to have the opposite aim: to keep a monopoly of the atomic bomb in U.S. and British hands, and to use it as a strong trump card in tough political bargaining with the Soviet Union. Wasn't he failing to take into account that the Russians could presumably duplicate our development and have

their own bomb within a few years? Had Truman indeed reversed Roosevelt's policy of conciliation?

Martin Sherwin's book shows that there was in fact no major
change of policy—that, on the contrary, Roosevelt himself, with
Churchill, had decided that the bomb should remain an Anglo-
American monopoly, and that this was necessary and desirable
in order to keep Britain a strong U.S. ally. France and the Soviet
Union were to be excluded from access to the weapon—even
though it was apparently clear to Roosevelt that the development of a bomb by the Soviets was only a matter of time.

Although certain aspects of this picture of atomic policy
have been revealed in the official history of the United Kingdom Atomic Energy Authority, Professor Sherwin has brought
into sharp focus many parts of the picture hitherto obscure and,
moreover, has filled it out with an enormous wealth of detail.
Some of this comes from correspondence between many of the
chief actors in the drama, like Vannevar Bush and James Conant,
the scientific directors of the Manhattan Project; the extensive
files of Robert Oppenheimer and General Leslie Groves; Churchill's atomic energy papers, just opened for public inspection;
Roosevelt's secret atomic energy files; and, especially valuable,
the diaries of Secretary of War Stimson. Sherwin's bibliography
is sometimes surprising, and all his conclusions are thoroughly
documented.

I had long been puzzled as to why there was seemingly so
little input to U.S. policy by the scientific community when it
was apparently well represented by two advisers to the President, Bush and Conant. Sherwin's detailed account of Conant's
advocacy, in October 1942, of restricted cooperation with Great
Britain on the development of the bomb, and of Roosevelt's
subsequent actions under the influence of Churchill, goes far
to explain this. While Roosevelt's decision to maintain a wartime partnership was the right one, it is a pity that after this
time Bush and Conant lost all influence on the development
of postwar atomic policy and were no longer even kept
informed. One wonders whether it was Churchill's influence
which made Roosevelt take fewer and fewer people into his
confidence—at any rate, this vastly increased the problems of
his successor.

To us, the scientists at Los Alamos, the most important initiative on postwar atomic policy came, as I have said, from Niels Bohr. As soon as Bohr heard of the initial successes of the U.S. atomic bomb program, he at once foresaw the postwar atomic arms race and the emergence of a "balance of terror"; the only way out was to neutralize the bomb, i.e., put it under international control. To achieve this, he urged that the Russians be informed immediately of the purpose of the Manhattan Project and of our intention, should we be successful in developing the weapon, to put it under such international control after the war. He did not propose that details of the bomb's development be revealed; he simply wanted to forestall any Russian idea that the bomb might be intended for use against them.

From 1943 until the end of the war, Bohr devoted all his energies to bringing his ideas to the attention of Churchill and Roosevelt. Sherwin gives us a graphic description of the interview between Churchill and Bohr, and of Churchill's inability to appreciate ideas out of harmony with the type of power politics he had been accustomed to all his life. Churchill's suspicions of Bohr were such that he even managed to turn Roosevelt against him. It strikes me as a special irony that the growing friendship between Roosevelt and Churchill, both great leaders of great countries, both intensely striving to do the best for their countries, should have had such bad side-effects. One is led to speculate how differently Truman might have acted at Potsdam had Roosevelt not become secretive, how differently Stalin might have acted had he been informed officially about the bomb.

Reading this account, I was again deeply saddened by the tragedy of the Potsdam meeting: Truman casually mentioning to Stalin that we had a weapon of unprecedented destructive power, but failing to express any desire to put the weapon under international control; Stalin answering equally casually—and, at this point, hopes for such control quite vanishing (if they had ever existed).

How did the atom and Truman interact? The author's analysis of Truman's personality and style and how they affected the fate of the atom in politics is highly illuminating and, like all parts of the book, well documented. For me it pulled together scattered memories, relating them to a sad whole.

Compared to the development of postwar policy, which involved great soul-searching (especially on the part of Stimson) and resolution of differences among policymakers, the decision to use the bomb militarily was quite simple. That the bomb would be used if it was ready seems to have been a foregone conclusion. Even Bohr separated the issue of wartime use from postwar policy. Individual scientists, and an *ad hoc* committee, pleaded for a demonstration of the bomb's power before it was actually employed. The so-called Interim Committee—which had been charged by Truman with making recommendations on both wartime and postwar atomic policy—did discuss this possibility, but no suitable demonstration could be thought of. In the final analysis, it was felt essential to "carry the [bomb's] impact effectively into Japan's war councils."

In this verdict (here I must differ with Professor Sherwin's judgment) I would myself concur—though it should be pointed out that the second strike, against Nagasaki, was in any case unnecessary, and came about because this decision was left to the commanders in the field.

The book contains much other information on the Manhattan Project. All the parts of which I have personal knowledge seem very accurate, and constantly bring to mind old times and concerns. It includes some letters which I had written and totally forgotten, an unimportant point, but testimony to the author's scholarship; his search of the available documents has been most thorough, and he has based on them a most coherent and comprehensive account of these complex developments. It is a story that should prove fascinating to both those who lived through it and those who are now witnessing its consequences.

HANS A. BETHE

Ithaca, New York
April 1975

ACKNOWLEDGMENTS

The completion of this book owes much to the generous support of the Program on Science, Technology and Society, and the Peace Studies Program, of Cornell University. I am especially grateful to Frank Long, George Quester, and Richard Rosecrance of Cornell, whose confidence in my work made that support possible.

I also wish to express my appreciation for the support I have received from the University of California, Berkeley, the Harry S. Truman Library, the Massachusetts Institute of Technology, and Princeton University.

It is a special pleasure to acknowledge the help of friends and colleagues who have selflessly offered their own valuable time to read and criticize the chapters that follow. The manuscript has been considerably improved as a result of their efforts. But before expressing my appreciation to each of them individually, I wish to thank my wife, Susan, and my children, Andrea and Alex, with whom I shared far too much of the agony and far too little of the pleasure involved in completing this book.

Three of my former teachers—Keith Berwick, Robert Dallek, and Richard Rosecrance—have each contributed to this book in a variety of ways for which I trust they realize I am deeply grateful. John Heilbron and Edward Segel read, criticized, and improved every chapter I wrote—and rewrote. Barton Bernstein, Daniel Kevles, Walter LaFeber, Robert Messer, and John Rosenberg, with whom I discussed ideas, traded documents, and exchanged manuscripts, have helped me over the years to achieve a clearer understanding of various issues and problems.

Others who offered advice and encouragement include: Bernard Bailyn, Richard Challener, Warren Cohen, Robert Divine, Gerald Feldman, Margaret Gowing, Roger Hahn, Richard Hewlett, David Hollinger, Marius Jansen, Lawrence Levine, Peter Lyon, Ernest May, Dorothy Nelkin, Gary Ostrower, Alice Kimball Smith, and Stephen Whitfield. Edward Agro saved me from a variety of errors, both factual and grammatical, and Howard Webber saved me from worse. I owe a special note of thanks to Hans Bethe, not only for his generosity in writing a preface for this book but also for his valuable comments on the sections concerning the atomic scientists. And, like all others fortunate enough to have Arno Mayer as a friend and critic, I am in his debt for many things intellectual—and in other ways as well.

This study could not have been written without a great deal of assistance from many librarians and archivists who answered questions, searched through their collections, replied to letters, returned telephone calls, and arranged for the reproduction of thousands of documents. I am grateful to them all, but wish to extend a special note of appreciation to Carolyn Sung at the Library of Congress, Joseph Howerton and Edward Reese at the National Archives, Lorna Arnold of the United Kingdom Atomic Energy Authority, and Judith Schiff at the Sterling Memorial Library, Yale University.

In the course of my research I conducted several formal interviews, many informal conversations, and some correspondence with Manhattan Project alumni. For their time and cooperation I am grateful to Hans Bethe, Lew Kowarski, J. Robert Oppenheimer, Glenn Seaborg, Emilio Segrè, Henry D. Smyth, Edward Teller, Harold Urey, Victor Weisskopf, and Eugene Wigner. I also wish to thank Owen Anderson and Stanley Levine for bringing the story of the American POWs killed at Hiroshima to my attention.

A note of appreciation to my editor, Angus Cameron, for his enthusiasm and wise counsel, to Melvin Rosenthal for his extraordinary editorial work, and to Bobbie Bristol for her patience and assistance. With skill and good cheer Glennis Cohen typed the manuscript and buoyed my spirits; I am grateful to her for both. Would that it could be otherwise, but, alas, for the errors that remain I am alone responsible.

MARTIN J. SHERWIN

Princeton, New Jersey
March 1975

A
WORLD
DESTROYED

INTRODUCTION

*[My] article ["The Decision to Use the Atomic Bomb"] . . .
has also been intended to satisfy the doubts of that rather difficult class of the community which will have charge of the education of the next generation, namely educators and historians.*
      —HENRY L. STIMSON to HARRY S. TRUMAN,
      January 7, 1947

The nuclear destruction of Hi-
roshima and Nagasaki dramatized the most important consequence of the Second World War: the survival of humanity
could no longer be assumed. The world had entered a new era
in which great-power diplomacy was conducted perilously close
to the abyss of nuclear war. By raising the stakes of war to this
ultimate pinnacle, scientists had altered the meaning of peace
and the relationship between weapons technology and world
affairs. This book is about the assumptions and decisions that
emerged from these changes and governed the atomic energy
policies of the United States from the discovery of nuclear fission to its military application. Its principal subjects are atomic
scientists who sought to save the new world while creating the
means of destroying the old, and policymakers who relied on
principles derived from the experience of the old world in their
struggle to ensure peace in the new.

To comprehend the relationship between atomic energy and
diplomatic policies that developed during the war, the bomb
must be seen as both scientists and policymakers saw it before
Hiroshima: as a possible means of controlling the postwar
course of world affairs. For this task the viewpoint of the present is conceptually inadequate. After more than a quarter-century of experience we understand, as wartime policymakers did
not, the bomb's limitations as a diplomatic instrument. But the
great expectations held for the bomb during the war were
based on the then-unchallenged assumption that its impact on

international relations would be decisive. For a proper assessment of the outlook and actions of the time, scientists' proposals need to be studied as closely as diplomatic policies;
British policies must be scrutinized as carefully as American;
the decision to use the atomic bomb against Japan must be
evaluated in the light of the entire history of the weapon's development; and the problems of impending peace must be considered along with the exigencies of war.

Throughout the war two successive Presidents of the United
States and their advisers viewed the atomic bomb as a *potential*
rather than an actual instrument of diplomatic policy. They
believed that its impact on diplomacy had to await its development, and perhaps even a demonstration of its power. As Secretary of War Henry L. Stimson, President Roosevelt's senior
atomic energy adviser, observed in his memoirs: "The bomb as
a merely probable weapon had seemed a weak reed on which
to rely, but the bomb as a colossal reality was very different."[1]
Historians generally agree that policymakers considered this
difference before Hiroshima, but whether they based wartime
diplomatic policies upon an anticipated successful demonstration
of the bomb's power remains a source of controversy.[2] The debate has centered on two issues: First, did the development of
the atomic bomb affect the way American policymakers conducted diplomacy with the Soviet Union? Second, did diplomatic considerations related to the Soviet Union influence the
decision to use the atomic bomb against Japan?

These important questions concerning the impact of the
atomic bomb on American diplomacy, and ultimately on the
origins of the cold war, have been considered almost exclusively
with respect to the formulation of policy during the early
months of the Truman administration. As a result, two anterior
questions of equal importance, questions with implications for
those already posed, have been generally overlooked: Did diplomatic considerations regarding postwar relations with the
Soviet Union influence the formulation of Roosevelt's atomic
energy policies? And, what was the effect of Roosevelt's atomic
legacy on both the diplomatic and the atomic energy policies
of his successor's administration? In seeking to isolate, for separate consideration, these two basic elements of policy that con-

verged during the war, we must first ask whether alternatives were in fact recognized.

One conclusion that emerges clearly from a close examination of wartime policy formulation is that policymakers never seriously questioned the assumption that the bomb should be used. From the first meeting to organize the atomic energy project in October 1941, Stimson, Roosevelt, and other members of the "Top Policy Group" conceived of the development and use of the atomic bomb as an essential part of the total war effort. Although the suggestion to build the bomb was initially made by scientists who feared that Germany might develop the weapon first, those with political responsibility for prosecuting the war accepted the very fact of the bomb's existence as sufficient justification for its use against any enemy.

Having acted upon this point of view, Stimson charged those who later criticized the use of the bomb with two errors. First, he insisted, these critics asked the wrong question: the issue was not whether surrender *could* have been obtained without using the bomb, but whether a different diplomatic and military course from that followed by the Truman administration would have achieved an *earlier* surrender. Second, the basic assumption of these critics was false: the idea that American policy should have been based primarily on a desire not to employ the bomb seemed to Stimson as "irresponsible" as a policy controlled by a positive desire to use it. The war, not the bomb, he argued, had been the primary focus of his attention; his responsibilities as Secretary of War permitted no alternative.[3]

Stimson's own wartime diary nevertheless indicates that from 1941 on the problems associated with the bomb itself moved steadily closer to the center of his own and Roosevelt's concerns. As the war progressed, the diplomatic implications of the weapon's development came steadily to the fore; recognizing that a monopoly on the atomic bomb would give the United States a powerful new military advantage after the war, Roosevelt and Stimson became increasingly anxious to convert it into a diplomatic advantage. In December 1944 they spoke of using the "secret" of the atomic bomb as a means of obtaining a *quid pro quo* from the Soviet Union.[4] But, still viewing the untested bomb as a potential rather than an actual instrument of diplomacy, they were not moved to formulate a concrete plan for carrying out this idea before the bomb was used. The weapon had "this unique peculiarity," Stimson noted several months later in his diary: ". . . success is 99% assured, yet only by the first actual war trial of the weapon can the actual certainty be fixed."[5]

Although Roosevelt left no definitive statement assigning a postwar role to the atomic bomb, his expectations for it can be constructed from the existing record. An analysis of the policies he chose from among the alternatives he faced suggests that the potential diplomatic value of the bomb began to shape his atomic energy policies as early as 1943. He may have been cautious about counting on the bomb as a reality during the war, but he nevertheless consistently chose policy alternatives that would promote its postwar diplomatic value if the predictions of the scientists proved true. These policies were based on the assumption that the bomb could be used effectively to secure postwar goals; and this assumption was carried over to Truman's administration.

Despite general agreement that the bomb would be an extraordinarily important factor in postwar affairs, the men closely associated with its development did not agree on how to use it most effectively as an instrument of diplomacy. Convinced that whatever wartime policies were adopted would ultimately have grave consequences, the eminent Danish scientist Niels Bohr tried to convince Roosevelt and Churchill to open negotiations with Stalin during the war for the international control of atomic energy. Bohr's proposal was not accepted, and for over two decades many who regretted that decision believed that Roosevelt and Churchill had misunderstood what Bohr had in mind. As J. Robert Oppenheimer, the wartime director of the Los Alamos Nuclear Weapons Laboratory, later wrote, "[it was] easy, as history has shown, for even wise men not to know what Bohr was talking about."[6] Bohr's effort to avert a postwar atomic armaments race between the great powers was explained as a tragedy; his obscure prose and barely audible speech were identified as the tragic flaws that prevented sympathetic statesmen from heeding his advice.[7]

Bohr's experience, however, suggests that tragic interpretations of history can result from incomplete evidence. During the past several years the curtain of secrecy that has hidden so many critical documents connected with important decisions taken during World War II has begun to open, allowing historians to fill out and in many cases revise the diplomatic history of the Grand Alliance—the wartime partnership among Britain, the Soviet Union, and the United States. Bohr's encounter with Roosevelt and Churchill can still be viewed as tragic, but not because he was misunderstood. His proposals were rejected because Roosevelt and Churchill were committed to the course he opposed.

While Bohr, and Roosevelt's science advisers, argued for the international control of atomic energy, Churchill urged the President to maintain the Anglo-American atomic monopoly as a diplomatic counter against the postwar ambitions of other nations—particularly those of the Soviet Union. Roosevelt's atomic energy policies thus emerged from the choices he made between two conflicting points of view. In 1943, he began to develop the diplomatic aspects of atomic energy policy in consultation with Churchill alone. As the war proceeded, the mutual advantages of continuing the atomic energy partnership after the war became increasingly obvious to the two leaders. While Britain became America's sentinel watching over the Old World, America would serve as its ally's arsenal, supplying it with power from the New World to remain strong and act effectively. Although Roosevelt's mode of decisionmaking and his sudden death have left his thoughts and motives elusive, the policies he pursued are clear: he consistently opposed international control and acted in accordance with Churchill's monopolistic, anti-Soviet views.

The findings of the present study challenge many generalizations historians have made about Roosevelt's diplomacy: that it was consistent with his public reputation for cooperation and conciliation; that he was naïve with respect to postwar Soviet intentions; that, like Woodrow Wilson, he believed in collective security as an effective guarantor of national safety; and that he made every possible effort to assure that the Soviet Union and its Western allies would continue to function as postwar partners.[8] The present work does not dispute the view that

Roosevelt desired amicable postwar relations with the Soviet Union, or, indeed, that he worked hard to realize this goal; but it does suggest that his confidence in its attainment, perhaps even his commitment to it—and certainly his willingness to risk seeking international control of atomic energy in order to achieve it— have often been exaggerated. His prescriptions for the diplomatic role of the atomic bomb, his most secret and among his most important decisions, reveal a carefully guarded skepticism regarding the Grand Alliance's prospects for surviving the war intact.

On April 12, 1945, just four months before the war ended, Franklin Roosevelt died unexpectedly. Without warning or preparation, Harry S. Truman—a Midwestern New Dealer who had devoted his decade of service in the Senate exclusively to domestic affairs—assumed the Presidency. Truman took office committed to the course Roosevelt had charted. But without his predecessor's tolerance for ambiguity and without experience in diplomacy, he steered the ship of state erratically, with little confidence in his ability to bring it safely to port. Leaning heavily upon trusted friends for moral support, upon inherited advisers for guidance, in implementing what he accepted as his diplomatic legacy, the new President increasingly came to believe that America's possession of the atomic bomb would, by itself, convince Stalin to be more cooperative. His advisers urged upon him a harsher, more forceful approach to the Soviet Union than Roosevelt had followed, with the result that Truman transformed FDR's concealed skepticism about the likelihood of continued cooperation into the explicit guiding principle of American-Soviet relations.

Thus, the question most frequently asked at the time of Roosevelt's death—what effect would his passing have on American-Soviet relations?—was soon transformed by events into another: Did Truman's policies destroy the possibility of cooperation between the two major allies? Although this latter query can be found at the heart of several studies seeking the origins of the Cold War, it cannot be completely resolved without access to Soviet records. As long as this debate depends upon extrapolating Stalin's ultimate objectives from actions that may have been taken chiefly in response to American policies, the issue of whether relations between the allies could have been substantially better had Roosevelt lived will remain a matter of conjecture. Nonetheless, our inability to deal fully with this issue should not preclude efforts to grapple with several important aspects of it: What were the assumptions, attitudes, and expectations that controlled Truman's diplomacy, and did they differ substantially from Roosevelt's? What were Truman's perceptions of Soviet actions and intentions, and how did he come to them? In seeking answers to such questions, the present work asks another: Were the policy considerations that governed diplomatic and military use of the atomic bomb during the final months of the war in conformance with Roosevelt's atomic legacy?

Roosevelt's commitment to a postwar atomic energy partnership with England died with him. More crucially, however, the new administration followed him in maintaining opposition to the idea of international control of atomic energy. In retrospect, it seems clear that wartime atomic policy produced fateful consequences beyond its immediate issue in the incineration of two Japanese cities. The lines from the *Bhagavad Gita* that flashed through Robert Oppenheimer's mind as he watched the first atomic explosion are apt: "I have become Death, Destroyer of worlds."

I
THE SECRET SITS

We dance round in a ring and suppose,
But the Secret sits in the middle and knows.

—ROBERT FROST

I

THE END OF
THE BEGINNING

In December 1938, less than a year before the outbreak of World War II, nuclear fission was discovered in Germany. Despite the potential military implications of this unexpected development, almost three years passed before the American government committed significant scientific and financial resources to develop an atomic bomb. While that commitment is generally believed to have been made by President Roosevelt in response to Albert Einstein's letter of August 1939 warning of German interest in the subject, the fact is that a long series of bureaucratic decisions separated Einstein's warning from the project's beginnings. During those years of turmoil and debate, of hasty preparations for war and unconvincing guarantees of peace, circumstances led a small number of émigré scientists in America and England to take the lead in urging support for nuclear research. But despite great efforts, their rewards were small, for they were unable to guarantee that such a weapon could be built quickly. Accordingly, under the criterion of "wartime use"—the policy of allocating resources only for weapons research that promised results in time for service during the impending war—work on atomic energy received little government support.

Late in the spring of 1941, however, the American government was informed that scientists in Britain had determined that it was possible to rapidly develop an atomic bomb, a weapon that might determine the outcome of the war. A major commitment to investigate that possibility was undertaken immediately, and an Anglo-American atomic energy partnership was agreed upon. The assumption that the weapon would be built quickly for use during the war was implicit in the decision to develop it.

I

An Unrecognized Question—and Its Discovery

The most important answers in the process of discovery, physicist Leo Szilard told the Senate Special Committee on Atomic Energy in 1945, are often answers to "unrecognized questions."[1] The discovery of nuclear fission is a case in point. Scientists from at least ten nations contributed to the theoretical insights and successful experiments that began with Becquerel's discovery of radioactivity in 1896 and came to fruition in Berlin in December 1938.[2] In spite of all the preceding work, however, the discovery of fission was made only when Otto Hahn and Fritz Strassmann—in defiance of then-prevailing scientific doctrine—raised a question that had never before been considered seriously: could the elements found after bombarding uranium with a stream of neutrons have been created by the fission of the uranium atom?

True, had that question not been asked in Germany in 1938, it is very likely that scientists elsewhere would soon have felt compelled to raise it. Research in this area was then going forward in several countries, and it is entirely possible that the discovery of nuclear fission might, for example, have been made in France or the United States. At the time Hahn and Strassmann were working on their experiment in Berlin, Frédéric Joliot* was making significant progress in Paris. And Philip Abelson, a doctoral candidate at the University of California in Berkeley, was trying to understand what was causing the "queer X rays" he had been detecting with his spectrometer. He assumed that his experiment with uranium had produced some new, heavier elements. But, in fact, by bombarding uranium atoms with neutrons he had split those atoms into nearly equal parts. "There is no doubt," according to Ernest Lawrence, the director of the Radiation Laboratory where Abelson was working, that had "this great discovery by Hahn and Strassmann been delayed a few weeks Abelson would have made it himself."[3] A distinguished research group had come very close four years earlier. In 1934 Enrico Fermi, Emilio Segrè,

---

* Best known, of course, as Joliot-Curie, the name he formed by adding his wife's maiden name to his own.

and their colleagues had collaborated on a series of experiments in Rome that placed them just one unrecognized question away from the discovery of fission. But the idea ran so completely counter to all contemporary understanding, Segrè has recalled, that despite an article by I. Noddack which "clearly indicated the possibility of interpreting the results as splitting of the heavy atom into two approximately equal parts," fission was discussed only in a "jocose mode."[4]

The consequences of the discovery of fission were staggering. Since Einstein's realization that matter and energy were different aspects of a single phenomenon, scientists had understood that if matter could be made to disappear, an equivalent energy would become available in quantities billions of times greater than the energy released by any other known method. But just how was matter constituted? And how could it be transformed into energy? During the second decade of the twentieth century a new answer to the first question came with a fresh description of elementary particles, or atoms, developed by Ernest Rutherford and Niels Bohr. Matter, according to their view—which proved to be correct—was largely associated with the nucleus, the central body of the atom. As the nucleus was studied and its properties revealed, scientists came closer to understanding the transformation of matter into energy. If a heavy element could be synthesized from lighter elements (fusion), or if one of the heaviest atoms could be broken into approximately equal fragments (fission), nuclear mass would disappear in the process and energy would be released. But while the release of energy in these ways could be considered as distant possibilities, no method of producing either fusion or fission was known.

In 1919 Rutherford made a significant breakthrough. He succeeded in transmuting one element (nitrogen) into another, heavier one (oxygen) by bombarding the first with alpha particles (nuclei of helium). As Einstein had predicted, energy was released in the process. But no power had been gained. To overcome the repulsion between the target nuclei and the bombarding particles, Rutherford had to supply the latter with enormous energies, and, as a result, the energy released in the experiments was infinitesimal compared to the total energy required to liberate it. So the possibility of obtaining large quantities of energy stored as mass in nuclei remained to be discussed only in Segrè's "jocose mode."[5]

In 1936 Rutherford himself labeled as "moonshine" talk about the transmutation of atoms as a source of power.[6] There is even reason to believe that Hahn and Strassmann themselves did not at first fully appreciate the nature of the reaction they observed in 1938. Rather than publish an explanation of their results immediately, Hahn wrote for assistance in interpreting his experiment to a former colleague, Lise Meitner, a Jewish refugee recently driven from Germany by Nazi persecution.

To understand the mystery Hahn and Strassmann faced in 1938, it is necessary to retreat for a moment to 1932 when experiments in Germany and France had led James Chadwick, Rutherford's close associate, to the discovery of a new elementary nuclear building block, the neutron. Unlike other particles, the neutron has no electric charge, a characteristic that allows it to penetrate nuclei without being repulsed by *their* electric charges. In the years that followed Chadwick's discovery, Fermi and his co-workers used neutrons to bombard the nuclei of one element after another; this procedure produced new nuclei, nuclei which had excess energy and were consequently radioactive—that is, they released some energy in the form of gamma rays, or they ejected electrons or other elementary particles in the process of transmuting themselves into more stable nuclei.

Even uranium, the heaviest atom then known, responded to this procedure, apparently producing new atoms heavier than uranium. Yet Hahn and Strassmann found that after uranium had been exposed to neutrons, there were among the reaction products radioactive elements whose masses were approximately half that of the original uranium atom. It was this inexplicable occurrence that Hahn wanted Meitner to explain.

Could the uranium atom have been split by the neutron into two more or less equal fragments? The time to recognize this question as a serious one had come. With the help of her nephew, Otto Frisch, an experimental physicist at the Niels Bohr Institute for Theoretical Physics in Copenhagen, Meitner tested the theory. It was correct.

Nine months after the discovery of nuclear fission, Nazi armies invaded Poland. This confluence of events in science and world affairs was to lead to other unrecognized questions . . . and, ultimately, to the destruction of Hiroshima and Nagasaki.

II

"One Day Earlier than Most"

Physicists viewed the discovery of nuclear fission like the finding of a lost treasure map. A feverish inquiry into its implications was underway even before the news was published in January 1939. By the end of the year nearly one hundred articles on the subject had appeared in science journals throughout the world.[7] For all the scientific questions it answered, however, the discovery raised other difficult issues that scientists could not easily resolve. What were the military implications of fission? Could it affect the course of the impending war? What were the responsibilities of scientists in this situation?

One of the myths that has grown up around these political questions is that scientists immediately recognized that an atomic bomb could be built. Like most myths, this one contains an element of truth distorted by oversimplification. It was clear even to many who were not scientists that unprecedented amounts of energy were released during fission. It was therefore easy to conclude that this energy might be harnessed someday as a source of power to light cities, or as a weapon to destroy them. But it required considerable scientific competence to recognize the full complexity of the problems to be surmounted before either dreams or nightmares could be realized. Thus, while journalists speculated easily about the imminent benefits and dangers of the new discovery,[8] nuclear physicists were more impressed with the theoretical and technical difficulties to be overcome before they could determine whether practical applications were possible.

Even the acknowledged leaders in nuclear research did not foresee the rapid progress that would be made. In 1939, less than three years before he conducted the first controlled nuclear chain reaction experiment, Enrico Fermi estimated as "remote"—"perhaps ten percent"—the chance that such a result was even possible.[9] In 1943, four years after bringing the news of the discovery to America, Niels Bohr remained skeptical about its uses. Writing from Nazi-occupied Denmark through the Danish underground to scientists in England, he stated his conviction that "in spite of all future prospects any immediate use of the latest marvelous discoveries of atomic physics is impractical."[10] And in August 1945, almost seven years after he had discovered fission, Otto Hahn at first refused to believe that the destruction of Hiroshima could have been caused by an atomic bomb. He and his German colleagues had concluded years before that such a weapon could not be constructed during the war.*

The predictions of Fermi, Bohr, and Hahn—all Nobel Prize winners—underscore the great distance that in 1939 divided theoretical speculations about atomic energy from experimental and technical realities. Although the obvious danger of war in 1939 caused scientists in every major country to think about the military potential of fission, they generally concluded that the scientific and technical problems were both too numerous and too complex to be solved in the near future, if indeed they could be solved at all.

Despite what seemed overwhelming odds, however, small groups of émigré physicists from Fascist Europe set energetically to work on the problem of fission in both Britain and America. Precisely because they were immigrants, they were not permitted to work on the most secret projects, such as radar, and were thus left free to work in the field they knew best, nuclear physics.†

* David Irving, *The German Atomic Bomb: The History of Nuclear Research in Nazi Germany* (New York, 1968), 11–18. The conversations of captured German scientists were covertly recorded by U.S. Army Intelligence. Irving blames the German failure on the disposition and temperament of German scientists, and the lack of military direction of their work: "Two forces militated against speed in the German project: the first, that the project was directed by scientists throughout its history, and not by military commanders as in America; and the second, that in Germany the emphasis was on the theory throughout the project" (p. 297). See below, pp. 34–5, for another view.

† According to Norman Ramsey, a Harvard University physicist who headed the Los Alamos Delivery Group that assembled the Hiroshima and Nagasaki bombs on the island of Tinian in August 1945, the Radar Laboratory at the Massachusetts Institute of Technology was named the "Radiation Laboratory" as a security cover. Scientists hoped to fool the Germans into thinking "that instead of our working on something really important and practical like radar, that we were wasting our time on

Their lingering respect for German men of science, moreover, fed their profoundest fear—a Nazi victory—and led at least some of them to assume the worst: that German scientists and engineers, regardless of the apparent difficulties, would attempt to develop an atomic bomb with the full support and encouragement of their government.

In America, however, a country still at peace, the émigrés' efforts to arouse official interest in their work encountered formidable obstacles. The government's preparations for war were conducted in the shadows of the political arena—isolationism was a force to be reckoned with, and President Roosevelt moved against it cautiously and, wherever possible, secretly.[11] The limited scientific and financial resources that could be mobilized under these conditions were directed, quite naturally, to the development of the most promising weapons. The atomic bomb was not one of these.

Those few who advocated work on the possibilities of nuclear fission were thus trapped in a vicious circle: to determine whether fission could be the basis for the development of an important weapon required a major investigation; such an investigation required considerable financial support; but neither the Army, the Navy, nor any civilian agency could offer such support without substantial evidence favoring a high probability of success. Suggestions regarding the profound significance of such a breakthrough availed little. Under these circumstances, the campaign for nuclear research came to focus upon making a convincing case for the émigrés' fears—upon the consequences for America of a breakthrough achieved in Germany.

The consequences for America . . . Few themes in American history have been as pervasive, despite the country's powerful isolationist bent, as the tendency to respond defensively to European actions. Americans have always been aware that they could not avoid the influence of Europe—of its political movements, its trade, its art, its science, and its wars. Even Washington's admonition to eschew entangling alliances was a warning to *postpone*, not to reject, the logic of the nation's past and future,[12] a logic

something completely impractical and useless like an atomic bomb," (Ramsey-Oral History Transcript [hereafter OHT], 35–6).

that Europe's émigrés—America's immigrants—periodically reinforced. Like each of the many other waves of immigration to the
United States, the 1930s migration of scientists from Fascist
Europe added to the American body politic still another element
involved with European affairs.[13] The concerns shared by émigré
scientists in 1939 made them consider more readily than American-born scientists the potential military value of the discovery
of nuclear fission.

One of the newcomers had even considered the problem while
residing in England almost four years before the discovery of
fission was made. "Whether or not the liberation of nuclear
energy and the production of radio-active material on a large
scale can be achieved in the immediate future," Leo Szilard wrote
to a colleague in 1935, ". . . I believe an attempt, whatever small
chance of success it may have, ought to be made to control this
development as long as possible."[14] Having recognized this possibility and having surmised that fission might be used in a weapon,
Szilard applied for a British patent describing the laws governing
a chain reaction. To keep his conjectures from becoming public,
he assigned the patent to the Admiralty.*

Szilard was a unique individual—not only a brilliant physicist,
but a scientist with a penchant for political soothsaying and para-
political activities. Born in 1898 in Budapest, the son of a civil
engineer, he studied electrical engineering in his native Hungary
until the exciting advances being made in physics led him, when
he was studying in Berlin, to change fields. After completing his
doctorate in 1922, he worked with Einstein, and taught at the
University of Berlin for a decade. But having concluded a few
days after the Reichstag fire in February 1933 that Nazi ambitions would not be contained, he fled the country with the intention of establishing an organization to seek academic positions

---

* Szilard's extraordinary foresight in 1935 is highlighted by the following, written by Ernest O. Lawrence in August 1945: "I know of no
record which indicates who first thought of this possibility [a chain re-
action]; probably it occurred to many (I heard it in this country *as early
as April 1939*, and Halban [Hans von Halban, Jr., an associate of Joliot]
spoke of it as a probable prospect in Paris in July 1939)" (italics added).
"Antecedents of the Metallurgical Project," August 9, 1945, Lawrence
mss., File 1015, Box 1, Folder 27.

abroad for anti-Nazi German intellectuals. Recalling years later that he left just one day before German border guards began checking passports at the frontier, he commented characteristically, "You don't have to be cleverer than other people, you just have to be one day earlier than most."[15]

By nature a futurist, by avocation a science fiction buff, Szilard found one of his greatest joys in life in using his gift of prescience to counter the lemming-like tendencies he discerned in the rest of the human species. Described as "an intellectual adventurer, likely to embark at any moment on some excursion far beyond the boundaries of science," he applied logic and imagination outside the laboratory in the same freewheeling manner he applied them within it.[16] If scientists may be said to function within a system of "social control," a system involving "characteristic types of behavior that produce conformity to . . . scientific norms and values,"[17] Szilard must be considered an unsocialized scientist. Although his political activities invariably related to some aspect of his scientific interests, his colleagues did not always appreciate his efforts. "Just rather not my style of person," one eminent scientist has remarked. "He was dashing about from one project to another, never staying in one place for any length of time. When I was at Chicago he was seldom there. When he was supposed to be in . . . he was seldom there. Leo was a very bright person, but he never settled down. . . ."[18]

Szilard had been in the United States about a year when news of the discovery of nuclear fission was announced. Recalling his earlier musings, it occurred to him that under carefully controlled conditions a chain reaction might be realized in a large mass of uranium. After discussing his ideas with Eugene Wigner and Edward Teller, two Hungarian colleagues and friends of many years, Szilard planned an experiment to test his hypothesis.* If more than one neutron was liberated in the disintegration of the uranium atom, then the possibility of a chain reaction was real,

* The Physics Department of Columbia University granted him permission to use their facilities. Columbia could not offer him the $2,000 he needed to rent a gram of radium for the experiment; Szilard, however, ever resourceful, formed the "Association for Scientific Collaboration" to fund his work through contributions raised from other physicists and a private donor.

and an explosive device was conceivable. In anticipation of such an outcome, Szilard urged Fermi, who was engaged in a similar investigation at Columbia, to cooperate with him in keeping any positive results secret.

Szilard's attempts to ensure secrecy reflected the political dimensions of the problem. Yet with every major nuclear physics group in the world pursuing the implications of fission, the effect of withholding publication on the subject in England, France, or America was problematical: Would it serve to keep useful information from scientists in Germany, or would it merely alert them to the possibility of intense Anglo-French-American interest in military applications? Would the exigencies of maintaining such secrecy retard work in the very countries that practiced it? Does secrecy in science ultimately serve any nation's interest?

In practice, responses to these kinds of questions were eventually imposed by governments; but even today the questions themselves remain unresolved among scientists. Given the circumstances, and his own personality and background, it is not surprising that at the time Szilard (who would emerge during the war as a leading critic of Army security regulations at atomic energy laboratories) should advocate such a break with scientific convention. Nor is it surprising that his proposal was not readily accepted. It is instructive, however, to follow the course of the debate that ensued, for it provides an early example of a recurring theme in the history of the atomic energy project, both in wartime and after: the efforts of scientists to preserve their traditional freedoms in the face of an unstable political environment made increasingly dangerous by their own work.

Writing on February 2, 1939, to Frédéric Joliot, whose work at the Laboratoire de Chimie Nucléaire was thought to be parallel to the experiments at Columbia, Szilard briefly explained how the experiments he and Fermi were planning elicited "some discussion here among physicists whether or not we should take action to prevent anything along this line from being published in scientific periodicals in this country, and also ask colleagues in England and France to consider taking similar action." He also expressed the hope "that there will be no, or at least not sufficient, neutron emission and therefore nothing to worry about."[19] His actions, however, suggested other expectations—which were realized one month later. Having set up his experiment, Szilard and his collaborator, Walter Zinn, went to the seventh floor of Columbia's Pupin Hall on the evening of March 3: "All we had to do was to lean back, turn on a switch, and watch the screen of a television tube," Szilard recounted after the war in a dramatized version of the event. "If flashes of light appeared on the screen it would mean . . . that the liberation of atomic energy was possible in our lifetime. We turned the switch, we saw flashes, we watched them for about ten minutes. . . . That night I knew that the world was headed for sorrow."[20]* Szilard would spend the last months of the war, and his life thereafter, exerting what influence he could to prevent the ultimate sorrow of nuclear destruction; until the defeat of Germany was at hand, however, his primary concern was to ensure that German scientists were not the first to develop whatever military potential inhered in nuclear fission.

The intensive discussions among physicists at Columbia during the following weeks over whether or not to publish Szilard's and Fermi's results provide an interesting insight into the influence that political, professional, and value judgments invariably exert upon science policy recommendations. The immediate question at issue—whether scientists in Germany would be advantaged by publication of the discovery that more than one neutron was released from a ruptured uranium nucleus—could not be isolated from judgments about the responsibility of scientists with respect to the crisis in Europe. Although differences of opinion among the émigré scientists were apparent from the beginning of the debate, as a group they were more inclined than their American-born colleagues to depart from accepted practice in this case. Not, to be sure, that they were less concerned about the implications of such a decision, but their experience with Nazism had made them more sensitive to the possible consequences of a contrary decision.

Those who favored publication focused only incidentally upon the necessity of upholding tradition, raising instead a variety of other arguments. Some opposed secrecy on the ground that it had

---

* At about the same time Fermi completed his separate series of experiments, which confirmed Szilard's conclusions. This led to a close collaboration between them in the ensuing months.

not actually been proved that a chain reaction could take place; they still did not believe it possible. Others opposed it on the ground that even if a chain reaction did take place, it was doubtful that it could be used in a military weapon. Still others argued simply that withholding publication was pointless, since word of the new findings would most likely spread by informal personal communications that, they maintained, would have the same effect as publication. Finally, some suggested that publication would stimulate further work in American laboratories which might otherwise not be carried out. Fermi, who initially opposed secrecy, accepted it after a meeting in Washington on March 19 with Szilard and Teller. Other émigré physicists who joined in the effort to convince colleagues in England, France, and America to withhold publication of their research were Wigner and Victor Weisskopf, who was then teaching at the University of Rochester.[21]

Just at the moment, however, when the advocates of secrecy appeared to have prevailed, it was learned that Joliot and his associates had published a note on the emission of neutrons in the fission of uranium, indicating that this might lead to a chain reaction.[22] Weisskopf sent a telegram to Joliot's laboratory on March 31, inquiring whether he was willing to follow the procedure of withholding publication while sending papers to science journals (to assure research credit). Joliot and his associates replied in a telegram of April 5 that they would not comply with that procedure.* This final refusal to collaborate proved to be the death-blow for the fragile, precariously constructed secrecy pact. Szilard still argued for his plan, insisting that Joliot would be forced to withhold future experimental results, because "otherwise . . . we would know his results and he would not know

* Joliot's decision to publish his initial findings, and his insistence upon continuing to publish the results of the research he was engaged in with H. von Halban, Jr. and L. Kowarski, provide an interesting sidelight on the political perspective from France and the influence exerted by professional interests there. Szilard's letter of February 2, it is true, was not followed by a notification to Joliot about the success of the experiment at Columbia University on March 3; yet it must be noted that Joliot made no effort, after completing his own experiment, to check on the status of the secrecy agreement.

our[s]"; but this argument failed to convince Fermi, who now once more reversed his stand and announced himself in favor of publication.

Thereafter Szilard stood alone at Columbia as a proponent of secrecy. His unyielding stand created an impasse. (I. I. Rabi, who was not involved in this work, gave Szilard a friendly warning that if he persisted in this stand he would probably be left without facilities for further work at Columbia.) Finally, at Fermi's suggestion, the decision was left up to the chairman of the Physics Department, G. B. Pegram, who resolved the dispute in favor of publication.[23]

"We both [Fermi and himself] wanted to be conservative," Szilard later recalled, "but Fermi thought that the conservative thing was to play down the possibility that this thing [a nuclear chain reaction] might happen, and I thought the conservative thing was to assume that it would happen and take the necessary precautions."[24] Szilard's position reflected his own estimate that atomic energy might well be used for military purposes. In contrast, Fermi had little confidence that anything militarily useful could result from their work. Beyond judgments based on their scientific intuitions, however, their temperamental differences also drew them in opposite directions. While it was Szilard's disposition to reevaluate traditional responses in the light of new circumstances, Fermi was by nature a conservative man disinclined at any time to deviate from customary practice. "Finally, withholding publication," one opponent of secrecy noted, citing Joliot's paper almost with a sense of relief, "sets a new and undesirable precedent among physicists."[25] Even Wigner, who had supported Szilard's proposal from the beginning, wrote that abandoning it was, "under the conditions, a wise decision as nothing really could be achieved in this matter."[26] It was now more important than ever, Wigner suggested, to awaken the government to the potential danger. But who could be contacted? How could émigré scientists gain entry into the corridors of power?

III

"This Requires Action"

The collapse in mid-April of Szilard's campaign for secrecy gave renewed impetus to the effort, already initiated a month earlier, to alert the United States government to the military potential of nuclear research. The scientists began by contacting the Navy Department in March; they got results only, however, after contacting the President directly in August. This outcome had a significant effect on Szilard. Although he never suggested himself that he had derived any particular lesson from this experience, his subsequent efforts to influence science policy decisions invariably followed the principle that even a bureaucracy was governed by the law of gravity. Ideas inserted at the bottom were likely to remain there, inactive, while those inserted at the top stood a good chance of getting results on their way down. The President of the United States was more likely to be interested in extraordinary ideas than the bureaucrats responsible for developing them.

Although nuclear studies and international affairs appeared to be moving toward frightening resolutions during the summer of 1939, no department of the government seemed concerned with their potential relationship. What would happen, Szilard and Wigner fretted in July, if the Germans shared their vision and seized the vast quantities of rich uranium ore in the Belgian Congo? Could such a move be preempted? How? Their thoughts turned to Einstein. He knew the Queen of the Belgians personally and might prove willing to write a letter warning her of the danger.

When Wigner and Szilard saw Einstein, he agreed to assist them in any way he could. A letter to a member of the Belgian cabinet, with a copy to be sent to the U.S. State Department, was decided upon. After Szilard returned to New York, however, he began to have second thoughts about the efficacy of this approach. Through a friend, Gustav Stolper, an economist and former member of the German Reichstag who was now a refugee living in New York, Szilard made contact with Alexander Sachs—a Russian émigré, a science buff, a consultant to the Lehman Corporation, and a New Dealer with access to the White House. Sachs was an ideal liaison. Imaginative, curious, egotistical, and determined, he was not the sort to forgo an opportunity to play the role of savior if given such a chance as Szilard now appeared to be offering. Even before Szilard approached him, Sachs has recalled, he had taken it upon himself to express his views on the potential importance of the discovery of nuclear fission to Roosevelt. If Szilard would obtain a letter from Einstein to the President explaining the gravity of the situation, Sachs promised to deliver it personally.[27]

It was Szilard who actually wrote Einstein's well-known letter. An astute and patriotic gesture in 1939, the letter became one of Clio's most revealing and cruelest ironies in 1945—revealing, because the shy scientist's willingness to lend his prestigious name indicates how important this matter appeared to him; cruel, because it associated Einstein with a historical event so clearly antithetical to his instincts and to his earlier pacifist position. "I made one great mistake in my life," Einstein told Linus Pauling years later, "when I signed the letter to President Roosevelt recommending that atom bombs be made, but there was some justification—the danger that the Germans would make them."[28]

About six weeks after the outbreak of war in Europe, Sachs delivered the letter signed by Einstein, with a supporting memorandum from Szilard, to the President. The letter was cautious in tone, stating no more about the likelihood of military applications than that "it is conceivable—though much less than fission as a source of power—that extremely powerful bombs of a new type may be constructed." It pointed out that "a single bomb of this type, carried by boat and exploded in port, might very well destroy the whole port together with some of the surrounding territory." Such bombs, however, might prove too heavy for aircraft. This description was a fair, analytical estimate of the situation as scientists understood it in the summer of 1939. Were it not for the final paragraph, the letter might not have seemed alarming: "I understand Germany has actually stopped the sale of uranium from the Czechoslovakian mines which she has taken over. . . ."[29]

Roosevelt passed the letter on to General Watson, his personal secretary, with the admonition that "this requires action."[30] His interest in the military possibilities that might result from nuclear research had been aroused, and his interest in the subject would play an increasingly important role in the bomb's development. At this point he encouraged further investigation into the two major problems posed by the discovery of nuclear fission: Were atomic bombs theoretically possible? If they were, could they be developed for use in the impending war?

In spite of the President's interest, however, there was little more he could do about it under the circumstances. Roosevelt was not qualified to make a personal judgment about the feasibility of nuclear research, and in 1939 he had neither a personal science adviser nor a standing science advisory committee to turn the problem over to. As a result, he found it necessary to create an *ad hoc* Uranium Committee to "study into the possible relationship to national defense of recent discoveries in the field of atomistics, notably the fission of uranium."[31] Lyman C. Briggs, the director of the National Bureau of Standards, was appointed the Committee's chairman.[32] Although Briggs was a physicist, his own experience and interests lay outside the field of nuclear physics, and his numerous other responsibilities proved to be serious distractions. Moreover, he was by nature "slow, conservative, methodical, and accustomed to operate at a peace-time tempo," qualities that the war in Europe and the possibility of developing an atomic bomb did not alter.[33]

The significance of the conversation between Roosevelt and Sachs in October 1939 thus lies in the President's decision to place under advisement the question of whether nuclear fission had potential military applications. But to learn the answer as quickly as possible obviously required a substantial commitment of resources from the federal government. Science advisers in a position to recommend such a commitment to the President had to be convinced that a major atomic energy research program was necessary, regardless of the cost in manpower and money. Such a conviction, of course, came naturally to Szilard—alerted by personal experience to the Nazi threat, unencumbered by bureaucratic complexities, and aware of the high caliber of German nuclear physicists. It came naturally to Roosevelt too—both his instincts and the weight of his responsibilities drew him willingly to the support of extraordinary ideas. But others in positions where they had less freedom to act on their instincts, for whom atomic energy was an area of scientific research whose possibilities had to be measured against opportunities in other fields, could not reach a decision as readily.

The speed with which the first meeting of the Uranium Committee was organized indicated that contacting the President had been an effective tactic. But the results of that and subsequent meetings suggested that the only way to keep the bureaucratic engine running was to refuel it periodically from the top. In February 1940, when Joliot published another paper which further reinforced the possibility of a chain reaction, not a single experiment aimed at studying the possibilities of such a reaction in natural uranium was underway in the United States. Explaining the situation to Einstein, Szilard proposed to write a paper for the *Physical Review* stating that the uranium-graphite system would be chain-reacting. He would then threaten to publish the paper unless the government asked him to withhold it and promised in return to take some positive action.[34]

Einstein wrote to Sachs, who wrote, in turn, to the President: "Dr. Szilard has shown me the manuscript which he is sending to the *Physics Review* [sic] in which he describes in detail a method for setting up a chain reaction in uranium. The papers will appear in print unless they are held up, and the question arises whether something ought to be done to withhold publication."[35] The tactic worked. The President's reply was positive and ordered that another meeting between the scientists and the Uranium Committee be arranged.[36] Within a few weeks Columbia received a grant of $6,000 for uranium-graphite experiments. Until the Uranium Committee was reorganized several months later, however, it initiated no other significant contribution to nuclear studies.

How can the Committee's lethargy be explained? Several reasons have already been suggested: the conservative disposition of its chairman, its *ad hoc* status, the inability of scientists to promise results. But an additional factor should be considered: whether or not it is fair to say that émigré scientists were not generally trusted, it is clear that many federal bureaucats, at least, were not willing to rely on their advice. Thus, after Fermi had discussed nuclear fission with the Navy an American-born scientist on the Committee received a call asking, "Who is this man Fermi? Is he a Fascist or what? What is he?"[37] A year later, in April 1940, Briggs told Sachs that Szilard and Fermi should not be invited to the Uranium Committee meeting ordered by Roosevelt because "these matters are secret."[38] The most telling event, however, occurred the following month: An advisory committee inspired by Szilard and composed of men appointed by Briggs on the advice of Harold C. Urey, professor of chemistry at Columbia, was informed at its first meeting that it would be disbanded because not all its members were U.S. citizens of long standing. If, they were told, the Briggs Committee supported a substantial research effort and it failed, the presence of Szilard, Fermi, and Wigner (who had in fact been a U.S. citizen for several years) would prove an embarrassment in case of a congressional investigation.[39] Such bureaucratic fears dogged the atomic energy project's decisionmaking process to the end of the war. This action of the Briggs Committee in May 1940 offers an early example of one consequence of this continuing theme: that the need to succeed would grow with the project's budget.

IV

"Probably a Wild Goose Chase"

Shortly after the Uranium Committee excluded émigré scientists from participation in its decisions, Roosevelt approved a proposal for a systematic mobilization of scientists in America for war, and the question of government support for atomic energy research was removed from the bureaucratic backwaters to which Briggs had consigned it. The atomic bomb was now in direct competition with other weapons research for financial support from the newly created science policy bureaucracy, the National Defense Research Committee (NDRC).

The NDRC was established by executive order on June 27, 1940, the day after Nazi armies occupied Paris. Its chairman was Vannevar Bush, who had been primarily responsible for bringing it into existence.[40] Grandson of a New England whaling captain and son of a Universalist minister, lean, shrewd, and energetic at fifty, Bush was an astute administrator. Not a research scientist, but an engineer and mathematician turned inventor, he had worked on submarine devices for the Navy during World War I. After the war he had served the Massachusetts Institute of Technology first as a professor, then as dean of engineering, and finally as its vice-president. Among his inventions Bush could list the justifying typewriter, an essential circuit for the automatic dial telephone, and the Bush differential analyzer, a prototype of the modern computer.[41]

In 1939 Bush accepted the presidency of the Carnegie Institution and moved to Washington. As head of the operating agency for the numerous scientific activities financed by the Institution, and as the new chairman of the National Advisory Committee for Aeronautics which he had joined in 1938, he had a close-up view of the government's then-stumbling defense efforts. Virtually nothing was being done to organize American science for the war that Bush was certain would soon involve the United States. In alliance with Karl T. Compton, James B. Conant, and Frank B. Jewett, the presidents respectively of M.I.T., Harvard, and Bell Telephone Laboratories, Bush developed a plan for a committee that would perform the same role in the general development of weapons technology that the National Advisory Committee for Aeronautics performed in aviation.[42]

The National Defense Research Committee was married to the past as a matter of institutional convenience—it was created under the authority of the World War I Council for National Defense from which it drew its funds—but it was free of old obligations. Its objective, Roosevelt wrote, was to stimulate "experimental investigations and reports, as may be found desirable in order to accelerate the creation or improvement of the instrumentalities of warfare."[43] Its sole purpose, it is important to emphasize here, was to search for new opportunities *to apply science to the demands of the impending war.*

Under Bush's direction, the NDRC exercised the right to independent judgment with regard to the selection of projects and their development. Although the Committee was created to serve the military, Bush insisted throughout the war—first as chairman of the NDRC and, after June 1941, as director of the Office of Scientific Research and Development (OSRD)—that the best method of rendering that assistance was ultimately a matter these organizations had to decide for themselves.[44] Even as he sought to preserve this administrative independence, however, he was naturally concerned as well with developing a close working relationship with the military. The achievement of this dual goal was perhaps his most challenging administrative task. He faced great difficulty in winning the confidence of military leaders who resented civilian "interference" and mistrusted civilian attitudes toward security. Bush's efforts to accommodate the military, however, created considerable resentment, in turn, among working scientists who objected to military regulation of their work.

The NDRC owed its birth to the foresight of Bush, Conant, Compton, and Jewett, not to the discovery of fission. But the importuning of Sachs, Szilard, and others aroused by the grim possibility of a nuclear chain reaction and its potential military consequences made the Committee's formation appear all the more vital to Roosevelt. The President's periodic reviews of the Briggs Committee's progress and his continued concern about the prospective creation of an atomic bomb led him, in establishing the NDRC, to place the Uranium Committee under its control. Briggs now reported directly to Bush.[45] The Uranium Committee had been in existence for less than a year when it thus came under new direction, in June 1940. During that time scientific advances had not been insignificant; but progress had in fact resulted only from the determined efforts of scientists working independently and the support they received as a result of Roosevelt's continuing interest.

The President's familiarity with atomic energy had been carefully nurtured. While Sachs kept Roosevelt informed about the need for both support and haste, Szilard kept Sachs alerted to the state of nuclear research. In March 1940, Sachs relayed to the White House a rumor that the Nazis had secretly intensified their uranium research, that Joliot had conducted an experiment of considerable importance, and that Szilard was making progress at Columbia. In May, Sachs reported to Roosevelt on the encouraging work of Fermi and Szilard, warning that something had to be done to safeguard the uranium ore in the Congo now that the Nazis were overrunning Belgium; he also suggested that the research project be placed under a more flexible organization.[46] The NDRC was designed to be that organization.

The integration of the Uranium Committee into the overall organizational framework of the military-scientific defense effort should have made it easier for nuclear scientists to gain support for their research efforts. In some ways it did; but the unanswered questions about the explosive potential of fission left these researchers at a disadvantage in the competition for funds. Although the NDRC was now providing a dynamic impetus for a previously languid group, the former's sole function was to support research that would result in weapons applicable to the present war. Bush had to be convinced, therefore, that the atomic bomb could be built and used within a reasonable time. If the fulfilment of its military promise lay beyond what then appeared to be the prospective temporal boundaries of the war, or if atomic energy could only be applied as a source of industrial power in the future, NDRC support would not be forthcoming.

In the year between June 1940 and July 1941 the Briggs Committee still held formal responsibility for formulating the atomic energy program. Although Bush soon reorganized the subordinate group, adding several top scientists and dropping the Army and Navy representatives, U.S. physicists still lacked the degree of support and encouragement—and the desperate sense of urgency—that came to characterize later work on the bomb.[47] In August 1940, for example, when Fermi and the chairman of the Physics Department outlined Columbia's research plans, they listed as their objectives power generation and large amounts of neutrons for making artificial radioactive substances for biological and therapeutic applications. The atomic bomb was not a primary goal. According to the official historians of the United States Atomic Energy Commission, this lack of interest in military uses was typical of the time. Scientists in America—Szilard, Wigner, and Teller here being exceptions—had not yet oriented their thoughts to weapons of mass destruction. Reports to Bush by scientists and engineers who undertook special reviews of the Uranium Committee's work in the spring of 1941 reflected a similar attitude: all were familiar with the possibility of a military application of atomic energy, but with the United States not yet at war, they did not see this as the major objective toward which all research should be directed. They ignored some essential facts and overlooked the military significance of others.[48]

That atomic weapons research was delayed in America until the fall of 1941 may be attributed to the relatively late date of actual United States engagement in World War II. Such an explanation, however, cannot account for a similar delay in embattled England, at war since September 1939. Although an atomic energy research program had been started almost immediately after the German discovery of fission was announced, the outbreak of war eight months later turned the attention of British scientists *away* from uranium research to "immediately urgent problems."[49] With regard to the possibility of an atomic bomb, the official historian of the United Kingdom Atomic Energy Authority reports that by 1940 "skepticism was almost universal and profound."[50] G. P. Thomson, professor of physics at Imperial College, London, who had initially shared Szilard's premonitions about the feasibility of the bomb, had practically concluded that the matter was not worth pursuing.

As in America, however, émigré physicists in England were barred by stringent security regulations from participating in the development of radar and other high-priority research. At least two of these men—Otto Frisch, who had left Bohr's institute in Copenhagen, and Rudolph Peierls—systematically pursued their study of the theoretical possibilities of a "superbomb." By April 1940 they had not only succeeded in outlining a method for developing an atomic bomb, but also suggested a means of detonating the device, had explained how the isotope uranium-235 might be separated from uranium-238, and had predicted the radiation effects of an atomic explosion.[51] Herein lies a remarkable demonstration of how, as in the U.S., the very restrictions and limitations imposed upon émigré scientists facilitated their leading roles in the bomb's development. Although American, British, and German scientists certainly possessed the talent to achieve the same progress, only the émigrés in America and Britain could devote enough time to the problem—a circumstance that correspondingly suggests another reason for the failure of German atomic scientists.

The work of Frisch and Peierls led to a reversal of the attitude of the British government toward atomic energy. A subcommittee of the Committee for the Scientific Survey of Air Warfare was formed under Thomson's chairmanship to oversee atomic energy research. It was the report of this group, codenamed the MAUD Committee, that reached America during the spring of 1941.[52]

Work on the atomic bomb in the United States had meanwhile proceeded slowly. When Professor A. V. Hill, the British scientific attaché in Washington, inquired about uranium research, he was told that it was not impossible that practical results might emerge in the end, but that there was no prospect of them at present. American scientists considered uranium research a waste of Britain's already strained resources: if anything valuable emerged from the work in this area in America the British would be informed. A large number of Americans, all well disposed toward England, were involved in the project and they had excellent equipment, Hill was told. It was far better for the work to continue in this country than for the British to be "wasting their time on what was scientifically very interesting but for the present practical needs probably a wild goose chase."[53]

The truthfulness of the Americans to whom Hill spoke is indicated by the limited support American scientists received for uranium research at the beginning of the new fiscal year. When Briggs sent Bush a summary of his Committee's work on July 1, 1940, he reported that a grant of $100,000 had already been made to study the separation of U-235. However, the remaining project—study of the possibility of a chain reaction—had yet to be funded. Briggs therefore recommended that the National Defense Research Committee set aside $140,000 for two lines of experimental work: the first, to determine more accurately the fundamental physical constants in the fission process; the second, to study the controlled-chain-reaction problem, still a crucial technical issue in the development of an atomic bomb. On September 6, however, Briggs was informed that the NDRC had agreed to assign only $40,000 to the atomic energy program.[54] This was sufficient to finance the work on physical constants, but it fell far short of the support required for the chain reaction experiments. The competition for money was keen, and until scientists in Britain suggested a method by which an atomic bomb might be built under the criterion of wartime use, work on atomic energy for military purposes made little progress in America.

V

"Its Use Might Be Determining"

Early in the summer of 1941 the British government forwarded to Bush a copy of the MAUD Committee's report entitled "The Use of Uranium for a Bomb." Based on the Frisch-Peierls memorandum, the report stated the premise that if pure U-235 were available in sufficient mass, any neutron produced—not just slow ones—could cause fission. Since the bulk of the neutrons would be fast, the chain reaction would cause an explosion of tremendous force. The report also held out the possibility that plutonium could be used for a bomb; that plutonium or uranium bombs could be made small enough to carry in existing aircraft; and, finally, that a bomb could be produced within two years.

Until his Committee had received the MAUD report, Bush informed Roosevelt on July 16, its members had believed the "possibility of a successful outcome was very remote," and therefore had not felt justified "in diverting to the work the efforts of scientists in considerable numbers, in view of the scarcity of highly qualified physicists for its other important work." Nevertheless, Bush had supported what he termed "a careful, but not an elaborate or expensive program" primarily as a safety measure, since it was known that "much work on this subject had been done on the Continent of Europe." However, an entirely different approach to atomic energy research was now necessary. Although the matter was still "highly abstruse," Bush considered "one thing certain: if such an explosive were made it would be thousands of times more powerful than existing explosives, and its use might be determining."[55]

Bush's report thus placed the issue of atomic energy in a completely new perspective for the President. If the British were pursuing such a promising line of research, it was entirely possible—indeed, considering the caliber of German physicists, it was probable—that atomic energy research in Germany had advanced in a similar direction. No one, certainly not Roosevelt, seemed willing to assume anything less. Thus, within the next few months the organization, the tempo, and the attitude toward such research in America altered dramatically.

Bush's July memorandum led to a White House meeting between himself, Vice-President Henry A. Wallace, and Roosevelt on October 9, 1941.[56] As a result of their discussion, the desultory Uranium Committee was replaced by a new group whose assignment reflected the sudden importance atomic energy had acquired. It was charged with the responsibility of "advis[ing] the President on questions of policy relating to the study of nuclear fission," and its membership included the government's top science administrators: Bush, now director of the recently formed Office of Scientific Research and Development (OSRD), and James B. Conant, chemist, president of Harvard University, and newly appointed chairman of the National Defense Research Committee. The War Department was represented by its senior civilian and military chiefs: Secretary of War Henry L. Stimson and Chief of Staff General George C. Marshall. And, as if to institutionalize his direct interest in the matter, Roosevelt assigned a personal liaison to the new committee —the Vice-President, whose attitude toward scientific research during the early New Deal years, when he was Secretary of Agriculture, had earned him a reputation among scientists as the most "clear-headed" member of the Cabinet.[57]*

In addition to this important administrative reorganization of atomic energy research, the participants in the October meeting discussed questions of secrecy, British progress in the field, the issue of postwar control, and the putative German atomic energy program. Roosevelt emphasized the importance of keep-

---

* The new committee was designated Section-1 (S-1) of the Office of Scientific Research and Development; thereafter the atomic bomb project was often referred to as "S-1."

ing knowledge of the project within the smallest possible circle, a theme he would stress again and again throughout the war. In March 1942, for example, he approved Bush's recommendation to turn the development of the atomic bomb over to the War Department, "on condition that you yourself are *certain* that the War Department has made all adequate provision for *absolute secrecy*."[58] Through the efforts of Sachs, Szilard, and Bush, Roosevelt had become keenly aware of the potential importance of the bomb even at this embryonic stage of its development.

What Bush continued throughout the war to refer to as the problem of "after-war control" or the "international situation" was reviewed "at some length" for the first time in October. Although there is no record of the details of this discussion, except that it included the problem of postwar sources of uranium, reports of later talks between Bush and the President on these issues indicate that the above phrases referred to the postwar sharing of atomic energy research and development with the British.[59]

The advanced state of British research in 1941 led Roosevelt to suggest to Churchill that their countries approach the development of an atomic bomb as full partners. "It appears desirable that we should soon correspond or converse concerning the subject which is under study by your MAUD Committee, and by Dr. Bush's organization in this country," he wrote to Churchill on October 11, "in order that any extended efforts may be coordinated or even jointly conducted."[60] Finally, there was the question of German progress, which at this time, and in the years that followed, remained an unanswered question of great concern to the President and his associates. At the October 9 meeting, as in all their subsequent discussions of the problem, Bush could say only that he knew "very little" about the progress of atomic energy research in Germany.

During the early months of 1942, the preliminary experimental work on the development of an atomic bomb went steadily forward, and the President was kept informed of its progress. In March, Bush was able to tell Roosevelt that "the stuff will apparently be more powerful than we then [in October] thought."[61] German progress remained a primary con-

cern, the relationship with the British appeared to be developing smoothly, and Bush began to plan for the War Department's takeover of the project by the summer of 1942. The
best estimate for completion was sometime in 1944. The President continued to be very interested in the project. In a memorandum to Bush, also in March, he stated that he wanted the
program "pushed not only in regard to development, but also
with due regard to time. This is very much of the essence."[62]
The criterion of wartime use had been satisfied by the work
of scientists in England, and what Bush called "the race toward
realization" was now underway after a delay of two years. Scientists entered this race convinced that the outcome of the war
depended upon their ability to recover the time lost.

2

SOLDIERS OUT
OF UNIFORM

The Manhattan Project, the wartime organization that developed the atomic bomb, stands out as the profoundest single experience in the history of the American scientific community. Its political, social, moral, intellectual, and professional repercussions had an enduring effect on the careers and political consciousness of all who participated. The pressures of war brought young Ph.D.'s into intimate contact with eminent nuclear physicists of both Europe and America; university scientists worked closely (if not always congenially) with men who had devoted their lives to industrial research; physicists and engineers, chemists and mathematicians pooled their knowledge to solve problems; the morally concerned came into contact with those who seldom considered the moral consequences of their work. Linking fundamental research to military applications, the project transformed scientists into weapons-makers and, at its end, introduced a world in quest of peace to history's deadliest weapon of war.

The alliance between science and government in America, like the Grand Alliance itself, was forged by the exigencies of war. The effectiveness of enemy air and sea forces provoked early crash programs to develop anti-aircraft and anti-submarine weapons. The scientists and engineers participating in these programs, the historian James P. Baxter has noted, "were daily conscious that time was the deciding factor of the conflict."[1] But none were more conscious of time than those who worked in the Manhattan Project. In the race for the atomic bomb—a race for survival against German scientists believed to have a two-year head start—all those associated with the enterprise, military and civilians alike, agreed that the bomb's rapid development was the single most important necessity of the war.

This common objective, however, became the cause of serious conflicts. As the experience of combat proved that success in the laboratory was a necessary precursor to victory in battle, scientists were brought into closer partnership with the military and with policymakers. While the nature of the war itself determined some aspects of their relationship, the preconceived attitudes of the new partners determined others. The initial administrative organization of the atomic energy program was profoundly influenced, for example, by the belief of science administrators that scientists ought to play an active role in the policymaking process; the wartime relationship between Manhattan Project scientists and the military was largely determined by the conflicting attitudes toward security held by research scientists and the Army officer in charge of their work; and the security regulations established by that officer were based primarily on his attitude toward the Soviet Union, an attitude that few scientists shared.

The conduct of scientists during the early organizational phase of the project reflected their intense involvement from the beginning. As the development of the atomic bomb got underway, the common commitment to speed came up against conflicting professional and political considerations. Science administrators in their Washington offices and research scientists in their Manhattan Project laboratories began fighting a two-front war: on the one hand, there were the enemies of the United States; and on the other, the potential enemies of science—men and institutions seeking to control research.

I

Vannevar Bush and the "Art of Management"

The effort to create the atomic bomb was the largest and most expensive weapons research and development project ever undertaken up to that time. Over a period of less than three years the program cost over $2-billion, required the construction and use of thirty-seven installations in nineteen states and Canada, employed approximately 120,000 persons, and absorbed a large proportion of the nation's scientific and engineering talent.[2]* The responsibility for the actual development of the bomb was turned over to the War Department in the fall of 1942, but the organizational edifice that gave form and life to this gigantic enterprise throughout the war was set up by science administrators: Vannevar Bush, as director of the Office of Scientific Research and Development (OSRD), and his assistant, James B. Conant, as chairman of the National Defense Research Committee (NDRC). The relationship between the research scientists who worked on the bomb and the policymakers who controlled its use was thus mediated by members of the American scientific community who could be counted on to represent what they considered to be the interests of American science.

The atomic energy administrative structure began to take shape at the White House meeting of October 9, 1941. There Roosevelt gave Bush and Conant, along with Stimson, Marshall, and Wallace, overall responsibility for the bomb's development. A year later, Brigadier General Leslie R. Groves, of the Army Corps of Engineers, joined this "Top Policy Group" as the officer-in-charge of the Manhattan Project. On May 1, 1943, Stimson, as Secretary of War, assumed direct responsibility for the administration of the entire project, and from that point on considered himself the "President's senior adviser on the military employment of atomic energy."[3] But Stimson's numerous other pressing responsibilities in fact left him little time to deal with the problems of the bomb's development, and it was not until very late in the war—the spring of 1945—

* As a recruiting aid, a list of nuclear physicists in America was compiled sometime in early 1943. Of the 33 nuclear physicists listed as "leaders in the field," 20 were then working with the Manhattan Project. Of the 150 designated as "men of ability and considerable experience in the field," 57 were with the Manhattan Project. Of the 225 physicists listed as "young men of ability and promise," 47 were employed by the project. OSRD, S-1, Personnel folder.

that atomic energy "ceased to be an *undertaking apart* and became the center of Stimson's official life."[4] Until then, his special assistants, Boston attorney Harvey Bundy and insurance executive George L. Harrison, handled routine atomic energy affairs for him. Chief of Staff Marshall similarly had no direct connection with the daily administration of the program; nor did Wallace, who served primarily as liaison and coordinator.

Thus it came about that Bush and Conant, on the one hand, and Groves, on the other, occupied the pivotal positions between the scientists actually engaged in the bomb's development and the civilian and military policymakers directly responsible to the President. It was these three men, standing administratively at one remove from the White House, who performed the critical tasks of interpreting and carrying out the President's decisions on atomic energy policy, and of bringing problems and suggestions to his attention. Their personalities, their political judgments, and their expectations about the postwar role of atomic energy would become increasingly important during the war.

The Top Policy Group of science administrators, presidential advisers, and military officers was assisted by the S-1 (atomic energy) Executive Committee of the Office of Scientific Research and Development. To ensure coordination, Conant acted as chairman of S-1. The other members of the Committee were Lyman C. Briggs, former chairman of the special atomic energy committee; Dr. E. V. Murphree, an engineer on leave from the Standard Oil Development Company of New York, who also served as chairman of the Atomic Energy Planning Board, a group primarily concerned with engineering matters; and the project leaders of the three major science research laboratories working on the bomb—Harold C. Urey at Columbia University, Arthur H. Compton at the University of Chicago, and Ernest O. Lawrence at the University of California Radiation Laboratory. Other bodies such as the Military Policy Committee and the Combined (American, British, Canadian) Policy Committee served as specialized advisory groups organized to facilitate decisionmaking within the U.S. government and among participating governments.[5]

After Groves became officer-in-charge of the Manhattan

Project, Conant's role as chairman of the S-1 Executive Committee slowly changed. In constant touch with every important aspect of the Project, he became an unofficial—but highly influential—science adviser to Groves. Bush, in turn, was informed of all important developments through numerous detailed memoranda from Conant. Over the course of the war the meetings of the S-1 Executive Committee became less frequent, and the administrative decisions made by Groves as Project head progressively more important. His actions were, however, subject to review by the Military Policy Committee, and it was this group that emerged from the tangled organizational web as the most important managerial committee of the Project. Bush was this group's chairman, and Conant attended all meetings as his alternate.[6]

Although Roosevelt set the specific criteria for the governance of the atomic energy project, Bush determined how those criteria would be implemented during the early years of the war. During the fall and winter of 1941 the President urged that the organization and administration of the project be designed to facilitate both strict security and utmost speed. But he left to Bush all decisions on how to implement his wishes in these respects, as well as the selection of the organizations and individuals necessary for carrying out the tasks.

In making these decisions Bush was strongly influenced by an additional consideration: his view that the advice of scientists was essential to efficient planning for modern warfare. He was determined that scientists should serve "as more than mere consultants to fighting men."[7] He believed that the nature of modern warfare required a coordinated and equal partnership among scientists, soldiers, and civilian policymakers as participants in strategic planning, and it was this partnership that he worked for throughout the war. "To plan scientific war without the presence of the scientist at the councils," he told Bundy in January 1942, "is to run a serious risk of drawing conclusions on incomplete premises. Yet, in the strategic level, and to some extent in the tactical level, that is just what is being done." If "scientific trends [were] becoming a determining factor in warfare," then it followed that scientists had to be accorded a permanent voice among planners.[8] It was because the

War Department encouraged such a role for scientists that Bush recommended that the Army be placed in charge of the development of the atomic bomb. He was aware that the ". . . Naval Research Laboratory was engaged on aspects of this [atomic energy] research . . . as early as any group anywhere," but for him this consideration paled before the Navy's lack of interest in the advice of civilian scientists.[9]

"The decision to take the [atomic bomb] program up with the Army rather than the Navy was my own," Bush explained after the war. "It was based on the general attitude of the Services in regard to relations with civilian research carried on in my own organization and also based on the fact that I had enormous respect for and confidence in Secretary Stimson. . . ."[10]* From the time Bush had first undertaken the task of organizing scientists for war in 1940, Stimson had demonstrated that he valued their counsel.[11] In contrast, Secretary of the Navy Frank Knox had shown no interest in civilian scientific advice. Early in 1941, for example, when Bush turned the attention of scientists to the problem of anti-submarine warfare, the Navy informed him that it "needed no help along these lines."[12] Nor did either the civilian or the military chiefs of the Navy Department change their views after Pearl Harbor. On several occasions Bush complained of this attitude to the coordinator of Naval Research, Rear Admiral Julius A. Furer. "As the head of the scientists who are attempting to aid in the war," Furer noted in his diary, "he [Bush] has been ignored at the higher levels. He has been called into consultation quite often by the Army, especially the Air Force High Command, and by the White House itself, but he has never been asked into consultation by Admiral King or Secretary Knox." Furer went on to note that Bush was so frustrated by the Navy's attitude as to consider "going to the mat on the subject with King"—deciding against this, however, on the assumption that it would serve only to further alienate the Navy's High Command.[13]

* Bush expressed the depth of his affection for Stimson in a letter of April 28, 1948: "During the war you were to me as a father to a son, and my greatest satisfaction of the whole war experience came from that relationship." Bush mss., Box 109, Folder no. 2552.

The formation of the Military Policy Committee (MPC) in September 1942 offers a further example of Bush's efforts to assure scientists a prominent voice in the determination of atomic energy policy. As the official historians of the Atomic Energy Commission have noted, it was Bush who initiated the idea of creating such a group,[14] conceiving of it as, in effect, the board of directors for a large "corporation." While Roosevelt was titular head of the corporation, and General Groves vice-president in charge of operations, Bush reigned as chairman of the board. The MPC was composed of three members: Bush, its chairman; Major General W. D. Styer, chief of staff for the Army's Services of Supplies; and Rear Admiral W. R. Purnell, assistant chief of staff to the Chief of Naval Operations. The creation of this advisory group thus brought into direct contact with the Manhattan Project high-ranking officers who could ease priority and procurement problems. The appointment of a Navy representative provided another military point of view, one not necessarily consistent with the Army's. This diminished the possibility of the Navy interfering with priorities and made access to Naval weapons development facilities easier to gain. As Bush's deputy, Conant attended all Committee meetings, and Groves—who was officially responsible to the Committee—worked closely with Conant. Overall, this arrangement served to ensure that scientists would always receive an adequate hearing.

It was such demonstrations of shrewd administrative and organizing skill that inspired Conant to label Bush a master of "the art of management," and to consider him "the most important" reason behind the numerous contributions scientists made to the war effort.[15] That, however, was the view from Washington; as seen from the various laboratories of the Manhattan Project, Bush's role appeared in a somewhat different light.

II

Scientific Pride and Prejudice

As in any complex organization, the decisionmaking processes within the Manhattan Project can be explained only partially by reference to administrative responsibilities, bureaucratic maneuvers, and organizational charts. The Project was too vast in scope, its tasks too unprecedented, the pressure for speed in the execution of those tasks too pervasive, for it to be governed by neat bureaucratic procedures. Science administrators' plans and Army security regulations alike had to be altered at times to accommodate the ideas of scientists with unique talents. The pressure for haste gave research scientists, as individuals or in small groups, a bargaining power that could not be traced on a table of organization. The importance of the atomic bomb to the war effort gradually led these scientists themselves, as well as science administrators, toward the idea that scientists ought to play a role in the policymaking process.

Even before the Army began to assume control over the atomic energy program late in 1942, participating scientists labored under a sense of heavy responsibility and anxiety—the fear that Germany was ahead in the race for the bomb. Arthur Compton, the director of the atomic energy project at the University of Chicago, was so distressed at the slow rate of progress that, in June 1942, he urged a program for researching and developing "counter measures" against a German atomic bomb.[16] In July Oppenheimer wrote despairingly that the war could be lost before an answer was found.[17] "What is wrong with us?" was Szilard's heading for a memorandum in September criticizing the rate of progress.[18]

The early months of work under the Army's jurisdiction did not relieve this concern of scientists; on the contrary, their anxieties deepened. Bush had to admit to the President in December that he still did not know "where we stand in the race with the enemy toward a usable result, but it is quite possible that Germany is ahead of us and may be able to produce superbombs sooner than we can."[19] At that time, in fact, Bush and Conant were still receiving complaints about the Project's organizational structure and the slow rate of progress for which it was held responsible.[20]

Despite the concern for speed expressed at the original White House meeting in October 1941, the actual development of a bomb had not yet started by the beginning of 1943; and only limited progress had been made in constructing the many facilities necessary for its creation. Groves was not appointed to head the Project until September 17, 1942. The site for the uranium separation plant at Oak Ridge, Tennessee, was acquired two days later. The land on which the bomb laboratory would be constructed outside of Los Alamos, New Mexico, was not even purchased by the government until November; and it was December 1942 before Oppenheimer was appointed director.[21] Thus, four years after fission had been discovered, scientists could not be confident that the United States was closing the lead the Germans were assumed to have. A feeling of desperate urgency grew with every passing month, and with it one of hostility toward any precautions that caused delays.

Unlike Bush, who labored in Washington for good relations with the War Department, many scientists in the Manhattan Project's laboratories showed open contempt for the Army's administration of the enterprise. They had little faith that that administration would do anything but impede their work, and the apparent rigidity and arbitrariness of the security regulations under which they lived reinforced this lack of faith. In contrast to their German counterparts, whose atomic energy research was conducted in relative complacency, scientists in America were driven by a profound sense of danger. They believed that nothing—not even security precautions—ought to be permitted to interfere with their work.

In this atmosphere it was natural that many scientists came to believe that they themselves, rather than the military, bore the ultimate responsibility for victory and the security of the nation. In August 1943, at Los Alamos, Hans Bethe and Edward Teller drew up a proposal for expediting the bomb's development by giving "full responsibility . . . directly to those [scientists] who are most experienced in various phases of the problem."[22] Echoing this call, Edward Creutz in Chicago introduced a similar plan with the warning: "We are engaged in what is undeniably the most far-reaching and significant project in the history of man . . . [which] may well be the determining factor in the continued existence of civilization itself. Since the responsibility for the success or failure of this venture lies with us, it becomes as much a part of our duty to seek the most reasonable and efficient administrative organization at it is to give out every ounce of training, technical ability, and creative energy to the solution of the scientific problems themselves." The development of the atomic bomb was far too important to be left to bureaucratic managers, military or civilian, and "however unseemly [such actions may be] for research workers," Creutz urged that they fight for an arrangement equal to the challenge.[23]

Military regulations and Washington bureaucrats were not the only impediments to progress that academic scientists criticized at this time. The unity of the scientific community in America as elsewhere had always been more apparent than real; for scientists were separated into two major categories, representing the different ventures of discovery and application.[24] In theory, all scientists shared a common intellectual tradition and values; in practice, however, the demands of financial competition guided the professional lives of industrial scientists, while researchers in the universities and foundations looked to academic distinction for their rewards. Now the more outspoken academicians began to complain that their colleagues in industry were too cautious, to the point of jeopardizing the safety of the nation. "In the past," Teller and Bethe observed in a letter to Oppenheimer, "the production program has been handled entirely by large companies. We believe that this has led to a considerable retardation of the program."[25] In addition to what these scientists perceived as overcautiousness, industrial values and attitudes constituted in themselves an additional cause of hostility.

At the Metallurgical Laboratory (Met. Lab.), the University of Chicago branch of the Manhattan Project, the tension between university and industrial scientists was particularly intense, and increased as Army security regulations, industrial safety precautions, and financial considerations began to complicate the work of the academics. Eugene Wigner reflected a general sentiment when he wrote that decisions "are taken by persons who have no adequate familiarity . . . with our project."[26] The academic members of the Chicago staff comprised a remarkable combination of eminent European refugees—Fermi, Szilard, Wigner, and James Franck, among others—with a brilliant, vigorous group of young Ph.D.'s launched out of their universities into the Manhattan Project's laboratories like marines onto Pacific island beaches. They were out to win the war, and they were determined that their contribution would be no less than that of the men serving their country in combat. They were, in the vernacular of the day, gung-ho, and very impatient with anyone who failed to share their *élan*.

Until very late in the war, progress on the bomb was measured against Germany's presumed head start. Project scientists, like administrators Bush and Conant, periodically felt more frustrated by their ignorance of German progress than by their own difficult scientific and technical problems. Spurred by their all-encompassing sense of responsibility for atomic energy matters, they developed some imaginative schemes for gathering intelligence on the status of work in Germany. In June 1942, Szilard suggested that a physicist be sent to Switzerland with diplomatic status for the purpose of contacting neutrals who attended German scientific meetings—an idea that was forwarded to Conant with the endorsement of Arthur Compton, the director of Met. Lab.[27] Likewise, in October 1943, Samuel K. Allison, Met. Lab.'s associate director, sent General Groves Philip Morrison's sophisticated intelligence-gathering proposal, designed to determine whether or not atomic energy research was being conducted in Germany on a scale large enough to have military applications. For this purpose Morrison outlined a series of surveys including analyses of the relevant literature and economic data, plant construction and auxiliary equipment usage, personnel allocation, and dispersion of selected chemical supplies.[28] But perhaps the most daring suggestion came from a young theoretical physicist privy to, though not then associated with, the work of the Manhattan Project. Having learned in October 1942 that Werner Heisenberg, the director of Germany's Kaiser-Wilhelm Institute, was scheduled to lecture in Switzerland at the University of Zurich, Victor Weisskopf wrote a letter to Oppenheimer, suggesting that Heisenberg be kidnapped, and volunteered to go himself on this dangerous assignment.[29] He added that he had discussed the matter with Hans Bethe, who had agreed that the risk—serious as it might be—was worth whatever price might have to be paid, presumably Weisskopf's life included. Although this cloak-and-dagger scheme was never actually attempted, the incident typifies the intensity of commitment and purpose that then prevailed among atomic scientists. And it explains, in part, the subsequent discontent of those who were not permitted to remain at the center of Manhattan Project activity.

The first major experimental barrier was breached on December 2, 1942, when, under Fermi's leadership, scientists at the University of Chicago produced the first self-sustaining chain reaction in history. There was now, at long last, definitive proof of the existence of such reactions. It remained to be determined, however, whether a self-sustaining chain reaction was possible under fast neutron bombardment. If fission only occurred with slow neutrons, as in the Chicago experiment, the bomb case would probably blow apart before the explosion had gone far enough. There were other basic questions that had to be answered, such as whether fast-neutron fission occurred in uranium-238 (U-238), the more plentiful isotope of natural uranium, or only in the rare isotope, uranium-235 (U-235). When U-235 proved to be the answer, scientists had to discover a method of separating the rare isotope in sufficient quantities, an extraordinarily difficult task. The engineering problems were as complex as the scientific ones.[30]

Between the fall of 1942 and February 1943, the orientation of the Manhattan Project shifted from one of academic research, centered at Chicago, to one of practical experimentation and engineering, at other sites. "From now on," as Conant reported to Bush on October 26, 1942, "it is a question of development and the solving of a multitude of mechanical problems."[31] With Fermi's successful chain-reaction experiment of December 2, 1942, the basic research required for the construction of an atomic bomb was virtually completed, and the research-oriented scientists not assigned to other sites were now relegated to a secondary role. Du Pont was selected as the Army's prime contractor for the next phase, and Wilmington, Delaware, became a site of major activity. "More than any other event," the historians of the Atomic Energy Commission have written, "that shift in authority engendered the undertones of discontent which pervaded the [Chicago] laboratory until the end of the war."[32] Chicago was being left behind; Oak Ridge in Tennessee, Hanford in Washington, and Los Alamos in New Mexico would now carry on the work. Isolated from the end-product of their labors so early and so suddenly, the Chicago scientists closely monitored the progress the industrial contractors were making. "In the[ir] sober judgment" matters were proceeding all too slowly. Unaccustomed to accepting administrative fiats, they did not hesitate to document their concerns in an unauthorized letter to Roosevelt in July 1943. Emphasizing the need for "all possible speed," they complained that "Army direction is conventional and routine. . . . Considerations of convenience and permanence [on the part of industry] obscure the main objective—speed." At once pleading and demanding, they called for a new approach: "Our enemy must not solve this problem first."[33]

At least some of the scientists' objections emerged as much from their pride as from their patriotism: "The program is delayed because of the lack of adequate consultation of the few scientific leaders which [sic] alone are competent in this new field. The life of our nation is endangered by such policy." As Philip Morrison summarized their views in a letter to Oppenheimer, the existing bad morale was due "to high policy, to the loss of responsibility by the lab, to the apparent obscurement of speed by objects of convenience and safety, to the business-as-usual-only-with-lots-more-money attitude of the contractors, to the unwillingness of the Army to trust men who know." It all added up to a plea for allowing the protesters to remain intimately involved with the Project, as well as a "desperate attempt at speed."[34] The fact that some of the most eminent nuclear physicists in the world were not being consulted by industry or confided in by the Army was proof enough to their young protégés in Chicago that both Army and industry were incompetent. It also guaranteed that in the future their opinions would be strong and vigorously expressed.

The immediate difficulties of 1942–43 were smoothed over by Arthur Compton, who obtained Groves's promise to keep Chicago as closely involved as possible in the work of the Manhattan Project.[35] But the sense of frustration and distrust did not disappear. It subsided temporarily, only to re-emerge later in attempts by Met. Lab. scientists to block the use of the bomb against Japan. Although their early concern for speed might appear inconsistent with these later efforts to prevent the dropping of the bomb, both views were actually derived from a single idea: that the scientists of the Manhattan Project were personally responsible for the development of the atomic bomb —and therefore also responsible for its use and control.

III

Manhattan Project Scientists: Soldiers Out of Uniform

The hostility of scientists to military control of the Manhattan Project did not originate in personal experience, although experience did serve to reinforce it. It arose, rather, from a deepseated prejudice—which surfaced during Oppenheimer's effort to recruit a staff for Los Alamos early in 1943—against a system that subordinated intellectual freedom to a formal chain of command. Isolated in the New Mexican desert for reasons of both security and safety, the laboratory where the bomb was to be assembled and tested was originally planned as a military installation to be manned by scientists in uniform: Oppenheimer was to hold the rank of lieutenant colonel, and each "section leader" was to be commissioned a major. For the architects of this arrangement, Groves and Conant, placing the laboratory under military control was an added security precaution, in a situation that required the maximum possible degree of security.[36]

In order to staff the Nuclear Weapons Laboratory at Los Alamos in 1943, scientists had to be recruited from other laboratories. By this time many of the country's most brilliant physicists had moved to Cambridge to work on radar at M.I.T.[37] But unless some of them could be brought into the Manhattan Project, "there was no chance whatever," Oppenheimer told Conant, of attaining the objective within the desired time.[38] There were two steps in the recruiting process. The first was to convince Bush and Conant that a given potential candidate was absolutely essential to the work of the Project. This was not a simple task, for, as Conant formulated the problem, it came down to this: "Should OSRD cripple the work of the Radiation Laboratory by taking one of the most important of eighteen group leaders in order to make Mr. Oppenheimer's work succeed?"[39]* If and when that difficult question was answered affirmatively, Oppenheimer then had to convince the candidate in question that his move to the barren desert would provide a greater scientific challenge than the work he was doing in Cambridge. And this argument, it turned out, would often be undermined by the scientist's belief that creative work would be stifled under a military chain of command.

In a letter to Conant written early in February 1943, Oppenheimer summarized what he called the "indispensable conditions for the success of the project." "At the present time," he wrote, "I believe that the *solidarity of physicists* is such that if these conditions are not met, we shall not only fail to have the men from MIT with us, but that many of the men who have already planned to join the new Laboratory will reconsider commitments or come with such misgivings as to reduce their usefulness." First among these conditions was that Los Alamos be demilitarized. Scientists feared that military control could lead to a situation in which the whole laboratory might be compelled to follow the instructions of military superiors "and thus in effect lose its scientific autonomy." The scientists were willing to leave the *execution* of security measures in the hands of the military, but they insisted that "the decision as to what measures should be applied must be in the hands of the Laboratory."

Although Oppenheimer did not share his potential recruits' fears about the loss of autonomy, it was clear to him that de-

---

* The intensity of the competition among project leaders for the best scientists is well illustrated by Karl T. Compton's letter to Conant of January 11, 1943: "If you take these men you will take two of the three most irreplaceable men [R. F. Bacher and I. I. Rabi] in the Radiation Laboratory under Dr. DuBridge, the remaining one being Dr. Ridenour. . . ." Oppenheimer eventually got Bacher. Bush-Conant mss., Oppenheimer June 1942–Feb. 1943 folder.

militarization was the only way to assure the scientists' cooperation and their "unimpaired morale." With "some sacrifice and considerable delay," he thought, the Laboratory might be able to "go, more or less," even without wholly fulfilling these conditions which four important scientists in particular—I. I. Rabi, R. F. Bacher, E. M. McMillan, and L. Alvarez—insisted upon. But Oppenheimer considered a "real delay" inevitable if the conditions were altogether ignored.[40]

Faced with such a stark choice between security and speed, Groves agreed on this occasion to modify his plans for security, at least temporarily. A compromise was worked out whereby the work at Los Alamos was divided into two phases, civilian and military, conforming to the sequential functions "concerned with the development and final manufacture of an instrument of war." In a letter written on February 25, Groves and Conant explained the details of the plan to Oppenheimer and authorized him to show the letter to those he sought to recruit. The civilian phase would include experimental studies in science, engineering, and ordnance with all personnel, procurement, and other arrangements to be negotiated, as specified in a contract between the War Department and the University of California. At a date no earlier than January 1, 1944, the military phase would be initiated, but there was to be no obligation on the part of anyone employed during the civilian period to accept a commission in the Army.[41]

In causing Groves and Conant to modify their plan, scientists had demonstrated their ability to exercise at least some measure of control over the conditions under which they had to work; they had proved that a determined stand (especially on the part of key men) could effect changes in what was supposedly inflexible policy. True, the February letter to Oppenheimer represented on its face merely a partial victory, since Groves and Conant had only agreed to delay, not eliminate, the complete militarization of Los Alamos. But in fact the Manhattan Project administrators never did alter the Laboratory's civilian status. Perhaps this was simply because it ran well under civilian control; or perhaps it resulted at least partly from concern that Bacher, who headed the Experimental Division, might make good his declared intention to resign as soon as he was obliged to don an Army uniform.*

Yet, beyond the immediate arguments that scientists presented for not working at Los Alamos as soldiers, there lay more general and more profound fears about the fate of free scientific inquiry. If, as Rabi wrote to Oppenheimer, the Project was "the culmination of three centuries of physics," this made autonomy in research all the more imperative.[42] Any other arrangement threatened to deliver science, along with the bomb, into the hands of the military. Oppenheimer also recognized this danger, but he did not, in 1943, perceive any alternative. "To me," he replied to Rabi, "[the issue] is primarily the development in time of war of a military weapon of some consequence. I do not think the Nazis allow us the option of carrying out that development."[43] Rabi agreed—he had not questioned in his letter the necessity of creating the bomb, but rather the conditions under which scientists had to work in building it. In his reply, Oppenheimer ignored this latter point, not out of any lack of concern, but simply because he was more deeply impressed by the immediate wartime imperative. Long-range considerations, he felt, could not be allowed to interfere. And while the tight security arrangements troubled him as much as they did others, as director of the Laboratory he was in a position to deal with them in a more flexible manner than Groves, Bush, or Conant had originally intended.

There also existed a less obvious danger, but one that several more politically sophisticated scientists actually found more worrisome. Groves's resistance to scientists' demands for autonomy was, after all, not unexpected, nor was it unmanageable, if Bush and Conant defended the interests of scientists. It began to appear, however, that they were willing to surrender important principles to ease their own difficult administrative problems. When Oppenheimer discussed the recruiting situation with Bush, he found him sympathetic but "completely unwilling to take jurisdiction over these considerations since General

* Rabi did not join the Los Alamos staff. Bacher did, but the letter of acceptance which he wrote was also his resignation, effective the day Los Alamos became a military installation. See Hewlett and Anderson, *The New World*, 232.

Groves had been given the authority to deal with them."[44] Although Bush and Conant did not share the General's confidence in the value of sharply drawn lines of authority, they did share his heavy responsibility for Project security. At one point during the war, Groves recalled years later, he "was told by Dr. Bush and Dr. Conant that they were not satisfied with the security—[they] didn't feel it was strict enough."[45] Without allies in Washington to protect their autonomy, Manhattan Project scientists feared that a creative environment would be lost—and with it perhaps the race for the bomb.

Thus, when Hans Bethe read Groves and Conant's letter of February 25 to Oppenheimer guaranteeing "through Dr. Conant complete access to the scientific world," Bethe was not altogether reassured. He had left M.I.T. under Oppenheimer's prodding to head the Theoretical Physics Division at Los Alamos, and he was finding both the challenging nature of this new assignment and his close association with Oppenheimer—whom he considered the best-educated man he had ever met—irresistible attractions.[46] But he did not believe he could work effectively if regulations isolated him from scientists at other Manhattan Project sites for the duration of the war. Did Conant's "guarantee" mean that any information Los Alamos scientists wished to receive from other sites or individuals could only be received in verbal or written form from Conant? "This would obviously be fatal," Bethe declared. A rather more optimistic interpretation was that any visit to another laboratory would have to be approved by Conant; if so, this would be "cumbersome but not impossible." What Bethe hoped it meant, of course, was that Conant was guaranteeing the top Project scientists access to *whatever* information they considered necessary for their work.[47]

Bethe's hopes, however, could not be realized under the system of information control established by Groves within the Manhattan Project. Under Roosevelt's mandate to prevent information leaks, the General set about creating a security system that prevented the free flow of information within the Project. The security system had two important effects: it assured that the issue of scientific freedom would become a political rallying cry for scientists after the war; and it effectively suppressed organized discussion of postwar atomic energy policy *during* the war.

IV

The Politics of Security: "Russia Was Our Enemy"

General Leslie R. Groves was a brusque, efficient career Army officer, an engineer by training and a field commander by temperament. After graduating fourth in his West Point class of 1918, he spent the next twenty-four years moving from company duty to construction work, from military schools to general staff assignments. He was the Army's Deputy Chief of Construction when he was selected in 1942 to organize the Manhattan Project. The assignment disappointed Groves—he had hoped that the war would bring him his first overseas field command. Yet one important consolation was held out to him: if successful, he was told, the atomic bomb could "win the war."[48] If this remark struck him as little more than pep talk in September, he had accepted it completely and literally before the year was out. Indeed, Groves became as obsessed with winning the war with the atomic bomb as scientists were with winning the race for it.

To university scientists, Groves seemed the embodiment of the military mind, a living stereotype who confirmed all their fears about the military control of science. A quarter-century after World War II they could look back upon his administration of the Manhattan Project and admit that he was an honest and exceptionally able administrator—an "eccentric administrative genius," in I. I. Rabi's words.[49] But during the war itself, struggling in an atmosphere of constant crisis against technical difficulties and administrative encumbrances, scientists were much less inclined toward such generous estimates. Arrangements that Groves considered both necessary and expeditious scientists often viewed as arbitrary and impeding.

The hostility manifested by Manhattan Project scientists after the war to any connection between the War Department and the Atomic Energy Commission—the so-called "scientists' movement"[50]—cannot be understood without reference to their wartime experience with "compartmentalization," a security system originally established by the Briggs Committee but refined and administered during the war by Groves. The idea behind compartmentalization was simple, Groves explained: "Just as outfielders should not think about the manager's job of changing the pitchers, and a blocker should not be worrying about the ball-carrier fumbling, each scientist had to be made to do his own work."[51] Compartmentalization dictated that the flow of scientific information among scientists be regulated on a "need to know" basis. This was not an unreasonable principle, indeed it was quite sound, from the security standpoint; the problem, however, was that it undermined many equally sound principles of scientific investigation. And Groves, moreover, determined more or less alone, without benefit of scientists' counsel, how the system was to be applied. Haunted by the specter of a German atomic bomb, scientists found the restrictions unbearable enough to provoke defiance. After the war Szilard testified before a congressional committee that in the interests of speed he and other scientists had purposefully violated Groves's security regulations.[52]

Manhattan Project scientists were, of course, not an undifferentiated group, with uniform views and attitudes. On the contrary, they were a diverse lot, including many who did not voice overt objections to the arrangements under which they worked. Nevertheless, the articulate minority's complaints about compartmentalization received the tacit support of the overwhelming majority. The point here is to take the measure of their critique: to understand how compartmentalization affected both their work and their attitude toward the military. While judgments on their work are by their very nature speculative—what might have been cannot be measured with any accuracy against what was—the effect of compartmentalization upon scientists' feelings toward the military is demonstrable.

The conflict between Groves and university scientists can be attributed in part to the General's difficult personality. If he did make an effort to hide his distaste for scientists' attitudes and his low opinion of their reliability, he failed in the attempt. "Here at great expense the government has assembled the greatest collection of crackpots," Groves was alleged by scientists to have told his military staff.[53] "All I asked of the civilian scientists in the Army," he remarked after the war, "was that they be able to wear the uniform, they be able to salute, and they be able to stand at attention and say, 'Yes Sir' when an officer spoke to them."[54] Groves viewed scientists as grown children—curious, undisciplined people, ready to wander from their tasks unless confined by enforceable rules. Without controlling the propensity of scientists to discuss their work, he explained with reference to Hiroshima, "we would have had a great university and more learned scientists but many more casualties."[55]

Much of the conflict over compartmentalization emerged from the naturally different perspectives of a military engineer and academic researchers. From the point of view of a scientist the compartmentalization of information reduced the opportunity to recognize important relationships. From Groves's standpoint, however, concern with and inquiry after those relationships appeared more likely to result in time-consuming searches for needless alternatives. Herein perhaps lay the nub of the matter, the most important source of mutual suspicion: what scientists viewed as the most important part of the creative process, Groves considered no more than idle chatter. "Compartmentalization of knowledge, to me, was the very heart of security. It forced scientists to mind their own jobs and not everyone else's."[56] "Adherence to this rule," Groves insisted, "greatly improved overall efficiency by making our people stick to their knitting."[57]

Whatever else may be said about compartmentalization, however, it is difficult to accept Groves's view that it expedited matters.[58] It was primarily designed, after all, as a counterespionage measure—to insure a minimum leakage of information—not as a way of accelerating the execution of engineering tasks by preventing scientists from distracting each other with extraneous ideas. Although engineering considerations may have outweighed scientific ones after the parameters of the chain reaction had been fixed, and the physics of the fast-neutron reaction for the bomb derived, the history of technology hardly suggests a negative correlation between access to ideas and the completion of technical tasks. Groves made this point himself in another context. Discussing alterations suggested by a team of British scientists and engineers for the gaseous diffusion plant at Oak Ridge, he remarked: "Their principal value lay in the stimulation the Kellex* engineers derived from discussing them. This is always of value in any scientific development."[59]

The fact is that nothing in the official history of the Atomic Energy Commission, in the files of the Manhattan Project, or in any other relevant source available, including Groves's own book, offers convincing support for his belief in the value of compartmentalization—indeed, quite the contrary. Even Oppenheimer, whose senior position afforded him access to a wide spectrum of information, complained to Fermi in March 1943 that the "background of our work is so complicated and information in the past has been so highly compartmentalized, that it seems that we shall have a good deal to gain from a leisurely and thorough discussion. My own view is that this is likely to contribute essentially toward our carrying out our directive in the simplest, fastest way."[60] Several months later a special reviewing committee for the Los Alamos project suggested that effectiveness could be improved "by systematizing the provisions for discrete interchange of all essential information between key personnel in the different groups."[61] Over a year later, however, the situation had, in the view of a British observer, hardly improved: "The extraordinary American ideas on security," Lord Cherwell wrote to Churchill, "which, although the Americans do not realize it, handicap them as much or more than they do us . . . debar people working in the different branches from discussing their work with each other."[62]

Nonetheless, American scientists who complained about the strict and seemingly arbitrary enforcement of the security system did miss part of its point. For Groves's efforts to ensure that they stuck to their "knitting" had an additional, political dimension. Though originally conceived mainly as a defense against German espionage, compartmentalization also came to be used to restrict discussion of the implications of the development of atomic bombs. Thus, when Groves learned in the spring of 1943 that a

---

* Kellex, a subsidiary engineering firm of the M. W. Kellogg Company, was established specifically to build the giant gaseous diffusion plant (later termed the K-25 project) at Oak Ridge, Tennessee.

series of weekly colloquiums had been organized at Los Alamos, he sought to have them canceled. Oppenheimer's persistent argument that scientists would work more efficiently and would be more conscious of security if they were aware of the significance of their tasks saved this innovation; but in striking a compromise, Groves extracted two promises: that Oppenheimer would severely restrict the number of those eligible to attend, and that he would limit discussions strictly to the scientific task at hand. In the delicate phrasing of the official history of the Atomic Energy Commission, Oppenheimer agreed "to avoid matters that, *whatever their importance in other ways*, were of little scientific interest."[63]

As a defense against German espionage the security procedures administered by Groves worked well. As a means for controlling discussions of the bomb's political implications, however, they worked too well. Hiroshima and Nagasaki may have been the price the world paid for their effectiveness. But security arrangements were less effective against Groves's primary target: the Soviet Union. "There was never from about two weeks from the time I took charge of this Project any illusion on my part but that Russia was our enemy," he stated, "and the Project was conducted on that basis. I didn't go along with the attitude of the country as a whole that Russia was a gallant ally. . . . Of course, that was so reported to the President."[64]

Although Groves made this statement in 1954, there can be no doubt that it accurately reflected his own wartime attitude and that of the Manhattan Project's security section. The available reports of the intelligence officers responsible for the Project's security are almost entirely devoted to the problem of Soviet espionage.[65] As the officer-in-charge of security and intelligence operations, Colonel John Lansdale, Jr., explained it, his job "was primarily concerned with the formation of judgment[s] as to who were or were not Communists in the loyalty sense in the Army." Every scientist with a left-wing background was brought under close surveillance, for, as Lansdale admitted, "in this problem of determining who is and who is not a Communist, determining who is loyal and who is not, the signs which point the way to persons to be investigated or to check on are very frequently political liberalism of an extreme kind."[66]

At least one scientist with a Communist background was drafted out of the Manhattan Project and into regular military duty on orders from Army Intelligence, despite the protests of Lawrence, Oppenheimer, and the man's draft board, which refused to comply with the "request" until both it and the state board were threatened with dissolution.[67] Another scientist was forced to resign from the Project after attending a small party given by the Soviet vice-consul in a San Francisco restaurant for the Russian violinist Isaac Stern.[68] Oppenheimer's own clearance, in fact, was granted only after Groves personally overruled the objections of Army Intelligence officers on the grounds that Oppenheimer was "absolutely essential to the Project."[69]*

In an important way, then, the Manhattan Project's security system served—as all such systems inevitably serve—as an extension and reflection of the policymaking process itself. Established to keep the secret of American efforts to develop atomic weapons from the Germans, it was soon transformed into a means for controlling the activities of scientists—and the flow of information about the Project to America's allies. Against the Soviet Union, Groves employed the security system, on orders from Roosevelt, much as he did against Germany: to conceal the fact that the military implications of atomic energy were being explored. And against Great Britain, as we will see in the following section, Bush and Conant sought to use security much as it was used by Groves against scientists: to seal off important areas of future research and development. Even during the early stages of the war, it is clear the policies governing the development of the atomic bomb were being formulated with an eye toward potential postwar implications.

---

* Major Peer de Silva, the security officer at Los Alamos, reported to Groves that Oppenheimer was "playing a key part in the attempt of the Soviet Union to secure, by espionage, highly secret information which is vital to the security of the United States." Quoted by C. A. Rolander, Jr. to Nichols, October 25, 1954, Oppenheimer mss, box 198.

II

THE ROAD NOT TAKEN

Two roads diverged in a yellow wood,
And sorry I could not travel both
And be one traveler, long I stood
And looked down one as far as I could
To where it bent in the undergrowth;

Then took the other, as just as fair,
And having perhaps the better claim,
Because it was grassy and wanted wear;
Though as for that the passing there
Had worn them really about the same,

And both that morning equally lay
In leaves no step had trodden black.
Oh, I kept the first for another day!
Yet knowing how way leads on to way,
I doubted if I should ever come back.

I shall be telling this with a sigh
Somewhere ages and ages hence:
Two roads diverged in a wood, and I—
I took the one less traveled by,
And that has made all the difference.

—ROBERT FROST

3

THE ATOMIC BOMB
AND THE POSTWAR WORLD

The assignment of responsibility
to the Army for the development of the atomic bomb in the fall
of 1942 inextricably linked atomic energy policy to the larger
wartime and postwar diplomatic policies of the Roosevelt administration. While the President and his atomic energy advisers remained cautious about counting on the bomb as a reality during
the war, they nevertheless assumed that it would have a profound
impact on diplomacy afterwards, and they formulated policy
accordingly. The fact that the bomb remained a closely guarded
secret simplified the policymaking process: bureaucratic bargaining was minimized, public pressures were eliminated, and the
decisionmaking structure was narrowly defined. Atomic energy
policy thus became a microcosm of the larger postwar concerns
of Roosevelt and his advisers, much as the administration of the
Manhattan Project's security policies reflected Groves's pre-
occupations, and the organization of Project laboratories those of
the scientists.

Although Secretary of War Stimson was nominally Roosevelt's senior atomic energy adviser, during the early part of the
war Bush and Conant wielded considerably more influence by
virtue of their closer association with the management of the
Manhattan Project. With his personal access to the White House,
Bush frequently communicated his own and Conant's views directly to the President. Nonetheless, even Bush's influence had
very definite limitations. Roosevelt would automatically accept
all recommendations of a primarily technical nature; on matters
of broad policy, however, he never allowed control to slip from

note

his grasp. The President at times made decisions on atomic energy in consultation with Churchill without the advice or knowledge of his advisers—while insisting that he be kept fully informed himself, he felt no obligation to keep Bush, Conant, or anyone else apprised of his own actions. This secretive, idiosyncratic approach led, naturally enough, to considerable confusion in Anglo-American atomic energy relations, as also in other aspects of foreign policy; but it assured Roosevelt a measure of freedom that he might otherwise have had to forgo. Moreover, it provided him with a degree of administrative camouflage which he used to cover his sympathy for Churchill's intention to use the atomic bomb to maintain British power after the war. Roosevelt made no explicit commitment to an Anglo-American postwar atomic energy monopoly until the fall of 1944. But, in the summer of 1943, when he signed the wartime atomic energy pact (Quebec Agreement) with Churchill, he was fully aware that the Prime Minister intended to use the bomb as a diplomatic bargaining counter against the Soviet Union after the war.

I

"Dr. Bush and Dr. Conant Were Now Anxious for Fuller Collaboration"

The Anglo-American atomic energy partnership was an unexpected consequence of a British proposal in the summer of 1940 for the "general interchange of secret technical information with the United States, particularly in the ultra short wave radio [radar] field." The proposition reflected Britain's beleaguered state and its desperate need for American technical assistance. "It is not the wish of His Majesty's Government to make this proposal the subject of a bargain of any description," the British ambassador wrote to Roosevelt on July 8, 1940. "Rather do they wish, in order to show their readiness for the fullest cooperation, to be perfectly open with you and to give you full details of any equipment or devices in which you are interested without in any way pressing you beforehand to give specific undertakings on your side. . . ." There was, of course, more than magnanimity behind this unusual offer. The British government hoped that the United States would reciprocate with secret information which, as their Ambassador said, the British were "anxious to have urgently."[1]

The American government's response was favorable. A series of exchange visits between groups of British and American scientists began almost immediately, and by the winter of 1941 scientific liaison offices had been established in both London and Washington.[2] At that time even Conant, who had often discussed atomic energy with the Briggs Committee, was "in complete ignorance of the prospects of a bomb."[3] But during these exchange visits he and other American scientists were informed unofficially by their British colleagues about the important discovery Frisch and Peierls had made in April 1940, and about the important experimental work then underway in England. In response, American scientists urged Bush to look more closely into the problem of developing an atomic bomb.[4] Finally, in June 1941, when the British completed their evaluation of the Frisch-Peierls memorandum, they sent Bush a copy of the vital "Report by MAUD Committee on the Use of Uranium for a Bomb."[5] Thus from the American, as well as the British, point of view, the agreement for scientific reciprocity already had resulted in substantial mutual advantage.

In the year that followed, British and American scientists were encouraged by their respective governments to cooperate to the fullest extent possible. Each nation needed the other's help in building an atomic bomb with the greatest speed. Although some members of the MAUD Committee had argued that atomic energy "was so important for the future that work should proceed in Britain . . . ," the strain on British resources and the danger to British project sites from German bombing led the Committee majority to recommend a coordinated effort on both sides of the Atlantic.[6] And, on October 11, 1941, Roosevelt signed a letter to Churchill, drafted by Bush, similarly suggesting that the two countries might wish to pool their resources in the race for the bomb: "It appears desirable that we should soon correspond or converse concerning the subject which is under study by your MAUD Committee, and by Dr. Bush's organization in this country, in order that any extended efforts may be coordinated or even jointly conducted."[7]

During the following months Roosevelt's proposal was implemented, and the Anglo-American atomic energy partnership produced close scientific ties. The advanced state of British work, the capability of American industrial plants, the high quality of American research laboratories, and, not least of all, the desperate need to work quickly, all combined to effectively override whatever considerations might normally have interfered with complete cooperation. Summarizing the situation in November 1941, a British memorandum noted "that Dr. Bush and Dr. Conant were now anxious for fuller collaboration in this field and for complete interchange of information between those who were at work on this project on both sides of the Atlantic. The President thought it desirable that this work should now be pressed forward with all possible speed, and he fully endorsed the view taken by Dr. Bush."[8]

By April 1942 the program had moved into high gear. Despite rising costs, every possible solution to the numerous remaining scientific problems was being pursued simultaneously.[9] In a letter to his counterpart in Britain, Sir John Anderson, Bush reported on April 20 that "all various aspects of the work are being given support and expedited," and that scientific interchange on specific problems "appears to be complete and I believe generally satisfactory." Bush emphasized his commitment to continuing collaboration both on technical matters related to the operation of uranium separation pilot plants and for the renewed period of planning that would follow. "The important matter," he told Anderson, "seems to me to be to insure that adequate interchange occurs at the time that pilot plants go into operation. I suggest, therefore, that we keep particularly in touch on this aspect of the subject." He urged that both British and American observers be present for any tests of the pilot plants, after which activities should, he felt strongly, be "considered jointly"; and he looked forward to "more explicit interchange of our plans when we arrive at that stage of progress."[10]

By the summer of 1942 the atomic bomb project had advanced to the point of departure which Bush had discussed in April. He reported to the President on June 17 that the work was being aggressively pursued, that a program for its continuation had been drawn up, and that the "results to be expected are still extraordinary." The time schedule called for the availability of atomic bombs early in 1944. "The principal feature" of the next stage was the transfer of responsibility to the Army for the construction of production plants and what Bush called "full-scale" efforts. He also noted that, "according to our policy," he would inform the British of the new technical and organizational plans, and he expected to receive reports on the program that the British had under consideration. "I feel sure these two plans will fit together adequately," he noted.[11] And they did, for several months.

II

"No Reason for a Joint Enterprise"

"From now on, it is a question of development and the solving of a multitude of mechanical problems," Conant reported to Bush after conducting a full-scale review of atomic energy research in October 1942. He was skeptical about several optimistic predictions that Project scientists had made to him, but Conant nevertheless expected "a couple of bombs (provided the critical size doesn't prove to be too large) by the fall of 1944. . . ." He seemed confident that the Radiation Laboratory at Berkeley could produce "a kilogram of material" by January 1, 1944. "This first kilogram is what we need most to find out whether indeed our theoretical physicists have been leading us down a blind alley or whether we are on the right track," he wrote. But he then indicated his confidence in their calculations. As for the organization as a whole, he felt that "everything considered it is running fairly smoothly."[12] There was, however, one arrangement that troubled him, about which he spoke at considerable length at this time, and for many months thereafter—the Anglo-American partnership.

Now that the project had moved beyond the stage of basic research, Conant saw "no reason for a joint enterprise as far as development and manufacture is concerned." He suggested that a new, limited arrangement with the British replace equal partnership. His argument rested upon three points: first, the project had been transferred from scientific to military control; second, the United States was doing almost all the developmental work; and third, security dictated "moving in a direction of holding much more closely the information about the development of this program. . . ." Under these conditions it was difficult, Conant observed, "to see how a joint British-American project could be sponsored in this country."[13] The "difficulty," however, actually arose not so much from the reasons Conant explicitly stated as from his view—which the other members of the Top Policy Group soon came to share—that the continuation of an equal partnership would be inimical to American postwar commercial interests. Conant perceived the British as displaying an inordinate interest in "information which appeared to be of value to them solely for postwar industrial possibilities. . . ."[14] But what right did the British have to the fruits of American labor? "We were doing nine-tenths of the work," Stimson told Roosevelt in October 1942.[15] Before the year was out the Top Policy Group and the Military Policy Committee had agreed that the British had no right at all.

With this concern in mind, Conant suggested that Bush emphasize the criterion of "wartime use" when he presented the issue to the President. There was "presumably only one reason for free interchange of secret military information between allied nations," Conant wrote, "namely, to further the prosecution of the war in which both are engaged." Noting that other instances of scientific cooperation with the British occurred only when the two countries were developing the same or similar devices, he pointed out that the British had no intention of producing uranium or plutonium for atomic weapons or atomic power *during the war*. The United States, therefore, had no obligation to provide them with any information, since "our passing our knowledge to them will not assist the British in any way in the present war effort."[16]

In December Conant wrote a long memorandum designed to reinforce his contention that atomic energy work in the United States was now based almost exclusively upon American research and American ideas. His conclusion was that Bush provide the President with the following alternatives regarding the future of Anglo-American atomic energy relations: a) Cessation of all interchange; b) Complete interchange not only in the research field but in development and production, including free interchange of personnel; c) Restricted interchange along clearly defined lines. In Conant's opinion, the best procedure was option c; his second choice was a.[17]

As this instance shows, Roosevelt's firm grasp on the reins of policy did not at this time exclude his science advisers from active participation in policy formulation. Conant's arguments and suggestions were incorporated into the "Report to the President by the Military Policy Committee," dated December 15, 1942.[18] The advantages of restricted interchange for the United States were so obvious, the case made for it so persuasive, that Roosevelt quickly approved the report's recommendations.[19] On January 13, 1943, the British were officially informed by Conant that the rules governing the Anglo-American atomic energy relationship had been altered: information would be passed on to the British or the Canadians only if they could "take advantage of this information in this war." Citing "orders from the top," the memorandum that Conant used in briefing the British representative stated that no further information was to be shared with either the British or the Canadians concerning the electromagnetic method, the production of heavy water, the manufacture of uranium fluoride gas, fast-neutron reactions, and all matters concerned most directly with "the bomb," such as use of fissionable material. Special approval was necessary for the interchange of information on the diffusion process and on certain kinds of more basic data. Only information on the use of heavy water in chain reactions was open to complete interchange, "inasmuch as the Canadian-British group will be working on the scientific branches of this subject in Montreal. . . ."[20]

The new policy threatened a complete breakdown of Anglo-American relations in the field of atomic energy research. The American government's decision, Churchill wrote to Roosevelt, "limits drastically interchange of technical information and entirely destroys the original conception of [here he quoted from Roosevelt's letter to him of October 11, 1941] 'A coordinated or even jointly conducted effort between the two countries.' "[21] "That we should each work separately," he warned, "would be a sombre decision."[22]

By approving the policy of "restricted interchange," Roosevelt rearranged the priorities that had been guiding American atomic energy policy: the desire for postwar control of the atomic bomb, and atomic energy generally, suddenly became as important as the need to build the bomb quickly—perhaps even more important, for the new policy was adopted despite the possibility that it might "slow down" work on the bomb.[23] Neither Bush nor Conant, nor any other member of either the Top Policy Group or the Military Policy Committee, was so naïve as to believe that the British would not object to the new, limited arrangement; to the contrary, they expected a distinctly angry response. They were even prepared to face the worst possibility: a refusal of the British and Canadian governments to continue to cooperate with the United States atomic energy program.

Conant's anticipation of adverse British and Canadian reactions to the new policy had been incorporated, along with his arguments for that policy, into the MPC's December report to the President. The report pointed out that the United States might lose the services of "a group of capable men" then being assembled in Canada to work on the heavy-water method of manufacturing the highly fissionable isotope plutonium-239. Among these men, the report states, was "an expert in the field (perhaps the man who has given the most thought to the problem in either the United States or the U.K.) [Hans von Halban]."* It would be advantageous to the United States if this group could be utilized, he admitted, "but it would not hamper the effort at all fatally if the cessation of interchange resulted in the withdrawal of this group from the effort."[24] This conclusion, however, was neither obvious to nor unanimously accepted by other scientists. Harold Urey, for example, became convinced several months later, after studying the subject, that the "use of heavy water would be the easiest, quickest, and cheapest method of accomplishing the production of element 94 [plutonium]."[25]

The report also mentioned the possibility of other, more serious reactions. The Canadian government might respond to the new restrictions by refusing to allow the production of its Trail Heavy

---

* When France was occupied, Joliot sent Halban to England with the laboratory's entire supply of heavy water—which at the time constituted the world supply. Hewlett and Anderson, *The New World*, 29.

Water Plant to cross the border. Such a decision would *"slow down* our development program but not cripple it," Roosevelt was informed. But a third prospect was the most worrisome: uranium ore shipments from Canada could be halted. "The question of the ore is more complicated," Conant wrote, for he could not express an opinion about the degree of American self-sufficiency "until the situation in respect to Colorado supplies has been further explored." The report then summarized Conant's conclusions as follows: there "would be *no unduly serious hindrance* to the whole project if all further interchange between the United States and Britain in this matter were to cease."[26]

This summary was noteworthy because it did not accurately reflect the possible consequences enumerated in the text of the report, but seemed deliberately designed instead to minimize those consequences. Unable to say that the loss of the services of the British-Canadian scientific team would have no effect at all on the American atomic energy effort, the MPC resorted to a heavily qualified formulation that it "would not hamper the effort at all fatally." Unable to preclude any detrimental effect on the American project if it could not have access to the Trail Heavy Water Plant's production, the qualification of "no unduly serious hindrance" was an equivocation based upon a gamble that the heavy-water separation technique would not be needed.*

The prospect that the most rapid possible progress on the atomic bomb would be endangered by this policy could not be hidden by these verbal twists and turns, and could not have eluded the President. Bush's covering letter to the report contained a succinct summary of his estimate of scientific progress on the bomb and its importance, its production schedule, and conjecture about the state of German atomic energy research. "There can no longer be any question that atomic energy may be released under controlled conditions and used as power," he

---

* The phrase "at all fatally" was substituted by Bush for "greatly," the term Conant had originally used. Either way, it is clear that the program would be delayed by restricted interchange. Another interesting change was the addition of the word "unduly" to Conant's phrase: "no serious hindrance." The changes were penciled onto the memorandum before they were incorporated into the MPC report. Conant to Bush, "U.S.-British Relations on S-1 Project," December 14, 1942, DHMP, Annex No. 6, MED files.

reported. "Furthermore, there is a very high probability that the same energy may be released under suitable conditions in such a small interval of time as to make a super-explosive of overwhelming military might." It now appeared, however, that the first bombs would not be ready until early in 1945. This setback in the production schedule was a worrisome matter, for the progress of German research remained unknown. "We still do not know where we stand in the race with the enemy toward a usable result, but it is quite possible that Germany is ahead of us and may well be able to produce superbombs sooner than we can."[27] The President and his advisers thus confronted a clear choice: a policy based upon a wartime and postwar partnership in order to develop an atomic bomb as quickly as possible, versus a policy of ensuring a postwar American monopoly of the weapon at the possible cost of delaying the bomb's production. In the event, the Top Policy Group and the Military Policy Committee recommended—and Roosevelt approved—the latter.* The postwar role of atomic energy had thus already become a major consideration.

III

"This Development Has Come as a Bombshell"

"This development has come as a bombshell, and is quite intolerable," Sir John Anderson told Churchill shortly after learning about the new American policy of "restricted interchange." He

---

* By June 1943, Harold Urey believed that this policy had led to a delay of six months: "I wish to emphasize the following points," he wrote to Conant: "1. It is my belief that our failure to establish satisfactory cooperation with the British and Dr. Halban, has certainly resulted in a delay of six months, and perhaps in a delay of a year or more, in establishing the feasibility of the homogeneous heavy water pile. 2. I believe that this failure to establish cooperation with the British and Dr. Halban had no justification on scientific or technical grounds. 3. If the decision not to cooperate fully with our principal ally was made on nationalist grounds by the highest authority, I hope this authority was advised of the possible delay that might result from our not being able to use the only considerable supply of heavy water available anywhere." June 21, 1943. For Conant's response, see his letter to Urey, June 29, 1943. Lawrence mss., file 1015, no. 1, box 1.

advised the Prime Minister to contact Roosevelt without delay and urge him to issue instructions that collaboration be renewed on a fully reciprocal basis.[28]

Just as the American policy grew out of postwar considerations, so did the British effort to reverse that policy. Six months before the new policy was approved, the British already had taken postwar factors into account. During the summer of 1942, Anderson recognized that Britain simply did not have the resources to build atomic bombs during the war. "Even the erection and operation of a pilot plant would cause a major dislocation in war production," he informed Churchill. Moreover, the Americans were pursuing atomic energy work "with enthusiasm and a lavish expenditure," working on four alternative methods simultaneously and making very good progress. Anderson still believed that the British method was probably the best, but he recommended, "with some reluctance," that their work, and the personnel concerned, be moved to the United States to pursue the development "as a combined Anglo-American effort."[29]

Given the limits of Britain's abilities, Anderson based his recommendations on three arguments, only one of which was related to the war: that the work was likely to be completed more expeditiously if pursued as a joint effort rather than separately in both countries. This consideration was clearly not uppermost in his mind, however. Most important was the necessity for the British to "face the fact that the pioneer work done in this country is a dwindling asset and that, unless we capitalise it quickly, we shall be rapidly outstripped. We now have a real contribution to make to a 'merger.' Soon we shall have little or none." Additionally, Anderson suggested, there was a more positive reason to transfer British scientists to the United States: while working with the Manhattan Project they would be able to "keep abreast of developments over the whole field." After the war they could be recalled, thus enabling the British "to take up the work again, not where we left off, but where the combined effort had by then brought it." Anderson's memorandum serves to confirm Conant's early suspicions about Britain's postwar interest in Manhattan Project research, although Conant was mistaken in thinking that the British government was primarily concerned with its potential commercial, as opposed to military, benefits.

When Conant originally suggested the policy of restricted interchange of scientific information in October 1942, he, along with the President's other atomic energy advisers, was completely uninformed about what arrangements, if any, Roosevelt had made with Churchill. From October 9, 1941, when the President had instructed Bush to draft a letter "to open discussions of the [atomic bomb] matter [with the British] at the top," until his death on April 12, 1945, he chose not to inform his advisers about the substance of his private discussions with Churchill on atomic energy matters. Roosevelt assumed and worked to maintain a distinction between the diplomatic and the scientific aspects of atomic energy policy. Thus, when Stimson told Roosevelt in October 1942 that "Bush and the others are anxious to know what foreign commitments [with the British] the President [has] made," Roosevelt answered vaguely. He had only talked with Churchill, he said, and "his talk was of a very general nature."[30]

Churchill's recollections suggest a rather different account. The two statesmen had discussed atomic energy matters at Hyde Park in June 1942, and Churchill had left the country with the impression that Roosevelt was committed to an Anglo-American partnership.[31] His impression appears to have been substantially accurate, for within three weeks after the Hyde Park meeting the President himself sent Bush a memorandum noting that he had "talked with Mr. Churchill in regard to this whole matter [atomic energy] and we are in complete accord."[32] From Churchill's point of view that could only mean a clear commitment to partnership.

Upon learning about restricted interchange in January 1943, Churchill did not hesitate to initiate a major effort to have the new policy reversed. Always sensitive to the nuances of influence in the formulation of American foreign policy, the Prime Minister took up the matter directly with the President and with Harry Hopkins, "Roosevelt's own, personal Foreign Office."[33] Bush and Conant soon found themselves on the defensive, constrained to justify the policy of restricted interchange to Hopkins. During the spring and early summer of 1943 the full complexity of the issue was delineated in the discussions that ensued between science administrators and diplomatic policymakers in Britain and America.

Restricted interchange clearly was not an isolated issue. On the contrary, it was related not only to the matter of wartime Anglo-American relations, but also to postwar relations between each of them and the Soviet Union. The specter of postwar Soviet power played a major role in shaping the attitudes of the British government on atomic energy policy during 1943, just as Bush and Conant's conception of conflicting British and American postwar commercial interests had played a major role in shaping the policy they had proposed. Nevertheless, the compromise that Roosevelt and Churchill eventually reached in the summer of 1943 indicates that the President was more inclined to act upon Churchill's fears of Soviet postwar intentions than upon Conant's fear of British commercial rivalry.

"When the President and I talked of this matter at Hyde Park in June, 1942," Churchill cabled Hopkins in February 1943, "my whole understanding was that everything was on the basis of fully sharing the results as equal partners." Although Churchill had no record of the conversation, he said he would be very surprised "if the President's recollection does not square with this." Until the new policy had been unilaterally adopted, he had believed that the basis of all interchange of information had been mutual confidence; from the project's initiation it had been based upon the premise that complete cooperation was the most expeditious way to build an atomic bomb. In fact, Churchill noted, a British suggestion for a formal agreement made in August 1942 "was concerned more with joint control and postwar arrangements than with wartime collaboration in actual work which, after the President's approach to me in October, 1941, had always been taken for granted."[34]

Subsequently, on February 27, Churchill sent Hopkins a long telegram summarizing the history of U.S.-British relations on the "project known as S-1 or tube alloys." It documented the information British scientists had passed on to Americans in 1940, Roosevelt's proposal that the atomic bomb project be "jointly conducted," Churchill's positive response, and the discussion between Roosevelt and Churchill at Hyde Park that had confirmed the Prime Minister's feeling that "all these communications assumed on both sides complete collaboration at all stages of the project." The telegram offered no explicit conclusion, but its implicit point was obvious: Britain had been unjustly cast aside after cooperating with the United States in good faith.[35]

By dealing with Hopkins, the Prime Minister skirted the normal channels of the Manhattan Project bureaucracy, thus insuring that the question would not be considered as an isolated matter, unrelated to other diplomatic issues. It was to Conant, as chairman of OSRD's Atomic Energy Executive Committee and as initiator of the policy of restricted interchange, that primary responsibility fell for its defense—though he was aided and abetted in this task by Bush. That Conant and Bush recognized the implications of Churchill's intervention, and of Hopkins's mediation, is clear from their memoranda. No longer did they concentrate on tortuous discussions differentiating between the scientific research stage and the manufacturing stage of the bomb's development; their primary objective now was to educate Hopkins and the President about the unique importance the atomic bomb would have after the war. "It seems to me of the greatest importance to be sure that the President understands the basic issue," Conant wrote to Bush. "The question is whether or not British representatives shall have full access to plans for the design and construction of the manufacturing plants which we are now building and full knowledge of their operation." Conant repeated his argument that Britain's inability to build bombs during the war invalidated "the basic underlying assumption of collaboration," and he advanced a variety of other reasons for restricted interchange, including better project security. These were minor considerations, however. "The major consideration must be that of national security and *postwar strategic significance*," he wrote. To provide the British with detailed knowledge of how to construct an atomic bomb "might be the equivalent to joint occupation of a fortress or strategic harbor in perpetuity. . . ."[36]

As early as December 1942, Conant had written Bush that the facts about the full military potential of atomic energy should "be established before the question of policing the postwar comes up for debate."[37] He now drew out the implications of this view. Information about the construction and operation of atomic energy plants was "a military secret which is in a totally different class from anything the world has ever seen. . . ."[38] A wartime atomic energy partnership would be likely to benefit the British alone and would permanently fuse U.S. and British foreign policy; there was no other basis upon which such a weapon could be shared. Nor did Conant relish the prospect of defending to Congress or to the American public after the war a permanent Anglo-American atomic energy partnership. Discussing the situation with Anderson months later, he insisted that the bomb had to be financed and controlled by the Americans themselves," as there still persisted the old myth that where they [Americans] worked anything jointly with the British, the British got ahead. It was not true but nevertheless a myth which would be effective in postwar times, once the government had to publicize or tell what had been done. . . ."[39] Although Conant of course understood that the ultimate decision would be taken by Roosevelt rather than by himself, Bush, or the Military Policy Committee, he considered it his duty "to see to it that the President of the United States, in writing, is informed of what is involved in these decisions."[40]

Bush forwarded Conant's memorandum to Hopkins with a long note of his own reviewing the policy of scientific interchange. In it he made it clear that, like Conant, he did not regard the most rapid development of the atomic bomb as the primary concern in the formulation of that policy. "The present unwillingness of the British to conduct certain scientific interchange, to which we have invited them," he argued, "merely means that our scientists do not have for the moment the benefit of their collaboration in the studies constantly being conducted. This is of much less importance than a clear understanding on a matter of the unique significance of this [atomic energy relationship with Great Britain]."[41]* The focus of attention in the contro-

---

* Bush was referring here to a request by the MPC that British scientists Chadwick and Peierls visit the United States as consultants. But a covering memo from Conant to Bush attached to a copy of the letter of invitation suggests a certain degree of writing for the record: "General Groves thought this letter should be written now in spite of your report to the President. Akers [British representative] told me informally he would probably refuse us as he felt the conditions of work set up by

versy over restricted interchange was thus shifted firmly to post-war considerations. As Bush summed it up to Hopkins: "We can hardly give away the fruits of our developments as a part of postwar planning except on the basis of some overall agreement on that subject, which agreement does not now exist."[42]

It was just such an agreement, of course, that was Churchill's objective at this time: if Britain could not build its own bombs during the war, Churchill wanted British scientists to share in the knowledge of the bomb's development. With their experience he expected to be able to insure Britain's ability to maintain its independence after the war.

In Britain, as in America, diplomatic policy in the sphere of atomic energy was formulated by the head of government in consultation with a few close advisers. But John Anderson and Lord Cherwell, unlike their American counterparts Bush, Conant, and Stimson, were kept informed about all atomic energy discussions and agreements between Churchill and Roosevelt. In Britain, atomic energy policy and diplomacy were treated as two sides of the same coin, the most discussed purpose of which was to buy postwar insurance against Soviet ambitions. "Can England afford to neglect so potent an arm while Russia develops it?" Cherwell asked Churchill rhetorically in the midst of the re-stricted-interchange controversy.[43] "We must always remember that the Russians, who are peculiarly well equipped scientifically for this kind of development, may well be working on the Tube Alloys [atomic bomb] project somewhere beyond the Urals and making great progress," Anderson warned Churchill in April.[44] "In my view, we cannot afford to wait," the Prime Minister re-plied.[45]

Churchill had in any case needed little persuasion. He had taken it upon himself during the interwar years to awaken his countrymen to the dangers Britain faced from Soviet Russia. His warnings were so well known, his feelings so strong, and his hostility to the Soviet government then so pervasive, that it was

Groves required so much secrecy as to make such a visit 'not worth-while.' I think it would be appropriate to get this [the invitation] on the record. . . . Do you agree?" Bush noted: "I agree." Conant to Bush, n.d., handwritten, attached to Conant to Akers, December 15, 1942, Bush-Conant mss., British, 1, 1942 folder.

now a credit to his own and to Stalin's statesmanship that they could deal with each other with civility on a personal level. Neither Anderson nor Cherwell had to remind the Prime Minister that those old perils he had envisaged only lay dormant, that they had not disappeared, and that atomic weapons would be a major factor in dealing with them after the war. "What are we going to have between the white snows of Russia and the white cliffs of Dover?" Churchill once asked.[46] The atomic bomb may well have been the answer he had in mind. Whatever the numerous other reasons Churchill could cite for his determination to acquire an independent atomic arsenal after the war, it was Great Britain's postwar position with respect to the Soviet Union that invariably led the list.

When Bush and Stimson visited London in July 1943, Churchill told them quite frankly that he was "vitally interested in the possession of all [atomic energy] information because this will be necessary for Britain's independence in the future as well as for success during the war." Nor was Churchill evasive about his reasoning: "It would never do to have Germany or Russia win the race for something which might be used for international blackmail." And he pointed out bluntly that "Russia might be in a position to accomplish this result unless we worked together."[47] In Washington two months earlier, Cherwell had explained the Prime Minister's views to Bush and Hopkins: the British government was considering "the whole [atomic energy] affair on an after-the-war military basis," intending to manufacture and produce the weapon.[48] Prior to the convening of the Quebec Conference in August, Anderson similarly outlined his own and Churchill's views to the Canadian Prime Minister, Mackenzie King: the British knew that "both Germany and Russia were working on the same thing." Moreover, he believed that the atomic bomb "would be a terrific factor in the postwar world as giving an absolute control to whatever country possessed the secret."[49]

While the focus of British attention thus remained upon atomic weapons as an instrument of postwar diplomacy, British strategy for renewing full collaboration concentrated on the criterion of wartime use. Certain that Britain's only "strong card" lay in the argument that wartime exigencies demanded collaboration, Anderson urged Churchill to insist upon this point, despite his own expectation that atomic bombs would not be produced before the end of the war in Europe: "We cannot afford after the war to face the future without this weapon and rely entirely on America, should Russia or some other Power develop it. However much, therefore, it may be tactically necessary to make use of the pretext of wartime collaboration, the Americans must realise that, failing collaboration, we shall be bound to divert manpower and materials from our work on radio, etc. in order to try to keep abreast." The commercial aspect, he added, was at present a secondary consideration.[50]

This was in fact the line of argument Churchill pursued during the spring of 1943. In telegrams he sent to Hopkins and Roosevelt, commercial interests were played down, Russia was played up; cooperation was the keynote, but the threat of independent British action was a theme too. In May, when Churchill arrived in Washington with the British Chiefs of Staff for an Anglo-American strategy conference (known as Trident), he discussed atomic energy matters face-to-face with Roosevelt. His arguments proved persuasive. Although there is no American record of their discussion, on May 26 Churchill sent a telegram to Anderson summarizing the outcome: "The President agreed that the exchange of information on Tube Alloys should be resumed and that the enterprise should be considered a joint one, to which both countries would contribute their best endeavours."[51]*

The significance of Roosevelt's acceptance of Churchill's position goes beyond the limited issue of an incident in Anglo-American wartime relations. It marks the point at which the President began to deal with atomic energy as an *integral* part of his general diplomacy, linking and encompassing both the current wartime situation and the shape of postwar affairs. It was precisely because Bush and Conant perceived this intimate connection in the fall of 1942 that they argued so vigorously in favor of their position during the spring and early summer of 1943. They were convinced that an Anglo-American atomic energy partnership during the war inevitably implied an Anglo-American military

* See Appendix A.

alliance afterwards. Such a decision had to be considered upon its merits, Bush insisted, not as an ineluctable offshoot of the development of atomic weapons.

Roosevelt certainly understood Bush's position; yet, on July 20, while Bush and Stimson were in London, the President confirmed and formalized his agreement of May with Churchill:[52] after receiving a note from Hopkins recommending the restoration of a full partnership, he cabled Bush, ordering him to "renew, in an inclusive manner, the full exchange of information with the British."[53] The cable was garbled, with the word "review" being substituted for the key term "renew"; and this gave Bush the opportunity to continue his negotiations in London with Churchill and to effect some modifications in the President's order. But Bush could not alter Roosevelt's intentions. When the two heads of state met in August at the Quebec Conference, they settled the matter between themselves.

IV

The Quebec Agreement

On August 19, 1943, at the Anglo-American summit conference in Quebec, Roosevelt and Churchill signed a secret agreement "governing collaboration between the authorities of the U.S.A. and the U.K. in the matter of Tube Alloys."[54] The Quebec Agreement reinstated the policy of complete interchange of atomic energy information between the two countries, albeit the British returned as junior rather than equal partners. For the remainder of the war this pact formed the basis for Anglo-American atomic energy cooperation, and for general diplomatic and military matters related to the bomb. It contained five points:

> First, that we will never use this agency against each other.
> Secondly, that we will not use it against third parties without each other's consent.
> Thirdly, that we will not either of us communicate any information about Tube Alloys to third parties except by mutual consent.

Fourthly, that in view of the heavy burden of production falling upon the United States as the result of a wise division of war effort, the British government recognize that any post-war advantages of an industrial or commercial character shall be dealt with as between the United States and Great Britain on terms to be specified by the President of the United States to the Prime Minister of Great Britain. The Prime Minister expressly disclaims any interest in these industrial and commercial aspects beyond what may be considered by the President of the United States to be fair and just and in harmony with the economic welfare of the world.

And fifthly, that the following arrangements shall be made to ensure full and effective collaboration between the two countries in bringing the project to fruition:

(a) There shall be set up in Washington a Combined Policy Committee. . . .

(b) There shall be complete interchange of information and ideas on all sections of the project between members of the Policy Committee and their immediate technical advisers.

(c) In the field of scientific research and development there shall be full and effective interchange of information and ideas between those in the two countries engaged in the same sections of the field.

(d) In the field of design, construction and operation of large-scale plants, interchange of information and ideas shall be regulated by such *ad hoc* arrangements as may, in each section of the field, appear to be necessary or desirable if the project is to be brought to fruition at the earliest moment. Such *ad hoc* arrangements shall be subject to the approval of the Policy Committee.

The President's commitment to Churchill was not a casual one, nor one taken in ignorance. As the official history of the Atomic Energy Commission notes: "Both Roosevelt and Churchill knew that the stake of their diplomacy was a technological breakthrough so revolutionary that it transcended in importance even the bloody work of carrying the war to the heartland of the Nazi foe."[55] The President was aware of Churchill's position, and he understood Bush's objections to it. Roosevelt was also aware of Cherwell's statement to Bush and Hopkins that the British government was considering "the whole [atomic energy] affair on an after-the-war military basis."[56] Although Roosevelt had said to Bush in June that such a position was "astounding," Bush nevertheless left the White House with the impression that "the President felt that the subject of postwar relationships on this matter was the subject at issue. . . ."[57] But how much closer Roosevelt was to Churchill in August 1943 than to his own advisers is suggested by a report written after the war by General Groves: "It is not known what if any American President Roosevelt consulted at Quebec. It is doubtful if there were any. All that is known is that the Quebec Agreement was signed by President Roosevelt and that, as finally signed, it agreed practically in toto with the version presented by Sir John Anderson to Dr. Bush in Washington a few weeks earlier."[58] There were some clauses in the agreement, Bush later complained, "with which we had nothing to do and which had postwar implications."[59]

The debate that preceded the Quebec Agreement is noteworthy for yet another reason: it led to a new relationship between Roosevelt and his atomic energy advisers. In the dispute over restricted interchange the President did not consult them—as Churchill did consult Cherwell and Anderson—about the diplomatic issues related to atomic energy policy. After discussing the matter with Stimson in July, for example, Churchill noted with some surprise that "the President had told him [Stimson] nothing of our discussions."[60]* Nor had Bush or Conant been in-

---

* Gowing reports that Anderson too was surprised to learn that "Marshall and Stimson knew very little about the project; in fact after he had given them a description of it Stimson said he began to understand for the first time what it was all about." *Britain and Atomic Energy*, 170. The extent to which Roosevelt had isolated his advisers from his discussions with Churchill became clear to Harvey Bundy, Stimson's special assistant for atomic energy affairs, when he tried to put the pieces of the atomic energy policy puzzle together. "Bundy said he feared that Stimson's records of President Roosevelt's discussion with the Prime Minister about T.A. [tube alloys—the atomic bomb] from the time of the Quebec

typical

formed either. Roosevelt listened attentively when any of his atomic energy advisers offered their views, but he acted decisively only in consultation with Churchill. Bush and Conant had exerted a large measure of their influence to oppose Churchill's position. But what they did not suspect was the extent to which the President had fallen into sympathy with the Prime Minister's view.

It can be argued that Roosevelt, political pragmatist that he was, renewed the atomic energy partnership to help keep relations with the British harmonious for the duration of the war, rather than disrupt them over matters of postwar concern. Indeed, it seems entirely reasonable to assume that the President did take this consideration into account, although the Quebec Agreement, according to the AEC historians, "was no mere concession to sweeten the pill the United States was asking its military partner to swallow."[61] For Roosevelt, it must be recognized, was perfectly comfortable with Churchill's concept of military power as a prerequisite to successful postwar diplomacy. As early as August 1941, during the Atlantic Conference, Roosevelt had rejected the idea that an "effective international organization" could be relied upon to keep the peace; an Anglo-American international police force would be far more effective, he told Churchill.[62] By the spring of 1942 the concept had broadened: the two "policemen" became four, and the idea was added that every other nation would be totally disarmed. "The Four Policemen" would have "to build up a reservoir of force so powerful that no aggressor would dare to challenge it," Roosevelt told Arthur Sweetser, an ardent internationalist. Violators first would be quarantined, and then, if they persisted in their disruptive activities, bombed at the rate of a city a day until they agreed to behave.[63] The President told Soviet Foreign Minister Molotov about this idea in May 1942, and in November he repeated it to Clark Eichelberger, who was coordinating the activities of American internationalists. A year later, at the Teheran Conference, Roosevelt again presented his idea, this time to Stalin.[64] As Professor Robert A. Divine

agreement onwards might be incomplete . . . ," Field Marshal Wilson wrote to Anderson, April 30, 1945, Prem 3/139-11A, 807.

has noted: "Roosevelt's concept of big power domination remained the central idea in his approach to international organization throughout World War II."[65]

Precisely how Roosevelt expected to integrate the atomic bomb into his plans for keeping the peace in the postwar world was not yet entirely clear. Against the background of his atomic energy policy decision of 1943 and his "police" approach to peace-keeping, however, his actions in 1944 suggest that he intended to take full advantage of the bomb's potential as a postwar instrument of Anglo-American diplomacy. If Roosevelt thought the bomb could be used to create a more peaceful world order, he seems to have considered the threat of its power more effective than any opportunities it offered for international cooperation. If Roosevelt was less worried than Churchill about Soviet postwar ambitions, he was no less determined than the Prime Minister to keep atomic energy information from the Soviets. There could still be four policemen, but only two of them would have the bomb.

4

THE TWO POLICEMEN

The atomic bomb promised to change the nature of military power in the postwar world and to become an extraordinarily important factor in diplomacy. As such, it created the potential for an atomic armaments race; for the Soviet government, while officially uninformed about the Manhattan Project, had become aware through espionage of its existence. Knowing this, Roosevelt confronted a difficult dilemma in the spring of 1944. On the one hand, he could continue to exclude the Russians from any connection at all with the bomb's development. But, although such a policy would strengthen America's postwar position, it would also encourage Soviet mistrust of Anglo-American intentions, a result that might undermine his stated objective of postwar cooperation with the Soviet Union. On the other hand, Roosevelt could try to use the atomic bomb project as an instrument of cooperation. He could try to assuage Soviet mistrust by informing Stalin of its existence, and of the American government's intention of cooperating with him in developing a plan for the international control of atomic energy—a proposal the Danish scientist Niels Bohr suggested in 1944.

Neither Roosevelt nor Churchill, however, was favorably disposed toward Bohr's idea. On the contrary, they agreed that the Anglo-American atomic energy partnership ought to be extended beyond the war to assure Britain's military position. The objective of Roosevelt's atomic energy policies, Bush noted in the fall of 1944, seemed to be "to control the peace of the world."[1] In this task a strong Britain was a useful ally, while a weak ally was a burden—and no one doubted that America and Britain would be allies in any future conflict. Just as the Royal

Navy had enabled Britain to serve as the arbiter of European diplomacy in the past, so the Royal Air Force, armed with Anglo-American atomic weapons, would allow her to play a similar and even greater role in the future—while simultaneously serving America's purposes. If Churchill wanted the bomb to bolster Britain's otherwise weak military position, Roosevelt wanted Churchill to have it as a hedge against the revival of isolationism within the United States. To the day of his death the President was never confident that his long battle against the isolationists had been won.[2]

I

Niels Bohr and the International Control of Atomic Energy

The longer scientists worked on the atomic bomb and the closer they came to making it a reality, the more they were forced to consider the long-range implications of the Manhattan Project. Their broader perspective, once achieved, was a troubled one—by 1944 the early anxiety about speed was complicated by a growing concern among laboratory scientists and science administrators with the international political ramifications of their work. At both Chicago and Los Alamos, small groups of scientists tried to study and discuss the potential problems.[3] The scientist in the most strategic position to influence policymaking was, of course, Vannevar Bush. But while Bush raised the issue of postwar control of atomic energy with the President as early as 1941, until very late in the war he offered no analysis of the weapon's probable impact on U.S.-Soviet relations.

The first serious attempt to analyze the postwar implications of the atomic bomb for relations with the Soviet Union was offered by Niels Bohr, who escaped to England from Nazi-occupied Denmark in September 1943. When Bohr learned of the Manhattan Project, he took steps to bring his own formulation of the postwar problem of the atomic bomb to the attention of policymakers. "That is why I went to America," he commented about his work as a consultant for the Project. "They didn't need my help in making the atom bomb."[4] As

Oppenheimer later said, "Officially and secretly he came to help the technical enterprise, [but] most secretly of all . . . he came to advance his case and his cause."[5] In the broadest sense, Bohr's cause was to ensure that atomic energy "is used to the benefit of all humanity and does not become a menace to civilization." More specifically, he warned that "quite apart from the question of how soon the weapon will be ready for use and what role it may play in the present war," some agreement had to be reached with the Soviet Union about the future control of atomic energy.[6]

Bohr's ideas on the international control of atomic energy remain significant today beyond any actual effect they might have had on policy at the time. He was universally admired by his colleagues both for his accomplishments as a scientist and for his qualities as a human being; and it was on account of both that he enjoyed great influence among them, even on political and social issues. He was responsible for several important advances in atomic physics—in particular, for the quantum theory of atomic systems—that had been crucial to the discovery of nuclear fission.[7] As a leader in the field of nuclear physics; Nobel Laureate in 1922; founder and director of an internationally renowned research institute in his native Denmark; and a major spokesman for the social responsibility of the international physicist community during the interwar years, Bohr's judgments on political matters always received a respectful hearing, and a respectable following. These judgments were based on his personal experience as a scientist and on a congeries of scientific values and attitudes held together by a commitment to internationalism. Whether or not other scientists ultimately agreed with his political proposals, most of them shared the basic view of science and its role in the world from which his political ideas grew. His proposals therefore reveal more than the insights and oversights of an individual scientist; one may say with conviction that they represent the transfer of the scientific ideal into the realm of international politics.

Bohr believed that the intellectual traditions of science preserved the fundamental values of Western civilization: individual freedom, rationality, and the brotherhood of man. Science and progress, science and rationality, science and peace, all went hand in hand. With reference to the discovery of nuclear fission and its consequences he once wrote, "Knowledge is itself the basis of civilization, [but] any widening of the borders of our knowledge imposes an increased responsibility on individuals and nations through the possibilities it gives for shaping the conditions of human life." His faith in science as a constructive force in the world was reinforced by a personal philosophy of social action, by a concern for the human condition that rested upon his belief that each individual shall strive to be a responsible member of society. Every person was obliged to confront the historical process, not merely as an observer, but as an active participant. In 1933 he remarked, "Every valuable human being must be a radical and a rebel for what he must aim at is to make things better than they are."[8]

Throughout Bohr's life his political interests and activities exemplified his commitment to these values. "The image of the scientist cut off from the world's problems was never true about father," wrote his physicist son Aage. "He always had a great interest in social problems and problems concerning the relationships between nations." Victor Weisskopf echoed the science community's sentiments when he said, "Bohr was not only a great scientist, he was also a man of unusual sensitiveness and feeling for the world in which he lived. The relation of science with the world of men was for him an important question."[9]

Bohr's concern for the influence of science on society was not suddenly aroused by the discovery of nuclear fission. Long before that discovery he had acted upon his belief that science should form a bridge rather than a barrier between nations. At the end of World War I he worked against the war guilt hysteria that excluded German scientists from international scientific societies. Throughout the interwar period, he helped to encourage peace through international science.[10] During the 1930s Bohr's institute in Copenhagen became the European haven for refugee scientists from Fascism. As the head of the Danish Committee for the Support of Fugitive Intellectuals and Scientists, which he helped to organize in 1933, Bohr became the head dispatcher of an "underground railroad" that delivered many of Europe's most brilliant scientists to England and America.

In 1944 Bohr's concerns and his understanding of the new discoveries that he had done so much to introduce into the world led him to reject traditional approaches to international relations for the postwar years. In his view, economic, ideological, territorial, and military questions all had to be reconsidered within the new framework of limitations imposed by the threat of a postwar nuclear arms race. In formulating his proposals, he did not ignore the role of traditional considerations in international relations; he sought only to reassess these in the light of this totally unprecedented situation. His proposals were based on his perception of the frightful insecurity of a nuclear-armed world—the consequence of the atomic arms race that he considered inevitable if attempts to institute effective international control of atomic energy were unsuccessful.

Simply put, Bohr believed that the development of the atomic bomb necessitated a new international order. At the heart of his plan was a scientist's natural distrust of secrecy, together with a Wilsonian desire to alter radically the means and methods by which nation-states had historically conducted their relations with each other. International control of atomic energy was only possible in an "open world," a world in which each nation could be confident that no potential enemy was engaged in stockpiling atomic weapons. He would urge Roosevelt to consider "any arrangement which can offer safety against secret preparations." International inspectors must be granted full access to all military and industrial complexes and full information about new scientific discoveries.[11] In essence, his argument was based on the proposition that the values of science—the very same values that had contributed to the discovery of fission—had to govern international relations after the war, if the accomplishments of scientists were not to destroy the world.

Behind Bohr's faith in the possibility of arranging such international controls was his estimate of the potential influence of statesmen over the course of international relations. He assumed that relations between states were guided by calculated decisions. The judgments of statesmen were often in error, and their perception of their own and the world's best interest often dangerously myopic; nonetheless, in Bohr's view, it was governments composed of men, not immutable laws of history or of international politics, that controlled the cycle of war and peace. He was convinced, therefore, that if statesmen could be made to understand the political and military implications of atomic energy, they would respond to a new international situation just as scientists responded to new discoveries. Bohr believed that under the threat of a nuclear arms race, creative statesmanship—diplomacy based on the possibility of a new and more hopeful future rather than on lessons from the past—could bring the great powers into harmony. There were no historical precedents to encourage him, but the lack of precedent seemed irrelevant—the threat of atomic warfare was also unprecedented. What was necessary, he once remarked to Oppenheimer in jest, referring to the quantum theory, was "another experimental arrangement."[12] But in a deeper sense he was not jesting, for his proposals called for a political quantum leap into the era of the atomic bomb. In 1944 such a leap did not seem impossible to Bohr; on the contrary, if the world was to survive, he considered it a necessity. Attempting to apply the ideals of science rather too directly to the conduct of human affairs, he took, as the components of his model, idealized versions both of international relations and of the international scientific community, with scientists responsible for educating statesmen to the necessity for a new diplomatic morality and a new international order.

A close examination of Bohr's proposals for the international control of atomic energy, as he expressed them in his numerous wartime memoranda and letters, is necessary for a clear understanding of what he proposed to Churchill and Roosevelt during the spring and summer of 1944. The problem that Bohr saw emerging with the development of the atomic bomb was (as noted above) an atomic arms race after the war. He never suggested that military use of the bomb in war might influence postwar relations with the Soviet Union one way or the other. "What role it [the atomic bomb] may play in the present war," he wrote to Roosevelt, was a question "quite apart" from any postwar considerations—a military rather than a political matter.[13] Looking beyond the war, however, Bohr argued that an agreement for international control could be accomplished only by promptly inviting Soviet participation in postwar atomic energy planning, *before* the bomb was a certainty and *before* the war was over. No other problem surrounding the atomic bomb—certainly not its use—posed so profound a dilemma for Roosevelt, and no proposal for the resolution of that dilemma was as prescient as the one Bohr offered.

Bohr's idea was based on two assumptions: first, the bomb was a creation out of proportion to anything else in human experience; second, such a thing could not be monopolized—its initial possessors would sooner or later be joined by rival nations. Under these conditions, traditional concepts of security through military protection became meaningless. Bohr saw the bomb, therefore, as drastically limiting the alternatives of statesmanship: on the one hand, a world in which each great power would feel confident that no other nation was producing nuclear weapons; on the other, a world dominated by the constant specter of total destruction. There could be no middle ground; the new weapon was too effective for that. If national security was not guaranteed to the great powers by some form of international control of atomic energy, he concluded, they would inevitably follow policies that planted the seeds of their own destruction.[14]*

Bohr's second point—the heart of his proposal—followed logically from his analysis. Since the atomic bomb in his judgment would be the critical factor determining the postwar international political climate, it was necessary that Stalin be informed about the existence of the Manhattan Project before the war ended. It had to be made clear to Soviet leaders that an Anglo-American alliance supported by an atomic monopoly was not being formed against them. Timing here was critical. Discussions had

---

* Bohr's memoranda to Roosevelt, especially his memorandum of March 24, 1945, suggest many of the control techniques later incorporated in the U.S. government's proposal to the United Nations Atomic Energy Commission (June 1946) for the international control of atomic energy. These include: (1) technical inspection, (2) advanced scientific research and development by the inspection agency, and (3) a distinction between "safe" and "dangerous" activities.

to be initiated before developments proceeded so far as to make an approach to the Russians appear more coercive than friendly.

Bohr understood that the initiative he urged did not guarantee the postwar cooperation of the Soviet Union; but he also believed that cooperation was impossible unless his proposal was adopted. He did not ignore the profound risks involved in executing his plan, but he was optimistic—overly optimistic under the circumstances—about the possibility of overcoming those risks. In any case, the stakes appeared to him great enough to justify the risk. He suggested that the Soviets be informed simply of the *existence* of the Manhattan Project, but not of the details of the bomb's construction. Should their response to this limited disclosure be favorable, then the way was open for further planning and increased cooperation. "In preliminary consultations [with the Russians]," he wrote to Roosevelt, "no information as regards important technical developments should, of course, be exchanged; on the contrary, the occasion should be used frankly to explain that all such information must be withheld until common safety against the unprecedented dangers has been guaranteed."[15]

Bohr wanted Roosevelt to offer Stalin, in effect, an atomic-age *modus vivendi*: international control of atomic energy and thereby security, in exchange for the surrender of the traditional national secretiveness that could offer but little such security in a nuclear-armed world.

It is worth noting that a modified version of Bohr's approach was adopted by Secretary Stimson during the last year of the war. And in June 1946, essentially the same concept emerged again in the United States government's plan for the international control of atomic energy—the Baruch Plan.[16] Bohr, however, was insisting in the summer of 1944 that the best time for making such an offer was *before* the weapon was a certainty and *prior* to the end of the war.

Bohr's third and final point revealed his idealized view of the political influence of the international community of scientists, and reflected how completely he had transferred the values of science to his judgments in the diplomatic sphere. He suggested to Roosevelt that "helpful support may perhaps be af-

forded by the world-wide scientific collaboration which for
years had embodied such bright promises for common human
striving. On this background personal connections between scientists of different nations might even offer means of establishing preliminary and non-committal contact."[17]* He was certain
that among the eminent scientists in Russia, "one can reckon
to find ardent supporters of universal cooperation."[18] That
their influence with the Soviet government on political matters
might be nil was a possibility that apparently did not occur to
him. The same scientific perspective that led him to envisage
so clearly the impact of the atomic bomb on the postwar course
of international affairs also led him to underestimate the very
difficult political obstacles that had to be overcome. These obstacles were not limited to Soviet views and attitudes; they
were, in the first instance, bound up with the atomic energy
policies of Roosevelt and Churchill.

II

Roosevelt: "Worried to Death"

Before Bohr left England for America late in 1943, he spent
several months discussing the postwar implications of the Manhattan Project with Sir John Anderson.[19] Anderson's high regard for the competence of Soviet physicists led him to consider seriously the advantages of Bohr's proposal for wartime
initiatives. His recent disagreements with American science administrators, however, left him skeptical about the likelihood of
Bush, Conant, or Groves cooperating on such a plan.[20] Having
been apprised of the British point of view in the conflict over
the exchange of atomic energy information, Bohr chose to

* Concerned that he had not emphasized the possible help of scientists strongly enough, Bohr wrote to the President in September: "As
a scientist it occurs to me that in this unique situation pre-war scientific connections may prove helpful in conveying, with entire regard
for security, an understanding of how much would be at stake should
the great prospects of atomic physics materialize, and in preparing an
adequate realization of the great benefit which would ensue from a
whole-hearted co-operation on effective control measures." Bohr to
Roosevelt, September 7, 1944, Roosevelt-OF mss, file 2240.

avoid the Manhattan Project's bureaucracy when he arrived in America as a consultant to the atomic energy program. Rather than approach Bush with his concerns and ideas, he sought out alternative means of bringing his proposals to the President's attention.

Bohr accomplished his difficult task with the assistance of Felix Frankfurter, a Roosevelt appointee to the Supreme Court and an unofficial adviser to the President. Bohr and Frankfurter were old acquaintances. They had first met in 1933 at Oxford University, and then in 1939 on several occasions in London and the United States. At these meetings Bohr had been impressed by the breadth of Frankfurter's interests and, perhaps, overly impressed with his influence on Roosevelt. In 1944 the Danish minister to the United States brought them together once again, at his home in Washington.

Some time before Bohr arrived in America, Frankfurter had learned about the Manhattan Project. He had been approached by a number of scientists and asked "to advise them on a matter [the atomic bomb] that seemed to them a matter of the greatest importance to our national interest." Thus, even before he and Bohr renewed their friendship in 1944, Frankfurter had become aware of "X," as he referred to the atomic bomb in his wartime correspondence. Spurred by a sense of curiosity that matched the depth of his intellect and the breadth of his ego, Frankfurter invited Bohr to lunch in his judicial chambers a few days after their Washington meeting. In the course of their conversation Frankfurter "made a very oblique reference to X"; Bohr replied in a similar vein, "but it soon became clear to both of us," Frankfurter recalled later, "that two such persons . . . could talk about the implications of X without either making any disclosure to the other." After a while, Bohr expressed his conviction that the atomic bomb and the potentialities it represented would be one of mankind's greatest advances or greatest disasters. It was Bohr's hope that disaster could be avoided by control of the bomb through political means. Bohr was a "man weighed down with a conscience and with an almost overwhelming solicitude for the dangers to our people," Frankfurter recalled.[21] Aage Bohr, who had come to the United States with his father, recalled the elder physicist's pleasure after he returned from his meeting with Frankfurter: "It was an exciting day. The result of the meeting corresponded to his best expectations."[22]

Moved by Bohr's dedication and insight, Frankfurter arranged an appointment with Roosevelt, probably late in February 1944. He gave the President a detailed description of Bohr's concerns, emphasizing his central worry: "that it might be disastrous if Russia should learn on her own about X rather than that the existence of X should be utilized by this country and Great Britain as a means of exploring the possibility of an effective international arrangement with Russia for dealing with the problems raised by X." Frankfurter also cited Bohr's belief that it would not be difficult for the Soviet Union to gain the information necessary for building her own atomic weapons.

After speaking with Roosevelt for an hour and a half, Frankfurter left the White House feeling that the President was "plainly impressed by my account of the matter." When Frankfurter had suggested that the solution to the problem of the atomic bomb might be more important than all the plans for a world organization, Roosevelt had agreed. Moreover, he had authorized Frankfurter to tell Bohr that upon his scheduled return to England he might inform "our friends in London that the President was most eager to explore the proper safeguards in relation to X." Frankfurter also vividly recalled Roosevelt's telling him that he was "worried to death" about the bomb and that he was very eager for all the help he could have in dealing with this problem.[23]

The winter of 1944 was not the first time Roosevelt had confronted the question of whether or not to inform the Soviet government about the atomic bomb. Something over a year earlier, on December 26, 1942, Secretary of War Stimson had learned that an Anglo-Soviet agreement for the exchange of scientific information had been signed three months before. Uneasy at the time even about British access to American atomic energy research, he informed Roosevelt on the following day that "this agreement seemed to put us in a very serious situation in regard to S-1 [the bomb]." The President concurred, and endorsed Stimson's judgment that it would be a

mistake to enter into any similar exchange pact with the Soviets. (It so happened that John G. Winant, U.S. ambassador to Great Britain, was crossing the Atlantic at that very
moment to urge just such an exchange. "I got here just in
time," Stimson remarked to the President).[24]*

One cannot realistically conceive of Roosevelt making any
other decision at that uncertain stage of the war. Although the
atomic bomb was expected to exert a tremendous influence on
international diplomacy after the war, exactly how the American government intended to wield that influence remained un-
settled. Plans for the postwar period were being formulated by
a committee of the Department of State,[25] but no one on that
committee was aware of the atomic bomb project, and no one
privy to the secret had any thought of suggesting that its members be notified. Moreover, Roosevelt, who believed that diplomacy, like politics, was fundamentally a personal rather
than an institutional matter, had yet to meet Stalin. It was not
until the Teheran Conference, in November 1943, that they
first came face to face.[26] But that conference was still eleven
months away, and victory and peace, like the atomic bomb,
still lay in the distant future. The fact that Roosevelt recoiled
from entering into an agreement in December 1942 that might
obligate him to inform the Soviet government about the Manhattan Project reflects little more than the obvious: that after
fighting together for only twelve months, the powers of the
Grand Alliance had failed to eradicate a quarter-century of
distrust between its two principal partners.

Nevertheless, the decision of December 27, 1942, was a por-
tent of future decisions and continued distrust, as well as a reflection of present uncertainties. Predictions of the bomb's
overwhelming power, periodic difficulties with the Soviet
Union, and the potential consequences, realistic or imaginary,
of sharing any information at all about the atomic bomb rein-

---

* Gowing states that the Anglo-Soviet agreement of September 1942
had been made "with the complete knowledge and approval of the
Americans, and it was intended that forthcoming Anglo-Russian discussions should take place only on a list of items approved by the Americans. Nevertheless, this was the first time Mr. Roosevelt or his Secretary
of War had heard of the Agreement." *Britain and Atomic Energy*, 155.

forced the natural inclination to guard the secret closely. Nor did time mellow the concern for secrecy; on the contrary, it became more intense as the war continued.

Yet, the message Frankfurter carried to Roosevelt contained a warning as well as a policy recommendation: whether the President chose to adhere to or to alter existing policy, his decision would have a profound impact upon postwar Soviet-American relations. Roosevelt therefore confronted a difficult dilemma. On the one hand, to continue to exclude the Soviet government from any official access to information about the development of the bomb until its power was demonstrated, was bound to affect the prospects for postwar cooperation; yet, the diplomatic and military advantages of such exclusion, with the implied coercion that was its corollary, might in the end render it desirable. On the other hand, to approach Stalin with a proposal for the international control of atomic energy had benefits too: such an initiative, if successful, would provide a meaningful basis for great-power collaboration after the war; if not, it would clarify the limitations of Soviet willingness to cooperate. Either choice involved serious risks. Roosevelt had to balance the diplomatic advantages of being well ahead of the Soviet Union in atomic energy production after the war against the advantages of initiating wartime negotiations for postwar cooperation. The issue here, it must be emphasized, is not whether the initiative Bohr suggested might in fact have led to successful international control, but rather to what extent, if any, Roosevelt demonstrated serious interest in laying the groundwork for such a policy.

Several considerations indicate that Roosevelt was inclined to reject Bohr's internationalist approach. Although it is unlikely that the President had reached a firm decision by the winter of 1944, there is reason to believe that he was well on his way to such a decision. First, Roosevelt had known for some time that the Soviets were finding out on their own about the development of the atomic bomb. As early as 1943 the President and members of the Top Policy Group received reports from the security section of the Manhattan Project, U.S. Army Intelligence, and the Federal Bureau of Investigation indicating that an active Communist cell existed in the Radiation Laboratory at the University of California. These reports noted that at least one scientist at Berkeley was selling information to Russian agents.[27] "They [Soviet agents] are already getting information about vital secrets and sending them to Russia," Stimson told Roosevelt in September 1943.[28] Yet, prior to his discussion with Frankfurter the President had made no effort to explore means of encouraging Soviet postwar cooperation on this problem; the danger of Soviet suspicion was accepted as unavoidable.

A second consideration is that Frankfurter appears to have been misled in his impressions of his White House interview. While the President's decision to authorize Bohr to discuss his proposal "with our friends in London" upon returning to England indicates positive interest, it also suggests that Roosevelt wished to avoid conveying the impression that he actually endorsed Bohr's proposal. "When faced with conflicting advice Roosevelt rarely made immediate clear-cut choices," his most recent biographer has observed.[29] But more than the President's tolerance for ambiguity was at work here. For, in addition to this oddly informal way of handling a matter that was "more important than all the schemes for a world organization," it is also notable that Roosevelt did not mention Bohr's ideas to Stimson, Bush, or anyone else until September 1944—and then only incidentally to his telling Bush that he was very disturbed that Frankfurter had learned about the project.[30]

There had been numerous opportunities for the President to discuss the issue with his atomic energy advisers prior to September. During the spring of 1944 (when Bohr had returned to England), Roosevelt conferred with Stimson on a variety of atomic energy matters: the procurement of uranium from the Congo, a trustee agreement proposed by the British, the cancellation of an antitrust suit against the du Pont Company to avoid "distracting these key people who are handling our most secret and important project," and the problem of getting through Congress an appropriations bill which included funds for the Manhattan Project without letting too many Congressmen in on the secret.[31] Yet the international control of atomic energy was never mentioned at any of these meetings.

To what alternative motivations might we ascribe the President's policy of refraining from discussion of international control, if we choose to discount an inclination to preserve the bomb as an instrument of Anglo-American postwar diplomacy? His concern, perhaps, for maintaining the tightest possible secrecy against German espionage. Or, he may have concluded, after considering Bohr's analysis, that Soviet suspicion and mistrust would only be further aroused if Stalin were informed of the existence of the project without promptly receiving detailed information about the bomb's construction. The possibility also exists that Roosevelt did not believe either Congress or the American public would approve a policy giving the Soviet Union any information about the new weapon. Finally, Roosevelt may simply have thought that the spring of 1944 was not the proper moment for such an initiative.

However, although it would be unreasonable to state categorically that these considerations did not contribute to his decision, they appear to have been secondary. Roosevelt was clearly and properly concerned about secrecy, but the most important secret with respect to Soviet-American relations was the existence of the Manhattan Project—and that secret, he was aware, already had been passed on to Moscow, so that Soviet mistrust of Anglo-American postwar intentions could only be exacerbated by continuing the existing policy. Moreover, an attempt to initiate planning for international control of atomic energy would not in itself have required the revelation of technical secrets. Nor is it sufficient to cite Roosevelt's well-known sensitivity to domestic political considerations as an explanation, since he showed himself willing on other occasions—at Yalta, for example—to take enormous political risks to further his diplomatic objectives.[32]

Had the President avoided all postwar atomic energy commitments, his lack of support for international control could be explained as merely a wish to reserve his options as to the best course to follow. But he had made commitments in 1943 in favor of Churchill's monopolistic, anti-Soviet position, and he continued to do so. Thus, on June 13, 1944, Roosevelt and Churchill signed an Agreement and Declaration of Trust, specifying that the United States and Great Britain would cooperate in seeking to control available supplies of uranium and thorium ore both during and after the war. The agreement declared that it is "the intention of the Two Governments to control to the fullest extent practicable the supplies of uranium and thorium ores within the boundaries of such areas as come under their respective jurisdictions . . . [and] in certain areas outside the control of the Two Governments and of the Governments of the Dominions of India and of Burma." The Declaration noted quite specifically that the arrangement would extend beyond the end of the war: "The signatories of the Agreement and Declaration of Trust will, as soon as practicable after the conclusion of hostilities, recommend to their respective Governments the extension and revision of this wartime emergency agreement to cover postwar conditions and its formalization by treaty or other proper method. This Agreement and Declaration of Trust shall continue in full force and effect until such extension or revision."[33]

The Agreement and Declaration of Trust was a document of much more than casual concern to the President. He had taken a close personal interest in the effort, begun under General Groves's direction in the spring of 1943, to gain for the United States as "complete control as possible" over the uranium resources of the world.[34] The President received periodic reports on Groves's progress and became interested enough to ask Bush for a map of the Congo designating the location of the mines.[35] If an atomic arms race did develop after the war, the Agreement and Declaration of Trust would provide the United States with an adequate supply of material to ensure superiority.

III

"We Did Not Even Speak the Same Language"

"It was with the greatest expectations that we came to London," Aage Bohr has recalled. "It was a fantastic matter for a scientist to try to affect the world's politics in this way, but it was hoped that Churchill, who had such an outstanding imagination, and who often had shown great foresight, would be able to be enthused about the new implications."[36] Their hopes were raised unrealistically by the excitement of their mission.

Beyond this, however, was a very deep personal stake and involvement on Bohr's part which he revealed many years later to a colleague and friend. "He [Bohr] had come to [the United States] with a plan, in the execution of which *he himself* would play an essential part," Bud Nielson remarked.[37] If scientists were to be the agents to usher in a new, peaceful world order, Niels Bohr, scientist-diplomat of the new age, was to lead the way. Had his mission been less of a personal crusade, Bohr might have been better prepared to deal with Churchill.

Upon Bohr's return to England in April 1944, he carried with him a letter written by Frankfurter containing a "formula" for discussion with Churchill—a summary of what Frankfurter presumed were Roosevelt's true interests in the postwar international control of atomic energy.[38] Before Bohr arrived, Anderson, Lord Cherwell, and Sir Henry Dale, President of the Royal Society, had already sought unsuccessfully to bring Churchill around to accepting the Danish physicist's position.[39] Others of influence, including the distinguished South African statesman Jan Christian Smuts, later added their names as well to a campaign waged in favor of Bohr's proposal.[40] But the Prime Minister, busy and difficult to persuade, was unmoved by any of their arguments. Churchill plainly preferred an Anglo-American monopoly of the atomic bomb to the postwar international control of atomic energy.

Bohr had to wait many weeks before he could see Churchill—and while he waited, his profoundest fears were realized: it seemed that the Soviets were indeed aware of the joint American-British-Canadian effort to build an atomic bomb. Bohr's suspicions were initially aroused by a letter he received from Peter Kapitsa, a Soviet physicist and long-time friend, inviting him to settle and work in Russia.[41] They were reinforced shortly afterward in a conversation with Counselor Zinchenko at the Soviet Embassy, where Bohr delivered his carefully worded reply, drafted with the assistance of British security agents.[42] Although, as Bohr later wrote to Roosevelt, "no reference was made to any special subject" by either Kapitsa or Zinchenko, the letter itself together with what was known of the prewar work of Russian physicists made it "natural to assume that nuclear problems will be in the center of [Russian] interest." The conversation with the Soviet official confirmed Bohr in his impression that the Russians were "very interested in the effort in America about the success of which some rumours may have reached the Soviet Union."[43] It was now more important than ever, Bohr reasoned, to demonstrate British and American good faith. The Soviets must not be panicked into choosing the path of an atomic arms race, which, his knowledge of the capabilities of Soviet science assured him, they were quite capable of entering.[44]

At last, around the middle of May, Bohr succeeded in obtaining an interview with Churchill.

It is no exaggeration to describe their meeting as a disaster. The Prime Minister showed little patience with a scientist intruding into his own jealously guarded arena of international affairs, especially one apparently so naïve as to urge him to inform the Russians about the development of the atomic bomb. Bohr's scheduled thirty-minute interview was not long underway before Churchill lost interest and became embroiled in an argument over the terms of the Quebec Agreement with Lord Cherwell, the only other person present. Bohr was left out of the discussion, frustrated and depressed, unable to bring the conversation back to what he considered the most important diplomatic problem of the war. The allotted time elapsed, and in a last attempt to communicate his anxieties and ideas to the Prime Minister, Bohr asked if he might forward a memorandum to him on the subject. A letter from Niels Bohr, Churchill bitingly replied, was always welcome, but he hoped it would deal with a subject other than politics. Bohr later succinctly summed up their meeting: "We did not even speak the same language."[45]

Churchill was unmoved by Bohr's argument because he rejected the assumption upon which it was founded: that the atomic bomb could change the very nature of international relations. To accept this, the Prime Minister would have had to execute a political and intellectual *volte-face* of which he was incapable. On the basis of his own perception of the bomb's potential menace, Bohr wanted Churchill to alter his understanding of international politics—to cast aside, in effect, the very principles that had guided him to the wartime leadership of his country. While Churchill certainly agreed that the atomic bomb would be a major factor in postwar diplomacy, he could not accept Bohr's view that it would invalidate traditional power considerations and so alter the basis of international relations; nor could he believe that international control was practicable, regardless of how straightforward and cooperative the United States and Britain might be. "In all the circumstances our policy should be to keep the matter so far as we can control it in American and British hands and leave the French and Russians to do what they can," he wrote in a memorandum less than a year later. "You can be quite sure that any power that gets hold of the secret will try to make the article [the bomb] and this touches the existence of human society. This matter is out of all relation to anything else that exists in the world, and I could not think of participating in any disclosure to third [France] or fourth [Russia] parties at the present time."[46]

Nothing could persuade the Prime Minister that his nation would be better served by exchanging familiar assumptions regarding political behavior and military power for a scientist's utopian-seeming forecasts. As Churchill strained to discern the shape of the future, his perceptions were largely governed by his understanding of the past. The monopoly of the atomic bomb that England and America would enjoy after the war would be a significant advantage in the geopolitical rivalries he anticipated arising between them and the Soviet Union. Churchill did not believe that anything could be gained by surrendering that advantage.

IV

"To Control the Peace of the World"

Less than a week after the Allied armies landed on the beaches of Normandy, Niels Bohr was back in the United States—less optimistic, perhaps, but still resolute. Once again, he contacted Frankfurter, who once again reported their conversation to the President. An interview between Bohr and Roosevelt was arranged for August 26, 1944, in preparation for which Bohr spent many long, hot summer evenings in his Washington apartment composing a summary of his ideas.[47]*

To Bohr's delight, though ultimately to his disillusionment, the meeting with Roosevelt presented a marked contrast to his confrontation with Churchill. The two men talked for over an hour about the atomic bomb, Denmark, and world politics in general. The President was as usual very agreeable. Regarding the postwar importance of atomic energy, Bohr told his son, Roosevelt agreed that contact with the Soviet Union had to be tried along the lines he suggested. The President said he was optimistic that such an initiative would have a "good result." In his opinion Stalin was enough of a realist to understand the revolutionary importance of this development and its consequences. The President was also confident that the Prime Minister would come to share his views. They had disagreed before, he said, but in the end had always succeeded in resolving their differences. Another meeting, Roosevelt suggested, might be useful after he had spoken with Churchill about the matter at the second Quebec Conference scheduled for the following month. In the meantime, if Bohr had any further suggestions, the President would welcome a letter.[48]

Roosevelt's enthusiasm for Bohr's proposals, however, was more apparent than real. The President did not mention them to anyone until, after the second wartime conference at Quebec, he again discussed atomic energy matters with Churchill on September 18 at Hyde Park. He then formally endorsed Churchill's point of view, agreeing as well that Bohr ought not to be trusted.

The decisions reached on atomic energy at Hyde Park were summarized and documented in an *aide-mémoire* signed by the

---

* After Bohr wrote the memorandum, he forwarded it to Frankfurter for editorial advice. The last paragraph underlined his deepest hope: "Should such endeavors be successful, the project will surely have brought a turning point in history and this wonderful adventure will stand as a symbol of the benefit to mankind which science can offer when handled in a truly human spirit." Bohr had doubts about the wisdom of such a "sentimental" passage; Frankfurter had none—he edited out the entire paragraph. See letters attached to Bohr's memorandum of July 3, 1944, Oppenheimer mss, box 34, Frankfurter-Bohr folder.

two leaders on September 19, 1944.[49]* The agreement bears all the marks both of Churchill's attitude toward the bomb and of his distrust of Bohr. "Enquiries should be made," the last paragraph reads, "regarding the activities of Professor Bohr and steps taken to ensure that he is responsible for no leakage of information particularly to the Russians." Whatever the specific reasons for Roosevelt's suspicions—Bohr's conversations with Frankfurter, his correspondence with Kapitsa, his interest in informing the Soviets about the Manhattan Project—there can be no doubt that the seeds of those suspicions were planted and nurtured by Churchill. "I did not like the man when you showed him to me, with his hair all over his head, at Downing Street," the Prime Minister wrote to Cherwell the day after signing the *aide-mémoire*. "How did he come into this business? He is a great advocate of publicity. He made an unauthorized disclosure to Chief Justice [sic] Frankfurter who startled the President by telling him he knew all the details. He says he is in close correspondence with a Russian professor. . . . What is this all about? It seems to me Bohr ought to be confined or at any rate made to see that he is very near the edge of mortal crimes."[50]

The *aide-mémoire* was just as explicit on the subject of Bohr's proposals for initiating an international control agreement with the Russians: "The suggestion that the world should be informed regarding tube alloys, with a view to an international agreement regarding its [sic] control and use, is not accepted. The matter should continue to be regarded as of the utmost secrecy." This was, of course, a misrepresentation of Bohr's position. He had never suggested that "the world" be informed about the atomic bomb, but had argued, rather, that peace was not possible unless one particular government, the Soviet, were officially notified about the project's existence—*only* its existence—before the time when any discussion would appear coercive rather than friendly.

It was the document's second paragraph, however, that revealed the full extent of Roosevelt's agreement with Churchill's point of view. "Full collaboration between the United States and the British Government in developing tube alloys for mili-

* See Appendix C.

tary and commercial purposes," it noted, "should continue after the defeat of Japan unless and until terminated by joint agreement."

The question of whether Roosevelt intended to promote such a collaboration had been uppermost in Churchill's mind when he visited Hyde Park. In a telegram of September 12, Cherwell had urged the Prime Minister to elicit from the President a statement of the broad outlines of American postwar atomic energy policy. "Do they wish, as we should like," Cherwell asked, "to go on collaborating after Japan is defeated—and could the two countries continue to cooperate in developing such a vital weapon unless they were united by a close military alliance?"[51]* Conant had effectively given the answer to Cherwell's question over a year and a half earlier, when he had likened a continuing atomic energy partnership to the joint occupation of a fortress or strategic harbor in perpetuity.[52] Just such an arrangement was in fact the object of Churchill's diplomacy, and on September 21 he cabled Cherwell of his success: "The President and I exchanged satisfactory initialled notes about the future of T. A. [tube alloys, i.e., atomic energy] on the basis of *indefinite collaboration* in the post-war period subject to termination by joint agreement."[53]†

Finally, the *aide-mémoire* offers some insight into Roosevelt's intentions regarding military use of the weapon during the war: "When a bomb is finally available, it might perhaps, after mature consideration, be used against the Japanese, who should be warned that this bombardment will be repeated until they surrender."

Churchill's hostility to Bohr's proposal, and to Bohr himself, grew ultimately out of the Prime Minister's determination to ensure Britain's future position as a world economic and military power. The atomic energy partnership he had worked for since 1942 had become a cornerstone of his postwar goals by 1944. Churchill would not allow Bohr or anyone else to alter the commitments he had secured. In March 1944, Anderson observed in a memorandum that there was "much to be said for communicating to the Russians in the near future the bare fact

* See Appendix B.
† See Appendix D.

that we expect, by a given date, to have this devastating weapon; and for inviting them to collaborate with us in preparing a scheme for international control"; Churchill penned in the memorandum's margin, "on no accounts."⁵⁴ And when Anderson noted that Cherwell agreed on the need to broaden the context within which the bomb was being considered, Churchill rejected the idea with a curt "I do not agree."⁵⁵ Just as restricted interchange had earlier threatened to deprive Britain of the advantages of its atomic alliance after the war, so, Churchill believed, would Bohr's concept of international control have the same effect.

In relation to the complex problem of the origins of the cold war, the Hyde Park meeting—overshadowed by the second Quebec Conference on the one hand, and by the drama of Yalta on the other—is far more important than historians have generally recognized.⁵⁶ Because our information about the decision-making process within the Kremlin is still incomplete (and is likely to remain so for generations), it is not possible to pass final judgment on the effect of the Hyde Park agreement on Soviet attitudes toward Anglo-American intentions. What *is* possible is to evaluate the wisdom of Anglo-American atomic energy policies with respect to Roosevelt's stated postwar diplomatic objectives. Along with arguments about the inevitability of Soviet hostility after the war, one must also consider the atomic armaments race Bohr predicted, Roosevelt's knowledge of Soviet espionage efforts, and the President's desire for postwar cooperation with the Russians.

The agreement reached in September 1944 reflected a set of attitudes, aims, and assumptions that guided the relationship between the atomic bomb and American diplomacy through most of the war. The basic alternatives had been recognized long before Roosevelt and Churchill drew up their *aide-mémoire*: the bomb could be used to initiate a diplomatic effort to work out a system for its international control, or it could remain isolated during the war from any cooperative initiatives and held in reserve should postwar efforts at cooperation fail. Neither choice was without serious risks—but Roosevelt consistently favored the latter alternative. With Churchill, he recognized that the bomb represented a unique departure in military power, a powerful diplomatic bargaining counter for as long as exclusive Anglo-American control could be maintained over the secret of its development.

The special relationship that Churchill had worked so hard to assure now appeared secure. Roosevelt's commitment to extend the atomic energy partnership seemed to guarantee the continuation of the Anglo-American wartime alliance; the bomb was simply too important to allow anything less. After all, Britain's value as an ally depended upon her strength, and Dr. Win the War (as cartoonists portrayed Roosevelt)[57] had no intention of abandoning his patient after the current crisis passed. His program for convalescence, and his prescription for preventing the outbreak of a new epidemic, included economic as well as military support for England. "The real nub of the situation is to keep Britain from going into complete bankruptcy at the end of the war," he wrote the Secretary of State ten days after signing the Hyde Park *aide-mémoire*. "I just can not go along with the idea of seeing the British empire collapse financially, and Germany at the same time building up a potential re-armament machine to make another war possible in twenty years."[58]* Economically and militarily secure, and armed with atomic weapons, Great Britain would be America's outpost on the European frontier, the sentinel for the New World in the Old. As Harry Hopkins told Lord Cherwell in October 1944, "It was vital for the United States to have a strong Britain because we must be realistic enough to understand that in any future war England would be on America's side and America on England's. It was no use having a weak ally."[59] Roosevelt himself was even more explicit in a conversation with Bush several days after the Hyde Park meeting. "The President evidently thought," Bush informed Conant, "he could join with Churchill in bringing about a US-UK postwar agreement on this subject [the atomic bomb] by which it would be held closely and presumably to control the peace of the world."[60]†

* See Appendix E.

† Support for British leadership in European affairs had been an important element of Roosevelt's foreign policy since the 1930's. Richard A. Harrison notes: "Having accepted the post-Wilsonian credo that the United States should not be the political leader of Europe, Roosevelt

By 1944 Roosevelt's musings about the four world policemen had faded into the background. But the underlying idea, the concept of guaranteeing world peace by the amassing of overwhelming military power, remained a prominent feature of his postwar plans.

counted on British leadership there. Accordingly, cooperation with Britain would be the fulcrum of the President's efforts to cooperate with the world." "Appeasement and Isolation: The Relationship of British and American Foreign Policies, 1935–1938" (Unpublished doctoral dissertation, Princeton University, 1974), 3.

5

A *QUID PRO QUO*

In the seven months between his meeting with Churchill in September and his death the following April, Roosevelt made no change in his atomic energy policies. Nor did he reverse his long-standing decision not to take his advisers into his confidence about diplomatic issues related to the new weapon. They were never told about the Hyde Park *aide-mémoire*, and they were never given an opportunity to discuss with him their ideas for the postwar handling of atomic energy affairs. Though officially uninformed, Bush suspected that Roosevelt had made a commitment to continue the exclusive atomic energy partnership with the British after the war, a continuation that both he and Conant opposed. They believed such a policy "might well lead to extraordinary efforts on the part of Russia to establish its own position in the field secretly, and might lead to a clash, say 20 years from now."[1] Unable to reach the President directly, they sought to influence his policies through Stimson, whose access to Roosevelt's office (though not to his thoughts on atomic energy) was better than their own.

The President's advisers were not alone in their struggle to influence his atomic energy policies. In the laboratories of the Manhattan Project scientists had become increasingly concerned during 1944 about the postwar implications of their work. To earlier anxieties about military control was now added an incipient realization that they might become victims of their own success. "There is a growing tendency in many quarters to maintain that science . . . is the servant of society and that all scientific activities should be under complete supervision and control by society or the state," observed the President of the American Physical Society, P. W. Bridgman, in 1943. "I believe," he warned, "that there is a probability that after the war this feeling will be intensified in proportion to the very success that physicists may have in helping to win the war."[2] If peace was not won in the process, scientists would most likely be enlisted—under strict military control—to re-create the military security their wartime accomplishments had rendered illusory. The question, therefore, was how they might most effectively contribute to winning the peace. Oppenheimer summed up the challenge they faced: "If one solves the problems presented by the atomic bomb one will have made a pilot plant for [the] solution of the problem of ending war."[3] Reduced to its essentials, that problem revolved around the best way to assure the cooperation of the Soviet Union. Should Stalin be approached with the carrot of international control before the bomb became a reality, or was it better to delay such an approach until the bomb was demonstrated, until it was clear that without international control the new weapon could be used as a terribly powerful stick? Given their background and their present responsibilities, it was Bush and Conant who, inevitably, came to be cast in the role of brokers between the recommendations of scientists and the inclinations of policymakers.

I

The Impact of "Nucleonics"

While Bohr's visits to Los Alamos during the spring of 1944 moved scientists there to consider the postwar implications of the atomic bomb for international relations, the atmosphere of criticism and distrust at the University of Chicago's Metallurgical Laboratory led quite naturally to similar concerns. Prior to the summer of 1944, however, even postwar considerations were tied to criticisms of compartmentalization, the policies of the participating industrial firms, and the slow pace of the bomb's development. No one was more persistent than Leo Szilard in bringing every reported instance of maladministration to Bush's attention. "In May of last year I wrote you because of my concern for the progress of our work. Today I am writing you again for the same reason," Szilard informed Bush in December 1943.[4] "What a pain in the neck Szilard was!" Groves blurted out to an interviewer after the war.[5] Conant was equally exasperated. "I think Szilard is interested primarily in building a record on the basis of which to make a 'stink' after the war is over," he told Bush.[6] When Szilard's most recent barrage of criticism failed to subside, Bush set aside an entire day in March to hear him out.[7] One reason for this rather extraordinary attention is obvious in retrospect: if Szilard was building a record from which to launch a critique of the administration of the Manhattan Project, Bush was going to build a defense against such an attack.

Szilard's criticisms amounted to a long list of past mistakes that had caused the loss of valuable time and an equally lengthy set of suggestions for avoiding such errors in the future. Bush listened patiently, assured Szilard that any constructive criticisms would be seriously considered, but indicated that Szilard's opinions might be different if he had information about other parts of the project (which the compartmentalization system prevented Bush from divulging). In essence, the meeting was an effort by Bush to keep his relations in order with the volatile Chicago group. The situation had already gotten out of hand once previously when Irving S. Lowen, a theoretical physicist who had worked with Wigner during the summer of 1943, complained about Groves to Eleanor Roosevelt and to Bernard Baruch. The President himself had taken time to talk with Lowen, had concluded that he was sincere about what he believed to be unnecessary delays, and had asked Conant to look into the problem.[8] Bush was doing all he could to avoid a similar incident.

By the beginning of 1944, however, Szilard's fertile mind had raced beyond the issues of the atomic bomb's development and its potential role in winning the war. What if the war ended before the bomb was developed and demonstrated? Would the American public be willing to make the sacrifices that a stable peace required? Szilard did not think so. Yet he was certain the weapon would be so powerful that an indissoluble political union would have to bind any two powers that simultaneously possessed it. "It would therefore be imperative rigidly to control all deposits [of uranium and thorium], if necessary by force," he wrote Bush on January 14, "and it will hardly be possible to get political action along that line unless high efficiency atomic bombs *have actually been used in this war* and the fact of their destructive power has deeply penetrated the mind of the public. This for me personally is perhaps the main reason for being distressed by what I see happening around me."[9] Seventeen months later, in June 1945, Szilard would advocate the diametrically opposite position, and, ironically, those then favoring the use of the bomb would rest their case in part on the position he had taken in January 1944.

Before the year was out, a group of Chicago scientists attacked the secrecy problem directly. Twenty-two of Met. Lab.'s leading physicists and chemists* called for a general statement to the American public revealing the existence of the Manhattan Project, the destructive potential of the bomb, and the fact that it was bound to affect relations between nations in the future. Beginning with the assumption that the vast array of plants constructed by the Manhattan Project made it practically impossible to keep the enemy unaware of the American effort to manufacture atomic bombs, they listed "three rather strong reasons which make the lifting of secrecy to a certain extent desirable." First, in the event Germany won the race for the bomb the populations of the Allied nations would undergo a profound shock which might degenerate into panic unless they had been forewarned. Second, if the bomb were employed against Germany, it would probably bring the war in Europe to a precipitous conclusion, leaving those responsible for organizing the peace unprepared to deal adequately with the advent of atomic weapons. Third, the strains involved in keeping the bomb's development secret necessarily played into the hands of the enemy, who was making every effort to fan the fires of suspicion between the Allied powers.[10]

Under the circumstances, this call for a public statement had little chance of being taken seriously in Washington. But the reactions it elicited from the director of the Metallurgical Laboratory show how the same premises and arguments could lead

---

* Samuel K. Allison, Walter Bartky, Farrington Daniels, A. J. Dempster, E. D. Eastman, James Franck, N. Hilberry, T. R. Hogness, L. O. Jacobson, Warren C. Johnson, Wendell M. Latimer, R. S. Mulliken, W. C. Munnecke, H. D. Smyth, F. H. Spedding, J. C. Stearns, R. S. Stone, J. C. Warner, William W. Watson, M. D. Whitaker, E. P. Wigner, W. H. Zinn.

to very different conclusions—the conclusions that in fact controlled atomic energy policy. For Arthur Compton, the scientists' fear of panic in America merely confirmed the value of secrecy: he noted "that surprise on the enemy will also be of psychological value." Public understanding seemed as important to Compton as it was to the twenty-two petitioners, "but why the rush?" As for relations among the Allies, Compton noted that "between U.S. and Britain this understanding is clear. Just what will be gained by telling Russia now?"[11] A chance to lay the foundations for an international control agreement, Bohr would have replied. But that would come in due course, if it came at all, Compton seems to have thought.

A variety of other proposals were forwarded to Compton, and through him to Bush during 1944. But the most sophisticated and far-reaching study of the problem of the atomic bomb for the postwar world was initiated by Zay Jefferies of General Electric, who wrote to Compton on July 14, urging him to "give favorable consideration to a prospectus on nucleonics." Jefferies's letter expressed the concerns of many of the younger scientists, who had been wondering aloud and anxiously about the future of their chosen field; and it owed a major part of its inspiration to Compton himself, who in June 1943 had asked some colleagues for ideas on postwar uses of atomic energy. It was, Jefferies reported, from that time on and with Compton's ongoing encouragement that they had devoted serious thought to the postwar problem.[12]

By the end of July, Jefferies had assembled a committee and received permission to proceed with his study. The group consisted of Fermi; James Franck, associate director of the chemistry division of Met. Lab.; Thorfin R. Hogness, director of chemistry for the Metallurgical Project; Robert S. Stone, head of Met. Lab.'s health division; Charles A. Thomas, research director of Monsanto Chemical Company and coordinator of plutonium research for the Manhattan Project; and Robert S. Mulliken, a physicist serving as information director of the Metallurgical Project.

"The Prospectus on Nucleonics," known more informally as the Jefferies Report, represented a broad spectrum of scientific opinion. It was assembled only after the views of group leaders throughout the Manhattan Project had been solicited, and both the quality and quantity of their responses suggest that not only the organization of postwar atomic energy research, but also the diplomatic and social implications of the new weapon, had been discussed in some detail by scientists at other laboratories.[13] The report, sixty-five typewritten pages in length, was submitted to Compton for forwarding through channels on November 18, 1944. It consisted of seven sections dealing with the background, progress, and potential of nuclear research in fields ranging from physics to explosives, and a set of recommendations for the postwar period. Of particular concern here is section VI: "The Impact of Nucleonics on International Relations and the Social Order."[14]

Section VI was a technological assessment presented in the form of a warning coupled with a set of recommendations: a world armed with nuclear weapons was analogous to two people armed with machine guns in a room; the attacker is certain to be victorious. The German atomic energy project was probably at about the same stage as the Anglo-American project, and "it would be surprising if the Russians are not also diligently engaged in such work." Thus, until a firm peace was achieved, the United States ought not to plan any relaxation of its work in the field of nucleonics; on the contrary, research should be broadened to include neglected possibilities and to assure a postwar lead in the field. A peace, however, based on uncontrolled and perhaps clandestine development of nuclear weapons was little more than an armistice and was bound to end, sooner or later, in catastrophe. A central authority for the control of atomic energy was necessary if the world was to avoid disaster.

Section VI, and a large part of Section VII, "The Post-War Organization of Nucleonics in America," were inspired by Eugene Rabinowitch, a Met. Lab. biophysicist who became the co-founder and editor of the *Bulletin of the Atomic Scientists* shortly after the war ended. Rabinowitch had left Russia after the Revolution of 1917, been trained as a chemist at the University of Berlin, and moved to England in 1933 and to the United States in 1938. In 1943 he came to Chicago from M.I.T. His broad international experience made him an acute and interested observer of world politics, and his substantial analytical powers were well supported by an ample facility with language. Although Rabinowitch was not a member of the Jefferies committee, Robert Mulliken, the committee secretary, was easily persuaded by his concerns. These were ideas, after all, that had been under discussion at Chicago for some time. Three months earlier, Arthur Compton had talked about the need for international control with the Metallurgical Project Council. It was at about the same time that the Jefferies Report was taking shape, that the petition to inform the public and the Allies about the bomb was drawn up.[15] And during the summer of 1944, on behalf of the Chicago scientists, James Franck had made a special trip to Washington to discuss postwar planning with Vannevar Bush.[16] Understandably, then, it was the expectation of Chicago scientists in 1944 that their recommendations would receive careful consideration and, it was hoped, be passed on to the President for action.

II

"The Success of Our Relations with Russia . . ."

Despite their numerous wartime duties, Vannevar Bush and James Conant had not ignored postwar considerations related to atomic energy. As early as October 1941 Bush had "discussed at some length after-war control" with the President, and the issue continued to be raised in subsequent communications between them. Conant was invariably informed by Bush about these exchanges, as he was about all matters related to atomic energy, and the issue was never far from his mind. Nevertheless, when Bush and Conant first put their thoughts about postwar policies into writing, they did not address the long-range issue already raised by Niels Bohr—the problem of the bomb's impact on Soviet-American relations. In a memorandum to Conant dated April 17, 1944, Bush summarized what he understood to be "our plans" on postwar policies. He noted only problems of publicity, congressional relations, and legislation for an atomic energy commission. A scientific summary of "this whole affair" was being prepared,* and plans were being formulated for two documents: one for the President, and another that Roosevelt might transmit to Congress and "release for use at the right instant." This would contain a plan for postwar management, and "our present thinking indicates that this might well be in the form of a commission with civilian members appointed by the [National] Academy [of Science] *and of course with military membership*, the commission to have rather complete control over many phases of the matter."[17]

In his reply to Bush, Conant revealed the still-embryonic state of his own thinking on the problem: "Of course, in *the very long run*, I'm inclined to think the only hope for humanity is an international commission on atomic energy with free access to all information and right of inspection."[18] At about the same time, however, Bohr was arguing in England that the only hope for humanity in the very long run depended upon an unprecedented act of statesmanship in the short run.

When Roosevelt called Bush to the White House on September 22, 1944, the limitations of his and Conant's tentative proposals became all too apparent.[19] The President first talked about the ideas of Bohr and Frankfurter, but in such a way as to leave Bush with the erroneous impression that Roosevelt had only recently become acquainted with them. It was clear, however, that he opposed Bohr's ideas. When the conversation turned to a general discussion of international relations and atomic energy after the war, Bush was "very much embarrassed." Lord Cherwell was present, and Roosevelt characteristically launched into a discussion of issues that he had not yet considered privately with his own advisers. The President indicated that he was "very much in favor of complete interchange with the British on this subject after the war in all phases, or not at all." He touched on certain aspects of his talks with Churchill at Quebec, but said nothing

* The scientific summary of the Manhattan Project to which Bush referred was written by Henry D. Smyth and published, shortly after the war ended, as *Atomic Energy for Military Purposes* (Washington, D.C., 1945). The idea for this report emerged from a conversation between Conant and Smyth. Whatever other reasons lay behind the issuance of the report, scientists were obviously anxious to have their various accomplishments acknowledged. Interview with Henry D. Smyth, April, 1967, Princeton, New Jersey.

about the decisions embodied in their Hyde Park *aide-mémoire*. "He pointed out," Bush wrote, "his belief of [sic] the necessity for maintaining the British Empire strong, and went into some of the methods by which this could be brought about. . . ."* But Bush was in no position to state what was on his own mind— "namely that too close collaboration with the British, without considering simultaneously the entire world situation, might lead to a very undesirable relationship indeed on the subject with Russia."[20]

Among the other issues the President raised at this White House meeting was the question of the use of the atomic bomb against the Japanese. Should it be dropped on Japan, or should it be used only as a threat after a full-scale demonstration in the United States? Bush considered the question a complicated and important one, but the answer, he felt, could wait. "Fortunately we did not need to approach it for some time," he told the President, "for certainly it would be inadvisable to make a threat unless we were distinctly in a position to follow it up if necessary. . . ." Although the matter obviously "warranted very careful discussion," he believed that it could be "postponed for quite a time."[21]† Roosevelt agreed, but without revealing that he had already discussed the military use of the bomb with Churchill. Raising the question in this way was either the President's method of probing for an opinion without giving his own judgment, or an attempt to reassure himself that his advisers were not opposed to the weapon's use. Nothing Bush had to say on the issue gave Roosevelt cause to reconsider what he and Churchill had already agreed upon.

---

* Roosevelt's remark on this occasion seems to contradict his expressed desire to eliminate British control of their overseas colonies. However, it is possible the President was using the term "British Empire" rather loosely and meant simply that he wished to see Britain remain a strong power. Either way, the context in which the remark appears further confirms the view that Roosevelt favored Churchill's intention to use the atomic bomb to maintain British military strength.

† Until this time Bush had simply taken the bomb's use for granted, and had not considered the questions Roosevelt raised. Other considerations were obviously more important to him, as is suggested by the fact that he forgot to include this discussion in his initial memorandum of the conference (AEC doc. no. 185).

Although Bush had thought about the problem of the atomic bomb and Soviet-American relations before September 22, he had felt no sense of urgency about the matter. "It is my strong feeling," he had written in August, "that we should not attempt to put any peacetime plans into effect at the present time."[22] Only three days before the meeting with Roosevelt, Bush and Conant had forwarded to the Secretary of War a memorandum covering their thoughts on postwar matters. Besides one point of wartime concern—a recommendation for an announcement to the public "simultaneously with their [atomic bombs'] use"—the memorandum included only two items: (1) national legislation controlling the production of and experimentation with atomic power, and (2) a treaty with Great Britain and Canada dealing with atomic power. With regard to the latter issue, they noted that "it would seem appropriate for the treaty to determine whether the interchange with the British of technical information should now be made complete and not confined to those aspects of the work concerned with winning the present war." No mention was made of the Soviet Union, of the probable impact of the atomic bomb on international relations generally, or of the need for action directed at avoiding a postwar race for atomic weapons.[23]

The hour and a half Bush spent at the White House on September 22 did give him new insight into Roosevelt's thinking about atomic energy policies. He left the meeting with the distinct impression that the President intended to maintain an Anglo-American atomic monopoly after the war—an objective that Bush considered unattainable, and therefore disastrous to pursue. Roosevelt's remarks had reflected his commitment to Churchill's point of view, but Bush could only guess at the extent of the commitment. He might have reacted even more vigorously had he been aware of what had actually been decided at Hyde Park. With Cherwell present, however, there had been little he could say without causing the President considerable embarrassment, although he did manage to suggest that after the war free and open publication on the scientific aspects of atomic energy would be inevitable. He had also added his view that the Russians should be encouraged to participate in the scientific discussions that would ensue upon this publication.[24]*

Until this conference with the President, Bush had been unaware how completely he had been isolated over the previous year from the diplomatic issues relating to atomic energy. The discovery upset him, as did the policies the President appeared to be following. Summarizing the situation the next day in a memorandum to Conant, he noted that they were not the President's "normal advisors . . . in regard to international relations of the subject [atomic energy] generally or on post-war matters, and he [the President] has not indicated that we have any duty thus to advise." Bush now believed, nonetheless, that their advice was needed. "The time has come when we should say quite definitely to those who are his normal advisors on such matters that we feel that they should insist upon giving their advice even if it is not called for."[25] Conant agreed, and within a few days Bush was discussing the situation with Stimson. Any attempt to monopolize atomic weapons, Bush now argued in phrases reminiscent of Bohr's, was likely to stimulate the Russians into an all-out effort to develop in secret their own atomic arsenal. If that happened, the possibility of another, far more devastating conflict within twenty years was a serious one. He therefore hoped that in the postwar period a policy of complete scientific reciprocity could be initiated to head off such an arms race. An international organization that would enable nations to share control of atomic energy ought to be given serious consideration.[26]

Bush obviously had not yet thought out these suggestions very carefully; they represented a point of view rather than a concrete proposal, his hopes for the future rather than a detailed plan for a diplomatic initiative. They required considerably more study and more discussion with the President. Stimson, however, was pessimistic about holding Roosevelt's attention long enough to

---

* Admiral William D. Leahy, Roosevelt's Chief of Staff, was also present at the meeting. He had been recently informed about the Manhattan Project, but remained singularly unimpressed. "While Professor Bush has evidently convinced the President and the Prime Minister of the effectiveness of this project," he commented in his diary, "his presentation . . . was not convincing to me." Leahy diary, September 22, 1944, Vol. 11, LC. See also his book, *I Was There* (New York, 1950), 269.

"get to the bottom of the subject." Even so, he did think the attempt should be made "if only for the record."[27] Stimson therefore agreed that Bush and Conant should draft a proposal outlining what they considered to be a reasonable approach to international control. Such a document, they all hoped, might bring the President's advisers back into the business of giving advice. Later that day, Stimson recorded his own sense of frustration in his diary: "Apparently the President has been discussing that problem without any conference with his own three American advisors who have had control of the big secret ever since it has been developed."[28]

The plain fact of the matter was that in the Roosevelt administration, controlling the administrative details of any project did not necessarily mean controlling, or even participating in, the major diplomatic decisions affected by that project. Bush, Conant, and Stimson were isolated because the President had taken sole personal responsibility for dealing with the issue, and felt no need or obligation to consult them. Now, they suddenly suspected the truth: that he had already committed the United States to what they recognized as Churchill's plan for maintaining a postwar Anglo-American monopoly of the atomic bomb. In their opinion, he had erred, and to correct his course they sought to recover their lost influence.[29]*

In less than a week, Bush and Conant sent Stimson two memoranda on the subject of the bomb and postwar relations with the Soviet Union. They predicted that a bomb equivalent to from one to ten thousand tons of high explosive could be "demonstrated" before August 1, 1945. They doubted that the present American and British monopoly could be maintained for more than three or four years thereafter, and they pointed out that any nation with reasonably good technical and scientific resources could catch up; accidents of research, moreover, might even put some other nation ahead. Furthermore, atomic bombs were only the first step along the road of nuclear weapons technology. In

* The summary of their recommendations makes no mention of approaching the Russians with a proposal for the international control of atomic energy. (See Appendix F.) Nor do any other documents seen by the author suggest that Bush and Conant were thinking about overtures for international control during the war.

the not too distant future, they observed, loomed the awesome prospect of a weapon perhaps a thousand times more destructive—the hydrogen bomb. Every major population center in the world would then lie at the mercy of the nation that struck first in war. Security, therefore, could be found neither in secrecy nor even in the control of raw materials, for the supply of heavy hydrogen was practically unlimited.[30]*

These predictions by Bush and Conant were more specific than, but not dissimilar to, Bohr's. They too believed that the only way to prevent a nuclear arms race after the war was to work for the international control of atomic energy before the war ended. Beyond urging a general commitment to international cooperation, however, they suggested no diplomatic initiatives likely to increase the probability of such cooperation. They certainly did not propose that Roosevelt inform Stalin of the existence of the Manhattan Project, as Bohr and the Chicago scientists had urged; on the contrary, although they did advocate disclosure of all but the military and manufacturing details of the bomb, they recommended such a disclosure only after the bomb was demonstrated. After the war the Soviet Union could be offered a free interchange of all scientific information on the subject, followed by free access to laboratories, industrial plants, and military establishments for the technical staff of an international control commission.

Opposition to such a radical measure would obviously be great both in Washington and in Moscow. But the magnitude of the danger might overcome that. Following Szilard's reasoning in his letter to Bush of January 14, 1944, they argued that to make an approach to the Russians after the bomb's use would improve the prospects of achieving international control in proportion to Moscow's fear of atomic war—a notion that suggests a lack of the sensitivity to the Soviet outlook that Bohr had exhibited. (Without such a weapon of their own, how could the Russians not feel threatened by its demonstrated effect?) On the other hand, Bush and Conant were, naturally enough, far more sensitive than Bohr to the exigencies of the American political system. Their appreciation of the potential domestic obstacles to inter-

---

* It should be noted, however, that an atomic (nuclear fission) explosion is necessary to detonate a hydrogen (nuclear fusion) bomb.

national control was apparent in their priorities. Having concluded that congressional approval would be required, they thought that only a cautious approach could eventually bring it about.

With regard to using the bomb against Japan, Bush and Conant then explained that the "demonstration" they were referring to "might be over enemy territory, or in our own country, with notice to Japan that the materials would be subsequently used against the Japanese mainland unless surrender was forthcoming."[31] This was one of the few times that the question of *whether* the bomb should be used in a surprise attack was raised with Roosevelt by a responsible government official, yet no specific recommendation was made. In the context of the memorandum, the issue appears to be almost an aside—a point worthy of future discussion, but not of immediate concern. It was raised after Roosevelt's death, in a committee formed to discuss atomic energy affairs, but again it received only cursory attention.

On October 9, about two weeks after Bush and Conant's memorandum on international control had been delivered to the Secretary of War, the bomb was discussed in another context. Stimson was concerned that introducing the proximity fuse for conventional explosives on the western front might give the Japanese an opportunity to manufacture it before the next summer. Bush, however, reassured him: "S-1 was in such a situation that we could use up the Japanese with that even if they got possession of the secret of the proximity fuse."[32]

When Bush and Stimson next discussed international control two weeks later, the Secretary failed to say what he planned to do. It seemed to Bush that he had not yet decided. The mood of optimism that prevailed after the apparent success of the Dumbarton Oaks Conference on a United Nations Organization encouraged Bush about the possibility of working with the Russians, and he was increasingly anxious to see the development of concrete proposals begun—so much, after all, depended upon these plans.[33] Stimson, however, was troubled by the general trend of Soviet-American relations: besides Dumbarton Oaks, there was Soviet behavior in Warsaw to consider; though hopeful of Soviet cooperation, he recognized the possibility of Soviet recalcitrance and hostility.[34]

Stimson's concern was heightened when Ambassador Averell Harriman returned to the United States. On the morning of October 23, 1944, Harriman described to Stimson his impressions of the recent conference in Moscow between Churchill and Stalin.[35] That evening, Stimson summarized in his diary Harriman's account of "the way in which the Russians were trying to dominate the countries which they are 'liberating' and the use which they are making of secret police in the process." He felt that a campaign of education on the problem of the secret police in the postwar world was necessary, and it seemed to him that "the success of our relations with Russia ultimately [would] largely depend [on the resolution of that problem]." He saw no difference between the Gestapo and the OGPU "which the Russians have historically used." Stalin would have to be induced to carry out the reforms he had promised the Russian people in his constitution and bill of rights if cooperation between the Allies was to continue.[36]

Harriman agreed in principle, but he was not sanguine about the possibility of liberalizing Soviet society. What he did, however, think possible—and necessary—was to prevent the Russians from introducing their secret police into the countries they were then invading, particularly Hungary. By way of confirming Harriman's view, Stimson wrote, "Hungary has not a Slavic population and I did not believe would willingly accept the methods of the OGPU. We should not allow them to be driven by the Russians into doing it. . . ." He concluded the day's entry by observing that the "two agencies by which liberty and freedom have been destroyed in nations, which grant too much power to their government, now seem to me clearly to be (1) the control of the press and (2) the control of the liberty of the citizens through the secret police. The latter is the most abhorrent of the two."[37] In the light of such considerations as these, the achievement of international control of atomic energy—so heavily dependent on inspection and access to industrial and military facilities—appeared far more problematic to Stimson than it did to Bush.

It was December 1944 before Bush and Conant had the opportunity to follow up their suggestions on international control with the Secretary of War. After returning from a trip to

England, Bush saw Stimson's Special Assistant, Harvey Bundy, and the Assistant Secretary of War, John J. McCloy, on December 8. Both men were very close to Stimson and capable of directing his attention to an issue in need of attention. After describing problems of the bomb's development, Bush suggested that an advisory committee be appointed to consider postwar atomic energy matters. Furthermore, the State Department, still unaware of the Manhattan Project, now had to be let in on the secret. Bundy reported these suggestions to Stimson on the following day, and four days later the Secretary and Bush reviewed them together. Although Stimson was noncommittal about an advisory committee, he did agree that State ought to be informed and promised to bring the matter to the President's attention. When their conversation turned to international exchange after the war, Bush received the impression that Stimson was still unsure of what he wanted to do. The decision was too complicated and far-reaching in its ramifications to be made without careful consideration of consequences.[38]

The consequences Stimson had in mind were related to his earlier discussions with Harriman about the nature of Soviet society. Over the course of the following months, the problem of opening up Soviet society, or at least of keeping the nations of Eastern Europe free from Soviet control, remained a central consideration for him. As other issues came to his attention, including that of postwar control of the atomic bomb, he considered them in relation to this all-encompassing goal. In a curious manner, he was coming around to Bohr's position. But whereas the Danish scientist sought to use the secret of the Manhattan Project to induce Soviet cooperation, Stimson was inclined to hold it in reserve as a reward. Their ultimate goal regarding the control of atomic energy was similar, but their means differed, as did their conceptions of the potential dangers in the postwar world. Nine months later, approximately one month after Hiroshima and Nagasaki had been obliterated, Stimson would embrace Bohr's position wholeheartedly: "I consider the problem of our satisfactory relations with Russia as not merely connected with but as virtually dominated by the problem of the atomic bomb," he wrote to President Truman on September 11, 1945.[39] In the winter of 1944, however, he was still struggling, as he continued to struggle throughout the remainder of the war, to find a means whereby the bomb could be used to serve the purposes of American policy. The ultimate irony of this policy was not yet apparent: holding the secret of the bomb during the war for use as a diplomatic instrument for shaping the peace was making cooperation with the Soviet Union more rather than less difficult to achieve.

III

"It Was [Not] Yet Time to Share It with Russia"

The memoranda submitted to Stimson by Bush and Conant were not brought to Roosevelt's attention until the last days of December 1944; but in the interim, however, other considerations regarding the atomic bomb were presented to him. Alexander Sachs had followed the development of the bomb with keen interest ever since he had first brought the discovery of atomic fission to Roosevelt's attention. In November 1944 he visited the White House with a series of recommendations on the problem of the atomic bomb in the postwar world. Unlike Stimson, Bush, Roosevelt, Szilard, or Bohr, Sachs worried that the military use of the bomb in war might adversely affect the postwar position of the United States. Concerned that the nation's moral leadership could be destroyed by an incautious use of the new weapon, he recommended four steps: first, a rehearsal-demonstration before a body of internationally recognized scientists, both Allied and neutral, and representatives of the major religious faiths; second, a report on the implications of atomic weapons; third, a warning by the United States, Britain, and Canada to Germany and Japan that selected areas of their countries would be struck with the new weapon if they did not surrender; finally, if all else failed, an ultimatum to these countries demanding immediate surrender on penalty of subjecting their peoples to atomic annihilation. Although Sachs later reported that his recommendations had been "favorably received by President Roosevelt," there is no evidence *typical FDR:*

that the President ever mentioned them to anyone else.[40] For the
third time in six months he gave the impression that he agreed
with an atomic energy proposal but then failed to discuss the idea
further or take action on it.

Another problem was soon brought to Roosevelt's attention
that, considering its larger implications, should have moved him
toward formulating a proposal for the international control of
atomic energy. Instead, it merely confirmed his determination to
keep the Manhattan Project isolated from Soviet-American diplomacy and thereby highlighted his refusal, and that of at least
some of his advisers, to face up to the growing impossibility of
doing so. What happened was that several French scientists employed by the British in the Canadian section of the Manhattan
Project had demanded, and received, permission to return to
France. It was expected that on their arrival they would speak
with the renowned scientist Frédéric Joliot—known to be a member of the Communist Party. Although American authorities
sought to prevent their visit home, the Frenchmen were under
British jurisdiction, and Sir John Anderson stated that he was
unwilling to treat them as prisoners. Discussing the matter with
Bundy on December 29, Stimson decided that it required the
attention of the President. The French were suddenly in a position to let Russia in on the secret development. That, at least,
was Stimson's overriding concern, and on the following day he
briefed Roosevelt about the situation.[41]

Stimson went to the White House at noon on December 30,
accompanied by Groves to, as he put it, "back me up."[42] His
argument to the President focused on what he considered Anderson's apparent interest in allowing the French the opportunity to
become full partners in the further development of atomic
energy. The President inquired about Churchill's position on the
matter and was told that the Prime Minister probably knew nothing about it. With obvious pride, Groves defended his security
goals: American money and genius had built the Manhattan
Project, and its secrets should be kept from France. Roosevelt
seemed to agree, remarking that France's unstable political situation made her a poor partner.[43] But even if the French government were dependable, there was no reason for sharing atomic

secrets with her. "The President acted as I fully expected he would," Stimson noted, "and agreed that it was impossible to let the French into the matter."*

Two other important points were discussed. Stimson suggested that Secretary of State Edward Stettinius be informed about the Manhattan Project. (Roosevelt personally notified him that evening.)[44] Finally, the President was shown a report prepared by Groves for General Marshall, outlining the expected schedule for the production of atomic bombs. At least one bomb that did not require testing would be ready by August 1, 1945. Another, less reliable weapon would be available in July for testing. Plans were already underway for training the crews of the 509th Composite Group for their mission against Japan.[45] All these items Roosevelt approved.

why no need for test?

Since Stimson had a number of other matters on his mind, another appointment was arranged for the following day. At this next meeting, the Secretary's main purpose was to discuss the German counterattack then proceeding on the western front (the Battle of the Bulge).[46] Roosevelt, however, talked freely about other problems. Touching on the approaching conference with Stalin and Churchill at Yalta, the President remarked that "Stalin had taken Britain's desire to have a *cordon sanitaire* of friendly nations around it in past years as an excuse now for Russia's intention to have Czechoslovakia, Poland, and other nations whom it could control around it."[47] The day before, he had written Stalin to protest Soviet determination to recognize the Lublin Committee as the provisional government of Poland.[48] "While we were on the question of troubles with Russia," Stimson noted in his diary, "I took occasion to tell him of [General John R.] Deane's warning to us in the [War] Department that we would not gain anything at the present time by further easy concessions

Yalta
Hiroshima

---

* General Groves and other members of the Top Policy Group considered this situation a "breach of the Quebec Agreement by the British." Prior to the summer of 1943, and without informing any U.S. officials, the British had agreed to allow French scientists employed in Canada to transfer restricted data to the French government. "Thus when the U.K. signed the Quebec Agreement it put itself in a position where it no longer had the power to carry out its prior commitment to France without violating its Quebec Agreement with us." DHMP, 21.

to Russia and recommending that we should be more vigorous in insisting upon a *quid pro quo*."*

It was at this point that Stimson linked up his two current major concerns: the atomic bomb and Soviet-American relations in the postwar years. "I told him of my thoughts as to the future of S-1 in connection with Russia," he wrote in his diary. Although the Soviets were known to be spying on the Manhattan Project, he did not believe that they had obtained any useful information; and while he was troubled about the possible effect of keeping them, even now, officially uninformed about the enterprise, he believed that it was essential "not to take them into our confidence until we were sure to get a real *quid pro quo* from our frankness." He had no illusions about the possibility of keeping such a secret permanently, but he did not think "it was yet time to share it with Russia." The President indicated that he agreed with Stimson.[49]

Time was now at a premium for Roosevelt, and for Stimson too. The wars in Europe and Asia, the French imbroglio, and the weight of his seventy-seven years left the Secretary of War little time to deal with the questions Bush had raised. In January 1945, most of the time he devoted to atomic energy matters was spent in settling his differences with Anderson over the status of the French scientists in Canada.† Bush became even more concerned that a planning committee for atomic energy matters be established as quickly as possible. He found the Secretary's priorities frustrating, but he was not easily discouraged. Unable to discuss the problem with Stimson, he turned to Bundy and to the State

---

* Although General Deane has been portrayed as crudely anti-Soviet (see, e.g., Alperovitz, *Atomic Diplomacy*, 30–33), he appears to have tried to maintain a balanced point of view throughout most of the war, as indicated by his book *Strange Alliance* (New York, 1946). Joseph E. Davies, who never failed to record any indications of anti-Soviet attitudes in his diary, was favorably impressed by Deane when they met and discussed Soviet-American relations in August 1944: "In Moscow, he [Deane] said, he had found the top officials very satisfactory to get along with, particularly the KKVD [sic] and the Air Force; but when he had to go through the lower echelons, there were exasperating delays." Davies also commented that Deane "seemed very friendly to the Soviets." Joseph E. Davies diaries, August 17, 1944, box 14.

† See Appendix G.

Department's recently appointed representative on atomic energy affairs, James C. Dunn. During January and early February, Bush pressed his case until the Secretary agreed in principle to set up such a committee.[50]

But Stimson was still skeptical. The problem of "S-1 and its possible connection with the Russians" continued to bother him, and he questioned Bush's apparent drift toward Bohr's idea of opening discussions with them on postwar control problems. The Secretary of War was "still inclined to tread softly and to hold off conferences on the subject until we have some much more tangible 'fruits of repentance' from the Russians as a *quid pro quo* for such a communication to them."[51] Before Stimson would tell the Soviets anything about the atomic bomb, he wanted some assurance of cooperation. (Bohr, of course, would have said he was putting the cart before the horse.)

When the President left the United States at the end of January to attend the Yalta Conference, the last of the wartime summit meetings between himself, Churchill, and Stalin, the policy of utmost secrecy agreed to at Hyde Park appears to have been the commitment he took with him. Despite the atmosphere of compromise and cooperation that pervaded Yalta, he did not alter his commitment to Churchill. Yet a series of events in January had brought the wisdom of maintaining the policy of secrecy into question by February. Hans von Halban, one of the French scientists employed in the Canadian section of the Manhattan Project, had been able to visit Joliot in France, despite Groves's recommendation that he be placed in confinement to prevent his departure.[52] Now Joliot, or possibly de Gaulle instigated by Joliot, could demand for France immediate participation in the Manhattan Project; and either of them could threaten to approach the Russians unless their demands were met.[53]

Under these circumstances Roosevelt raised the question with Churchill whether it might not be better to seize the initiative. But the Prime Minister was adamant. He was "shocked at Yalta," Churchill wrote about a month later, "when the President in a casual manner spoke of revealing the secret to Stalin on the grounds that de Gaulle, if he heard of it, would certainly double-cross us with Russia." Maintaining the Anglo-American partnership was Churchill's sole concern. "I am getting rather tired of all the different kinds of things that we must do or not do lest Anglo-French relations suffer," he noted. "One thing I am sure [of is] that there is nothing that de Gaulle would like better than to have plenty of T. A. to punish Britain, and nothing he would like less than to arm Communist Russia with the secret. . . . I shall certainly continue to urge the President not to make or permit the slightest disclosure to France or Russia. . . . Even six months will make a difference should it come to a show-down with Russia, or indeed with de Gaulle."[54]*

Roosevelt's ready acceptance of Churchill's view effectively ended any possibility that the question of postwar control of atomic energy might be raised with the Russians *during* the war. The Anglo-American leaders' publicly professed expectations for continued cooperation with the Soviet Union, it is now obvious, were somewhat less firm than has been heretofore recognized.[55]

IV

"Liberalization in Exchange for S-1"

The problems associated with the atomic bomb took up an increasing amount of Secretary Stimson's limited time in the weeks that followed the Yalta Conference. He was in need of rest every afternoon. Yet his numerous responsibilities pressed in upon him inexorably, while Bush maintained constant, though sympathetic, pressure for the programs he believed had to be initiated. Bush discussed atomic energy with Stimson on February 15, 1945, and again suggested the idea of an international pool of scientific research to include everything susceptible to military use after the war. This was the only way to prevent secret research for weapons development such as that conducted during the 1930s by German scientists. Bush was thinking along the "right lines," Stimson believed, but was in the Secretary's view too anxious. "It would be inadvisable to put it into full force yet until we had gotten all we could in Russia in the way of liberalization in exchange for S-1," he noted. Biological research, he thought, would be a good place to start.[56]

* See Appendix H.

In spite of Stimson's hesitations about timing, Bush felt that he could now bring his views on the future of the atomic bomb to the President's attention directly. He therefore outlined his plan in a letter to Roosevelt recommending that the United Nations Charter include a section devoted to international scientific research. It was necessary to create an international atmosphere of trust, he said, and it therefore followed that in a world threatened with an atomic arms race there had to be an agency that could guarantee that no nation was engaged in the secret production of atomic weapons. If this plan worked, it could then serve as a model for the complete interchange and control of all scientific work that might have military applications. The ultimate goal was the removal of all major weapons systems from national to supranational control. The atomic bomb was to serve as a test case.[57]

These proposals needed more study and official sanction, which could best be accomplished, Bush believed, by creating the sort of committee he had already recommended to Stimson. But on March 3, when he saw Harvey Bundy again, he was disappointed to learn that no action had been taken on his idea. Unless plans were drafted immediately for public statements, legislation, international control, and the postwar technical program, Bush argued, chaos would reign when the secret of the bomb was revealed. Bundy was impressed. On Monday morning, March 5, he had a long discussion with Stimson. For two hours he held the Secretary's attention while he outlined the entire range of problems raised by Bush on Saturday. "We're up against some very big decisions," Stimson belatedly concluded, and mused that "the time is approaching when we can no longer avoid them and when events may force us into the public on the subject." Their talk must have strayed far beyond the immediate question at hand, for the Secretary recorded that their thoughts "went right down to the bottom facts of human nature, morals, and governments."[58]

Stimson was at last grasping the full magnitude of the problem the atomic bomb would create after the war. As if to confirm his discovery, he went immediately to discuss the matter with Army Chief of Staff Marshall, whose judgment he held in high regard. But Marshall had never deeply considered the diplomatic aspects of atomic energy, and though he listened carefully, he did not add anything to what the Secretary had already concluded.

From this point on, the atomic bomb dominated Stimson's thinking, and he took it as his most important responsibility. "This matter now is taking up a good deal of my time and even then I am not doing it justice," he remarked a few days later. "It is approaching its ripening time and matters are getting very interesting and serious."[59] The problems included not only the Russians and postwar control, but domestic politics and finance as well. James F. Byrnes, director of War Mobilization, sent the President a memorandum on March 3, pointing out that the Manhattan Project's costs were approaching $2-billion, and it seemed to him that achievement of the final product remained in doubt. Although the administration might well avoid embarrassment during the war, afterwards public and congressional criticism would be uncontrollable if the project were a failure. If Stimson had needed an incentive to see Roosevelt, the Byrnes memorandum offered it.

The two elder statesmen saw each other on March 15—it was to be their last meeting. After making his case as to how "jittery and nervous and rather silly" were Byrnes's concerns, Stimson outlined the future prospects and problems posed by the bomb, as Bush, Conant, and Bundy had explained them to him. He pointed out that there were two schools of thought about control after the war. One approach called for continued secrecy and an attempt to maintain the Anglo-American monopoly; the other was the idea of international control based upon freedom of both scientific study and inspection. The issue had to be decided promptly, not left unresolved before the bomb was used; and neither Stimson nor Roosevelt expressed any doubts as to whether it would or should be used. It was also necessary to work more closely with Congress at this point. Roosevelt raised no objection to anything the Secretary said, and Stimson concluded that "on the whole the talk . . . was successful."[60]

As on several previous occasions, however, Roosevelt failed to move decisively on this matter of immediate importance.

Perhaps he was too busy with other problems, or perhaps just too tired to initiate something new. But it is more likely that he simply remained committed to keeping the atomic bomb a secret against the possibility of Soviet postwar intransigence.

The difficulties developing between the United States and the Soviet Union after Yalta did not help the efforts of those interested in planning for the international control of atomic energy. Stimson himself became something of a sounding board for his colleagues who were worried about Russian behavior. On April 2, Stettinius and Secretary of the Navy James Forrestal came to the War Department to take up the "trustee question," but the conversation turned to the "increasing strain of the relations between us and Russia."[61] Stettinius described a recent sharp exchange of messages between Stalin and Roosevelt.* One source of irritation was the unwillingness of the Russians to let the United States send planes and officers behind their lines in Poland and Germany to pick up liberated American prisoners. The Soviets, in turn, were furious about the refusal of the Americans and the British to allow them full participation in what they believed were surrender negotiations, then proceeding in Berne. Another sore point was the Soviet refusal to allow Allied bombers, whose missions originated in France, to land behind Russian lines.[62] And the impending Conference on the United Nations Organization raised further difficulties.

But the most important matter, "the principal one," as Stimson referred to it, was the Polish question. Although the Soviet-American disagreement over the future government of Poland was very serious, Stimson told Stettinius that "we simply cannot allow a rift to come between the two nations without endangerous [sic] the peace of the world." Marshall, he noted, had anticipated these troubles and thought they would be diffi-

---

* *Stalin's Correspondence*, I, msg. nos. 273–90, covers the post-Yalta-Roosevelt days. Stalin and Roosevelt exchanged eighteen messages between the Yalta Conference and the President's death on April 12. The first complaint communicated to Stalin came on March 4 with regard to "the difficulties which are being encountered in collecting, supplying, and evacuating American ex-prisoners of war and American aircraft crews who are stranded east of the Russian lines." No. 276.

cult to resolve, but he too felt they had to be tolerated. After all, Russia had been very cooperative on the "large issues." She had "kept her word and carried out her engagements. We must remember that she has not learned the amenities of diplomatic intercourse and we must expect bad language from her."[63]

Reflecting on the attitudes of the Secretaries of State and Navy, Stimson decided on the following day that it *"is time for me to use all the restraint I can on these people* who have been apparently getting a little more irritated." Tempers had to be controlled; rash actions had to be prevented. If the United States stated the facts with "perfectly cold-blooded firmness," things would work out.[64] Thus, on April 3, Stimson resolved to be the voice of moderation and restraint within the administration. Just ten days after that decision was made, its importance suddenly magnified; Roosevelt was dead. Relations with the Soviet Union had deteriorated even further. No action had been taken on Bush's atomic energy proposals. A new President, uninformed and unsure of himself, yet impulsive, was faced with the most delicate and difficult diplomatic problems of the war. From Stimson's point of view, the atomic bomb was chief among them. But "it has this unique peculiarity," he mused the day before Roosevelt died, "although every prophecy thus far has been fulfilled by the development and we can see that success is 99% assured, yet only by the first actual war trial of the weapon can the actual certainty be fixed."[65] Truman did not inherit the question of whether that certainty ought to be fixed; he inherited the answer.

III

FIRE AND ICE: FROM WORLD WAR TO COLD WAR

Some say the world will end in fire,
Some say in ice.
From what I've tasted of desire
I hold with those who favor fire.
But if it had to perish twice,
I think I know enough of hate
To say that for destruction ice
Is also great
And would suffice.

—ROBERT FROST

6

THE NEW PRESIDENT

On the afternoon of April 12, 1945, Franklin Roosevelt suddenly died. That evening his Vice-President, Harry S. Truman, took the oath of office and assumed the formidable burdens of the Presidency: as Commander-in-Chief, he was responsible for the military policies of a nation still at war; as chief executive officer, for the diplomatic policies that would guide the nation through the difficult transition to peace. During his first weeks in office, however, Truman—emotionally unprepared and generally uninformed—had no diplomatic program of his own. The suddenness of Roosevelt's passing thus effectively left policymaking in the hands of his inherited advisers, who, for the most part, viewed Soviet intentions in a more sinister light than Roosevelt had. Under the circumstances, they easily persuaded Truman to adopt a harsher, less conciliatory stance toward the Russians than his predecessor had pursued. The result was a serious crisis in American-Soviet diplomacy—within two weeks rapport between the allies had declined precipitously. This led Stimson, whose attitude differed from that of the other advisers, to warn the new President (as Bush and Conant had warned Stimson) that the postwar implications of the atomic bomb made cooperation with Stalin a necessity, not a choice.

I

The Atomic Legacy

The most controversial and significant element of Roosevelt's atomic energy policies at the time of his death—his commitment to continue the Anglo-American atomic energy partnership after the war—died with him. His atomic energy advisers, of course, remained uncertain as to the nature of the personal understanding the late President had reached with Churchill: they had never been informed about the Hyde Park agreement, nor about other private discussions on this subject between the two leaders.[1]* Insofar as they suspected the truth, however, they opposed the idea of such an exclusive partnership. In any event, in the absence of a well-defined atomic energy policy that they could present to the new President, the need to formulate a coherent postwar policy was pressing.

The question of the use of the bomb against Japan was more clearly settled than was general policy: no one except Alexander Sachs had ever questioned the assumption that the weapon should be used during the war if it became available. But it does not necessarily follow that a surprise atomic attack against the Japanese was therefore unalterably set. Assumptions made during the early years of the war were not necessarily valid or appropriate near the war's end. Indeed, the Hyde Park *aide-mémoire* itself put the matter very tentatively: the atomic bomb "might perhaps, after mature consideration, be used against the Japanese. . . ." Had this carefully worded and qualified statement been available to Truman, which it was not, he could hardly have considered it an irreversible declaration of intention. In fact, three days after signing the document Roosevelt had asked Bush whether he thought the atomic bomb "should actually be used against the Japanese or whether it should be used only as a threat with full-scale experimentation in this country." Bush treated the question in the same way that Roosevelt had raised it—as a matter not of immediate importance.

*The Hyde Park *aide-mémoire* came to Stimson's attention on June 25, 1945. He made the following notation in his diary entry for that day: "At eleven o'clock Sir Henry Wilson came in bringing me a hitherto unseen paper on S-1 which was signed by Roosevelt and Churchill at Hyde Park on the latter's visit there I believe. The Roosevelt duplicate has evidently been mislaid among Mr. Roosevelt's papers, so this was the only one available. It, however, did not bring any bombshell. I called in Bundy and Roger Makins of the British embassy who were outside and we all four discussed the matter together, together with future plans for the S-1 test."

There were many aspects to the matter that could not be considered until the bomb was ready, Bush noted; it would be foolish to threaten the Japanese with an atomic attack until the blow could be delivered: "The matter warranted very careful discussion, but this could be postponed for quite a time. . . ."[2] It was. No further discussions about the matter ever took place between them.

During the seven months between the Hyde Park Conference and Roosevelt's death, steady progress had been made on the development of the bomb at Los Alamos and the other facilities of the Manhattan Project. In a memorandum written about two weeks before Roosevelt died, General Groves expressed his confident opinion that atomic weapons would be available in time to use against Japan. He was certain that the weapon would bring the war to a rapid conclusion, thereby justifying the years of effort, the vast expenditures, and the judgment of the officials responsible for the project. Two bombs would be ready by August 1, 1945.[3] Even before Truman took office, the race for the bomb had already changed from a race against German scientists to a race against the war itself. "I don't think there was any time where we worked harder at the speed-up than in the period after the German surrender [May 8] and the actual combat use of the bomb," Oppenheimer recalled after the war.[4]

When Truman took office, then, no policy in the sphere of atomic energy was definitely settled: The President had the option of deciding the future of the Anglo-American alliance according to his own estimate of what was fair; although the policy of "utmost secrecy" had been confirmed at Hyde Park the previous September, neither Bush nor Conant nor Groves nor Stimson knew the substance of atomic energy agreements between Roosevelt and Churchill; although the assumption about the bomb's wartime use was shared by members of the Manhattan Project's Top Policy Group, Bush had already indicated that he, at least, did not consider this a matter beyond discussion; and finally, no group of advisers had been formally assigned by the Executive to study the probable impact of the atomic bomb on postwar diplomacy. The final decisions on these questions were the responsibility of the new President.

Truman was, however, bound to the past by his own uncertain position and by the prestige of his predecessor, who had initiated the Manhattan Project. Since Roosevelt had refused to open negotiations with the Soviet government for the international control of atomic energy, and since he had indicated his intention to use the new weapon to help win the war, it would have been difficult indeed for Truman to reverse these decisions. Roosevelt himself had shrunk from the effort at Yalta, and such a reversal would have been far easier for him. So Truman's atomic energy legacy, while it included several options, did not necessarily entail complete freedom to choose between them. "Roosevelt had such immense prestige politically arising from his four successful campaigns for President," Stimson wrote in his diary on April 13, 1945, "that he carried a weight with the Congress and with general politicians of the country which Truman could not possibly have."[5] The new President was constrained in his choices by the very occurrence that had created them—Roosevelt's sudden and unexpected death.

II

The New President

Roosevelt's death necessarily precipitated a major review of American wartime diplomacy. This was not initiated with the intention of reversing current policies; on the contrary, Truman had no idea just what those policies were. Roosevelt had been in Washington for less than a month during the eighty-two days since the inauguration and had conferred with his Vice-President on only two occasions. Truman himself estimated that he saw the President perhaps eight times during the final year of Roosevelt's life, and these meetings added little to his preparation for the responsibilities he inherited.[6] Truman, in turn, had avoided any attempt to prepare himself for higher office. "I had been afraid for many weeks that something might happen to this great leader," he recalled years later, "[but] I did not allow myself to think about it after I became Vice-President."[7] General Harry H. Vaughan, Truman's friend and assistant, has confirmed this: "Mr. Truman . . . just didn't want to think of it. . . ."[8]

After his inauguration as Vice-President on January 20, Truman's responsibilities were limited to trivial matters.[9] According to Vaughan, Roosevelt "never talked to Mr. Truman a minute on what happened at Teheran, and what happened at Yalta, and what happened at Casablanca, so Truman was not prepared at all. He didn't know any of the commitments we had made to Russia or to France or to Great Britain."[10] Nor did Truman's experience in the Senate assist him in dealing with foreign policy.[11] His stated views on foreign affairs reflected an outlook widely associated with Midwestern America. Although they do not represent a consistent underlying philosophy, they do offer an insight into his political style. A notorious example of his careless rhetoric, and the one most frequently cited as evidence of an anti-Soviet bias, was a glib comment made two days after Germany had attacked the Soviet Union: "If we see that Germany is winning we ought to help Russia and if Russia is winning we ought to help Germany and that way let them kill as many as possible. . . ."[12] But new circumstances elicited new opinions. "I'm for Russia," Senator Truman proclaimed in 1943.[13]

Candor and openness were distinguishing features of Truman's character. He never entertained false notions about his intellectual abilities or his background. After succeeding to the Presidency, he accepted gracefully the hallmark of "common man," a theme his supporters put forward almost from his first day in office. "The sheer fact that he is the average man, understands the average man and his quality," the Kansas City *Star* editorialized, "is probably Truman's greatest asset as he undertakes these new overpowering responsibilities." The editor hoped that Truman would heed the wisdom of the people. "Personal government" was over; "government by consultation" had once again returned.[14]

The image of Truman as a tough-minded, confident President, the man who displayed a sign on his desk reading "The Buck Stops Here!," was one he cultivated after the war was over. During the war he revealed no sense of confidence, but rather a shrewd understanding that he could not survive politically—or live comfortably with himself—if he did not *appear* decisive, confident, and in control of events. Yet in this period he was in fact at the mercy of events, and to compensate for his lack of experience, his inadequate knowledge, and his profound concern over his ability to do the job so suddenly thrust upon him, he relied upon those advisers who offered decisive advice. Years later, he elevated his preference for decisiveness into an interpretation of American history—a transparent defense of his own political style. Referring once to Andrew Jackson's role in the nullification controversy of the 1830s, he remarked, "We know now what they could not know then. We know what a pliant, supple man in the White House in that crisis might have cost us."[15] Here, as in many other references to the past, Truman saw history as guided by men of strong will acting upon principle: "I learned [from reading history] that in those periods . . . when there [is] no leadership, society usually gropes through dark ages of one degree or another. I saw that it takes men to make history, or there would be no history. History does not make the man." In sum: "Do your duty and history will do you justice."[16]

During the early months of his Presidency, Truman made a conscious effort to appear decisive. Like Roosevelt, he under-. stood the dynamics of leadership, but unlike FDR, he was not a charismatic leader. Until the war ended, until he freed himself from his predecessor's encumbering legacy, Truman felt compelled constantly to prove himself to those around him. On the evening of April 12, 1945, as he stood in the crowded Cabinet Room of the White House, he was the center of attention, yet terribly alone—ignorant of problems and policies, without a personal ally among his chief advisers, unsure to whom he should turn for guidance, certain only that whatever experience and knowledge he possessed had not prepared him for the tasks ahead. He was an outsider in his own administration, an intruder with little if any standing in the eyes of those who were officially his subordinates. It was symbolic of his situation that, when a few days later, President Truman entered the East Room of the White House for Roosevelt's funeral service, no one stood up. As Robert E. Sherwood has noted, "All they could think of was that the President was dead. But everybody stood up when Mrs. Roosevelt came in."[17]

Truman's first days in office were chaotic and agonizing; the mask of certainty and decisiveness could not be set in place immediately. "It was the only time in my life, I think, that I ever felt as if I'd had a real shock," he wrote to his mother.[18] The task before him appeared so awesome that on the afternoon of his first full day as President, he publicly expressed his lack of confidence. "Boys," he said to a group of reporters, "if you ever pray, pray for me now. I don't know whether you fellows ever had a load of hay fall on you, but when they told me yesterday what had happened, I felt like the moon, the stars, and all the planets had fallen on me. I've got the most terribly responsible job a man ever had."

"Good luck, Mr. President," a reporter called out. "I wish you didn't have to call me that," Truman replied, and there is no reason to doubt that he meant it.[19] When Alben Barkley, the Senate Majority Leader, later paid a call on Truman, he listened to him "deprecate his situation." Barkley has recalled Truman as "extremely humble and modest about it all and finally I thought a little too much so, because he very frequently said he wished he hadn't been President, wished he hadn't been Vice-President, wished he were not President and that he never wanted to be." Rumors and stories of Truman's attitude circulated around Washington, and Barkley felt compelled to return in a few days to tell the new President that if he did not display confidence in himself, "the people [would] lose confidence" in him.[20]

As if immediately to emphasize the primacy of foreign affairs, the first Cabinet meeting, hastily convened after Truman was sworn in, was interrupted by Press Secretary Steve Early, who asked if the San Francisco conference on the United Nations would meet as planned on April 25. The press was anxious to know. More than anything else agreed to at the Yalta meeting in February, the prospect of a United Nations Organization was a symbol of continued Allied cooperation. Truman responded accordingly; his answer was affirmative. It was his first and without doubt his easiest decision. His intention, he then told his inherited advisers, was to continue both the foreign and the domestic policies of the Roosevelt administration.[21] As we have seen, lacking any policies of his own, he really had little alternative.

When the brief Cabinet meeting was adjourned, Stimson remained behind. He would explain the details later, he said, but before departing he wanted to inform the President of "a new explosive [under development] of almost unbelievable destructive power . . ."; that was all he wished to say at the moment.[22] Although this statement left Truman understandably puzzled, the matter was not pursued. Stimson then took his leave, profoundly anxious about the sudden turn of events. Problems related to the atomic bomb suddenly took on a new sense of immediacy for him. He may well have pondered that evening over the irony that the ultimate responsibility for the new weapon should now belong to Harry Truman. As chairman of the Senate Committee to Investigate the National Defense Program, the Senator from Missouri had come annoyingly close on two occasions, in June 1943 and March 1944, to uncovering Stimson's most closely held secret. Both times his probing had been successfully parried; but on the latter occasion, it must have taken some tedious persuasion, for Stimson had noted in his diary that "Truman is a nuisance and pretty untrustworthy man. He talks smoothly but acts meanly."[23]

Whether or not Stimson recalled that entry on the evening of April 12, it is unlikely that he felt confident about his new chief. His enigmatic remarks to Truman after the first Cabinet meeting had been impulsive and very much out of character. They reflected the tensions of the moment and his sudden realization that the problem of the atomic bomb required immediate and considerable attention. However, he did not try to pursue the matter with the President for almost two weeks. Trained as a trial lawyer under the eminent attorney and statesman Elihu Root, Stimson had been inculcated with "the need for infinite pains in preparation." For Stimson, his biographer has noted, "preparation was . . . almost everything"[24]—and he characteristically decided to delay any further discussion with the President about the bomb until he had carefully reviewed and studied the entire atomic energy program. His first step in this regard was to order Groves and his special assistants Harvey Bundy and George Harrison to draw up a memorandum on "the whole [atomic energy] situation."[25]

III

"The Harassing Question of Poland"

During the daily meetings and briefings that filled Truman's first ten days as President, most of his time was devoted to foreign affairs in general and the "harassing question of Poland" in particular. The impression he received from his advisers, from Churchill's messages, and from State Department reports was that Stalin was not keeping his word. The new President's first official visitor on April 13 was Secretary of State Edward R. Stettinius, Jr., an official with little influence under Roosevelt, but a man who represented the rising tide of mistrust of the Soviet Union then flowing through high government circles. His report to the President on the "background and the present status of the principal problems confronting this government in its relations with other countries" viewed American-Soviet affairs almost exclusively with reference to events since the Yalta Conference. Stettinius declared that "Churchill fully shares this government's interpretation of the Yalta Agreements on Eastern Europe and liberated areas." He reported, however, that the Soviet government had "taken a firm and uncompromising position on nearly every major question that has arisen in our relations," and he enumerated just what those issues were. "The most important of these are the Polish question, the application of the Crimea [Yalta] Agreement on liberated areas, the agreement on the exchange of liberated prisoners of war and civilians, and the San Francisco Conference [United Nations Organization meeting]. . . . in the politico-military field, similar difficulties have been encountered in collaboration with the Soviet authorities." With regard to Poland, Stettinius stated that "the Soviet authorities [are] consistently sabotaging Ambassador Harriman's efforts in the Moscow Commission to hasten the implementation of the decisions at the Crimea Conference."[26]

The Yalta agreement on Poland reached by Churchill, Roosevelt, and Stalin represented, as Truman came to understand it, a compromise: The Warsaw Provisional Government then functioning in Poland was to be broadened by the inclusion of "certain democratic leaders who were still in Poland and by others who were living abroad [the Polish government in exile —known as the "London Poles"]." The expanded government would then be pledged to hold free and unfettered elections as soon as possible on the basis of universal suffrage and the secret ballot. "Properly carried out, this compromise might very well have solved the problem," Truman noted. "We were now faced, however, with the failure of the Russians to live up to this agreement."[27] That Roosevelt and Churchill had also agreed to Stalin's demand that the Polish government be "friendly" to the Soviet Union—and that the London Poles and their supporters were decidedly anti-Soviet—were facts that Truman's advisers ignored.

During this period of familiarization it was, of course, impossible for Truman to investigate fully any major issue on his own. As a result, he accepted without question the hostile interpretation of Soviet behavior presented by his advisers. On the afternoon of his fifth day in office, for example, Truman cabled a four-point proposal on the complicated and volatile Polish issue to both Churchill and Stalin.[28] The first three points spelled out the American demand that the London Poles be consulted on the composition of the future government of Poland. Point four was the heart of the matter: "We do not feel that we could commit ourselves to any formula for determining the new Government of National Unity in advance of consultation with the Polish leaders [the London Poles] and we do not in any case consider the Yugoslav precedent [an arrangement that assured a pro-Soviet government] to be applicable to Poland." This document had been fully prepared in advance by the State Department; yet Churchill later commented that it was "remarkable that he [Truman] felt able so promptly to commit himself to it amid the formalities of assuming office and the funeral of his predecessor."[29]

On the contrary, considering the circumstances and his own personality, it would have been remarkable had Truman hesitated to follow the advice of the experienced men around him. Agreement among his advisers and the opportunity to act de-

Truman's accession was enabling factor in destroying FDR's tolerance[?] for ambiguity, or allowing anti-Soviet advisers to prevail

153

The New President

cisively upon their advice was exactly the kind of support Truman needed during his trying first days and weeks as President, and he took full advantage of their recommendations. "It was necessary for me to begin making decisions an hour and a half before I was sworn in, and I've been making them ever since," he wrote to his mother after nine days in office.[30] A more accurate description would be that he restricted himself to confirming policies formulated by others.

The Soviet government's response to Roosevelt's death was in diplomatic terms ambiguous. While continuing to insist upon arrangements that would ensure a pro-Soviet Polish government, Stalin accepted a suggestion put forward by Harriman and reversed an earlier decision not to send his Foreign Minister, V. M. Molotov, to the San Francisco Conference.*[31] But if the President was to assess the Polish question calmly, if he was to have the chance to consider the consequences of an inflexible position on his own part, Stalin would have had to initiate a temporary moratorium on his diplomatic maneuvers in Poland. Time, however, was a gift that Stalin did not choose to offer, and both the rush of events and their direction swept the President into a diplomatic corner. Soviet policies were being viewed, and explained to Truman, in terms of what Henry Kissinger has described as an "inherent bad faith" model. Such a perspective, Kissinger observes, is "clearly self-perpetuating, for the model itself denies the existence of data that could disconfirm it. At the interpersonal level such behavior is characterized as abnormal—paranoia. Different standards seem to apply at the international level. . . ."[32] Underplaying the intrinsic ambiguity of the Yalta agreements, Truman's advisers chose to

note — both US + Sov had it, esp. after Truman came in

---

* Stalin's decision to withdraw Molotov from the Soviet delegation had worried Roosevelt. He had written to Stalin on March 24, urging him to change his mind: "All sponsoring powers and the majority of the other countries attending will be represented by their Ministers of Foreign Affairs. In these circumstances I am afraid that Mr. Molotov's absence will be construed all over the world as a lack of comparable interest in the great objectives of this Conference on the part of the Soviet Government." *Stalin's Correspondence*, I, No. 280. But Stalin's March 27 reply to Roosevelt had been adamant: "We highly value and attach great importance to the San Francisco Conference . . . but present circumstances preclude V. M. Molotov's attendance." *Ibid.*, No. 282.

interpret the Soviet position as duplicitous. As each day passed, Truman became further convinced that the Russians were ignoring what he took to be the plain meaning of the Yalta accords. Although today the Kremlin's attitude on this issue is not necessarily viewed as unreasonable, few U.S. policymakers at that time accepted this interpretation.

Harriman's reports from Moscow reinforced the opinions of the analysts in Washington. Disagreements with the Soviets that to Roosevelt were "minor," Harriman viewed as "major," and he wanted them understood in the Kremlin as such.[33] Although an advocate of Soviet-American cooperation, he was convinced that meaningful agreements with the Soviets could only be won by dealing with them in kind: stern policy for stern policy. Harriman believed that Stalin's final communications with Roosevelt had not helped to resolve the Polish problem. He recommended, therefore, that the United States adhere to its interpretation of the Yalta decisions under which the provisional government then functioning in Poland should be reorganized on a broad democratic basis.[34] In Harriman's view, Stettinius told Truman on April 16, "Stalin essentially is asking us to agree to the establishment of a thinly disguised version of the present Warsaw regime and [Harriman] recommends that we continue to insist that we cannot accept a whitewash of the Warsaw regime."[35]

In the following days, this view received what Truman considered strong substantiation. First of all, he learned that the Soviet government had informed Harriman of a "great public demand" for the conclusion of a treaty of mutual assistance between the Soviet Union and the existing Polish government. Stalin was about to play his trump card and recognize a committee of Polish Communists, the "Lublin Poles," as the legitimate government of Poland. Faced with the possibility of a *fait accompli* on an issue that had been defined as the symbolic test of Soviet willingness to cooperate with the United States, Truman indeed felt he was being backed into a diplomatic corner.[36] A few days later, with Harriman back in Washington, the President was briefed on Soviet problems by the Ambassador, Stettinius, Under Secretary of State Joseph Grew, and Soviet affairs specialist Charles Bohlen. This meeting, reported in great detail by Truman, must have been extremely important to him. Harriman presented the President with a view of Soviet policy which left him a choice between either assuming an inflexible stance with regard to Poland or developing a different analysis of Soviet aims and behavior independent of the consensus his advisers presented.[37]

Averell Harriman was a respected diplomat with an imposing presence, a man able to present his opinions with great skill and vigor. His diplomatic experience and his frequent meetings with Stalin gave him an air of authority that no Washington observer could command. When they met, Truman acted, in effect, as if Harriman were in charge. The Ambassador began by arguing that the Soviet Union was pursuing a dual policy: on the one hand, cooperating in a variety of matters of mutual concern to the Allies; on the other, extending Soviet control over neighboring states through unilateral actions. He indicated that certain elements around Stalin saw U.S. gestures toward compromise as indications of softness, implying that any American effort to cooperate with the Soviet Union would lead to further Soviet encroachments. In the Ambassador's opinion, however, the Soviet Union had no desire to break with the United States because American economic assistance was vital to their reconstruction program. For this reason, he believed that the President could stand firm on important issues without running serious risks. At this point in the briefing, Truman interjected a revealing comment. "I stopped Harriman," he reports in his *Memoirs*, "to say that I was not afraid of the Russians and that I intended to be firm. I would be fair, of course, and anyway the Russians needed us more than we needed them."[38]

The exchange between the President and the Ambassador continued in this vein throughout. When Harriman suggested that some Russians foolishly believed that it was a matter of life and death to American business to increase exports to Russia, Truman declared that he too thought it was ridiculous and repeated that he intended to be firm. Harriman went on to suggest that the Russians were conducting a "barbarian invasion of Europe." He was sure that Soviet control over foreign countries meant that their influence would be paramount in those countries' foreign relations. In his view, it was necessary to decide on a policy that took account of these unpleasant facts. He was not pessimistic, however; if the government surrendered its remaining illusions about Soviet aims, negotiations might prove fruitful. Once again, Truman expressed agreement. He did not expect to get one hundred percent of what he proposed, but he did feel "we should be able to get eighty-five percent."

Harriman argued that Stalin had discovered that an honest execution of the Yalta agreement would mean the end of the Soviet-backed Lublin group's control over Poland. The policy of the United States toward its Soviet ally had to take this into account; it had to be grounded on the assumption that the Russians were likely to prove adamant. After some discussion of the relationship between the United Nations Organization and the Polish issue, Truman brought the meeting to a close. "I intend to be firm in my dealings with the Soviet government," he assured his advisers. Then, as Truman reports it, "Before leaving *Harriman took me aside* and said: 'Frankly, one of the reasons that made me rush back to Washington was the fear that you did not understand, as I had seen Roosevelt understand, that Stalin is breaking his agreements. My fear was inspired by the fact that you could not have had time to catch up with all the recent cables. But I must say that I am greatly relieved to discover that you have read them all and that we see eye to eye on the situation.' "

"I am glad," Truman replied, "that you are going to be available to our delegation in San Francisco."[39]

The Foreign Minister of the Soviet Union, V. M. Molotov, arrived in Washington on Sunday, April 22. He was preceded by the announcement that a Soviet-Polish treaty had been concluded, despite Truman's urgings against it.[40] Molotov and the President met twice during the next two days. At their first conference, at Blair House, Truman brought up the Polish issue, but only in general terms. He stated that "a proper solution" to the issue was of great importance because of its impact on American public opinion. "The Polish question had become for our people the symbol of the future development of our international relations," Truman noted. Molotov in turn reminded the President of Poland's geographical proximity to the Soviet Union and its consequent importance to Russian interests. After some formalities, further discussions were scheduled at the Department of State the next day, and the meeting ended.[41]

The second meeting, which Truman did not attend himself, was similarly unproductive; it deadlocked over Soviet insistence that the Lublin government be seated at the San Francisco Conference. Truman thereupon held an unscheduled meeting that same afternoon with his top military and foreign policy advisers. Stettinius, Bohlen, Harriman, and Dunn represented the Department of State; Stimson, Forrestal, Marshall, King, and Leahy, the military. In his memoirs, Truman presents this meeting as one called to help him formulate a response to the existing impasse. However, other accounts of the gathering, in the diaries of Leahy, Forrestal, and Stimson, suggest or explicitly state that the President was *already* convinced of the need to explain his position to Molotov "with rather brutal frankness."[42] After saying this, the President told the group what he intended to tell Molotov. Then he asked Stimson, who had not been forewarned that Poland would be discussed at the meeting, for his comments.

Remaining true to his pledge of April 2 that he would argue for "restraint," Stimson pointed out that in major military matters the Soviet government had always kept its word and, in fact, often exceeded its promises. Furthermore, before acting precipitously, it was important to make an accurate assessment of Soviet motives in Eastern Europe, an area that was, after all, vital to Russian security.[43] Stimson stressed the great danger of a confrontation over Poland at this point. He suggested that rather than antagonize Molotov with undiplomatic language and an ultimatum, the President proceed cautiously. Stimson's argument was weakened, however, by what he felt obliged to leave unsaid. He could not point out the "real difficulties of the situation without reflecting on [his] colleague in the State Department [Stettinius] or the young men who were urging him on." Stimson believed that the Department of State had gotten itself into a "mess." They had failed to settle the major problems between the Allies prior to going ahead with the San Francisco Conference, and now they felt "compelled to bull the thing through." The President, Stimson noted, was "evidently disappointed at my caution."[44]

If the President was only "disappointed" by the Secretary of War's caution, almost everyone else present was strongly opposed to it. Forrestal, who had discussed the issue with Harriman three days earlier, argued that Poland was part of a pattern of unilateral Soviet action. He felt that they "might as well meet the issue now as later on."[45] Harriman spoke to Stimson's point about Soviet motives by offering the explanation he had suggested earlier to Truman: that when Stalin realized after Yalta what free elections would bring, he was determined to avoid them. As for Soviet military cooperation, that was a necessary result of self-interest, and he was therefore not impressed by it. Leahy felt there was nothing surprising about Russian actions, considering the ambiguity of the Yalta agreements. Stettinius objected: there was nothing ambiguous about Soviet obligations; to prove his point he read the parts of the agreement relating to the formation of the new Polish government and free elections. He felt that they were open to only one honest interpretation. Marshall finally allied himself with Stimson, agreeing that the possibility of a rupture in relations with the Soviet Union should not be considered lightly. He pointed to the advantage of securing Soviet cooperation in the war against Japan.

Although, as Leahy has recorded, there was "[no] consensus of opinion," at least a clear majority agreed with Harriman that the "time [had] arrived to take a strong American attitude toward the Soviet Union, and that no particular harm [could] be done to our war prospects even if Russia should slow down or even stop its war effort in Europe and Asia."[46] The most important point to stress here, however, is that the President had apparently accepted Harriman's view even before the meeting was called. He was to consider a cautious approach later—but only after he was faced with the unexpected results of his blunt, uncomplicated diplomacy.

Stettinius, Harriman, Dunn, and Bohlen remained to assist the President in preparing for his conference with Molotov that evening. When the Foreign Minister arrived, Truman chose to dispense with protocol, and "went straight to the point."* He was

---

* Truman looked back on this incident while writing his memoirs and stated that he had decided to "lay it on the line with Moscow." Truman, *Year of Decisions*, 50.

disappointed, he said, over the lack of progress in solving the Polish problem. He then proceeded to explain the position of the United States government on the matter. The four-point program sent to Stalin almost a week earlier was "eminently fair and reasonable," and he would not be a party to the formation of a Polish government that was not representative of all the people. As far as the United Nations Organization was concerned, the United States would proceed no matter what difficulties or differences arose over other matters. American economic assistance to the Soviet Union, however, was a different matter; that depended upon Soviet cooperation on other matters of mutual interest. "No policy in the United States, foreign or domestic, could succeed unless it had public confidence and support," Truman told Molotov. This applied to economic as well as political collaboration. It was Truman's hope that the Soviet government would keep this in mind. He then handed Molotov a message for Stalin that outlined the American position.[47]

In response, Molotov asked permission to make a few observations about the Soviet position. Truman listened impatiently, and retorted that he was only asking the Soviet government to carry out the Yalta decision on Poland. Molotov repeated his government's intention to do no less: "It [is] a matter of honor." Truman "replied sharply" that an agreement had been reached, and that Stalin ought to carry it out. Molotov reminded the President that the Premier's views on the agreement had been set out in detail in an earlier cable to Roosevelt. Truman again retorted that an agreement had been reached on Poland and the Soviets ought to keep their word. Molotov seemed to be "avoiding the main issue," Truman said, adding this time that he "wanted it clearly understood that [cooperation between their countries] could be only on a basis of the mutual observation of agreements and not on the basis of a one-way street."

"I have never been talked to like that in my life," protested Molotov.

"Carry out your agreements and you won't get talked to like that," the President answered.[48] The conference was over.

If Harriman's appraisal of Soviet behavior had been accurate, Truman's frank statement of American policy to Molotov should have led to a more cooperative Russian attitude. But a far differ-

and be expected maybe . . . ?
✓

ent result followed. Within two days Truman received a message from Stalin which he later referred to as "one of the most revealing and disquieting messages to reach me during my first days in the White House." Citing Britain's determination to have sympathetic governments in Belgium and Greece as a recognized precedent, Stalin insisted that the security of the Soviet Union had to be acknowledged as the primary criterion for a settlement of the Polish question. He reaffirmed his willingness to do everything possible to bring about a settlement, but he made it clear that any settlement had to be in line with Soviet interests. "I think there is only one way out of the present situation," he concluded, "and that is to accept the Yugoslav precedent as a model for Poland."[49] According to this formula, approximately eighty percent of the ministers of the new Polish government would have to be sympathetic to the Soviet Union.

Truman had rejected this same proposal in his earlier four-point proposal to Stalin, and the Soviet Premier's blunt response grated on the President's sensibilities. "Without any attempt to hide his role in diplomatic niceties," Truman complained, "Stalin for the first time in addressing Churchill and me used the 'Big I am.' "[50] This was not the first time, moreover, that Truman had felt personally insulted by Stalin's messages. According to Leahy, even before the meeting with Molotov "the insulting language" of Soviet communications had been "an affront to the solid, old-fashioned Americanism possessed by Harry Truman. . . ."[51] In light of the existence of the atomic bomb, however, both the tone and the substance of Truman's diplomacy seemed all wrong to Stimson, a point he intended to make when he spoke about it to the President two days later.

IV

"The Most Terrible Weapon . . ."

After meeting with the President on the afternoon of April 23, Stimson returned to his office deeply troubled, fearful that Truman was being maneuvered into an ill-advised confrontation with Molotov. The Secretary's innate sense of caution, his aversion to

making decisions without careful preparation, and his own understanding of the profound complexity of the issues involved, all
contributed to his distress. He related the details of the meeting
to Assistant Secretary of War John J. McCloy, but cautioned
him not to initiate any discussion about it with members of the
State Department. "Sooner or later," he remarked, "we will find
out what happened." He did not wish Stettinius, Forrestal, or any
of the others who favored an uncompromising policy toward the
Russians to be alerted to his continuing concern, for he intended
to counsel the President against their approach. Even before
Roosevelt's death, Stimson had been anxious to apply all the influence he could muster against the policies recommended by
Forrestal and Stettinius. It had appeared to him then—and the
meeting from which he had just returned confirmed him in his
view—that they were reacting emotionally and precipitously at a
time when it was necessary to be "very careful in order to avoid
a head-on collision." Poland was "the most important and difficult
question we and Russia have got between us," Stimson noted,
and he was "very much alarmed for fear that we were rushing
into a situation where we would find ourselves breaking our
relations."[52]

One reason Stimson was particularly upset about the April 23
conference was that it had been "sprung on me at a time and in
a method in which I could not give the considered and careful
answer to the President which I wanted to give." That yet-to-be-
proffered answer was based—in addition to the considerations he
had cited at the White House meeting—upon his understanding
of the implications of the atomic bomb. When he returned from
that meeting, he found that Bundy, Harrison, and Groves had
completed the memorandum he had asked them to compose.
"They have drawn up a very interesting summary . . . and I read
that and talked with them about it."[53]

Stimson's preparations for briefing Truman continued on the
following day. He reviewed reports on the status of the Manhattan Project and, with the assistance of Harvey Bundy, drew up
a memorandum of his own on the bomb's postwar significance.
He then wrote to the President requesting an early appointment.
As he had learned to do early in his legal career, he directed his

first efforts "at making the court want to decide for you." Whatever the nature of the case, Root had taught him, "you set up your data . . . in such a way that you prepare the mind of the judge emotionally" to decide for you.[54] "Dear Mr. President," Stimson wrote, "I think it is very important that I should have a talk with you as soon as possible on a highly secret matter. I mentioned it to you shortly after you took office but have not urged it since on account of the pressure you have been under. It, however, has such a bearing on our present foreign relations and has such an important effect upon all my thinking in this field that I think you ought to know about it without further delay."[55]

With his memorandum on the "political aspects of the S-1 performance"* in hand, and General Groves in reserve, Stimson went to the White House on April 25. The document he carried with him was the distillation of numerous decisions already taken, each one the product of attitudes developed along with the new weapon. The Secretary himself was not entirely aware of how various forces had shaped these decisions: the speculations of Manhattan Project scientists, the recommendations of Bush and Conant, the policies followed by Roosevelt, the uncertainties inherent in the wartime alliance, the oppressive concern for secrecy, in addition to his own incessant concern with long-range implications. At this point, Roosevelt's death, the fact that work on the bomb was nearing completion, and the exigencies of war and diplomacy had brought all these considerations and forces together.

The memorandum was a curious document.[56] It displayed Stimson's sensitivity to the historic significance of the atomic bomb, but did not question the wisdom of using it against Japan. Nor did the Secretary suggest any concrete steps for developing a postwar policy. His objective was to acquaint Truman with the salient problems in general and their bearing on Soviet-American relations in particular: the possibility of an atomic arms race, the danger of atomic war, and the necessity for some form of international cooperation in the field of atomic energy if the United Nations Organization was to work. "If the problem of the proper use of this weapon can be solved," he wrote, "we would

* See Appendix I.

have the opportunity to bring the world into a pattern in which
the peace of the world and our civilization can be saved."* To
cope with this difficult challenge, Stimson suggested the "establishment of a select committee" to consider the postwar problems
inherent in the development of the bomb. Bush's suggestion of
December had taken almost five months to reach the White
House.

When Stimson returned to the Pentagon after the meeting, he
was pleased; the talk "worked very well," he noted in his diary
that evening. But what had been accomplished? The President
had indeed approved the formulation of a committee to study
and advise him on atomic energy matters. Beyond that, Stimson
had increased his influence with the President by making it clear
that in addition to his normal responsibilities as Secretary of War,
he was the Cabinet officer who had been responsible for "the most
terrible weapon ever known in human history, one bomb of
which could destroy a whole city."[57] If Stimson's presentation
had been a "forceful statement" of the problem, as the historians
of the Atomic Energy Commission have called it, its "force"
simply inhered in the problem itself, not in any bold formulations
he offered for its solution.[58] If, as another historian has claimed,
this meeting led to a "strategy of delayed showdown," requiring
"the delay of all disputes with Russia until the atomic bomb had
been demonstrated," there is no evidence in the extant records of
the meeting that Stimson had such a strategy in mind or that Truman interpreted the Secretary's remarks as recommending such a
policy.[59]

What emerges from a careful reading of Stimson's diary, his
memorandum of April 25 to Truman, a summary by Groves of
the meeting,† and Truman's own recollections is a case for overall
caution in American diplomatic relations with the Soviet Union—[60]
it was an argument against *any* showdown. Since the atomic
bomb was potentially the most dangerous issue facing the postwar
world and since the most desirable resolution of the problem was
some form of international control, Soviet cooperation was indis-

---

* The context here makes it clear that Stimson's reference to "the
problem of the proper use of this weapon" relates to postwar policy,
not to military use of the bomb during the war.
† See Appendix J.

pensable. It was imprudent, Stimson suggested, to choose a policy that would undermine the possibility of international cooperation on atomic energy matters after the war ended. Truman himself summed up the meeting by stating his impression that the Secretary of War was "at least as much concerned with the role of the atomic bomb in the shaping of history as in its capacity to shorten the war."[61] These were indeed Stimson's dual concerns on April 25, and he could see no conflict between them.

7

PERSUADING RUSSIA
TO PLAY BALL

Events had moved swiftly through April. Too swiftly for Truman. His efforts to gain a measure of influence over Stalin's policies demonstrated how little control he had over his own. Lacking Roosevelt's tolerance for ambiguity, Truman could only adapt, he could not emulate, his predecessor's diplomacy. By highlighting differences between the allies, the new President's penchant for clarity made them more difficult to resolve. While in Washington the substance of Truman's diplomacy could be distinguished from his style, no such distinction could be counted on or even expected from Moscow. In less than a month Truman's conduct of Soviet-American relations had become politically dangerous as well; reports began to circulate that he was reversing Roosevelt's policy of accommodation.[1]

The new President needed time, and he needed diplomatic leverage. He needed, in addition, an alternative set of assumptions to guide him. His lack of success since April 13 offered the most persuasive argument for modifying his diplomacy, and this argument was reinforced by Stimson's warning about the implications of the atomic bomb—and, as well, by the surrender of Germany. A Soviet declaration of war against Japan was now a pressing objective of American diplomacy; unconditional surrender was too costly a burden to take on alone.

A different view of Soviet behavior came to the President's attention during the critical month of May. Its source was Joseph E. Davies, a former ambassador to the Soviet Union (1937–39), who advanced a benign interpretation of Soviet foreign policy.

Before the month was out, Harry Hopkins had left for Moscow
with instructions from Truman to heal the breach with Stalin;
a summit conference was arranged for July. The President had
gained time. How did he use it?

Truman struggled during this difficult period of adjustment to
strike a balance between the foreign policy objectives he had
accepted as his inheritance, and the means at his disposal for attaining them. The surrender of Germany placed the allies at a
diplomatic crossroads. Could two hostile political systems united
in battle against a common foe continue to cooperate with their
mutual antagonist removed? Notwithstanding the widespread
suspicion and antagonism toward the Soviets within the Truman
administration, only one high official, Under Secretary of State
Joseph C. Grew, was convinced that they could not; and pru-
dence dictated that he keep his conviction secret.[2] True, the potential for the dissolution of the Grand Alliance had been all too
apparent for years, even to those who entertained an optimistic
view. The Soviet Union had now achieved its primary goal, the
defeat of Germany, and its secondary goal, political control of
Eastern Europe, was theirs for the taking. It was the Soviet
Union's third objective—obtaining desperately needed economic
assistance for reconstruction—that led Harriman and others to
believe not only in the possibility of the Alliance holding together
for the remainder of the war, but in the prospect of America
gaining, and maintaining, a measure of influence over Soviet policies afterwards.[3]

At about the same time that Truman was beginning to consider
such an application of economic leverage as an instrument of
American diplomacy, a committee under Stimson's direction was
taking up the difficult task of developing policy with regard to
the atomic bomb. Having already discussed with Roosevelt in
December the idea of using the new weapon as a bargaining
counter in postwar negotiations with the Soviet Union, Stimson
quite naturally pursued the same line of reasoning with Truman
in May. One important factor encouraging this notion in Washington of atomic leverage was the prevailing imbalance between
American objectives and current military realities in Europe. As
the President's diplomatic problems mounted, the atomic bomb
became an increasingly important consideration in the formula-

tion of American diplomacy. A hint of the role the bomb would play emerged when Truman scheduled the Potsdam Conference to coincide with the first test of the new weapon.

Potsdam

I

"I Am Appointing an Interim Committee on S-1"

Despite what he had told the President about the importance of the atomic bomb, Stimson did nothing for almost a week after the meeting in which he counseled Truman to form an advisory committee on atomic energy. It is difficult not to conclude that the multitude of problems requiring his attention during this tumultuous period were just too much for the seventy-seven-year-old Secretary of War. They would have drained the energy reserves of a young man in good health, and Stimson was neither young nor healthy, a fact that he recognized only too well. His work schedule, geared to the limitations of his body rather than to the demands of his office, left him only enough time to deal with the most urgently pressing issues. At the end of April, however, Stimson was persuaded to act, after Bush prodded George Harrison and Harvey Bundy into bringing another memorandum from Niels Bohr to the Secretary's attention.

On the same day that Stimson briefed Truman, Bohr had visited Bush at the headquarters of the Office of Scientific Research and Development. Reading from a copy of the memorandum he had used during his interview with Roosevelt, and a supplementary paper composed in March, he outlined his concerns: the San Francisco Conference was about to convene, and world peace hung in the balance; yet the delegates charged with ensuring postwar stability remained totally ignorant of the atomic bomb. He warned that a postwar atomic arms race could be prevented only by an international agreement with the Soviet Union. Then, expressing once again the hope that had sustained him through the disappointments of the previous year, he concluded with the thought that through the bomb's creation, science might have helped to construct a solid foundation for peace.[4]

This was Bohr's last effort to bring his ideas to the attention of responsible officials. To do it, he had to modify the main thrust of his initial analysis. A year before, he had warned that an *early* approach was necessary to ensure the achievement of post-war cooperation with the Soviet Union on international control of atomic energy. Now the first atomic explosion was less than three months away. If Bohr's judgments had been correct in 1944, was it not now too late for such an initiative in the spring of 1945? Perhaps, but the effort was still worthwhile. In any case, Bush was impressed. Like Bohr, he was convinced that time was running out, but he was less concerned with winning the confidence of the Soviet government by informing them about the bomb than he was with laying the groundwork in America for international control before the passions engendered by public debate complicated the issue.

Bush forwarded Bohr's memorandum to Bundy with a strong letter of endorsement. He agreed with the general thesis that immediate steps toward international control were advisable, though his remarks lacked Bohr's sense of urgency. To ensure the correct international atmosphere, Bush advocated preliminary discussions with the Soviet Union before knowledge of the bomb became public. The country's best minds ought to be put to work on the issue, and it was important that an advisory committee be formed rapidly in order to deal with the matter in time.[5] Stimson, however, never saw either Bohr's memorandum or Bush's endorsement. These were replaced with a composite memorandum Harrison and Bundy presented to the Secretary on May 1.* Although it concentrated on the international implications of atomic energy, it failed to mention an early approach to the Soviet Union. Like the document Harrison and Bundy had drawn up for Stimson's use on April 25, this latest paper was cast in the most general terms: "If properly controlled by the peace loving nations of the world this energy should insure the peace of the world for generations. If misused it may lead to the complete destruction of civilization."[6] What "properly controlled" meant, and whether or not the Soviet Union was to be considered among the "peace loving nations," were questions Harrison and Bundy did not explicitly discuss. Presumably, these were points to be considered by the members of the advisory committee they urged Stimson to form. Stimson reacted to this memorandum with warm ap-

* See Appendix K.

proval. He liked it so much that he showed it immediately to Marshall, who was "one of the very few men that know about S-1."[7]

During the following week, the atomic bomb absorbed a significant share of Stimson's time, but he was still not occupied with questions of policy. Rather, he was concerned with the membership of the "Interim Committee," as his political acumen led him to call the proposed advisory group.[8]* Its responsibilities were enumerated in the letter Stimson sent to those he invited to serve as members: "With the approval of the President, I am appointing an Interim Committee on S-1 to study and report on the whole problem of temporary war controls and later publicity, and to survey and make recommendations on post war research, development and controls, as well as legislation necessary to effectuate them."[9]

In setting up the Committee, Stimson sought to keep it small enough to carry on meaningful discussions but sufficiently varied in its membership to represent all the relevant policymaking segments of the executive branch, to include individuals familiar with atomic energy problems, and, finally, to have influence with the President. The Committee had seven official members: Stimson, as chairman (with Harrison his alternate); Ralph A. Bard, an Under Secretary, representing the Navy Department; William L. Clayton, an Assistant Secretary, the State Department; and the experienced science administrators Bush, Conant, and Karl T. Compton, president of M.I.T. In addition, in response to Conant's suggestion a "Scientific Panel" was appointed, consisting of Oppenheimer, Lawrence, Arthur Compton (the project leaders of Los Alamos, Berkeley, and Chicago, respectively), and Enrico Fermi. The seventh, and last, official member was the President's personal representative. After the other members had been chosen, Stimson informed Truman on May 2 that he wished to add one other member, someone "(a) . . . with whom the President had close personal relations, and (b) who was able to keep his mouth shut."[10] Later that day Harrison suggested James F. Byrnes, who, according to Washington rumors, had already been selected by Truman to replace Stettinius as

---

* The term "Interim" was meant to assure legislators that the Executive was not trying to usurp congressional authority.

Secretary of State. On May 3 Stimson telephoned the President, who approved Byrnes: "So my committee is now complete," Stimson wrote in his diary that evening. "Bundy and Harrison were tickled to death with this Byrnes selection and now we can start at work on preparing for the many things that must be planned for S-1."[11] Within two weeks those plans began to take diplomatic relations with the Soviet Union into account—a consideration that became increasingly important as the war drew to its close.

II

The Shadow of a Doubt: "Did I Do Right?"

By the end of April 1945 the deterioration in the state of Soviet-American relations had reached crisis proportions. "We were making very little headway with Stalin over the explosive Polish question," Truman noted in retrospect, permitting himself a degree of understatement. Churchill had fared no better in his attempt to repair diplomatic relations between the Allies than had the U.S. leader. The Prime Minister had addressed a personal plea to Stalin urging him to be more cooperative, lest the quarrel over Poland "tear the world to pieces" and shame the Allied leadership before history. It was an eloquent message, pleading in tone yet ominous in its forecast of future possibilities. "I heartily backed the British Prime Minister's pleas to establish a free Poland and prevent a divided world," Truman wrote of his reaction to Churchill's message. "But I was afraid it would do little to change Stalin's attitude." On the morning of April 30, Secretary of State Stettinius sent Truman a message confirming this judgment: discussions on Poland at the San Francisco meeting of the United Nations Organization had reached an impasse.[12]

After only eighteen days in office, Truman was confronted by a major decision: he could respond in kind to Stalin and risk further and perhaps irreparable damage to American-Soviet relations, or he could accept Stimson's advice to proceed more cautiously. The dangers of strong or precipitous action were becoming more apparent to him daily, as was the complexity of postwar international affairs. In addition to Stimson's warnings, he received similar advice on April 30 from former Ambassador

Joseph E. Davies, one of Washington's most vociferous advocates of Russian-American cooperation.

Davies had played a unique role in U.S.-Soviet relations during the Roosevelt administration. Although he held no official position during the war, he had occasionally acted as Roosevelt's personal liaison with Soviet officials.* Publicly and privately since the days of his ambassadorship, he had crusaded for good relations between the two countries, heaping "fulsome praise" upon the Soviet Union.[13] While his uncritical approach to the Soviet leaders and their policies had earned him the hostility of his Foreign Service staff officers during his "Mission to Moscow," it had led to a special relationship with the men in the Kremlin, who considered Davies an advocate of their legitimate interests.[14] After Roosevelt's death Davies's close ties with the Russians took on new significance, for, like Harry Hopkins, who was then seriously ill, he was a symbol of American cooperation with them.

It was not too surprising, therefore, that before Molotov saw Truman on the evening of April 23, he first discussed Soviet-American relations with Davies, "unofficially and very frankly," though obviously not without the hope that his views would be communicated sympathetically to the new President. Molotov emphasized the uncertainties that Roosevelt's death had increased —citing, for example, the unexpectedly rapid deterioration of German resistance, which gave a new urgency to the Polish question. Regardless of the consequences, however, his government was "going to stand pat on having a friendly government in Poland." With Roosevelt alive, he said, the Russians had been confident that their security needs would be recognized and respected. Now they were not sure. He had come to the United States, therefore, not primarily for the San Francisco Conference, but to "sound out, size up and determine what the attitude of the new President was going to be."[15]

Molotov's discussion with Davies appears to have been part of his effort to influence that attitude. A few hours later, however, Truman stripped away whatever ambiguity still shrouded Amer-

---

* In May 1943, for example, Roosevelt sent Davies to Moscow, and in October of that year to Mexico City to consult with the former Soviet ambassador to the U.S., Constantine Oumansky, then serving as ambassador to Mexico.

ican policy on Poland. Considering the Kremlin's stiff reaction to the meeting, it seems that Truman's firm position and his blunt statements served only to confirm the position of those in the Soviet Union who argued for a hard line.[16]* Indeed, the messages Truman exchanged with Stalin on April 30, the day Davies first spoke with the President, suggest that the Soviet Premier had in fact settled upon an even firmer position.[17] It was against this background that the discussion between Davies and Truman took place—the first of several meetings they held on Soviet-American relations.[18]

As recounted by Davies, their conversation began with a review of his liaison work under Roosevelt, after which Truman vividly described his own recent confrontation with Molotov: "I gave it to him straight. I let him have it. It was the straight one-two to the jaw. I wanted him to know that our cooperation had to be two-sided; and not a one-sided street. . . . We would live up to our commitments. They should live up to theirs." The President seems clearly to have relished telling this story of how he stood up to the Russians. Yet, almost immediately thereafter, he gave voice to the nagging uncertainties of the week just past. "I want to know what you think," he queried. "Did I do right?"

Davies could express his disapproval no more directly than to suggest that Truman's "statement might serve helpfully to show them the quality of direct, straight-forwardness of the President and the kind of square-toed dealing which could be expected from you." He then proceeded to recount in detail his own conversation with Molotov, presenting a point of view that few government officials entertained, but one that appeared more striking in light of the events of the past week. Davies repeated Molotov's remarks about Soviet confidence in Roosevelt, and the new con-

---

* Close observers of the Soviet political system suspected that Soviet diplomacy, like U.S. diplomacy, was subject to internal governmental pressures and influence. In a memorandum of May 15, 1945, Charles E. Bohlen, assistant to the Secretary of State and a Soviet specialist, suggested this very point: "Even at Yalta we all had felt that the Soviet failure to carry out the agreement reached there had been due in large part to opposition inside the Soviet Government which Stalin had encountered on his return." FRUS, *The Conference of Berlin*, I, 13; Adam Ulam, *Expansion and Coexistence: The History of Soviet Foreign Policy, 1917–67* (New York, 1968), 314–77.

ditions and problems that had arisen with regard to Poland. He went on "in an effort to give a picture, not necessarily of the facts, but of the point of view as to these facts which the Soviets might have and did have." While the details of the Yalta accords were not known to him, he did know that the Polish question represented a matter of physical security for Russia and that she therefore would not entertain the idea of a "strong independent Poland." Moreover, he pointed out, the Soviets, "sticklers for reciprocity as between allies," had gone along with U.S. and British policies toward the Vichy government in Africa, the Badoglio government in Italy, and the Royalists in Greece, even though they did not believe that those regimes represented the anti-Fascist elements of those countries.[19] They had accepted, however reluctantly, the argument that these were "vital interests" to America and Britain; now, they expected reasonable cooperation in return in matters of their vital security like Poland.

Beyond these direct arguments for adopting an attitude of open cooperation, Davies suggested to the President a number of more subtle reasons. The Russians were aware of the existence of considerable anti-Soviet sentiment in some U.S. military circles, the lower levels of the State Department, and other departments of the government. It was important that the President not give them the impression that he was in agreement with these views.[20]* Davies also noted that the Soviets were aware of the desire on the part of certain members of the U.S. and British governments to use the Soviet request for a $6-billion loan for reconstruction to win concessions. "It would be a desperate gamble to proceed on any such theory," he believed. The Russians were at the "zenith

* Davies's diaries and journal contain numerous scattered entries recording anti-Soviet attitudes and acts. Among the more dramatic of these is a report of a colonel who handled the Soviet Desk at Army Intelligence conferring with Senators Wheeler and Nye, anti-Soviet columnist Constantine Brown, and others to discuss the "Soviet menace." The colonel was reported to be "sabotaging" the war effort in Europe (journal, December 28, 1944). For Davies's notes on the "sabotaging of Lend Lease aid to Russia by War and State Department personnel," see his journal entry for September 23, 1943. Accounts of other anti-Soviet actions by members of the U.S. government can be found in the following entries: diary: October 15, 1943, March 14, 1944; journal: May 10, 1945.

of course

of their effectiveness," and they would "go it alone" rather than surrender vital interests in exchange for a loan.[21]

In conclusion, Davies stated his belief that the next few months would probably be decisive in determining the direction of Soviet policy. Whether they would trust the United States and go along with an effort to maintain collective security depended on American diplomacy. "Well, what should be done?" Truman asked. "What can I do?" The answer returned to Davies's general theme: "Your conference with Molotov commanded their respect. You must now command their confidence in our good will and fairness." He suggested a meeting with Stalin, while scrupulously avoiding any actions that might give the Russians the impression that the United States and Britain were "in cahoots" against them. Truman was sufficiently impressed by the end of their meeting to suggest that Davies call the White House any time he was concerned about Soviet-American relations.

It is not likely that Davies changed the President's mind about Soviet duplicity over the Yalta agreements; yet his remarks did reinforce the arguments for caution put forward by Stimson, and the President did appear amenable to his views. Davies left the meeting convinced he had a mandate to initiate his own diplomatic attempts to smooth over the disagreements between Stalin and Truman. Within two days he had sent Molotov a personal letter explaining that the President had told him about their meeting, and in his view, cooperation could be ensured if Molotov and Stalin came to know Truman better. "The important thing is that the President should come to know you and the Marshal personally, and that you both should come to know him."[22]

This letter, however, reflected Davies's own understanding of the nature of diplomacy, not Truman's. Like Roosevelt, Davies appears to have believed that real differences among nations could be settled on the strength of warm personal relations among statesmen, that problems between the United States and the Soviet Union resulted from ignorance and misunderstanding rather than conflicting objectives. Solutions were therefore always within the reach of men of good will if they could only get to know and trust each other. Davies believed that Roosevelt had held the alliance together by personally committing himself to that goal;

Truman could be equally successful if he followed his predecessor's course. It never seems to have occurred to Davies that Truman might be disposed toward a quite different general approach to diplomacy, or that the challenges of peace posed more profound problems than the exigencies of war—or that his whole conception of diplomatic relations was faulty. Davies remained convinced that a meeting between heads of state would repair differences between allies—and the course of events during the following two weeks served to reinforce him in this conviction.

The precipitous collapse of Germany during the first days of May compounded the difficulties of the last weeks of April. It simultaneously intensified the need for a settlement in Eastern Europe and made such a settlement unlikely. The discussions over the United Nations Organization in San Francisco continued to reflect disagreements among the Allies without illuminating new ways of solving them. Messages between Moscow and Washington intensified Truman's frustration. In response to his message to Stalin on Poland on May 4, the President received the simple and disturbing reply that his attitude ruled out the possibility of an agreement.[23]

On the morning of May 8, shortly before announcing the unconditional surrender of Germany, Truman wrote to his mother and sister about the incredible number of "momentous decisions" he had been forced to make in less than a month. "So far luck has been with me," he mused, adding his hope that it might stay with him for a while longer. "I hope when the mistake comes it won't be too great to remedy."[24] The tone of resignation here and his invocation of good fortune reflected more than the President's understanding that the course of world affairs lay so largely outside his control; more to the point, he was becoming increasingly aware that he did not have a firm grasp on the reins of the executive bureaucracy. He was learning more about military affairs and diplomacy every day, but he had to work very hard just to keep up with the daily round of new problems that were now his responsibility. He handled this enormous workload by generously (perhaps even carelessly) delegating authority to eager subordinates. "He delegates!" Davies would soon comment approvingly. "A complete and definite contrast to F.D.R."[25]

Joseph Grew wrote in a similar vein to a friend on May 2: "When I saw him [Truman] today I had fourteen problems to take up with him and I got through them in less than fifteen minutes with a clear directive on every one of them. You can imagine what a joy it is to deal with a man like that. . . ."[26]

As long as Truman's staff used their new freedom cautiously and wisely, he was lucky indeed. Shortly after the German surrender on May 8, however, his luck ran out.

III

Background for Atomic Leverage: The Lend-Lease Imbroglio

Since 1941 the United States had shipped to the Soviet Union almost 17 million tons of supplies, valued overall at nearly $10 billion. But billions more were needed to rebuild a war-ravaged nation that had lost perhaps 20 million people in four years of fighting. Russia's need was America's leverage, Harriman had argued for months; and the opportunity had to be seized.[27]

It was. On May 12, in response to orders issued by the subcommittee in charge of shipping lend-lease supplies, officials of Atlantic and Gulf ports immediately stopped the loading of goods for the Soviet Union and called back ships at sea bound for Russia. While the U.S. government clearly had every intention of using its economic leverage to reinforce its diplomacy,[28] evidence indicates that the crude execution of this initiative was the result of Truman's careless delegation of authority rather than his attempt to bludgeon the Soviets into submission. Only two days earlier, Harriman and Stettinius had agreed that adjustments in the lend-lease program should be made as tactfully as possible "without any hint of relationship with the Polish or other political problems with the Soviet Union."[29] There were good reasons for their caution. Harriman was about to propose that he approach Stalin directly with a new proposal for breaking the deadlock over Poland. In the meantime, he and Stettinius agreed, "no specific acts of pressure or retaliation should be suggested or even considered. . . ."[30] But what turned out to be a quite startling and provocative cessation of lend-lease outraged Stalin, embarrassed Truman, and undermined any possibility thereafter of introducing any subtlety into attempts to apply economic leverage to diplomatic ends.[31] How did it happen?

On May 10, Harriman had discussed lend-lease with the President and with the departments and agencies involved in the Soviet aid program. A memorandum, ready for approval on the following day, was presented to the President by Foreign Economic Administrator Leo Crowley and Grew, who predicted a sharp response from the Russians. Nevertheless, Truman was prepared to defend his position, for according to the stipulations of the Lend-Lease Act general aid was not to be extended beyond the conclusion of war, which had ended for the Russians with the surrender of Germany. Truman was very aware that both public and congressional opinion was manifestly hostile to any loose interpretation of the act. As Vice-President, he had cast the tie-breaking vote in the Senate on April 10, 1945, against an amendment to the Lend-Lease Act offered by Senator Robert A. Taft, calling for *automatic* cessation of *all* lend-lease assistance the instant war ended. According to the arrangement approved by Truman on May 11, however, the Soviet Union would, indeed, continue to receive lend-lease aid, but it would be limited to equipment necessary for the completion of industrial plants already under construction and items required for Soviet operations in the Far East. Other requests would be evaluated separately.[32] Some American newspapers even considered this proposal a bold and friendly gesture toward the Soviet Union, given the generally prevailing feeling domestically on this issue.*

What appeared to the Soviets as distinctly unfriendly, however, was the provocative *manner* in which lend-lease was

---

* *The New York Times* treated the cutoff as an automatic result of the end of the war in Europe. It reported assurances that shipments being loaded and en route would not be stopped. May 13, 1945, 1. On May 12 the Chicago *Tribune* printed a front-page color cartoon of Stalin and others in the back of a jeep with a G.I. driver who was saying, "All out—everybody who isn't going my way"; it was labeled "Lend-Lease Joy Riders." See also May 15, 23, and 24. On May 20, 1945, Walter H. Waggoner wrote in *The New York Times*, p. 1, that the purpose of the lend-lease cutoff was to pressure the USSR *into* the war against Japan.

terminated. Yet neither Truman, Stettinius, nor Harriman had anything to do with the way in which policy was carried out in this case. When the Subcommittee on Shipping of the President's Soviet Protocol Committee had debated the issue on the morning of May 12, it had decided that lend-lease was to be "cut off immediately as far as physically practicable." This phrase was then interpreted literally by the Foreign Economic Administration representative on the Subcommittee. It was, in Stettinius's own words, "particularly untimely," and he called Grew from San Francisco to urge him to discuss it with the President. Harriman and Assistant Secretary of State William Clayton quickly moved to have the order countermanded. Ships at sea were once again turned around toward their original destinations, and dockside cargoes already scheduled for the Soviet Union were reloaded and shipped. However, as the Secretary of State later wrote, "the psychological damage had been done."[33]

When Joseph Davies learned about the lend-lease imbroglio, his worst fears were confirmed: Truman, he believed, had decided upon "the tough approach." The consequences to his mind were obvious: a sharp Soviet rejoinder intended to "out-tough" the United States, which could only lead to a final dissolution of any hopes for postwar cooperation. In a long letter to the President on May 12, Davies restated his view that the Soviets could not be bullied into acquiescence; on the contrary, only friendship could beget cooperation. Beneath the obsequious and simplistic tone which marked so much of Davies's writing, there remained a sound argument. Peace was an economic necessity for the devastated Soviet economy (as Harriman had argued earlier). But if Russia felt threatened by capitalistic encirclement, she would opt for a *cordon sanitaire* of her own not only in Eastern Europe, but in the Far East as well. A tough policy would only ensure the very thing it sought to prevent. "What is required is realistic common sense, boldness, strength, and an approach that is not dogmatic, intolerant, or lacking in respect for the other fellow's point of view."[34]

Davies was not the only admirer of Roosevelt's foreign policy to be distressed by recent events. Felix Frankfurter, whose knowledge regarding the atomic bomb made him doubly sensitive to matters affecting the course of Soviet-American relations, had learned of the White House conference on April 23 that had preceded Truman's talk with Molotov. Frankfurter contacted Davies to see what he knew about it, and on Sunday morning, May 13, they met to discuss Soviet-American relations and the policies of the Truman administration. Davies showed him the letter he had written the day before, described his correspondence with Molotov, and recounted his conversation with the President. Frankfurter encouraged him to continue his efforts and suggested that Davies speak with Stimson and other like-minded persons of influence in order to "galvanize" them into action to prevent the "possible impending disaster." It was imperative, Frankfurter suggested, that Truman be brought around to accepting Roosevelt's cooperative attitude toward the Russians.[35]

Davies nowhere suggests that Truman was personally at fault, yet it is clear that he was convinced, like Frankfurter, that it was the change of Presidents that had widened the gulf between the wartime allies. Truman was recognized as a man of limited ability compared to Roosevelt, but Davies never doubted his good intentions. If the President knew the truth about the Russians, if he could be made to understand Roosevelt's approach, as Davies and Frankfurter believed they understood it, that would lead Truman toward a conciliatory, and successful, policy.

During these first months of Truman's Presidency, various factions of his official and unofficial advisers were waging a vigorous struggle behind the scenes to win the President to their respective views. In such a contest, respect for Truman's privacy offered no advantage, and Davies decided to telephone the White House late on Sunday afternoon. He was rewarded with an invitation to spend the remainder of the day discussing Soviet-American relations.

The Davies papers contain two detailed memoranda of this meeting with Truman: an eight-page diary entry and a nine-page expanded summary of the meeting for his journal.[36] The significance of these documents goes beyond the informative conversation they preserve. For they provide an insight into the President's warm personal feeling for Davies, his willingness to listen at length to his point of view, and his confidence in Davies's ability to act as an effective liaison for the United States government in its relations with the Soviet Union.[37] Beyond that, they reveal that Truman was still uncertain in his own mind just what the best approach to the Soviet Union might be; that he was willing to try a cooperative approach in light of the frustrations that had plagued his every initiative since April 13; and that he was troubled by press reports of the diplomatic situation.

When Davies arrived, he found the President very much disturbed over the Russian situation. "These damn sheets [newspapers]" were making things worse, he complained; but he admitted that relations were in truth extremely bad. All signs pointed to an aggressive Soviet policy. Tito, for example, had stated his intention to take Trieste, the adjacent territory, and all of southern Austria that he could secure. It appeared to Truman that Stalin was "out of control" and that the generals were dominating the situation. Tito would not act this way, he surmised, without the Kremlin's approval. Although Davies disagreed with this analysis, Tito's actions did reinforce his fears that the Soviets might have decided that the United States and Britain would not work with them along what he termed "practical lines." Now they were securing their position. He referred to a broadcast by Churchill and a recent speech by Jan Christian Smuts that hinted at the British government's intention to "load" Europe in a balance of power against Russia after the war. In answer to Truman's query: "What could be done?" Davies repeated some suggestions from the letter he had written the day before (but had apparently not yet mailed to Truman). These suggestions, he said, could be judged only against the background of diplomatic events from June 22, 1941, and with the President's encouragement he recounted this history. What followed was the first exposure Truman had to an analysis of Soviet policy that was both comprehensive and favorable.

Davies began with British Foreign Secretary Anthony Eden's visit to Moscow in the fall of 1941 to secure an agreement eliminating the possibility of a separate peace with Germany. Stalin had urged that a second front be opened on the Continent and that any treaty include a recognition of Soviet claims to the Baltic states and Polish territory east of the Curzon line; Roosevelt, however, had opposed the inclusion of such a clause. Nonetheless, throughout the spring of 1942, when Molotov arrived in London to sign the agreement with the British, the Russians stood firm on the Polish boundary issue. Although the British tried to accommodate Roosevelt in this matter, they were determined to do all they could, including signing the treaty with the clauses Stalin insisted upon, to avoid a repetition of the disastrous consequences of Brest-Litovsk in 1918. At the last minute, however, Molotov withdrew his requirement, according to Davies, "out of consideration for Roosevelt." "They did that?" Truman asked, in evident surprise.

Davies then described in detail the basis for the Soviet view that for two years the British and Americans had backed out of their commitment made in the summer of 1942 to open a second front on the Continent. The Russians were facing 3,000,000 Germans along a 1,600-mile front during 1943 while the total number of all troops in North Africa—German as well as British and American—amounted to approximately 600,000.[38] At the same time, the Combined Military Staffs of the United States and Great Britain were planning global strategy without the Soviets. "They resented that."[39] Davies related the long record of hostility between the London Polish Government and Moscow, concluding with the Soviets breaking diplomatic relations when the London Poles demanded an impartial investigation of the wholesale massacre of captured Polish officers in the Katyn Forest.[40]

In March 1943, Soviet-American relations were abruptly shaken when the U.S. ambassador to the Soviet Union, William Standley, publicly charged that the Kremlin was not giving proper credit to his country for its lend-lease aid; however, Davies believed Standley was wrong on this point.[41] "It was the accumulation of these and other suspicious situations which made the situation most serious and much similar to the present," Davies told Truman. Such a comparison was grossly inaccurate of course, for the imminent conclusion of the war made the problems of 1943 very different from present difficulties. However, Davies's objective was not analytical accuracy, but the President's sympathy. Having set the historical stage, he then continued with his own version of the script.

"During the eight months prior to that time [March 1943], Roosevelt and Churchill, and Roosevelt alone, had been trying to induce Stalin to meet with them. But without success." After Standley's public outburst, Roosevelt had wanted Davies to return to Moscow as ambassador, but, he said, he had had to refuse for reasons of health. He consented, however, to go to Moscow "if only to stay 10 days." The object of his visit was to persuade Stalin to attend a summit conference—which he initially agreed to, only to renege in August 1943. Roosevelt contacted Davies once again, this time sending him to Mexico to talk with Soviet Ambassador Constantine Oumansky, "who had influence with Molotov and Stalin." Davies related that he "gave Oumansky a personal message from me to Stalin giving him my personal guaranty that a meeting with Roosevelt would result in an understanding, that [Roosevelt] would not ultimately object to the Curzon Line and the Baltic States. . . . The result was Teheran."

At that meeting, and afterwards, Davies went on, Roosevelt composed differences between Britain and the Soviet Union. But in the last six weeks the situation had changed: "It is now Britain which is composing differences between us and the Soviets." The successful American effort to bring Fascist Argentina into the United Nations over Soviet opposition was only one example of "British influence making us pull their chestnuts (British food and trading interests) out of the fire." He then added that there were only two members of Stettinius's entire staff in San Francisco not hostile to the Russians. Reminding Truman of his confrontation with Molotov, he remarked that the Foreign Minister had "taken it hard." The President inquired whether Davies thought that Molotov had gone to San Francisco to make trouble. No, replied Davies, he had gone to see whether Soviet security interests could be trusted to such an organization, or whether the cards were stacked against his country. Molotov's behavior at the conference meant nothing compared to what the Russians might do if the Politburo and Stalin made up their minds that a hostile capitalistic alliance was ganging up on them. He then reminded Truman that in 1939 Stalin had made a pact with Germany less than two weeks before the war broke out, when Poland refused to allow the Soviet army to take over the defense of the Polish-German border. "This impressed him," Davies noted. "He got it more clearly, it appeared, than when I talked to him last."

Davies then discussed the letter he had written to Molotov on May 2. The answer he had received contained an encouraging sentence: "I think that personal contact of the heads of our governments could play in this matter an extremely positive part."[42] Truman agreed that he and Stalin ought to meet, but explained how difficult it was for him to get away before July because he had the budget to get out. Nor did he want to go all the way to Moscow.

Sometime near the end of their discussion, Truman asked Davies if he could undertake a trip to Moscow to urge Stalin's cooperation for such a meeting, but Davies said his doctor would never permit such a strenuous trip. He offered instead to send Stalin a personal message through Molotov, as he had done on a number of previous occasions. The President agreed to this. But what would happen if Stalin refused to come? Truman asked. Davies would not admit such a possibility. At this point Truman's lack of confidence surfaced once again: "It is no wonder that I am concerned of [sic] this matter. It is a terrible responsibility and I am the last man fitted to handle it and it happened to me. But I shall do my best," he said and recited the following verse:

> Here lies Joe Williams, he did his best.
> Man can do no more.
> But he was too slow on the draw.

On that pensive note, Truman invited Davies to dinner.

It was a pleasant family affair. Truman's mother, his sister, and his daughter were all there, along with Mrs. Henry Wallace and her maternal grandmother. The President indulged his guests with some of his favorite Calvin Coolidge stories. Davies left shortly after dinner, no doubt pleased that he had called the President that afternoon. He was comforted by the knowledge that Truman had accepted his suggestion of April 30 that he meet with Stalin; although Davies had had to decline to undertake a preliminary conference with the Soviet Premier, the fact that he had been asked indicated to him that he had won a major battle in the struggle for Truman's allegiance.

Exactly when Truman decided to send a special envoy to Moscow remains unclear.[43] Truman has written that he first raised the possibility of such a trip with Hopkins on the journey to and from Hyde Park for Roosevelt's funeral. But Hopkins said he had to discuss it with his doctor and suggested Harriman as an alternate. On May 4, Truman repeated his request to Hopkins, and this time "Hopkins said he understood the urgency of the situation and that he was prepared to go." This gave Truman the opportunity, he noted, to sound out former Secretary of State Cordell Hull, Secretary of State-designate Byrnes, and others about sending Hopkins to Moscow and Davies on a special mission to London.[44]* The two aging diplomats, both stalwart supporters of Soviet-American cooperation, were dispatched on their historic assignments during the last week of May. Upon the outcome of their meetings, most especially upon the results of Hopkins's discussions with Stalin, rested the feasibility of arranging a meeting between Churchill, Stalin, and Truman.

Davies had been the first to suggest a summit meeting, but others, who did not share his confidence that personal contact between the Allied leaders would necessarily lead to agreement, also advocated the idea. The conflicts over Poland and the impasse at the United Nations Organization conference moved Churchill in this direction. On May 4, in a communication to Eden, then representing the United Kingdom in San Francisco, he declared, "The Polish deadlock can now probably only be resolved at a conference between the three heads

* Hull endorsed the Hopkins mission, but it was opposed by both the State Department and Byrnes. This may explain why Truman raised the possibility of Davies's going to Moscow on May 13. Davies, after all, was also a link between Roosevelt and Stalin, and he might succeed as well in convincing Stalin that Truman intended to carry out Roosevelt's policies.

of government. . . . It is to this early and speedy show-down and settlement with Russia that we must now turn our hopes."[45] On May 6, Churchill forwarded to Truman a similar suggestion: "Matters can hardly be carried further by correspondence. . . . As soon as possible, there should be a meeting of the three heads of government"; and on May 10, Eden also told the President the same thing.[46] Admiral Leahy added his opinion that a summit meeting was necessary.[47] On May 15, Grew and Harriman voiced similar views, both emphasizing that such a conference should not be delayed.* Grew told Truman that the State Department believed that "it was of the utmost importance that the Big Three meeting should take place as soon as possible. . . ."[48]

Even before Eden, Leahy, Harriman, and Grew had registered their enthusiasm for the suggestions of Davies and Churchill, the President had agreed in principle to such a meeting. Answering Churchill's communiqué on May 9, he had replied that a summit conference would be desirable.[49] Recognizing the desirability for a conference, however, and making a definite commitment to it were entirely separate matters, and the President treated them as such. Davies, Grew, Harriman, and Churchill all urged haste. But just what did haste mean? Could a conference be arranged in a week? A month? Two months? The answer to that question ultimately depended upon two considerations: first, the results of Hopkins's talks with Stalin; and second, the schedule for the initial test of the atomic bomb in the New Mexican desert.

---

* Harriman accompanied this recommendation with the suggestion of another form of leverage. He "assumed of course that we were not prepared to use our troops in Europe for political bargaining; nevertheless if the meeting could take place before we were in a large measure out of Europe he felt the atmosphere of the meeting would be more favorable and the chances of success increased." FRUS, *Conference of Berlin*, I, 13.

IV

Poker Diplomacy: Stimson, the Atomic Bomb, and the Timing of the Potsdam Conference

The prospect of negotiating with Stalin and Churchill in a foreign land with the eyes of the world (and the American press) firmly fixed upon him—the man whom fate, rather than the American electorate, had placed among the Big Three—was not an experience Truman relished after little more than three weeks in office. Nor was it the sort of conference that any President, much less a new one, would approach without assurance that mutually acceptable agreements were at least possible. During the first weeks of May, that was not an assumption that anyone could make with confidence. In judging whether a summit conference was likely to be successful (as measured, of course, in terms of American objectives), Truman first had to believe that Stalin was willing to compromise on the issues under dispute between Washington and Moscow. It was the purpose of Hopkins's mission to ascertain whether that was a reasonable expectation. By May 28 he had indicated that it was, informing Truman on that day that Stalin was anxious to meet with him. Then, as the official history of the Atomic Energy Commission notes, the President, "thinking of the latest estimates from Los Alamos [the schedule for the first test of the atomic bomb], suggested July 15."[50]*

Why did Truman schedule the test of his diplomatic skills at Potsdam to coincide with the test of the first atomic bomb in New Mexico? The answer depends upon understanding the nature of the challenge he envisioned as well as the support he believed he would need to meet it successfully. Inexperienced and insecure in the world of diplomacy, Truman was preparing to face the most demanding and potentially the most po-

---

* It is interesting to note that Stalin could not in any case have left the Soviet Union for a summit meeting until after June 28, 1945, though Truman did not know this when he chose a date in the middle of July. FRUS, *Conference of Berlin,* I, 53.

litically damaging single experience of his adult life. He was readying himself to sit down with Stalin, a tough negotiator of considerable experience, the director, in Harriman's words, of a "barbarian invasion of Europe." Their deliberations would cover the great issues between the Allies: the future of Germany, reparations, the extent of Soviet control over Eastern Europe, the division of the spoils of war in Asia, and the number of soldiers America would have to sacrifice to obtain the unconditional surrender of Japan. They would, in effect, decide how the war would be fought to its conclusion, and how the peace would be brought into existence. The stakes could be no higher; the dangers could be no greater. Each man would bring his own cards to the negotiating table. How they played them depended upon the value each placed upon his entire hand. Early in May, Harriman assured Truman that America's economic leverage was worth a great deal; several weeks later, Stimson informed him that he held another high card, the atomic bomb. These two bargaining counters were "a royal straight flush and we mustn't be a fool about the way we play it," the Secretary of War confided in his diary on May 14. "They [USSR] can't get along without our help and industries and we have coming into action a weapon which will be unique."[51]

The advantage of hindsight suggests how unfortunate this approach was. It encouraged reckless bets against the future to avoid losses in the present. It was cynical rather than sinister, damaging rather than destructive, the product of frustrated expectations and the insecurity of the new President. Though Truman adopted this stance quite naturally, the position was developed for him slowly. He was the recipient rather than the instigator.

In the two weeks between Davies's first and second meeting with Truman, the President was hardly concerned with atomic energy matters. When he spoke with Stimson on May 2, 3, and 4, he simply approved the membership of the Interim Committee. "They would be sufficient even without a personal representative," the President had told Stimson on May 2, but Stimson preferred to have such a liaison.[52] Their brief conversations on May 3 and 4 concerned only Byrnes, whom Stimson had recommended for this position.* During this same period Stimson became deeply involved with atomic energy matters, and he began to integrate his thoughts about the bomb with considerations about the war in the Far East and American-Soviet diplomacy. There is no indication, however, that he discussed any of this with Truman until May 16.

The first meeting of the Interim Committee convened on May 9, and Stimson's diary entry of the following day contains his first direct reference connecting the atomic bomb with current problems of diplomacy and wartime strategy. Discussing the proposed invasion of Japan with Marshall, he inquired "whether or not we couldn't hold matters off from very heavy involvement in casualties until after we had tried out S-1." Later that same day, he discussed Soviet affairs with Harriman. The Ambassador was not sanguine about the possibility of liberalization within the Soviet Union or the areas under its control. However, he thought that Russia would stop short of rejecting the United States. "She is going to try to ride roughshod over her neighbors in Europe," Stimson recorded Harriman as saying, "[but] he thought that she really was afraid of us." He and Harriman then "talked over very confidentially our problem connected with S-1 in this matter."[53] Exactly what "our problem" was is not clear. It might have been international control or the myriad problems that went

* The conversation on May 3 was conducted over the telephone. "I called up the President to suggest that Jimmy Byrnes would be a good man to put in the position on the committee for S-1 . . . and late in the afternoon the President called me up himself and said that he had heard of my suggestion and it was fine." The May 4 conversation was also about Byrnes. "After the Cabinet [meeting] I asked the President for the details of the Byrnes acceptance of membership on my committee and he said that he had accepted. I told the President that we were at work on the agenda so as to get the thing started as soon as Byrnes was available." Ibid., May 3 and 4, 1945. Alperovitz's description of Stimson's activities during the first week of May is in error. He writes: "In fact, the Polish issue and the atomic bomb now became inextricably bound together as Stimson discussed the implications of the weapon with the President almost every day of the tense first week of May." Alperovitz, Atomic Diplomacy, 64. He is also wrong about May 1. Stimson did discuss the atomic bomb on that day, but only with Bundy, Harrison, and Marshall. Stimson diaries, May 1, 1945.

along with it, issues that had been raised at the Interim Committee meeting the day before.[54] Or it might have been the relationship between a summit conference and the testing of the atomic bomb, a subject that Stimson discussed with the President on May 16.[55] Either way, however, it is clear that the meeting of the Interim Committee and Stimson's discussions with Marshall and Harriman had advanced the Secretary's thinking about the atomic bomb. During the following week, after he returned to Washington from an extended weekend rest at his estate on Long Island, these new considerations were translated into policy decisions.

On Sunday, May 13, at about the time Davies and Frankfurter were discussing the deterioration of relations with the Soviet Union, Stimson arrived back in his office. He had hardly begun work when Assistant Secretary of War John J. McCloy handed him a memorandum from Grew which raised four basic questions about American policy in the Far East. The time was fast approaching when it would be necessary to inform Chiang Kai-shek of the agreements on Chinese territory that Churchill, Roosevelt, and Stalin had reached at Yalta. Some questions that had to be considered were: (1) How much pressure could the United States afford to put on the Soviets to assure that they kept their side of the bargain? (2) Was Soviet assistance in the Pacific war at the earliest possible moment of such vital importance to the United States as to preclude any attempt to obtain Soviet agreement to certain desirable political objectives in the Far East prior to their entry? (3) Should the Yalta accords regarding Soviet political desires in that area be reconsidered or put into effect completely or in part? (4) If the Soviets should demand to participate in the military occupation of Japan, should the United States acquiesce, or would such occupation adversely affect our long-term policy for the treatment of Japan in the future? It was the opinion of the State Department, Grew wrote, that this country ought to obtain a number of specific commitments before carrying out its end of the Yalta agreements. It should have guarantees of Soviet cooperation in the unification of China under Chiang, the return of Manchuria to Chinese sovereignty, the trusteeship of Korea, and the right to land U.S. aircraft in the Kuriles. These were vital questions, Stimson noted, and he was glad that he had been given an opportunity to comment on them. They "cut very deep and in my opinion are powerfully connected with our success with S-1. Certainly they indicate a good deal of hard thinking 'before the early part of this week' when they are to be discussed."[56]

By Tuesday morning, however, at the meeting between the Secretaries of State, War, and the Navy, after Stimson had reviewed these questions with Grew and Marshall, he told Grew and Forrestal that he "thought it was premature to ask those questions; at least we were not yet in a position to answer them." The trouble, he informed his colleagues—mistakenly— was that the President had "promised apparently to meet Stalin and Churchill on the first of July and at that time these questions will become burning."* He thought it might be necessary then "to have it out with Russia over relations to Manchuria and Port Arthur and various other parts of North China." It seemed to Stimson that "over any such tangled wave of problems the S-1 secret would be dominant and yet we will not know until after that time probably, until after that meeting, whether this is a weapon in our hands or not." It seemed "a terrible thing to gamble with such big stakes in diplomacy without having your master card in your hand."[57]

Here was the connection that Stimson had been slowly moving toward, the *quid pro quo* he had suggested to Roosevelt in December—the connection between the atomic bomb and American diplomacy. Stimson did not intend to threaten the Soviet Union with the new weapon, but certainly he expected that once its power was demonstrated, the Soviets would be more accommodating to the American point of view. Territorial disputes could be settled amicably, and a policy for the international control of atomic energy could be agreed upon. From these considerations Stimson argued that it was not yet time to answer Grew's questions. "The best we could do

---

* Stimson had probably concluded from the message traffic between Churchill and Truman that the President's tentative commitment to July was a firm commitment to the first of the month. In fact, however, no specific date was agreed upon until Hopkins spoke with Stalin in Moscow thirteen days later.

today," he noted in his diary, "was to persuade Harriman not to go back [to Moscow] until we had had time to think over these things a bit harder."[58]

A conference with the President to review a series of diplomatic issues was scheduled for the following day, May 16, and Stimson took advantage of this meeting to press his views. He was entirely successful. He opposed the proposal of T. V. Soong, the Chinese Foreign Minister, who was in Washington arguing that the best way to defeat Japan was first to face her army on the Chinese mainland.* Another problem involved the transfer of American troops from the European theatre to the Pacific. Churchill had sought vigorously to delay any such transfer until Soviet cooperation in Eastern Europe was assured, but Stimson saw no cause for alarm. The redeployment was a slow process and would therefore provide "more time for your necessary diplomacy with the other large allies than some of our hasty friends realize. Therefore I believe that good and not harm would be done by the policy towards your coming meeting which you mentioned to me. We shall probably hold more cards in our hands later than now."[59]† The policy Stimson referred to could be none other than a summit meeting timed to coincide with or follow the test of the atomic bomb. The conclusions Stimson had reached on May 14 and 15 had now become part of the effort to "find some way of persuading Russia to play ball."‡ As the setbacks of April led to adjustments in May, the seeds of atomic diplomacy** were

---

* Stimson wrote in his diary that Americans would land in China "over my dead body." May 16, 1945.

† Truman confirmed the connection between the bomb and the timing of the Potsdam Conference several days later, when he spoke with Joseph Davies. Davies diary, May 21, 1945.

‡ This remark appeared in the context of a discussion on the rehabilitation of Europe. That discussion, however, included a wide range of issues, including the atomic bomb. Stimson's diary suggests that by May 16 he and Truman were attempting to integrate direction and action on these issues into a coherent policy. Stimson diaries, May 16, 1945.

** I have defined "atomic diplomacy" to mean either the overt diplomatic or military brandishing of atomic weapons for the purpose of securing foreign-policy objectives, or a covert diplomatic strategy based

sown in the process. They did not bear fruit until after the war, but the assumption of a profitable harvest was accepted without question before it was over.

---

upon considerations related to atomic weapons. Martin J. Sherwin, "The Atomic Bomb and the Origins of the Cold War: U.S. Atomic-Energy Policy and Diplomacy, 1941–1945," *The American Historical Review*, 78 (October 1973), 947 *n.* 6.

8

THE BOMB, THE WAR, AND THE RUSSIANS

Despite Truman's diplomatic initiatives of May, time continued to march with the Russians during June and July. Each day afforded them additional opportunities to consolidate their objectives in Eastern Europe, and left the United States with less leverage to promote its interpretation of the Yalta agreements. Even the capitulation of Germany appeared likely to weaken the American position since the struggle to win the unconditional surrender of Japan required the redeployment of troops to the Far East. Under these circumstances it was natural for Truman and his advisers to cast about for means to strengthen their diplomacy. By the middle of May they were considering the atomic bomb; by the end of the month they were counting on it. As preparations for the summit conference got underway, assurances that the weapon would work became increasingly important to the President. On June 6 he told Stimson that he had "postponed" the Potsdam Conference "until the 15th of July on purpose to give us more time."[1]

Encouraged by Truman's preference for straightforward solutions, and his tendency to accept the most palatable advice, his advisers' estimates of the bomb's diplomatic value soared. The more frightful it seemed as a weapon of war, the more useful it appeared as an instrument of peace. Discussing "further *quid pro quos* which should be established in consideration for our taking them [the Soviet Union] into partnership," Truman and Stimson agreed that after the first bomb had been successfully used against Japan a fitting exchange would be "the settlement of the Polish, Rumanian, Yugoslavian, and Manchurian problems."[2] Even before, James F. Byrnes, the President's representative on the Interim Committee, had told Truman that the bomb "might well put us in a position to dictate our own terms at the end of the war."[3] It is not clear whether Byrnes was referring on this occasion to Japan or the Soviet Union, but it is clear that the Secretary of State-designate had joined the ranks of those viewing atomic weapons as a panacea for the nation's military and diplomatic problems.[4] Believing that the bomb should be used if it was ready before the Japanese surrendered, Truman, Stimson, and Byrnes reasoned that such a clear demonstration of its extraordinary power would induce the Soviets to exchange territorial objectives for the neutralization of this devastating weapon.

Scientists at the University of Chicago, however, reasoned quite differently, their analysis flowing from alternative assumptions formulated during the closing months of the war. Far removed from the policymaking process, and free of the responsibilities imposed by participating in it, they uttered a prescient warning to a deaf audience: The indiscriminate military use of the atomic bomb would undermine the possibility of achieving the international control of atomic energy.[5]

I

"The Bottom Facts"

Many of the questions that have plagued later commentators on the atomic bombings of Hiroshima and Nagasaki simply do not seem to have occurred at the time to the policymakers responsible for those decisions. Nowhere in Stimson's meticulous diary, for example, is there any suggestion of doubt or questioning of the assumption that the bomb should be used against Germany or Japan if the weapon was ready before the end of the war. From the time of the first organizational meeting for the atomic energy project held at the White House on October 9, 1941, members of the Top Policy Group conceived of the development of the weapon as an essential part of the total war effort. They asked whether it would be ready in time, not whether it should be used if it was; what were the diplomatic consequences of its development, not the moral implications of its military use.

This was not simply due to an absence of reflection. Stimson, for one, began to ponder seriously the revolutionary aspects of the atomic bomb during the winter of 1944–45. By March he was convinced that its development raised issues that "went right down to the bottom facts of human nature, morals and government."[6] And yet this awareness of its profound implications apparently did not lead him to raise the sort of questions that might naturally seem to follow from such awareness. He never suggested to Roosevelt or Truman that its military use might incur a moral liability (an issue the Secretary did raise with regard to the manner in which conventional weapons were used), or that chances of securing Soviet postwar cooperation might be diminished if Stalin did not receive a commitment to international control prior to an atomic attack on Japan. The question naturally arises, why were these alternative policy choices not considered? Perhaps what Frankfurter once referred to as Stimson's habit of setting his mind "at one thing like the needle of an old victrola caught in a single groove"[7] may help to explain how he overlooked exactly what he sought to avoid—an atomic energy policy that contributed to the destruction of the Grand Alliance. Yet it must be pointed out that Bush and Conant never seriously questioned the assumption of the bomb's use either. Like Niels Bohr, they made a clear distinction between, on the one hand, its military application, which they took to be a wartime strategic decision, and, on the other, its moral and diplomatic implications, which bore on the longer-range issues of world peace and security and relations among nations. "What role it [the bomb] may play in the present war," Bohr had written to Roosevelt in July 1944, was a question "quite apart" from the overriding concern: the need to avoid an atomic arms race.[8]

The preoccupation with winning the war obviously helped to foster this dichotomy in the minds of these men. But a closer look at how Bohr and Stimson respectively defined the nature of the diplomatic problem created by the bomb suggests that for the Secretary of War and his advisers (and ultimately for the President they advised) the dichotomy was, after all, more apparent than real. As a scientist, Bohr apprehended the significance of the new weapon even before it was developed, and he had no doubt that scientists in the Soviet Union would also understand its profound implications for the postwar world. He also was certain that they would convey the meaning of the development to Stalin, just as scientists in the United States and Great Britain had explained it to Roosevelt and Churchill. Thus the diplomatic problem, as Bohr analyzed it, was not the need to convince Stalin that the atomic bomb was an unprecedented weapon that threatened the life of the world, but the need to assure the Soviet leader that he had nothing to fear from the circumstances of its development. It was by informing Stalin during the war that the United States intended to cooperate with him in neutralizing the bomb through international control, Bohr reasoned, that it then became possible to consider its wartime use apart from its postwar role.

Stimson approached the issue differently. Without Bohr's training and without his faith in science and in scientists, atomic energy in its *un*developed state had a different meaning for him. Memoranda and interviews could not instill in a non-scientist with policymaking responsibilities the intuitive understanding of a nuclear physicist whose work had led directly to the Manhattan Project. The very aspect of the atomic bomb upon which Bohr placed so much hope for achieving a new departure in international affairs—its uniqueness—made it unlikely that non-scientists would grasp its full implications and therefore act upon his proposals. In this sense Bohr was correct when he said that he did not speak the same language as Churchill, or as any other statesman, for that matter.

It was only after Bohr's proposal was rejected at the Hyde Park meeting in September 1944 that events forced Stimson to think deeply about the weapon under his charge. Beginning with the fixed assumption that the bomb would be used in the war, he developed a view of the relationship between it and American diplomacy that reinforced that assumption, or at least gave him no cause to question it. For he could not consider an untried weapon an effective diplomatic bargaining counter; on the contrary, its diplomatic value was related to, if not primarily dependent upon, its demonstrated worth as a military force. Only when its "actual certainty [was] fixed," Stimson believed, could it carry weight in dealings with the Soviet Union.[9]

The need for assurance that the bomb would work raises the central question: Did Stimson's understanding that the bomb would play an important diplomatic role after the war actually prevent him from questioning the assumption that the bomb ought to be used during the war? It must be stressed, in considering this question, that Stimson harbored no crude hatred or racial antagonism for the Japanese people. Nor was he blind to moral considerations that might affect world public opinion. On May 16 he reported to Truman that he was anxious to hold the Air Force to "precision bombing" in Japan because "the reputation of the United States for fair play and humanitarianism is the world's biggest asset for peace in the coming decades."[10] But his concern here, it is evident, was not with the use as such of weapons of mass destruction, but simply with the manner in which they were used. "The same rule of sparing the civilian population should be applied as far as possible to the use of any new weapon," he wrote in reference to the bomb.[11] The possibility that its extraordinary and indiscriminate destructiveness represented a profound qualitative difference, and so cried out for its governance by a higher morality than guided the use of conventional weapons, simply did not occur to him. On the contrary, the problem of the bomb as he perceived it was how to effectively subsume its management under the existing canons of international behavior. His diary suggests why:[12]

May 13, 1945: Having copied into his diary Grew's memorandum raising questions about the role of the Soviet Union in the Far East during and after the war, Stimson noted: "These are very vital questions. . . . [They] cut very deep and in my opinion are powerfully connected *with our success with S-1.*"

May 15, 1945: Recounting the meeting between the Secretaries of State, War, and the Navy, he described "a pretty red hot session first over the questions which Grew had propounded to use in relation to the Yalta Conference and our relations with Russia." He then remarked: "Over any such tangled wave of problems the S-1 secret would be dominant and yet we will not know until after that time [the beginning of July] probably, until after that meeting [the Potsdam Conference] whether this is a weapon in our hands or not. We think it will be shortly afterwards, but it seems a terrible thing to gamble with such big stakes in diplomacy without having your *master card* in your hand."

Stimson's diary reveals further that following that May 15 meeting, he discussed the war against Japan with Marshall. He noted that while the Navy did not favor an invasion, Marshall "has got the straightforward view and I think he is right and he feels that we must go ahead," adding, "Fortunately the actual invasion will not take place until after my secret is out. The Japanese campaign involves therefore two great uncertainties; first whether Russia will come in though we think that will be all right; and second, when and how S-1 will resolve itself."

May 16, 1945: Summarizing the discussion with Truman about precision bombing and new weapons noted above, he wrote: "We must find some way of persuading Russia to play ball."

Was the conveying of an implicit warning to Moscow, then, the *principal* reason—as some historians have argued—for deciding to use the atomic bomb against Japan?[13] The weight of the evidence available suggests not. Stimson's own account of his decision seems more accurate: "My *chief purpose*," he wrote in 1947, in defense of the bombings of Hiroshima and Nagasaki, "was to end the war in victory with the least possible cost in the lives of the men in the armies which I had helped to raise."[14] But if the conclusion of the war was Stimson's *chief* purpose, what other purposes were there? And did they prevent him from questioning the assumption that the bomb ought to be used?

The problem raised by these latter questions—the influence of secondary considerations reinforcing the decision—defies an unequivocal answer. What can be said, however, is that, along with Truman and Byrnes and several others involved, Stimson consciously considered two diplomatic effects of a combat demonstration of the atomic bomb: first, the impact of the attack on Japan's leaders, who might be persuaded thereby to end the war; and second, the impact of that attack on the Soviet Union's leaders, who might then prove to be more cooperative. It is likely that the contemplation together of the anticipated effects upon both Japanese and Soviet leaders was what turned aside any inclination to question the use of the bomb.

In addition, however, to the diplomatic advantages policymakers anticipated, there were domestic political reactions they feared, and these, too, discouraged any policy other than the most devastating and rapid use of the bomb. Everyone involved in administering the atomic energy program lived with the thought that a congressional inquiry was the penalty he might pay for his labors. It was in preparation for just such an eventuality that the Briggs Committee, even before the Project was underway, had excluded émigré and even recently naturalized scientists from its meetings.[15] At the time the Army assumed responsibility for the development of the bomb, and on several occasions thereafter, Under Secretary of War Robert P. Patterson informed Groves that the "greatest care should be taken in keeping thorough records, with detailed entries of decisions made, of conferences with persons concerned in the Project, of all progress made and of all financial transactions and expenditures . . . [for] the most exact accounting would be demanded by Congress at sometime in the future."[16] Even Bohr's association with the Manhattan Project was a product of this concern. He was invited to join the Project, Richard Tolman wrote to Conant in October 1943, because Groves "would like to be able to say that everything possible had been done to get the best men."[17] That these anxieties were not the result of mere bureaucratic paranoia is made clear by the wartime correspondence between the Secretary of War and the chairman of the Senate Special Committee Investigating the National Defense Program. "The responsibility therefore [sic] and for any waste or improper action which might otherwise be avoided rests squarely upon the War Department," Senator Harry Truman warned Stimson in March 1944.[18] Then there was the warning to Roosevelt a year later from the director of the Office of War Mobilization, James Byrnes: "If the project proves a failure, it will then be subjected to relentless investigation and criticism."[19] It is all the more necessary to remember the possible influence of these warnings by Truman and Byrnes in the ironic aftermath of events.

Beyond reasons directly related to the war, to postwar diplomacy, or to domestic politics, there was another, more subtle consideration moving some advisers to favor a combat demonstration of the bomb. "President Conant has written me," Stimson informed news commentator Raymond Swing in February 1947, "that one of the principal reasons he had for advising me that the bomb *must be used* was that that was the only way to awaken the world to the necessity of abolishing war altogether. No technological demonstration, even if it had been possible under the conditions of war—which it was not—could take the place of the actual use with its horrible results. . . . I think he was right and I think that was one of the main things which differentiated the eminent scientists who concurred with President Conant from the less realistic ones who didn't."[20]

Among the most prominent of the "less realistic" scientists Stimson was referring to here was, of course, Leo Szilard, a premature realist on atomic energy matters since the thirties. On May 28, 1945, Szilard and two associates (Walter Bartky, Associate Dean of the Physical Sciences at the University of Chicago, and Harold Urey, head of the Manhattan Project's Gaseous Diffusion Laboratory at Columbia) traveled to Spartanburg, South Carolina, to discuss atomic energy matters with Byrnes. They were directed there by Matt Connelly, the President's appointments secretary, after an unsuccessful attempt to speak personally with Truman.[21]

Since March 1945, Szilard had been applying his analytical energies to the problem of predicting the impact of the new weapon on American security, and on devising a workable plan for the international control of atomic energy. In a remarkably perceptive memorandum written in March he had discussed a number of central problems: the transition of nuclear weapons technology from atomic to hydrogen bombs, the greater vul-

nerability of an urbanized nation to nuclear attack, systems of
control that ought to be considered, including control of raw
materials and on-site inspection, and several other issues basic
to any international control program.[22] Having concluded that
there was "no point" in trying to discuss his ideas with Groves,
Conant, or Bush, he contacted Einstein. He needed a letter of
introduction to the President, Szilard told his colleague, for
there was "trouble ahead." A request for an interview with
Roosevelt was then sent to Mrs. Roosevelt, who had intervened
earlier in the war to bring the criticisms of the Chicago scientists
to her husband's attention. "Perhaps the greatest immediate
danger which faces us is the probability that our 'demonstration' of atomic bombs will precipitate a race in the production of these devices between the United States and Russia,"
Szilard warned in a memorandum prepared for a conference
with Roosevelt scheduled for May 8. The United States government was about to arrive at decisions, he warned, that would
control the course of events after the war. Those decisions
ought to be based on careful estimates of future possibilities,
not simply "on the present evidence relating to atomic bombs."
Always conscious of power considerations, and well aware of
the potential diplomatic weight of the bomb, Szilard concluded
a series of questions with the query: "Should . . . our 'demonstration' of atomic bombs and their use against Japan be delayed
until a certain further stage in the political and technical development has been reached so that the United States shall be in
a more favorable position in negotiations aimed at setting up a
system of control?"[23]

Szilard's reasoning here was not very different from Stimson's. They both looked to the bomb's power to persuade the
Soviets to accept an American blueprint for world peace. But
whereas the Secretary of War expected the early demonstration of that power to suffice to produce the desired effect, Szilard reasoned that the American lead in development would
have to be overwhelming and unapproachable before such a
demonstration had even a chance of having the desired effect.

At the Spartanburg interview the hopelessness of having
such a calculated policy adopted became clear to Szilard.
Byrnes seemed grossly ignorant about the implications of atomic

energy and its diplomatic value. In response to the Secretary of
State-designate's view that "our possessing and demonstrating
the bomb would make Russia more manageable in Europe,"
Szilard argued that the "interests of peace might best be served
and an arms race avoided by not using the bomb against Japan,
keeping it secret, and letting the Russians think that our work
on it had not succeeded." Byrnes responded that the nation had
spent $2-billion on its development and Congress would want
to know the results. "How would you get Congress to appropriate money for atomic energy research if you do not show
results for the money which has been spent already?" he asked
the astonished scientists.* They returned to Chicago convinced
that Byrnes was inclined toward a policy that would make a
postwar atomic arms race inevitable.[24] As a direct result of the
Spartanburg interview, Szilard initiated a movement among
scientists at the University of Chicago to prevent the use of the
atomic bomb against Japan. In the meantime, however, decisions were being taken that would outdistance any attempt to
block the military use of the bomb.

II
"Looking at This like Statesmen"

On May 31, 1945, three days after Truman set the date for the
Potsdam Conference, the Interim Committee submitted a formal recommendation that the atomic bomb be used without
warning against Japan. The Committee had met officially on
three previous occasions—May 9, 14, and 18.[25] Its members had
reviewed the history of the Manhattan Project; received background briefings from Groves, Bush, Conant, and others; discussed the Quebec Agreement and the Combined Development
Trust; appointed a Scientific Panel; considered the appointment of industrial and military panels; and designated William

---

* Byrnes was not the only person associated with the Manhattan
Project to express this attitude. Irving Stewart, a special assistant to
Bush, suggested: "if the military importance [of the atomic bomb] is
demonstrated, it may provide the necessary Constitutional [sic] sup-
port [to create a Commission on Atomic Energy]." Stewart to Bush,
Aug. 25, 1944, AEC doc. no. 299.

L. Laurence, science editor of *The New York Times*, to prepare statements to be issued *after* the atomic attacks. Yet the
question of whether the bomb should be used at all had never
actually been discussed. The minutes of the Interim Committee
suggest why. The committee members had come together as
advocates, the responsible advisers of a new force in world affairs, convinced of the weapon's diplomatic and military potential, aware of its fantastic cost, and awed by their responsibilities.
They were also constrained in their choices by several shared
but unstated assumptions reinforced for scientists and policymakers alike by the entire history of the Manhattan Project:
First, that the bomb was a legitimate weapon that would have
been used against the Allies if Germany had won the race to
develop it. Second, that its use would have a profound impact
upon Japan's leaders as they debated whether or not to surrender. Third, that the American public would want it used
under the circumstances. And fourth (an assumption from
which one member of the Committee subsequently dissented),
that its use ultimately would have a salutary effect on relations
with the Soviet Union. These assumptions suggested, at least
obliquely, that there were neither military, diplomatic, nor domestic reasons to oppose the use of the weapon. On the contrary, four years of war and the pressures to end it, four years
of secrecy and the prospect of more; $2-billion and the ques-
tion "For what?"; Japan's tenacious resistance and America's
commitment to unconditional surrender; Soviet behavior and
the need for international control—all these factors served to
bolster the accepted point of view. And the structure of the
Committee itself made the introduction of alternatives extremely
difficult: its tight organization and its crowded agenda; its wide-
ranging responsibilities for atomic energy policy and its limited
knowledge of the military situation; its clear mandate to recommend postwar programs and the ambiguity, at best, of its
responsibility for wartime decisions.

Stimson organized, chaired, and drew up agendas for the
Committee's meetings. Although he did seek to create an atmosphere in which everyone felt free to discuss any problem
related to atomic energy, the minutes of the meetings indicate
that discussions closely adhered to the questions Stimson present-

ed. The task before the Committee was enormous, and time was short. There was little inclination to pursue unscheduled issues.

Stimson had prepared very carefully for the meeting of May 31, to which Arthur Compton, Enrico Fermi, Ernest Lawrence, and Robert Oppenheimer, the membership of the Scientific Panel, had been invited. He was anxious to impress upon them "that we were looking at this like statesmen and not like merely soldiers anxious to win the war at any cost."[26] He had worked with Harrison, Bundy, and Groves throughout the previous day preparing the agenda, which included a statement summarizing the Committee's purpose in general—"to study and report on the whole problem of temporary controls and publicity during the war and to survey and make recommendations on post-war research, development and controls, both national and international"—and a second statement explaining a major purpose of this meeting in particular—"to give the Committee a chance to get acquainted with the [invited] scientists and vice versa." The memorandum also contained a list of questions that might arise. These included future military prospects, international competition, future research, future controls, the possibility that "they might be used to extend democratic rights and the dignity of man," and future nonmilitary uses.[27] There is no suggestion in the memorandum, or in the questions the Secretary placed before the assembled group, that his memory was serving him well when he wrote in his autobiography: "The first and greatest problem [for the Interim Committee] was the decision on the use of the bomb—should it be used against the Japanese, and if so, in what manner?"[28] The fact is that a discussion of this question was placed on the agenda only after it was raised casually in the course of conversation during lunch.

At 10:00 A.M. the members of the Interim Committee, the Scientific Panel, and invited guests Marshall, Groves, Bundy, and Arthur W. Page (a friend and assistant to Stimson) assembled in the Secretary of War's office.[29]* For the benefit of the Scientific Panel, Stimson opened the meeting with a general explanation of his own and Marshall's responsibility for recommendations on military matters to the President; he went on to assure them that the Committee did not regard the bomb "as a

* See Appendix L for minutes of this meeting.

new weapon merely but as a revolutionary change in the relations of man to the universe" and that he wanted to take advantage of this; it might be "a Frankenstein which would eat us up" or it might be a project "by which the peace of the world would be helped in becoming secure."[30] The implications of the bomb, he understood, "went far beyond the *needs* of the present war."

After these introductory remarks the members of the Scientific Panel expressed their views on questions related to postwar planning. Their orientation was toward expansion. Arthur Compton sketched the future of military weapons by outlining three stages of development. The bombs currently under production would soon be surpassed by a second generation of more powerful weapons. "While bombs produced from the products of the second stage had not yet been proven in actual operation," the minutes report, "such bombs were considered a *scientific certainty*." And a "third stage" for which nuclear fission would serve merely as a detonator, though far more difficult to achieve, might—Oppenheimer reported—reach production within a minimum of three years. There is no hint in the minutes that the eventual development of even the hydrogen bomb lay in doubt: the question was merely how soon it could be developed.

Oppenheimer's review of the explosive force for each stage must have strained the imaginations of the non-scientists present. A single bomb produced in the first stage was expected to have an explosive force of 2,000–20,000 tons of TNT. The second generation of weapons would yield the equivalent of 50,000–100,000 tons of TNT. It was possible that a bomb developed in the third stage might produce an explosive force equal to 10,000,000–100,000,000 tons of TNT.

No one, then, sitting at that table in the Pentagon on May 31 could have entertained serious doubts that atomic weapons would be available within months. Of this, the scientists were absolutely certain. Even a year earlier, Ernest Lawrence had confidently written: "The primary fact now is that the element of gamble in the overall picture no longer exists."[31] The uncertainty that remained in May 1945 was merely as to how efficiently the initial bombs would work. Under these circumstances the sort of atomic energy programs the United States chose to pursue after the war was a pressing issue. Lawrence, as always, urged development on every front, and in the discussion that ensued, his opinion found support. Within a short time Stimson was able to conclude that there was general agreement that after the war the industrial facilities of the atomic energy program should remain intact, that a sizable stockpile of material for military, industrial, and technical use should be acquired, and that the door to industrial development should be opened.

During the remainder of the morning, as the Committee moved from a general discussion of control and inspection to the problem of how to obtain international control, the "question of paramount concern was the attitude of Russia." Adopting the line of reasoning that Bohr had advocated during his visits to Los Alamos, Oppenheimer suggested that the United States approach the Russians about international control without giving them details of the progress achieved. He firmly believed that the Russian attitude in this matter should not be prejudged; they had always been friendly to science.

Marshall supported this general point of view by drawing on his own experience. The history of charges and countercharges that were typical of American-Soviet relations, he related, were based on allegations that had generally proved to be unfounded. The seemingly uncooperative attitude of Russia in military matters resulted from their felt necessity to maintain security. He had accepted this and had acted accordingly. As to the postwar situation, and in matters other than purely military, he was in no position to express a view. He was inclined, however, to favor the buildup of a coalition of like-minded powers that could compel Russia to fall in line. He was confident that the United States need not fear that the Russians, if they were informed about the Manhattan Project, would disclose this information to the Japanese. Finally, he raised the question whether it might be desirable to invite two prominent Russian scientists to witness the first atomic bomb test scheduled for July at Alamogordo, New Mexico.

Byrnes, who heretofore had said little, strenuously objected. If information were given to the Russians, even in general terms, he feared that Stalin would ask to be brought into the partnership. This likelihood, he felt, was increased in view of American commitments and pledges of cooperation with the British, though he did not explain how the Soviets would know about them. Although Bush noted that not even the British had any blueprints of our plants, Byrnes could not be dissuaded. He did not explain his position further, yet subsequent events suggest that he believed the bomb's diplomatic value would be diluted if Stalin were informed of the weapon prior to its use. The most desirable program for him was to maintain superiority by pushing ahead as fast as possible in production and research, while at the same time making every effort to better our political relations with Russia. In any case, the issue appears to have been settled by his forthright stand. The morning session ended shortly afterwards, at approximately 1:15 P.M., after Arthur Compton summarized as the Committee's consensus that the United States had to assure itself a dominant position while working toward political agreements. No one saw any conflict between these two objectives. "Throughout the morning's discussion," Arthur Compton has written, "it seemed to be a foregone conclusion that the bomb would be used. It was regarding only the details of strategy and tactics that differing views were expressed."[32]

There are two extant accounts of how the luncheon conversation turned to the question of using the bomb against Japan: a letter of August 17, 1945, from Lawrence to a friend, and a description published by Compton in 1956. Lawrence claims that Byrnes asked him to elaborate on a brief proposal he had made for a nonmilitary demonstration during the morning session;[33] Compton recalls that he asked Stimson whether it might not be possible to arrange something less than a surprise atomic attack that would so impress the Japanese that they would see the uselessness of continuing the war.[34] Whatever the case, the issue was discussed by those at the table, including at least Byrnes, Stimson, Compton, Lawrence, Oppenheimer, and Groves. Various possibilities were brought forward, but were discarded one after the other. Inured to the brutality of war by conventional means, someone countered that the "number of people that would be killed by the bomb would not be greater in general magnitude than the number already killed in fire raids [on Tokyo]."* Another problem was that Oppenheimer could not think of a sufficiently spectacular demonstration. Groves and others at the table were convinced that a real target of built-up structures would be the most effective demonstration.[35]

There were other considerations as well, Compton reports. If the Japanese received a warning that such a weapon would be exploded somewhere over Japan, their aircraft might create problems that could lead to the failure of the mission. If the test were conducted on neutral ground, it was hard to believe that the "determined and fanatical military men of Japan would be impressed."[36] No one could think of any way to employ the new weapon that offered the same attractive combination of low risk and high gain as a surprise attack; and no one was willing to argue that a higher risk should be accepted.

When the Committee members returned to Stimson's office at 2:15 P.M., the Secretary altered the agenda. The first topic he now wanted considered was the effect of the atomic bomb on the Japanese and their will to fight. The initial discussion revolved around the explosive force of the weapon. One atomic bomb, it was pointed out, would not be very different from current Air Force strikes. But Oppenheimer suggested that the visual effect of an atomic bomb would be tremendous. It would be accompanied by "a brilliant luminescence which would rise to 10,000 or 20,000 feet," and the neutron effect would be lethal for a radius of nearly a mile.

There was also a discussion of attempting several simultaneous attacks. Oppenheimer considered such a plan feasible, but Groves objected on the grounds that the advantage of gaining additional knowledge by successive bombings would be lost, and that such a program would require too much of those assembling the bomb.

After considerable discussion of types of targets and the de-

---

* On March 9–10 a quarter of that city had been destroyed by incendiary bombs; 83,000 persons were killed and 40,000 were injured in the most destructive conventional air raid in history. A. Russell Buchanan, *The United States and World War II*, 2 (New York, 1964), 577–8.

sired effect, Stimson expressed the conclusion, on which there was general agreement, that the Japanese would not be given any warning; and that the bombing would not concentrate on a civilian area, but that an attempt would be made to make a profound psychological impression on as many Japanese as possible. Stimson accepted Conant's suggestion that the most desirable target would be a vital war plant employing a large number of workers and closely surrounded by workers' homes. No member of the Committee spoke to the contradiction between this conclusion and their earlier decision not to concentrate on a civilian area.

This critical discussion on the use of the bomb was over. It had not only confirmed the assumption that the new weapon was to be used, but that the *two* bombs that would be available early in August should be used. The destruction of both Hiroshima and Nagasaki was the result of a *single* decision. On the following day Byrnes suggested, and the members of the Interim Committee agreed, that the Secretary of War should be advised that, "while recognizing that the final selection of the target was essentially a military decision, the present view of the Committee was that the bomb should be used against Japan as soon as possible; that it be used on a war plant surrounded by workers' homes; and that it be used without prior warning."*

* The grounds for planning to use the atomic bomb against Japan rather than Germany remain unclear. Although racism has been charged on occasion, no *direct* evidence has been found to support this thesis. The following reasons, probably in descending order of importance, appear to have been the cause of the decision, which was settled on late in the spring of 1944: (1) The war in Europe was expected to end first; and since the training of the "509th Composite Squadron" promised to be an extremely arduous and lengthy matter, it was more reasonable to pick Japan as a target; (2) assembling an atomic bomb on a Pacific island to bomb Japan was safer than assembling it in England; (3) the war in the Far East was primarily an "American" war, and the bomb was primarily an American product. Groves (and perhaps others as well) wished to use an American aircraft to deliver the weapon. Using the bomb in the Far East guaranteed employment of the B-29 rather than the British Lancaster.

Bush makes an ambiguous reference to the use of the bomb on June 24, 1943: "We [he and FDR] then spoke briefly of the possible use against Japan, or the Japanese fleet, and I brought out, or I tried to, because at this

On June 6 Stimson informed Truman of the Committee's decision.[37]

III

The Ghost in the Bottle

Early in June, scientists at the University of Chicago's Metallurgical Laboratory were also considering the military use of atomic weapons. Szilard returned to Chicago from Spartanburg to find "the project in an uproar."[38] Groves was as furious at Szilard for having made the unauthorized trip as Szilard was appalled by what Byrnes had told him. To meet both the Army's demand that scientists adhere to the chain of command and the scientists' concern that policymakers consider their opinions about the use of the bomb, Arthur Compton organized a series of six committees to study and report on the implications of the new weapon's development. The most important of these committees was the one on Social and Political Implications, chaired by the distinguished émigré physicist James Franck. The primary concern of its members was "the conditions under which international control is most probable"; their basic assumption was that the "manner in which this new weapon is introduced to the world will determine in large part the future course of events."[39]

A report was assembled by June 11, seven days after the committee's first official meeting. Known as the Franck Report, this document proved to be a perceptive study.[40] It predicted the almost limitless destructive power of nuclear weapons, the uncertain security that an attempt at monopoly would bring, and what methods of international control might be feasible. Its primary purpose, however, was less to predict the hazards of the postwar atomic age than to recommend wartime policies

point I do not think I was really successful in getting the idea across, that our point of view or our emphasis on the program would shift if we had in mind use against Japan as compared with use against Germany." "Memorandum of Conference with the President," AEC doc. no. 133. However, on April 23, 1945, Groves informed Stimson that "the target is and was always expected to be Japan." MED-TS, folder 25, tab M. See also Hewlett and Anderson, *The New World*, 252–3.

that might help to avoid those hazards. The central argument of the report was that a surprise atomic attack against Japan was inadvisable from any point of view—whether one was optimistic or pessimistic about the possibility of international control of atomic energy:

> If we consider international agreement on total prevention of nuclear warfare as the paramount objective, and believe that it can be achieved, this kind of introduction of atomic weapons to the world [surprise attack] may easily destroy all our chances of success. *Russia*, and even allied countries which bear less mistrust of our ways and intentions, as well as neutral countries may be deeply shocked. It may be very difficult to persuade the world that a nation which was capable of secretly preparing and suddenly releasing a weapon as indiscriminate as the [German] rocket bomb and a million times more destructive, is to be trusted in its proclaimed desire of having such weapons abolished by international agreement.

The report also made the converse case for not using the atomic bomb even "if one takes the pessimistic point of view and discounts the possibility of an effective international control over nuclear weapons at the present time. . . ." In this case, the Franck Committee concluded, "the advisability of an early use of nuclear bombs against Japan becomes even more doubtful—quite independently of any humanitarian considerations. If an international agreement is not concluded immediately after the first demonstration, this will mean a flying start toward an unlimited armaments race. If this race is inevitable, we have every reason to delay its beginning as long as possible in order to increase our head start still further."

In summary, the members of the Franck Committee considered an *unannounced* attack against Japan to be "inadvisable" on any grounds—moral, political, or diplomatic. Not only would the indiscriminate destruction wrought in such an attack sacrifice public goodwill for the United States throughout the world, but it would "precipitate the race for armaments, and prejudice the possibility of reaching an international agreement on the future control of such weapons."

It is interesting to note that the members of the Franck Committee shared a basic assumption with Truman, Stimson, and Byrnes—that an atomic attack against Japan would "shock" the Russians—but their reasoning about the effect of such a shock was very different. As we have seen, Stimson did not consider an untested weapon a usable diplomatic bargaining counter, regardless of his belief that it would revolutionize "the relations of man to the universe." Byrnes and Truman shared this point of view. Moreover, they all believed that an actual combat demonstration would make a far greater impression on both the Japanese and the Soviet government. It was this *impression*— the psychological impact of a single bomb dropped from a lone aircraft causing damage equal to that caused by thousands of bombs dropped from hundreds of aircraft—upon which they based their policy. From their point of view, the greater the "shock" effect in Tokyo, the more quickly the war would be concluded; and the greater the "shock" effect in Moscow, the more interested the Soviets would be in reaching an accommodation with the United States.

The members of the Franck Committee, on the other hand, drew the diametrically opposite conclusion: the more awesome the bomb's power, the more likely an arms race. The most important demonstration needed was some means of conveying to the Soviets an American commitment to international control. Szilard, on his way to Chicago from Spartanburg, saw Oppenheimer in Washington and made this point to him. "Don't you think," Oppenheimer rejoined, "if we tell the Russians what we intend to do and then use the bomb in Japan, the Russians will understand it?" "They'll understand it only too well," Szilard replied.[41]

Once the Franck Report was completed, its authors, fearful that it might never reach policymaking circles in time if it were transmitted through channels, persuaded Franck to carry it to Washington on June 11. There he met Compton the following day, and together they tried to see Stimson. They were informed by an aide that the Secretary was out of the city (which was not true).* The report was left, therefore, with a covering

---

* Stimson was definitely in Washington that day: his diary records that he had a conversation with Frankfurter in his office. Ironically,

letter by Compton—a letter, however, that was more of a dissent from than an endorsement of the report's conclusions. In effect, he stated that the report had failed to consider the most important issue at hand. "While it called attention to difficulties that might result from the use of the bomb, [the report] did not mention the probable net saving of lives, nor that if the bomb were not used in the present war *the world would have no adequate warning as to what was to be expected if war should break out again.*"[42] Here was the same argument that had led Conant to recommend to Stimson that the bomb "must be used"; both scientists shared the hope that the last and most terrible act of the Second World War would serve notice to the world that there must be no third great war. It must be assumed, Conant wrote in November 1945, "that in another war atomic bombs will be used. For us to plan otherwise would be the height of folly."[43] It was an assumption that terrified those who contemplated it, yet one that carried its own strange, desperate message of hope in the spring of 1945 and for some time after: "The development of atomic energy holds great, but as yet unexploited, promise for the well-being of civilization. Whether this promise will be realized depends on whether the danger of swift and unprecedented destruction can be removed from the earth," Stimson wrote in March 1946.[44] "My own view," Oppenheimer asserted later, "is that the development of atomic weapons . . . can make the problem more hopeful . . . because it intensifies the urgency of our hopes—in frank words, because we are scared."[45]

Four days after Franck and Compton had tried to see Stimson in Washington, the Scientific Panel met at Los Alamos. While Fermi, Compton, Lawrence, and Oppenheimer were discussing the future of nuclear research, Harrison called from Washington to explain that before the Interim Committee

---

Frankfurter had come to tell Stimson about Bohr's concerns: "Felix Frankfurter plead for an interview at ten thirty and came in and spent half an hour to tell me about the great Dane, Professor Bohr, most of which I knew already. However, he, Bohr, is a fine old fellow and I am willing to give some time to ease his worries. He made through Frankfurther some good suggestions too on which I called in Bundy and got them injected into our plans in S-1." Just what those suggestions were is unknown. Stimson diaries, June 12, 1945.

would consider the views expressed in the Franck Report, he wanted to have the Panel's opinion on the question of the immediate use of nuclear weapons. Compton has summarized the atomic dilemma as he and his colleagues defined and faced it:

> We thought of the fighting men who were set for an invasion which would be so very costly in both American and Japanese lives. We were determined to find, if we could, some effective way of demonstrating the power of an atomic bomb without loss of life that would impress Japan's warlords. If only this could be done!
>
> Ernest Lawrence was the last one of our group to give up hope for finding a solution. The difficulties of making a purely technical demonstration that would carry its impact effectively into Japan's controlling councils were indeed great. We had to count on every possible effort to distort even obvious facts. Experience with the determination of Japan's fighting men made it evident that the war would not be stopped unless these men themselves were convinced of its futility. . . .[46]

The Scientific Panel thus reported to Stimson on June 16 that they could "propose no technical demonstration likely to bring an end to the war . . . no acceptable alternative to direct military use."[47]* The end of the war rather than the impact of the bomb after the war had received primary consideration. To have decided otherwise under the circumstances would have required a farsightedness and political courage, the lack of which at least one member of the Panel—Oppenheimer—regretted in later years.

The issues raised by the members of the Franck Committee, which Compton summarized for his colleagues on June 16, led the Scientific Panel back to the argument which Niels Bohr had first introduced to Los Alamos almost fifteen months earlier: that the Russians (the Scientific Panel added France and China) be informed about the bomb prior to its use. Then, having made their recommendations, they questioned their own competence to consider these matters: "With regard to these general aspects of the use of atomic energy, it is clear that we, as

* See Appendix M.

scientific men, have no proprietary rights. It is true that we are among the few citizens who have had occasion to give thoughtful consideration to these problems during the past few years. We have, however, no claim to special competence in solving political, social, and military problems which are presented by the advent of atomic power."[48]*

In spite of this disclaimer, or perhaps because the Franck Report showed that scientists were already considering many aspects of atomic energy, the Interim Committee reversed itself on June 21 and accepted the Scientific Panel's recommendation that America's allies be informed about the bomb's imminent use. The British already had been so notified. They had been asked—in accordance with the Quebec Agreement—to give their obligatory approval. But the Interim Committee now took the incredible step of seeking to eliminate that obligation, unanimously passing a motion "that the Secretary of War be advised that the Interim Committee favored revocation of Clause Two [the Quebec Agreement's provision for Britain's consent before the bomb was used]."[49] France and China were dismissed as irrelevant; the major concern was the Soviet Union. Bush and Conant vigorously defended the Scientific Panel's view, arguing that such disclosure would help to gain Soviet cooperation for international control after the war.[50] The recommendation was unanimously adopted late in the afternoon and recorded in the minutes as follows:

> In the hope of securing effective future control and in view of the fact that general information concerning the project would be made public shortly after the conference, the Committee unanimously agreed that there would be considerable advantage, if suitable opportunity arose, in having the President advise the Russians that we were working on this weapon with every prospect of success and that we expected to use it against Japan.
>
> The President might say further that he hoped this matter might be discussed some time in the future in terms of insuring that the weapon would become an aid to peace.

* See Appendix N for memorandum to Stimson about concerns of Chicago scientists.

The Committee added further that should the Russians ask for details, they should be told that no additional information could be furnished. Furthermore, in view of the Quebec Agreement, this recommendation should be discussed with Churchill.[51]

In these recommendations of June 21, the Interim Committee had brought together the three major considerations that had guided atomic energy policy throughout most of the war: the criterion of wartime use, the role the British should play in the atomic energy partnership, and the postwar impact of the atomic bomb on international affairs. They had confirmed their earlier recommendation that the bomb should be used if the Japanese continued to resist after the weapon was available for delivery; they had also made it quite clear that the British no longer could count on the special relationship Churchill had secured from Roosevelt—they were to be consulted merely to confirm American decisions; finally, the Committee had recommended that the President take the first step to introduce the new weapon into the whole complex of postwar diplomatic relations with the Soviet Union—the recommendation Bohr had made over a year earlier. But this last recommendation for international control does not appear to have been taken very seriously by those responsible for atomic energy policy; at least, that was the thrust of John Anderson's analysis. Preparing Churchill for the Potsdam Conference, Anderson explained that the American attitude toward international control "appear[s] to be much in line with yours. They cannot imagine any system of international control which did not involve strict inspection; they doubt whether this could be made effective in Russia even if the Soviet Government accepted it; moreover, this being so, they doubt whether Congress would agree to strict inspection in the U.S.A."*

---

* The minute goes on to state: "It seems the Americans are rather attracted by the proposal to say in response to any enquiries from other Governments that we have not been able to think of any effective methods by which we could ensure that this new development inured to the benefit of mankind but that we should be glad to consider any practical proposals which others might be able to put forward." Anderson to Churchill, Prem 3/139-8A, 296.

For all practical purposes the issue of whether the bomb should be used was now closed.

In truth, it had never really been opened, even though opportunities to do so had arisen on several occasions. Now, however, such opportunities no longer existed. When Under Secretary of the Navy Ralph Bard changed his mind about the wisdom of using the bomb without first publicly warning the Japanese, Truman merely assured him during an interview that the matter of a warning had received very careful attention. Bard's argument concerning "the position of the United States as a great humanitarian nation" simply carried no weight with the President.[52]*

After the Interim Committee's June 21 meeting the inevitability of the surprise use of the bomb did not escape Szilard, who was in the process of circulating a petition protesting such an unannounced attack against Japan.[53] "I hardly need to emphasize that such a petition does not represent the most effective action that can be taken in order to influence the course of events," he wrote to Oppenheimer. "But I have no doubt in my own mind that from a point of view of the standing of the scientists in the eyes of the general public one or two years from now it is a good thing that a minority of scientists should have gone on record in favor of giving greater weight to moral arguments and should have exercised their right given to them by the Constitution to petition the President."[54] Szilard had urged his friend Edward Teller to sign the petition, and Teller gave the matter a great deal of thought. Finally, however, he decided that he could not join those who wished to record their objections to the bomb's use. He wrote to Szilard explaining his reasons: "Since our discussion I have spent some time thinking about your objections to an immediate military use of the weapon we may produce. I decided to do nothing. I should like to tell you my reasons."

Teller then explained that he had no hope of clearing his conscience, for the things they were working on were "so terrible that no amount of protesting or fiddling with politics will save our souls." He had not worked on the project for selfish

* See Appendix O for Bard's dissent.

reasons, he said, and the experience had given him more trouble than pleasure. He had simply "worked because the problems interested me and I should have felt it a great restraint not to go ahead." He did not even wish to claim that he had worked to do his duty. Indeed, a sense of duty could keep him out of such work, but it could not get him into it against his inclinations. If Szilard could succeed in convincing him as to the validity of his moral objections, he would quit working. However, Teller noted, it was unlikely that he would start protesting.

But Teller was simply not convinced by Szilard's objections. There was no chance of outlawing any single weapon and therefore the slim chance of survival lay in the possibility of eliminating wars. He believed that the more decisive a weapon was, the more surely it would be used in any real conflict and no agreements would help prevent its use. The only hope for survival appeared to be in getting the facts about atomic energy before the people. If this was accomplished, it might convince people that the next war would be fatal. *"For this purpose,"* he thought, *"actual combat-use might even be the best thing."*

The main point, however, was that the "accident that we worked out this dreadful thing should not give us the responsibility of having a voice in how it is to be used." In the final analysis, the facts had to be made known because the responsibility had to be shifted to all the people. This was the only cause for which Teller felt entitled to do something.

"All this may seem to you quite wrong," he noted in conclusion. "I should be glad if you showed this letter to Eugene [Wigner] and to [James] Franck who seem to agree with you rather than with me. I should like to have the advice of all of you whether you think it is a crime to continue to work. But I feel that I should do the wrong thing if I tried to say how to tie the little toe of the ghost to the bottle from which we just helped it to escape."[55]*

* Teller has written (and on numerous occasions stated in public) that he originally favored Szilard's petition, but had been talked out of it by Oppenheimer. "In the spring of 1945," he has written, "I did become worried about the way the atomic bomb might be used. My apprehension reached a high plateau several months before Hiroshima [actually one month] when I received a letter at Los Alamos from Szilard. He asked

my support for a petition urging that the United States not use the atomic bomb in warfare without first warning the enemy.

"I was in absolute agreement, and prepared to circulate Szilard's petition among the scientists at Los Alamos. But it was my duty, first, to discuss the question with the director of the Los Alamos Laboratory, Dr. J. Robert Oppenheimer. . . .

"Oppenheimer told me, in a polite and convincing way, that he thought it improper for a scientist to use his prestige as a platform for political pronouncements. . . . I did not circulate Szilard's petition. Today I regret that I did not." Edward Teller and Allen Brown, *The Legacy of Hiroshima* (New York, 1962), 13–14.

However, there is evidence to suggest that Teller's views were never in conflict with Oppenheimer's on this matter. When Teller received Szilard's petition he wrote to Oppenheimer as follows:

"You may have guessed that one of the men 'near la Franck' [James Franck] whom I have seen in Chicago was Szilard. His moral objections to what we are doing are in my opinion honest. After what he told me I should feel better if I could explain to him my point of view. This I am doing in the enclosed letter. What I say is, I believe, in agreement with your views. At least in the main points. I hope you will find it correct to send my letter to Szilard." Oppenheimer mss, Teller folder, box 71.

9

DIPLOMACY—AND DESTRUCTION

On the eve of the Potsdam Conference the most widely accepted attitude toward the atomic bomb was an extension of how it was seen and valued earlier—as a potential instrument of military and diplomatic policy. Caught between the remnants of war and the uncertainties of peace, policymakers and scientists were trapped by their own unquestioned assumptions. Not only the conclusion of the war but the organization of an acceptable peace seemed to depend—for Byrnes, Stimson, and Truman as well as for Conant, Oppenheimer, and Teller—upon the success of the atomic attacks against Japan. The secret development of this terrible weapon, during a war fought for total victory, created a logic of its own: a quest for a total solution to a set of related problems that appeared incapable of being resolved incrementally. As Szilard first suggested in January 1944,[1] the bomb might provide its own solution—a military demonstration held out the possibility of literally blasting old diplomatic calculations out of existence.

The senior American policymakers who traveled to Potsdam were imbued with this hope. Fervent believers in the rightness of their course, convinced that world peace depended upon Soviet acceptance of their views, they waited for the results from Alamogordo to learn whether they had the means at their disposal to ensure Soviet compliance with their plans for the postwar world. "The bomb as a merely probable weapon had seemed a weak reed on which to rely, but the bomb as a colossal reality was very different," Stimson wrote, recalling his own reaction to news of the flawless test. American diplomacy had *an equalizer (!)*

gained "a badly needed 'equalizer,'" and further diplomatic efforts to bring the Russians into the war against Japan suddenly appeared "largely pointless."[2] The decision to use the bomb to end the war could no longer be distinguished from the desire to use it to stabilize the peace.

The news from Alamogordo instilled a new sense of confidence in the American delegation. Arguments that the Japanese should be offered specific inducements to surrender,* or that the negotiators should compromise with the Soviets, disappeared. Within weeks this new power would be demonstrated to the world under combat conditions. Then Tokyo and Moscow would surely reconsider their stubborn policies; America's sole possession of this extraordinary weapon promised their acquiescence. Having invested so much in the performance of the bomb, it is perhaps not surprising that Truman, upon learning of the outcome of the raid against Hiroshima, made the vile remark: "This is the greatest thing in history."[3]   *quote!*

I
"A Blind Woman Who Saw the Light"

Truman carried a heavy burden of anticipation to Potsdam. This first major test of his diplomatic skills promised to engage some of the most difficult issues of the war. Did Stalin intend to join the final assault against Japan in time to save a significant number of American lives? If he did, would he expand his territorial demands in the Far East? Could American-Soviet differences over Eastern Europe be resolved harmoniously? Would Stalin compromise in exchange for American economic assistance? How was Germany to be ruled? Finally, beyond these issues of policy, Truman faced a question more personally pressing: how well would he measure up against Stalin and Churchill at the negotiating table?[4]

As late as July 3, the unfamiliar formalities of international

* Grew and Stimson had argued that the war could be ended sooner by assuring the Japanese that the Emperor would not be removed if the people of Japan wished him to remain as a constitutional monarch. Grew, *Turbulent Era,* 1428–31, and Stimson and Bundy, *On Active Service,* 626.

diplomacy and the uncertainties of the outcome of the conference found him less than enthusiastic about the challenge.
"Wish I didn't have to go," he wrote his mother and sister,
"but I do and it can't be stopped now."⁵ Coating a hard grain
of truth with a soft Midwestern colloquialism, several aides described the political environment to the President on the day of
his departure: "We think that as a well known Missouri horse
trader, the American people expect you to bring something
home to them."⁶ It was an expectation he needed to fulfill. By
the early morning hours of July 7, when he departed for Potsdam from Newport News, Virginia, aboard the U.S.S. *Augusta*, he had come to believe that the results of the test at
Alamogordo would determine to a large measure how well he
could accomplish that goal. He had no intention of employing
the bomb explicitly as an instrument of diplomacy during the
conference, but a successful test would assure him at the very
least that he need make no politically embarrassing concessions
there.

Truman and his closest advisers therefore placed a high value
on knowing with complete certainty that they possessed the
bomb as a backstop for their diplomatic policies—a value underlined by their efforts to have the test conducted prior to
the opening of the conference. When Oppenheimer reported to
Groves on July 2 that the preferred date, July 14, entailed un-
acceptable risks and a "frantic" situation, and therefore could
not safely be met, his request for a mere three-day delay was
denied. There were other reasons why it was extremely important that the test be performed by the earlier date, Groves
informed him that morning. And again at 5:45 in the evening,
after discussing the situation with Harrison and Bundy,
Groves called Los Alamos to confirm his earlier decision. The
"upper crust want[s] it as soon as possible," he said. Although
he was not in agreement with their decision, he had to "stress
the urgency of having it done the 14th."⁷

Despite Oppenheimer's best efforts to comply, the bomb was
not ready for testing until the early morning hours of July 16.
News from Alamogordo reached Potsdam in stages between
July 16 and 21. The reports came to Stimson, who passed them
on to Truman, Byrnes, and Churchill. As each document filled

in more details of the extraordinary, successful performance of the first atomic bomb, the spirits of the Anglo-American leaders rose. Churchill was "intensely interested and greatly cheered up" by the first reports, while Truman was "evidently very greatly reenforced," Stimson wrote in his diary.[8] The full impact of the historic explosion on the Potsdam negotiators was delayed, however, until the sixth day of the conference, July 21, when a complete report from Groves arrived by courier.* Stimson was deeply impressed: "It was an immensely powerful document, clearly and well written and with supporting documents of the highest importance."[9] Eschewing formal military language, Groves described the event in vivid detail:

> At 0530, 16 July 1945, in a remote section of the Alamogordo Air Base, New Mexico, the first full scale test was made of the implosion type atomic fission bomb. . . . The test was successful beyond the most optimistic expectations of anyone. Based on the data which it has been possible to work up to date, I estimate the energy generated to be in excess of the equivalent of 15,000 to 20,000 tons of TNT; and this is a conservative estimate.

Groves then reviewed the bomb blast's effects: an incredible fire ball as bright as several midday suns; a mushroom cloud that shot 41,000 feet into the substratosphere; a tremendous crash that broke a window 125 miles away; a crater 1,200 feet in diameter; a forty-ton steel tower one-half mile from the explosion destroyed. The Pentagon (whose construction Groves had directed) was not a safe shelter from such a bomb, he concluded. "With the assistance of the Office of Censorship we were able to limit the news stories to the approved release supplemented in the local papers by brief stories from the many eyewitnesses not connected with our project. One of these was a blind woman who saw the light."[10]

At 3:30 that afternoon at the President's quarters in Potsdam, "the Little White House," Stimson reviewed Groves's report with Truman and Byrnes. "They were immensely pleased," he recalled. "The President was tremendously pepped up by it and spoke to me of it again and again when I saw him.

* See Appendix P.

what a worm Truman was

He said it gave him an entirely new feeling of confidence and he thanked me for having come to the Conference and being present to help him in this way."[11]

Fortified by this news, the President left at 5 P.M. for the fifth plenary session, where he took command of the debate with a vigor he had not displayed at previous meetings.[12] "I shall state frankly what I think," he told Stalin.[13] "He stood up to the Russians in a most emphatic and decisive manner," Churchill observed, "telling them as to certain demands that they absolutely could not have and that the United States was entirely against them."[14] "Now I know what happened to Truman yesterday," the Prime Minister remarked after reading Groves's report. "I couldn't understand it. When he got to the meeting after having read this report he was a changed man. He told the Russians [and the British, he should have added] just where they got on and off and generally bossed the whole meeting."[15] Harriman perceived the change in attitude too. Despite a general feeling among the American delegation that the Russians were recklessly expanding their demands, he commented to Stimson on July 23 about "the increasing cheerfulness evidently caused by the news from us [about Alamogordo]."[16] Truman directly confirmed the influence of the bomb on his attitude and his negotiating position that same day when he discussed the situation with Stimson. The President assured him that despite Soviet demands he was standing firm and "he was apparently relying greatly upon the information as to S-1." It appeared to Stimson that the "program for S-1 is tying in what we are doing in all fields."[17]

Several days later Byrnes explained to Special Ambassador Joseph Davies, who had been invited to the conference by Truman, how important the bomb had become to him. Byrnes "was having a hard time with reparations," Davies wrote, but the "details as to the success of the atomic bomb, which he had just received, gave him confidence that the Soviets would agree as to these difficulties." Davies was deeply disturbed. "Byrnes' attitude that the atomic bomb assured ultimate success in negotiations disturbed me more than his description of its success amazed me," he wrote in his diary. "I told him the threat wouldn't work, and might do irreparable harm."[18]

But Davies did not make policy, and to remain faithful to the historical record the views of those who did need to be taken seriously. To recognize that the President and his advisers weighed the implications of the successful test in relation to all aspects of American policy does not *ipso facto* justify ascribing diabolical motivations to them. Historians who have chosen to ignore, or more recently those who have sought to explain away, the effect of Alamogordo on the Potsdam negotiators have not succeeded in correcting the exaggerated influence of the bomb described by others.[19] Under the circumstances, how could American policymakers have failed to be affected by Groves's description of that historic explosion? The experience of war at once blinded them to any moral constraints against using the new weapon and encouraged them to seek whatever military or diplomatic advantages its use might incur. The United States was in control of a "final arbiter of force."[20] At the crossroads of war and diplomacy the temptation to seize this advantage was irresistible.

Truman's decision to reopen the question of whether the Soviets were needed to conclude the war against Japan provides the clearest example of the bomb's influence on American policy. As early as May 1945, Acting Secretary of State (and former ambassador to Japan) Joseph C. Grew had urged the President, the Secretaries of War and the Navy, and high State Department officials to modify the insistence on "unconditional surrender."[21] The Japanese would never give up, he argued, without assurances that the present dynasty and the institution of the Emperor would not be destroyed. Without such a guarantee, even members of Japan's peace faction were powerless before the weight of national tradition and the determination of the armed forces to continue the struggle. Unconditional surrender, however, had become a political shibboleth by the time Truman took office, a slogan that embodied for the American public what the sacrifices of war seemed to be all about. Neither Truman nor Byrnes, consummate politicians to the core, was ready to retreat publicly from this path that Roosevelt had blazed.[22] Grew's suggestion was therefore set aside, and Truman came to Potsdam hoping to secure a Soviet declaration of war against Japan.[23] With the invasion of the Japan-

ese mainland scheduled for November 1945, there was still
time for the Soviets to divert the powerful Japanese Manchurian Army.

By the end of the first week of the Potsdam Conference,
however, the negotiating position assumed by the Soviets created second thoughts about the consequences of their assistance. Considering the generally hostile attitude toward the
Russians pervading the American delegation, those second
thoughts are not surprising. Even before the conference
opened, Davies found Special Ambassador Edwin Pauley and
his reparations negotiators determined to "out-trade the so and
so's—or else." He was told by Byrnes that the Russians could
only be dealt with in a tough manner, and that Truman was
"constantly being hammered on the idea that this was the only
way to handle them." Leahy and Harriman were forcefully advocating the idea that it was essential to be tough with the Russians. "The fact is," Davies commented on July 15, "that the
anti-Soviet prejudices in the [State] Department and in other
departments has [sic] surrounded the President to a degree where
it makes the situation very dangerous."[24]

Dangerous indeed, for the inevitable tough bargaining at
Potsdam led the American delegates quickly to the conclusion
that the Soviets were living up to their worst expectations
(while the Soviet delegates no doubt reached the same conclusions about the Americans). They were "throwing aside all
their previous restraint as to being a continental power . . .
seeking to branch in all directions," Stimson wrote in his diary.
Although Truman considered many of their new demands a
bluff, the feeling grew among senior American officials that the
Russians were out to absorb as much as they could get. They
were trying to extend their influence in Eastern Europe, Stimson reported, in Turkey, in the Italian Mediterranean colonies,
and elsewhere. Even an effort to obtain solitary control over
Korea seemed possible.[25] Stimson Diaries is source; j.P. Papers
What could be done? Truman instructed Stimson to find out
whether "Marshall felt that we needed the Russians in the war
or whether we could get along without them."[26] The answer,
that they were not needed, was relayed to the President as follows: The massing of Soviet troops along the Chinese border

was already tying up Japan's forces in Manchuria, and now that the atomic bomb was a reality the value of Soviet assistance had declined. Moreover, if the Soviets intended to enter the war they could not in any case be stopped.[27] Truman decided not to request their help. The conference notes of Walter Brown, press secretary to Byrnes, explain his motives in advocating that decision: the Secretary was "still hoping for time, believing after atomic bomb [sic] Japan will surrender and Russia will not get in so much on the kill, thereby being in a position to press for claims against China."[28]

Although the combination of news of the successful test and the expansion of Soviet territorial demands changed the attitude of American policymakers toward Soviet participation in the Far Eastern war, it did not incline them to lay the bomb on the negotiating table. Their policy of letting the weapon speak for itself in the next week or two remained unaltered. Only Churchill, who had earlier opposed any revelation about the bomb to Stalin, changed his mind. Not only did he agree after reading Groves's report that the Russians should be informed about the existence of the project as the Interim Committee had recommended, but he was "inclined to use it as an argument in our favor in the negotiations."[29] But Truman was not. Following the letter of the Committee's recommendation rather than its spirit, which embodied the hope that an overture to Stalin would initiate the process toward international control, Truman "casually mentioned to Stalin, after the plenary session on July 24, "that we had a new weapon of unusual destructive force." Stalin's reply was unexpectedly brief: "He was glad to hear it and hoped we would make 'good use of it against the Japanese,' " Truman reported.[30] A letter from Charles Bohlen confirms the President's description of this colloquy: "My recollection and impression . . . is that he [Truman] wished to make his statement as casual as possible and for this reason without taking me, his interpreter, with him he strolled over to Stalin. . . ."[31]

The steady course toward a postwar atomic armaments race that Bohr had sought to alter passed several important markers at Potsdam. Not only were Soviet fears about the consequences of an American atomic bomb heightened, but on the American

side, what little commitment there was among high officials for
the international control of atomic energy all but vanished.
Stimson, the most determined advocate of international control
within the Truman administration in June, had executed a
complete *volte face* on the issue by July 26. In a long memorandum to the President, "Reflections on the Basic Problems
Which Confront Us," he outlined a new position and the considerations that brought it about.[32] The nature of the Soviet
government—a police state—precluded the possibility of effective international control. He was unwilling to abandon hope
altogether, but the atmosphere the Soviets had created at Potsdam led him to believe that, at the present juncture, even "with
the best of efforts we cannot understand each other." Fearing
that a new war and the destruction of civilization would result
if a hostile relationship became permanent, he urged that his
government direct its thoughts "constantly to the time and the
method of attacking the basic difficulty and the means we may
have in hand to produce results." How, in other words, could
Soviet society be liberalized? Until free speech was granted, it
was necessary to proceed along the path toward international
control slowly "and constantly explore the question how our
headstart in X [the atomic bomb] and the Russian desire to
participate can be used to bring us nearer to the removal of the
basic difficulties. . . ." The Secretary was still thinking in terms
of the *quid pro quo* he had first advocated in December 1944; but
the terms of the trade had now escalated from geography to ide-
ology, from the modification of Soviet foreign policy to the
reconstruction of Soviet society. *exactly . . . and
Stalin knew it all along*

II

"A Graveyard with Not a Tombstone Standing"

A similar purpose guided American policy toward Japan. The
democratization of Japanese society remained an undisputed
goal throughout the war, though there existed strong differences of opinion over how to achieve it. While Grew and Stimson argued in the spring and summer of 1945 that the Emperor's
remaining was a necessary corollary to the process, Assistant

Secretaries of State Dean Acheson and Archibald MacLeish insisted that the institution itself was fundamentally antidemocratic and had to be eliminated.[33] This debate—which bore closely on the question of whether or not to modify the demand for unconditional surrender—was temporarily settled by Byrnes, who sided with Acheson and MacLeish on the advice of the ailing former Secretary of State, Cordell Hull.[34] Having blocked what appeared under the circumstances to be Japan's last viable exit from the war, U.S. policymakers concentrated on ways to open another: a severe psychological shock inflicted by successive atomic bombings held out the possibility of altering the Japanese government's determination to continue the hopeless struggle. The selection of targets reflected this intention, which had been guiding the Air Force's bombing strategy since March; the central purpose of the terrible fire bomb raids on Tokyo was not so much to destroy Japanese fighting capability as to weaken the will of the people and government to continue the war.

Guided by instructions from Groves, a Target Committee composed of Manhattan Project scientists and ordnance specialists studied the available options, and developed criteria for their selection.* The report of the Committee's second and third meetings, held in Oppenheimer's office at Los Alamos on May 10 and 11, provides a straightforward summary of its orientation. The minutes record their conclusion that any small, strictly military target should be located in a much larger area subject to blast damage "to avoid undue risks of the weapon being lost due to bad placing of the bomb." The members of the Committee agreed, too, that psychological factors in the target selection were of great importance. "Two aspects of this," the report states, "are (1) obtaining the greatest psychological effect against Japan and (2) making the initial use sufficiently spectacular *for the importance of the weapon to be internationally recognized* when publicity on it is released."[35]

One city stood out above all others in light of the Commit-

---

* Members present included: General T. Farrell, Colonel Seeman, Captain W. S. Parsons, Major J. Derry, Dr. J. Stearns, Dr. R. Tolman, Dr. J. R. Oppenheimer, Dr. C. Lauritsen, Dr. N. F. Ramsey, Dr. Dennison, Dr. J. Von Neumann, Dr. R. R. Wilson and Dr. W. Penney.

tee's criteria—Kyoto, the ancient capital of Japan and the center of her civilization for more than a thousand years. Located 300 miles southwest of Tokyo, part of the Osaka-Kobe industrial complex, its numerous shrines, palaces, temples, and universities were surrounded on three sides by ranges of high hills, *insanity* at the northern end of a plain. "Kyoto has the advantage," the Committee observed in terms that utterly defy logic, "of the people being more highly intelligent and hence better able to appreciate the significance of the weapon."[36]

The Target Committee's concern that the full implications of the bomb be recognized reflected a pervasive anxiety among all who worried about the role of the bomb in the postwar world. As an instrument of peace based upon the international control of atomic energy, or as an instrument of diplomacy to be used in postwar negotiations, the influence of the weapon depended upon a general recognition that pre-atomic age calculations had to give way to new realities. If the Japanese did not accept this view, the war would continue; if the Russians ignored it, the peace would be lost. In this sense the bomb became its own message, and within the context of the war those who participated in the decisionmaking process were consumed by a single objective—to transmit the message in the most dramatic fashion possible.

Here Stimson dissented. The residents of Kyoto were spared their assigned role because he refused to accept this last assumption. "This is one time I'm going to be the final deciding authority. Nobody's going to tell me what to do on this. On this matter I am the kingpin," he told Groves as he struck Kyoto from the list.[37] After explaining the city's history to the startled and disappointed general, he rejected Groves's argument that Kyoto's large industrial area and geographic layout dictated its selection.

Almost six weeks later, Harrison wired Stimson at Potsdam that his military advisers wanted his "pet city" reinstated as a target.[38] But the old man stood firm. "Aware of no factors to change my decision," he wired back. "On the contrary new factors here tend to confirm it."[39] Already planning to groom Japan as an outpost for American interests in the Far East, he feared that the "bitterness which would be caused by such a wanton act might make it impossible during the long postwar period to reconcile the Japanese to us in that area rather than to the Russians." He pointed out to Truman, who agreed with him, that "it might thus be the means of preventing what our policy demanded, namely a sympathetic Japan to the United States in case there should be any aggression by Russia in Manchuria."[40] That he failed to question as well *any* use of the bomb indicates how deeply rooted were his assumptions about the appropriateness of that decision, and how firmly he had integrated them into the context of the war. It never occurred to Stimson that the destruction of any city, or two cities, might be considered "wanton."

By July 23 the schedule for the atomic attack was settled. Stimson was notified that a uranium bomb would be available soon after August 1. The first plutonium bomb, the type tested at Trinity (Alamogordo), would be ready for delivery about August 6, and a second plutonium bomb was expected by August 24. Additional ones would be produced at an accelerating rate from possibly three in September to perhaps seven or more in December. The specially trained B-29 crews of the 509th Composite Group were to deliver the first bomb as soon as weather permitted visual bombing after August 3. The targets were: Hiroshima, Kokura, Niigata, and Nagasaki.[41]

On July 23, Oppenheimer informed General Thomas Farrell, Groves's executive officer, and Captain William S. Parsons, the Manhattan Project's ordnance specialist who would arm both bombs aboard the attacking aircraft, that the bombs were expected to perform well. "As a result of the Trinity shot we are led to expect a very similar performance from the first Little Boy [uranium bomb] and the first plutonium Fat Man." Oppenheimer predicted that the energy release of either bomb would fall between 12,000 to 20,000 tons, and that the blast effect would be equivalent to from 8,000 to 15,000 tons of TNT. The fireball would be of greater brilliance and longer duration than that of the Trinity shot, since no dust would be mixed with it at the detonation altitude of 2,000 feet. Yet lethal radiation from the bomb would reach the ground. "The possibilities of a less than optimal performance of the Little Boy are quite small and should be ignored," he noted, while the possibility that the plutonium bomb would give a less than optimal performance was about twelve percent. While there was about a six percent chance that the energy release would be under five thousand tons TNT equivalent, he did not expect it to be less than one thousand tons unless a component actually malfunctioned.[42]

Two weeks later Hiroshima was destroyed: "The gun type [uranium] bomb was ready at Tinian on 31 July awaiting the first favourable weather," Groves reported to General Marshall on August 6, 1945. "The daily 24 hour advance forecasts kept indicating unsatisfactory conditions until 3 August when there was a prediction of possible good weather over the targets for 4 August at 2200Z (5 August 0700 Tinian or 4 August 1800 EWT). Later predictions delayed this a day. At 5 August 0415Z General LeMay finalized the take-off time, final assembly of the bomb proceeded and take-off actually occurred on schedule at 1645Z 5 August. Two B-29's with recording instruments and special scientific observers accompanied the vital plane. The anticipated weather over the targets was not certain to be good but only fair."[43]

The initial report from the attack plane was succinct and unambiguous. "Target at Hiroshima attacked visually ⅒th cloud at 052315Z. No fighters no flak." The results were clear-cut. The visible effects were greater than in the New Mexico test, the crew reported.[44] The city was totally destroyed. Perhaps 100,000 of its citizens were killed immediately, and tens of thousands more left dying of radiation poisoning—among them, two U.S. Navy fliers imprisoned in the city jail.*

* The details surrounding the deaths of these fliers, Brissette and Neal, were first reported to the author by former Lieutenant Stanley Levine (USAAF), the radar officer of the *Sad Tomato*, a B-29 that ditched off the coast of Japan on August 8. Levine and nine other members of its crew were with the men in Hiroshima when they died. He does not recall being debriefed after repatriation—"No one seemed to care"—but he is under the impression that other members of the crew did report the deaths of Brissette and Neal to authorities on Guam. A Japanese witness has confirmed Levine's story: Nobuichi Fukui, then a military police captain, saved the lives of the crew, and was with them while they were in Hiroshima. He reports describing the entire story in detail to members of General Douglas MacArthur's staff who called him to Head-

Two days later, as the radioactive dust settled over Hiroshima, Ambassador Naotake Sato entered Foreign Minister Molotov's study in the Kremlin at 5 P.M. Moscow time. Having arrived hoping to enlist the Soviets as mediators between the Anglo-American and Japanese governments, he was unprepared for the message he received: a state of war would exist between the Soviet Union and Japan on the following day. Two hours later (1 A.M. August 9, Tokyo time), Soviet forces crossed the Manchurian border driving back the depleted forces of Japan's once powerful Kwantung army.[45] Japan's moment of decision had arrived, but before it was recognized and acted on, a second city was to be destroyed.

The rationale that had loosed the first atomic attack was about to unleash the second one too—unconditional surrender had to be accepted immediately or, as Truman announced, the Japanese "may expect a rain of ruin from the air, the like of which has never been seen on this earth. . . ."[46] Yet the first atomic attack together with the Soviet declaration of war had marshaled the end-the-war advocates within the Japanese government to action despite the danger of assassination these advocates faced. "In short," the leading student of Japan's decision to surrender has written, the peace advocates "recognized in the atomic bomb and the Soviet entry into the war not just an imperative need to give in but actually a supreme opportunity to turn the tide against the die-hards and to shake the government loose from the yoke of military oppression under which it had been laboring so long."[47] By August 9 the decision to sue for surrender had become inevitable, though the tragedy's Japanese protagonists needed time to recite their lines. If Washington had maintained closer control over the scheduling of the atomic bomb raids, the annihilation of Nagasaki could have been avoided. But as it happened, the initiative had been left with the bomber command on the island of Tinian. Norman Ramsey, the leading physicist on the island, described to Oppenheimer the sequence of events that led to the second

quarters on two separate occasions. To this day, however, the U.S. government has never officially acknowledged that Americans were killed at Hiroshima.

atomic attack before the Japanese government had absorbed
the shock and implications of the first:

> Our original schedule called for take off on the morning
> of 11 August local time (10 August Washington time).
> However, on the evening of 7 August we concluded that we
> could safely advance the date to August 10. When we pro-
> posed this to [Colonel Paul W.] Tibbets [commander of
> the 509th Composite Group] he said it was too bad we
> could not advance the date still another day since good
> weather was forecast for 9 August with at least five days of
> bad weather forecast to follow. We agreed to try with the
> understanding we might miss our schedule since we were
> unwilling to speed any operation which might conceivably
> affect either safety or reliability. Finally at 11 P.M. on 8
> August the unit was in the plane and completely and thor-
> oughly checked out. Take off was at about 3 A.M. We all
> aged ten years until the plane cleared the island. We were
> scheduled to receive a strike report at 10:30 A.M. 9 August,
> but all we heard until 12:30 was the very worried query
> from the fastax ship, "Did the strike plane abort?" Finally
> we received the message from Ashworth that the secondary
> target had been bombed largely by radar and that at least
> technically the unit functioned even better than Hiroshima
> although there was some doubt as to the location of the
> bomb.[48]

There was some doubt too about its victims—the likelihood
that, here again, among the tens of thousands in this "graveyard
with not a tombstone standing"[49] were American prisoners of
war. This is suggested by a message from Headquarters, U.S.
Army Strategic Air Forces, Guam, to the War Department on
July 31: "Reports prisoner of war sources, not verified by photos,
give location of Allied prisoner of war camp one mile north of
center of city of Nagasaki. Does this influence the choice of this
target for initial Centerboard operation? Request immediate reply." The reply came quickly: "Targets previously assigned for
Centerboard remain unchanged."[50]

What effect did this second holocaust delivered only three days after the first have on the decision of the Japanese to surrender? The fact that Nagasaki was destroyed before Japan's leaders had absorbed the shock of Hiroshima, or the shock and implications of the Soviet declaration of war, precludes an accurate assessment. The rapid succession of crises blurred the significance of each. "The machinery of [the Japanese] government," Professor Butow has observed, "had ground to a halt [on August 9] not because it had been damaged but because it had been thrown off balance. The factors which should have urged speedy and smooth operation had engendered exactly the opposite results."[51] Yet the argument that the second bombing gave the Emperor the opportunity to convince the military that Allied surrender terms had to be accepted is not convincing; it assumes that until the Emperor was informed about Nagasaki he was not inclined either to accept or to advocate surrender.[52] Nothing could be further from the truth. The surrender movement began soon after the fall of Saipan in July 1944, and as early as June 22, 1945, the day Okinawa was wrenched from Japanese control, the Emperor took his first cautious step toward undermining those committed to continue the useless struggle. At an Imperial Conference called to discuss the course of events and their implications, he requested the Cabinet or the Supreme Command to consider alternatives to the decision to fight to the end.[53] Ambassador Sato's mission to Moscow was a direct response to that request, and by July 13 Japan's willingness to capitulate became clear: "Unconditional surrender is the only obstacle to peace . . . ," Foreign Minister Shigenori Togo wired Sato.[54]

Having broken the Japanese code before the war, American Intelligence was able to—and did—relay this message to the President, but it had no effect whatever on efforts to bring the war to a conclusion. The need to provide the Japanese with a positive, specific commitment preserving the throne paralyzed any further American initiative, and the anticipated effect of the atomic bombs made an American compromise appear unnecessary, or even undesirable. The Potsdam Declaration of July 26 calling for the surrender of Japan was decidedly unhelpful to those Japanese who were searching for a means of bringing the war to a conclusion.[55] "Following are our terms. We will not deviate from them. There are no alternatives. We shall brook no delay," it firmly stated. Calling for the elimination of the authority and influence "of those who have deceived and misled the people of Japan into embarking on world conquest" and warning that "stern justice shall be meted out to all war criminals, including those who have visited cruelties upon our prisoners," the proclamation offered the military die-hards in the Japanese government more ammunition to continue the war than it offered their opponents to end it. Was there any evidence here that the leaders of the United States, Great Britain, and China did not consider the Emperor one of those who had "deceived and misled the people of Japan"? Was there any guarantee that the Emperor would not be considered a war criminal? The statements that a new government would be formed "in accordance with the freely expressed will of the Japanese people," and the call for the unconditional surrender of "all Japanese armed forces" (rather than the government of Japan or the Japanese people) offered scant support for those who wanted peace without sacrificing the throne. The Japanese government's response to the Potsdam Declaration was to "mokusatsu" it—literally "to kill with silence," or, more idiomatically, "to take no notice of," "to treat with silent contempt," or "to ignore."[56] It was an unfortunate reply, for the Americans concluded that the Japanese were determined to fight on. "In the face of this rejection," Stimson wrote in his autobiography, "we could only proceed to demonstrate that the ultimatum had meant exactly what it said when it stated that if the Japanese continued the war, 'the full application of our military power, backed by our resolve, will mean the inevitable and complete destruction of the Japanese armed forces and just as inevitably the utter devastation of the Japanese homeland.' For such a purpose," the Secretary continued, "the atomic bomb was an eminently suitable weapon."[57]

Yet a painful question remains even for those who accept the exigencies of war as the terrible rationalization for the first atomic bomb: Did the destruction of Nagasaki significantly hasten Japan's decision to surrender?

In the early morning hours of August 10, in the Emperor's bomb shelter adjoining the imperial library, Premier Kantaro Suzuki startled his divided colleagues on the Supreme Council with the announcement, "Your Imperial Majesty's decision is requested. . . ." That decision, "to accept the Allied proclamation on the basis outlined by the Foreign Minister," brought the war to its conclusion—on the condition that the United States guarantee the survival of dynasty and Emperor.[58] That unconditional surrender remained an obstacle to peace in the wake of Hiroshima, Nagasaki, and the Soviet declaration of war—until the government of the United States offered the necessary (albeit veiled) assurance that neither Emperor nor throne would be destroyed*—suggests the possibility, which even Stimson later recognized,[59] that *neither* bomb may have been necessary; and certainly that the second one was not. *he leaves this hanging*

III
"Man Has Mounted Science"

What effect did the atomic bomb have on American wartime diplomacy?

The diplomacy of atomic energy came to rest during the war on a simple and dangerous assumption: that the Soviet government would surrender important geographical, political, and ideological objectives in exchange for the neutralization of the new weapon. Warnings from Bush and Conant that the Russians might be able to reach atomic parity within three to five years were ignored in favor of Groves's estimate that it would take the Soviet Union twenty to fifty years to catch up. Even if the Russians had the scientific talent, Groves argued, they could not possibly possess the necessary industrial capability. Although Groves and those who heeded his advice were aware that a similar kind of arrogance had led atomic scientists in Germany to underestimate American potential during the war, their low opinion of the So-

* On August 10 the Japanese Government offered to surrender on condition that the Potsdam Declaration "does not comprise any demand which prejudices the prerogatives of His Majesty as a Sovereign Ruler." Stimson notes that "while the Allied reply made no promises other than those already given, it implicitly recognized the Emperor's position by prescribing that his power must be subject to the orders of the Allied supreme commander. These terms were accepted on August 14 by the Japanese, and the instrument of surrender was formally signed on September 2, in Tokyo Bay." Stimson and Bundy, *On Active Service*, 626–7.

viets blinded them to the validity of such an analogy.[60] As a result, those who conducted the foreign policy of the United States became too confident, too certain, that through the accomplishments of American science, technology, and industry they could alone make the "new world" into one better than the old. American diplomacy and prestige suffered grievously in the process: an opportunity was missed during the war to gauge the extent of Soviet interest in the international control of atomic energy, and the need for a comprehensive postwar policy on atomic energy was ignored. No one thought to consider how the bomb would be used to restructure international relations if the Soviets did not choose to "cooperate."

And they did not cooperate. At the London Foreign Minister's Conference in September, Molotov engaged in a strategy of "reverse atomic diplomacy," joking about the bomb and underplaying its value.[61] Byrnes, who had gone to the conference expecting that "the presence of the bomb in his pocket" (as he told Stimson) would "get [him] through," was thrown completely off balance.[62]* Three months and a day after Hiroshima was bombed, on the eve of the Anglo-American-Canadian atomic energy conference in Washington, Bush wrote that the whole matter of international relations relating to atomic energy "is in a thoroughly chaotic condition."[63] The technology of war was already being hailed as the symbol of peace, and it was becoming increasingly clear that instead of promoting American postwar aims, wartime atomic energy policies had made them more difficult to achieve. As American-Soviet relations deteriorated, Hiroshima and Nagasaki rose as symbols of a new American barbarism, and as explanations for the origins of the cold war.[64] A century before, Henry Adams had tersely phrased the truth that had now received a final, unequivocal confirmation: "Man has mounted science, and is now run away with."

* See Appendix Q.

NOTES

his earlier point about U.S. & allies
ganging up on Soviets

AEC doc. no.—Atomic Energy Commission document number. These documents, obtained by the author from the AEC in 1970, were moved in 1973 to the National Archives, Washington, D.C. They are located throughout the Office of Scientific Research and Development, Section-1 (S-1) files.

ASC-Ad. files—Atomic Scientists of Chicago, Addenda files, Regenstein Library, University of Chicago, Chicago, Ill.

Bush mss—Vannevar Bush manuscripts, Library of Congress, Washington, D.C.

Bush-Conant files—Vannevar Bush–James B. Conant files, Office of Scientific Research and Development, Section-1 files (Record Group 227), National Archives, Washington, D.C.

Byrnes mss—James F. Byrnes manuscripts, Clemson University Library, Clemson, S.C.

CAB 90—British War Cabinet Scientific Advisory Committees' files, Public Records Office, London, England.

Cherwell-OS mss—Lord Cherwell (F. A. Lindemann) Official Series manuscripts, Nuffield College Library, Oxford University, Oxford, England.

Cherwell-PS mss—Lord Cherwell Personal Series manuscripts, Nuffield College Library, Oxford University, Oxford, England.

Davies diaries—Joseph E. Davies diaries, Library of Congress, Washington, D.C.

Davies journals—Joseph E. Davies journals, Library of Congress, Washington, D.C.

DHMP—Diplomatic History of the Manhattan Project, Manhattan Engineer District files (Record Group 77), National Archives, Washington, D.C.

Feis mss—Herbert Feis manuscripts, Library of Congress, Washington, D.C.

Fermi mss—Enrico Fermi manuscripts, Regenstein Library, University of Chicago, Chicago, Ill.

Forrestal diaries—James Forrestal diaries, Firestone Library, Princeton University, Princeton, N.J.

Frankfurter mss—Felix Frankfurter manuscripts, Library of Congress, Washington, D.C.

FRUS—Foreign Relations of the United States, Department of State, Washington, D.C.

Furer diary—Rear Admiral Julius A. Furer diary, Naval Historical Foundation, Washington, D.C.

Grew mss—Joseph C. Grew manuscripts, Houghton Library, Harvard University, Cambridge, Mass.

Groves diaries—General Leslie R. Groves diaries, Manhattan Engineer District Records (Record Group 77), National Archives, Washington, D.C.

Hopkins mss—Harry L. Hopkins manuscripts, Franklin D. Roosevelt Library, Hyde Park, N.Y.

Lawrence mss—Ernest O. Lawrence manuscripts, Bancroft Library, University of California Berkeley, Berkeley, Cal.

Lamont-OHT—Lansing Lamont, oral history transcript, Harry S. Truman Library, Independence, Mo.

Leahy diaries—Admiral William D. Leahy diaries, Library of Congress, Washington, D.C.

MED—Manhattan Engineer District Records (Record Group 77), National Archives, Washington, D.C.

MED, H-B—Manhattan Engineer District, Harrison and Bundy files (Secretary of War's MED files) (Record Group 77), National Archives, Washington, D.C.

MED-TS—Manhattan Engineer District–Top Secret. A section of the MED records set aside by Groves as "Top Secret, Special Interest to General Groves" (Record Group 77), National Archives, Washington, D.C.

Met. Lab. files—Metallurgical Laboratory, University of Chicago files, Argonne National Laboratory Archives, Argonne, Ill.

Millikan mss—Robert A. Millikan manuscripts, Library of the California Institute of Technology, Pasadena, Calif.

Oppenheimer mss—J. Robert Oppenheimer manuscripts, Library of Congress, Washington, D.C.

Oppenheimer tapes—J. Robert Oppenheimer tape recordings, part of the Oppenheimer manuscripts, Library of Congress, Washington, D.C.

OSRD, S-1 files—Office of Scientific Research and Development, Section-1 files other than the Bush-Conant files (Record Group 227), National Archives, Washington, D.C.

Prem. 3—Premier 3 files of Winston Churchill, Public Record Office, London, England.

Provost Marshal General files—Records of the Office of the Provost Marshal General, 1941–1945 (Record Group 389), National Archives, Washington, D.C.

Ramsey-OHT—Norman Ramsey, oral history transcript, Oral History Research Department, Butler Library, Columbia University, New York, N.Y.

Roosevelt-MR—Franklin D. Roosevelt Map Room file, Franklin D. Roosevelt Library, Hyde Park, N.Y.

Roosevelt-OF—Franklin D. Roosevelt Official file, Franklin D. Roosevelt Library, Hyde Park, N.Y.

Roosevelt-PPF—Franklin D. Roosevelt President's Personal file, Franklin D. Roosevelt Library, Hyde Park, N.Y.

Roosevelt-PSF—Franklin D. Roosevelt President's Secretary's file, Franklin D. Roosevelt Library, Hyde Park, N.Y.

Roosevelt-Truman mss—Roosevelt Papers Pertaining to Truman, Harry S. Truman Library, Independence, Mo.

Rosenman mss—Samuel I. Rosenman manuscripts, Harry S. Truman Library, Independence, Mo.

Rush mss—J. H. Rush manuscripts, Regenstein Library, University of Chicago, Chicago, Ill.

Shalett mss—Sidney Shalett, oral history transcript of interviews with Alben Barkley, Harry S. Truman Library, Independence, Mo.

Smith diary—Harold D. Smith (Director, Bureau of the Budget), Diary, Franklin D. Roosevelt Library, Hyde Park, N.Y.

State Dept. doc.—Department of State documents (Record Group 59), National Archives, Washington, D.C.

Stimson diaries—Henry L. Stimson diaries, Sterling Memorial Library, Yale University, New Haven, Conn.

Stimson mss—Henry L. Stimson manuscripts, Sterling Memorial Library, Yale University, New Haven, Conn.

Sweetser mss—Arthur Sweetser manuscripts, Library of Congress, Washington, D.C.

Szilard mss—Leo Szilard manuscripts, in possession of Gertrude Weiss Szilard, M.D., La Jolla, Calif.

Truman-OF—Harry S. Truman, Official File, Harry S. Truman Library, Independence, Mo.

Truman-PP—Harry S. Truman, Personal Papers, Harry S. Truman Library, Independence, Mo.

Vaughan-OHT—Harry H. Vaughan, oral history transcript, Harry S. Truman Library, Independence, Mo.

INTRODUCTION

1. Henry L. Stimson and McGeorge Bundy, *On Active Service in Peace and War* (New York, 1947), 637.

2. Conflicting interpretations are found in: Gar Alperovitz, *Atomic Diplomacy: Hiroshima and Potsdam* (New York, 1965); Herbert Feis, *The Atomic Bomb and the End of World War II* (Princeton, 1966); Len Giovannitti and Fred Freed, *The Decision to Drop the Bomb* (New York, 1965); Richard G. Hewlett and Oscar E. Anderson, Jr., *The New World, 1939/1946: A History of the United States Atomic Energy Commission*, I (University Park, Pa., 1962); Lisle A. Rose, *After Yalta* (New York, 1973) and his *Dubious Victory: The United*

States and the End of World War II (Kent, Ohio, 1974); Walter Smith Schoenberger, *Decision of Destiny* (Athens, Ohio, 1969).

3. Stimson and Bundy, *On Active Service*, 628–9.

4. Stimson diaries, Dec. 31, 1944.

5. *Ibid.*, Apr. 6–11, 1945.

6. J. R. Oppenheimer, "Niels Bohr and Atomic Weapons," *The New York Review of Books*, Vol. 3 (Dec. 17, 1966), 6.

7. See, for example, Ruth Moore, *Niels Bohr: The Man, His Science and the World They Changed* (New York, 1966), 344.

8. These views are represented in the following books and articles: Alperovitz, *Atomic Diplomacy*, 12–13; William H. Chamberlain, *America's Second Crusade* (Chicago, 1953), 206; Arthur Schlesinger, Jr., "Origins of the Cold War," *Foreign Affairs*, 46 (1967), 26–9; and Herbert Feis, *Churchill, Roosevelt, Stalin: The War They Waged and the Peace They Sought* (Princeton, 1957), 596–8.

CHAPTER I

1. U.S. Senate, *Hearings Before the U.S. Senate Special Committee on Atomic Energy*, 79th Cong., 1st Sess., November–December, 1945, Part 2, 294 (hereafter cited as *Senate Hearings on Atomic Energy*).

2. For a brief and interesting survey of the history of discoveries that led up to the discovery of nuclear fission, see Kenneth Jay, "A Glance at Prehistory," introduction, Margaret Gowing, *Britain and Atomic Energy, 1939–1945* (London, 1964), 3–30.

3. Ernest O. Lawrence, "Historical Notes on My Early Activities in Connection with the Tuballoy [sic] Project," March 24, 1945, Historical Documents folder, Lawrence mss.

4. Emilio Segrè, "Fermi and Neutron Physics," *Reviews of Modern Physics*, 27 (July 1955), 262–3; *Enrico Fermi: Physicist* (Chicago, 1970), 76.

5. A. H. Compton, "Statement to the National Policy Committee," May 28, 1945, 2–6, Bush-Conant files, "Report to National Committee" folder.

6. Cited in Daniel S. Greenberg, *The Politics of Pure Science* (New York, 1967), 211 *n.*

7. Gowing, *Britain and Atomic Energy*, 24–6.

8. *New York Times*, May 5, 1940, 1, cited in William L. Laurence, *Men and Atoms* (New York, 1962), 43–4.

9. As quoted in Leo Szilard, "Reminiscences," edited by Gertrude Weiss Szilard and Kathleen R. Winsor, in Donald Fleming and Bernard Bailyn, eds., *The Intellectual Migration: Europe and America, 1930–1960* (Cambridge, Mass., 1969), 107.

10. Bohr to James Chadwick, ca. early 1943, in "Niels Henrik David Bohr, 1885–1962," *Biographical Memoirs of Fellows of the Royal Society*, November 9, 1963, Oppenheimer mss, box 21.

11. William L. Langer and S. Everett Gleason, *The Challenge to Isolation, 1937–1940* (New York, 1964), 45–51 *passim*. Robert E. Sherwood, *Roosevelt and Hopkins: An Intimate History* (New York, 1948), 101–2, 131–33.

12. Felix Gilbert, *The Beginnings of American Foreign Policy: To the Farewell Address* (New York, 1961), 121–36.

13. On the immigration of scientists to America prior to World War II, see Laura Fermi, *Illustrious Immigrants: The Intellectual Migration from Europe, 1930–41* (Chicago, 1968); and Charles Weiner, "A New Site for the Seminar: The Refugees and American Physics in the Thirties," in Fleming and Bailyn, eds., *The Intellectual Migration*, 190–234.

14. Szilard to F. A. Lindemann, June 3, 1935, Cherwell-PS mss, folder 13, III; Szilard, "Reminiscences," 101–:.

15. Szilard, "Reminiscences," 97. For additional sketches of Szilard, see Edward Shils, "Leo Szilard, a Memoir," *Encounter*, 23 (December 1964), 35–41; John McClaughry, "The Voice of the Dolphins," *The Progressive*, 29 (April 1965), 26–9; Eugene Rabinowitch, editorial in *Bulletin of the Atomic Scientists*, 20 (October 1964), 16–20; Alice Kimball Smith, "The Elusive Dr. Szilard," *Harper's Magazine*, 221 (July 1960), 77–86; "I'm Looking for a Market for Wisdom," *Life*, 51 (September 1, 1961), 75–6; *Time*, 79 (March 23, 1962), 43–4.

16. Smith, "The Elusive Dr. Szilard," 77.

17. Warren O. Hagstrom, *The Scientific Community* (New York, 1965), chap. I, "Social Control in Science."

18. Confidential letter to author, February 23, 1967.

19. Szilard to F. Joliot, February 2, 1939, Met. Lab. files, doc. no. NDN55352.

20. Leo Szilard, "We Turned the Switch," *The Nation*, 161 (December 22, 1945), 718.

21. Szilard, and W. H. Zinn to Pegram, "Agreement about Secrecy," n.d.; Wigner to P. Dirac, March 30, 1939, and Weisskopf to P. M. S. Blackett, March 1939, Met. Lab. files, doc. no. NDN55352.

22. H. von Halban, Jr., F. Joliot, and L. Kowarski, "Liberation of Neutrons in the Nuclear Explosion of Uranium," *Nature*, 143 (March 18, 1939), 470–2. Copies of all telegrams and letters exchanged between Szilard *et al.* and Joliot's laboratory can be found in OSRD, S-1 files, 11-24-41, Report to President by NAS folder.

23. Szilard, "Collapse of Secrecy," Met. Lab. mss NDN55352.

24. Szilard, "Reminiscences," 108–10.

25. Zinn to Pegram, n.d., Met. Lab. files, doc. no. NDN55352.

26. Wigner to Szilard, April 17, 1939, Met. Lab. files, doc. no. NDN55352.

27. Szilard, "Reminiscences," 108–13; Hewlett and Anderson, *The New World*, 14–17; see also Pegram to Admiral Hooper, March 16, 1939,

Fermi mss, box 9, folder 7, and Szilard, "Second Approach to the Navy," Met. Lab. files, doc. no. NDN55352.

28. Quoted in Ronald W. Clark, *Einstein: The Life and Times* (New York, 1971), 554.

29. Einstein to Roosevelt, August 2, 1939, Roosevelt-PSF, Confidential File, Alexander Sachs folder. This file also contains a letter from Sachs to Roosevelt, October 11, 1939, a memorandum from Szilard that Sachs used in discussing the issue with the President, a letter to Einstein from Roosevelt's personal secretary thanking the scientist for his letter, and reprints of two articles from *The Physical Review*: H. L. Anderson, E. Fermi, and Leo Szilard, "Neutron Production and Absorption in Uranium" (August 1, 1939) and Leo Szilard and Walter H. Zinn, "Interaction of Slow Neutrons with Uranium" (April 15, 1939). See also Sachs's testimony before the U.S. Senate Special Committee on Atomic Energy (hereafter "Atomic Energy Hearings"), 79th Cong., 1st Sess., November 27, 1945, 2–29 and the appendix, 553–58.

30. Sachs, "Atomic Energy Hearings," 9.

31. Irving Stewart, *Organizing Scientific Research for War: The Administrative History of the Office of Scientific Research and Development* (Boston, 1948), 9.

32. The other members of the committee included: Colonel K. R. Adamson, Army Ordnance Department, and Commander G. C. Hoover, Navy Bureau of Ordnance. See also Hewlett and Anderson, *The New World*, 19; Szilard, "Reminiscences," 114.

33. Karl T. Compton to Bush, March 17, 1941, AEC doc. no. 292.

34. Szilard to Briggs, October 26, 1939, Report to President by NAS folder, and Szilard, "Memorandum, Meeting of Oct. 21, 1939, Washington, D.C." in Dr. Szilard's Reports, S-61 folder, OSRD, S-1 files; see also Szilard to John Tate, February 6 and 14, 1940, Met. Lab. files, doc. no. NDN55352; Szilard, "Reminiscences," 115–17.

35. Szilard, "Reminiscences," 118–20 and 119, *n.* 36.

36. Roosevelt to Sachs, April 5, 1940, Met. Lab. files, doc. no. NDN-55352.

37. Szilard, "Reminiscences," 114.

38. *Ibid.*, 119. After Sachs exploded in anger, Briggs reversed his decision.

39. *Ibid.*, 121.

40. Stewart, *Organizing Scientific Research*, 7; James Phinney Baxter, II, *Scientists Against Time* (Boston, 1946), 13–14; Bush to Briggs, June 18, 1940, OSRD, S-1 files, NDRC–Bush, Dr. V. folder.

41. Baxter, *Scientists Against Time*, 13; "The Great Science Debate," *Fortune*, 33 (June 1946), 119–20, 236; *Newsweek*, 27 (March 11, 1946), 58–9; S. J. Woolf, "Chief of Staff on the Science Front," *The New York Times Magazine*, January 23, 1944, 16; J. D. Ratcliff, "War Brains," *Collier's*, 109 (January 17, 1942), 28; *Current Biography*, 1947, 80–2.

42. Hewlett and Anderson, *The New World*, 24–5.

43. Roosevelt to Bush, June 15, 1940, Hopkins mss, A-bomb folder; Stewart, *Organizing Scientific Research*, 8.
44. *Ibid.*, 18.
45. Roosevelt to Briggs, June 15, 1940, Roosevelt-OF, file no. 4010; Stewart, *Organizing Scientific Research*, 7–9; Baxter, *Scientists Against Time*, 14–16; Sherwood, *Roosevelt and Hopkins*, 153–4.
46. Sachs, "Atomic Energy Hearings," 15–21; for documents associated with Sachs's activities see OSRD, S-1 mss, Sachs–Nuclear Fission folder; 11-24-41 Report to President by NAS folder and Szilard, Leo folder.
47. Stewart, *Organizing Scientific Research*, 9–12.
48. Hewlett and Anderson, *The New World*, 27, 37–40, 43. For reports to Bush see Bush-Conant files, S-1 OSRD Research Program Exec. Comm., Planning Committee no. 2 folder and S-1 Historical file, Section A folder.
49. Gowing, *Britain and Atomic Energy*, 37.
50. *Ibid.*
51. *Ibid.*, 40–1, and Appendix 1, "The Frisch-Peierls Memorandum," 389–93.
52. *Ibid.*, Appendix 2, "The Maud Reports," 394–436; Hewlett and Anderson, *The New World*, 42–4.
53. Gowing, *Britain and Atomic Energy*, 43–4.
54. Hewlett and Anderson, *The New World*, 26–7.
55. Bush to Roosevelt, July 16, 1941, Roosevelt-PSF.
56. Bush to Conant, October 9, 1941, Bush-Conant files, S-1 Historical file, Section B folder.
57. Isaiah Bowman to W. W. Campbell, July 27, 1933, Millikan mss, box 6, National Research Council folder.
58. Roosevelt to Bush, March 11, 1942, Roosevelt-PSF, Bush folder.
59. Bush to Conant, December 16, 1941, Bush-Conant files, S-1 Historical file, Section B folder; Bush to Roosevelt, June 19, 1942, Roosevelt-PSF, Safe file; Bush to Sir John Anderson, September 1, 1942, AEC doc. no. 51; Conant to Bush, October 26, 1942, AEC doc. no. 295.
60. Roosevelt to Churchill, October 11, 1941, Roosevelt-MR, box 1.
61. Bush to Roosevelt, March 9, 1942, Bush-Conant files, S-1 Historical file, Section B folder.
62. Roosevelt to Bush, March 11, 1942, Roosevelt-PSF, Bush folder.

CHAPTER 2

1. Baxter, *Scientists Against Time*, 3.
2. Robert P. Patterson to Stimson, February 25, 1945, MED, H-B files, box 147, folder no. 2.
3. Stimson and Bundy, *On Active Service*, 612–13.
4. *Ibid.*, 468–9 (italics added).
5. Leslie R. Groves, *Now It Can Be Told* (New York, 1962), chap. 1; Hewlett and Anderson, *The New World*, chaps. 2 and 3.

6. James B. Conant, *My Several Lives: Memoirs of a Social Inventor* (New York, 1970), 288.

7. Vannevar Bush, *Modern Arms and Free Men* (New York, 1949), 6.

8. Bush to Bundy, January 26, 1942, Bush mss, box 17, folder 389.

9. Bush to Hopkins, March 31, 1943, Hopkins mss, A-bomb folder. To Rear Admiral Julius Furer, coordinator of Naval Research, Bush frequently expressed his displeasure with the Navy Department's attitude toward scientists; see Furer diary, March 12, 21, 1942; April 9, 1942; January 15, 1944; May 24, 1944; October 12, 1944; May 29, 1945. I wish to thank Professor Daniel Kevles for his generosity in making excerpts from this diary available to me.

10. Vincent Davis, *Postwar Defense Policy and the United States Navy, 1943–1946* (Chapel Hill, 1962), 338, *n.* 112.

11. Stimson diaries: August 27, 1940; October 2, 1940; April 28, 1941; September 1, 1942; October 28, 1942; November 11, 1942; March 22, 1944.

12. Davis, *Postwar Defense Policy*, 338, *n.* 112.

13. Furer diary, April 9, 1943.

14. Hewlett and Anderson, *The New World*, 81–3.

15. Conant, *My Several Lives*, 246.

16. Compton to Wallace, June 23, 1942, Roosevelt-PSF, Bush folder; Bush sent his reply directly to Roosevelt, June 24, 1942, Roosevelt-PSF, Bush folder.

17. Oppenheimer to J. Manley, July 14, 1942; to M. McKibben, June 10, 1942, to E. Segrè, June 10, 1942, Oppenheimer mss, boxes 49 and 50.

18. Hewlett and Anderson, *The New World*, 179.

19. Bush to Roosevelt, December 16, 1942, AEC doc. no. 121.

20. Szilard to Bush, December 13, 1943, OSRD, S-1 files, Szilard folder.

21. Hewlett and Anderson, *The New World*, 71–83, 119, 174, 229–30; Groves, *Now It Can Be Told*, 3–5.

22. Teller and Bethe to Oppenheimer, August 21, 1943, Oppenheimer mss, box 20, Bethe folder.

23. E. Creutz, September 18, 1942, Szilard mss, bbs-40A; see also Szilard to Bush, May 26, 1942; Conant to Bush, May 29, 1942, and Briggs to Bush, June 9, 1942, in OSRD, S-1 files, Szilard folder.

24. A. Hunter Dupree, *Science in the Federal Government: A History of Policies and Activities to 1940* (New York, 1957), chaps. 17 and 18; Margaret Smith Stahl, "Splits and Schisms, Nuclear and Social" (unpublished doctoral dissertation, University of Wisconsin, 1946), 168–73. This sociological study investigates the respective reactions of "pure" and "applied" scientists to the development of the atomic bomb.

25. Teller and Bethe to Oppenheimer, August 21, 1943, Oppenheimer mss, box 20, Bethe folder.

26. Wigner, September 17, 1942, Szilard mss, bbs-40A.

27. Szilard to Compton, June 1, 1942; Compton to Conant, June 2, 1942, Bush-Conant files, Espionage folder. Other interesting plans are in this folder.

28. Morrison to S. Allison, September 23, 1943, doc. no. DCV55078; Allison to Groves, October 11, 1943, doc. no. DCV55079; A. H. Compton to A. V. Peterson, June 2, 1943, doc. no. DCV55077; Met. Lab. files.

29. V. Weisskopf to Oppenheimer, October 28, 1942, Oppenheimer mss, box 77, Weisskopf folder. Already aware of Heisenberg's plans, Oppenheimer thanked Weisskopf for the information and promised to submit the letter to proper authorities. Oppenheimer to Weisskopf, October 29, 1942. On the same subject, see Teller to A. H. Compton, October 16, 1942, and Oppenheimer to Bush, July 15, 1942, Oppenheimer mss, box 23, Bush folder.

30. Hewlett and Anderson, *The New World*, 22, 112.

31. Conant to Bush, October 26, 1942, AEC doc. no. 295.

32. Hewlett and Anderson, *The New World*, 198.

33. Unsigned copy of letter to Roosevelt from Met. Lab. scientists, July 29, 1943. Oppenheimer mss, box 51, Morrison folder.

34. Morrison to Oppenheimer, July 29, 1943, *ibid.*

35. Hewlett and Anderson, *The New World*, 198–204.

36. Conant and Groves to Oppenheimer, February 25, 1943, AEC doc. no. 66; see also Hewlett and Anderson, *The New World*, 231.

37. Stewart, *Organizing Scientific Research*, chap. 9.

38. Oppenheimer's view reported in Conant to Bush, November 20, 1942, Bush-Conant files, Oppenheimer, June 1942–February 1943 folder.

39. *Ibid.*

40. Oppenheimer to Conant, February 1, 1943 (italics added), AEC doc. no. 296.

41. Conant and Groves to Oppenheimer, February 25, 1943, AEC doc. no. 66.

42. Quoted in Oppenheimer to Rabi, February 26, 1943, Oppenheimer mss, box 59, Rabi folder. Rabi had apparently suggested this to Oppenheimer in a prior letter or conversation.

43. *Ibid.*

44. Oppenheimer to Conant, February 1, 1943, AEC doc. no. 296.

45. Groves, interview by John K. M. McCaffery, September 9, 1964, Oppenheimer tapes, no. 5355-22.

46. Stephane Groueff, *Manhattan Project: The Untold Story of the Making of the Atomic Bomb* (Boston, 1967), 235.

47. Bethe to Oppenheimer, March 3, 1943, box 20, Bethe folder, and Rabi to Oppenheimer, March 2, 1943, box 59, Rabi folder, Oppenheimer mss.

48. Groves, *Now It Can Be Told*, 4; Groueff, *Manhattan Project*, 3.

49. Abraham Pais *et al.*, *Oppenheimer* (New York, 1969), 8.

50. Alice Kimball Smith, *A Peril and a Hope: The Scientists' Movement in America, 1945–47* (Chicago, 1965); Donald A. Strickland, *Scientists in Politics: The Atomic Scientists Movement, 1945–46* (Lafayette, Ind., 1968); Robert Jungk, *Brighter Than a Thousand Suns: A Personal History of the Atomic Scientists* (New York, 1958).

51. McCaffery interview, Oppenheimer tapes, no. 5355-22.
52. Testimony of Leo Szilard, December 10, 1945, U.S. Congress, Senate, *Hearings on Atomic Energy*, 79th Cong., 1st Sess., part 2, 293.
53. Quoted in Nuell Pharr Davis, *Lawrence and Oppenheimer* (New York, 1968), 173-4.
54. Lamont-OHT, no. 2, 258.
55. McCaffery interview, Oppenheimer tapes, no. 5355-22.
56. *Ibid.*
57. Groves, *Now It Can Be Told*, 140.
58. For critiques of compartmentalization, see: Ramsey-OHT, 66-7; H. Urey to Conant, April 2, 1943, Lawrence mss, file 1015, no. 11; Wigner, "Brief History of Planning for W," January 7, 1944, Met. Lab. files, doc. no. DCV55212; Oppenheimer to Groves, October 4, 1943, OSRD, S-1 mss, Oppenheimer folder; "Report of Special Reviewing Committee on Los Alamos Project," May 10, 1943, OSRD, S-1 files, Los Alamos Review Committee folder; Cherwell to Churchill, July 25, 1944, Prem. 3/139-11A, 744.
59. Groves, *Now It Can Be Told*, 119.
60. Oppenheimer to Fermi, March 11, 1943, Oppenheimer mss, box 33, Fermi folder.
61. "Report of Special Reviewing Committee on Los Alamos Project," May 10, 1943, OSRD, S-1 files, Los Alamos Review Committee folder.
62. Cherwell to Churchill, July 25, 1944, Prem. 3/139-11A, 744.
63. Oppenheimer encouraged general discussions of the scientific problems. Hewlett and Anderson, *The New World*, 237-9 (italics added); see also Groves, testimony: *In the Matter of J. Robert Oppenheimer— Transcript of Hearing Before Personnel Security Board, Washington, D.C., April 12, 1954, to May 6, 1954* (Washington, D.C., 1954), 166 ff. (hereafter cited as *Oppenheimer Hearings*).
64. Testimony of Groves, *Oppenheimer Hearings*, 173.
65. *Ibid.*, 273-8.
66. *Ibid.*, 172.
67. *Ibid.*
68. Herbert Childs, *An American Genius: The Life of Ernest Orlando Lawrence* (New York, 1968), 354.
69. Groves to the District Engineer, United States Engineer Office, Manhattan District, Station F., July 20, 1943, in *Oppenheimer Hearings*, 170.

CHAPTER 3

1. Lord Lothian to Roosevelt, July 8, 1940, Annex No. 1, DHMP. For the responses of the departments of State, Navy, and War, see *ibid.*, Annexes Nos. 2a, b, c, and d.
2. For Anglo-American atomic energy cooperation prior to formal agreement, see Minutes of the War Cabinet Scientific Advisory Commit-

tee, March 4 and December 9, 1941, CAB 90/2; and September 16, 17, and 19, 1941, CAB 90/8. See also Conant, *My Several Lives*, 250–1; Gowing, *Britain and Atomic Energy*, 64–7; Hewlett and Anderson, *The New World*, 256–9.

3. Conant, *My Several Lives*, 276.

4. Marcus Lothrop, "A History of the Radiation Laboratory Activities in Berkeley," November 17, 1945, Lawrence mss; Karl T. Compton to Bush, March 17, 1941, AEC doc. no. 292; Hewlett and Anderson, *The New World*, 32–9.

5. Gowing, *Britain and Atomic Energy*, see 115–20 and app. 2 for the entire report; Hewlett and Anderson, *The New World*, 40–4.

6. Gowing, *Britain and Atomic Energy*, 73.

7. Roosevelt to Churchill, October 11, 1941, Roosevelt-MR.

8. Norman Brook, "Tube Alloys," November 27, 1941, Prem. 3/139-8A, 572. See also Hewlett and Anderson, *The New World*, 256–9, Gowing, *Britain and Atomic Energy*, 64–7; Conant, *My Several Lives*, chap. 20.

9. Conant, *My Several Lives*, chap. 22.

10. Bush to Anderson, April 20, 1942, AEC doc. no. 307.

11. Bush to Roosevelt, June 17, 1942, Bush-Conant mss, Reports to and Conferences with President folder.

12. Conant to Bush, "Some thoughts concerning the S-1 project," October 26, 1942, AEC doc. no. 295; see also AEC doc. no. 114, which appears to be another draft of this memo, OSRD, S-1 mss, 11-24-41 Report to President by NAS folder.

13. *Ibid.*

14. DHMP, 9. For source of Conant's suspicions, see also Conant to Bush, "International complications of the S-1 project," November 13, 1942, AEC doc. no. 310, and Hewlett and Anderson, *The New World*, 271.

15. Stimson memo, October 29, 1942, DHMP, Annex No. 5.

16. Conant to Bush, "U.S.-British Relations on S-1 Project," December 14, 1942, AEC doc. no. 149 (italics added).

17. *Ibid.*

18. "Excerpt from Report to the President by the Military Policy Committee, December 15, 1942, with Particular Reference to Recommendations Relating to Future Relations with the British and Canadians," DHMP, Annex No. 6.

19. Roosevelt to Bush, December 28, 1942, Roosevelt-PSF, Bush folder.

20. Conant, "Memorandum on the interchange with the British and Canadians on S-1," January 7, 1943, AEC doc. no. 152. A marginal note reads: "Discussed in detail with Gen. Groves and Mr. Akers [British representative] on Jan. 26, 1943 . . ." Informally, however, Akers had learned about the new policy some weeks earlier. Related documents can be found in Bush-Conant files, British, 1, 1942 folder and International Situation folder.

21. Churchill to Roosevelt, February 27, 1943 (1744Z), Hopkins mss, A-bomb folder.

22. Sherwood, *Roosevelt and Hopkins*, 704; Churchill to Roosevelt, April 1, 1943, Hopkins mss, A-bomb folder.

23. "Excerpt from Report to the President by the MPC," December 15, 1942, 3, DHMP, Annex No. 6.

24. *Ibid.*, 2.

25. Urey to Conant, April 2, 1943, Lawrence mss, file 1015 no. 1, box 1. Conant's critique and Urey's response are located in the same folder.

26. Bush to Roosevelt, December 16, 1942, AEC doc. no. 121 (italics added).

27. *Ibid.*

28. Anderson to Churchill, January 11, 1943, Prem. 3/139-8A, 562–3.

29. "Minute from Sir John Anderson to Prime Minister," July 30, 1942 in Gowing, *Britain and Atomic Energy*, Appendix no. 3.

30. Roosevelt's attitude is reflected in Bush to Conant, October 9, 1941, AEC doc. no. 17, and Bush to Conant, September 23, 1944, AEC doc. no. 186. For Roosevelt's answer to Stimson, see Stimson memo, October 29, 1942, DHMP, Annex No. 5.

31. Churchill to Roosevelt, February 27, 1943 (1744Z), Hopkins mss, A-bomb folder.

32. Roosevelt to Bush, July 11, 1942, Roosevelt-PSF, Safe file.

33. Sherwood, *Roosevelt and Hopkins*, 202.

34. Churchill to Roosevelt, February 27, 1943 (1744Z), Hopkins mss, A-bomb folder.

35. Churchill to Roosevelt, February 27, 1943 (1807Z), *ibid.*

36. Conant to Bush, "Some thoughts concerning the correspondence between the President and the Prime Minister on S-1" (hereafter cited as "Some thoughts"), March 25, 1943, Hopkins mss, A-bomb folder. (Italics added.)

37. Conant to Bush, December 15, 1942, Bush-Conant files, Reports, White House folder.

38. Conant to Bush, "Some thoughts," March 25, 1943, Hopkins mss, A-bomb folder.

39. Quoted in J. W. Pickersgill, *The Mackenzie King Record, 1939–1944*, 1 (Chicago, 1960), 532.

40. Conant to Bush, "Some thoughts," March 25, 1943, Hopkins mss, A-bomb folder.

41. Bush to Hopkins, "Interchange on S-1," March 31, 1943, Hopkins mss, A-bomb folder.

42. *Ibid.*

43. Cherwell to Churchill, "Notes on Tube Alloys," n.d., Prem. 3/139-8A, 494.

44. Anderson to Churchill, April 29, 1943, Prem. 3/139-8A, 500.

45. Churchill to Anderson, April 15, 1943, Prem. 3/139-8A, 503.

46. Quoted in William L. Neumann, *After Victory: Churchill, Roosevelt, Stalin and the Making of the Peace* (New York, 1967), 89.

47. Harvey Bundy, "Memorandum of Meeting at 10 Downing Street," July 23, 1943, DHMP, Annex No. 11.

48. Bush, "Memorandum of Conference with Mr. Harry Hopkins and Lord Cherwell at the White House, May 25, 1943," Hopkins mss, A-bomb folder.

49. Quoted in Pickersgill, *Mackenzie King*, 532.

50. Anderson to Churchill, July 21, 1943, Prem. 3/139-8A, 454–55.

51. Churchill to Anderson, May 26, 1943, Prem. 3/139-8A, 491; Winston S. Churchill, *The Hinge of Fate* (New York, Bantam ed., 1962), 703.

52. Roosevelt to Churchill, July 26, 1943, Hopkins mss, A-bomb folder; FRUS, *Conferences at Washington and Quebec*, 1943 (Washington, 1970), 636.

53. Roosevelt to Bush, July 20, 1943, Hopkins mss, A-bomb folder.

54. Gowing, *Britain and Atomic Energy*, app. 4. For discussion of the Quebec Conference, see Herbert Feis, *Churchill, Roosevelt, Stalin: The War They Waged and the Peace They Sought* (Princeton, 1967), 149–51.

55. Hewlett and Anderson, *The New World*, 280.

56. Bush, "Memorandum of Conference with the President," June 24, 1943, AEC doc. no. 133.

57. Bush, "Memorandum for file," August 4, 1943, AEC doc. no. 168.

58. DHMP, 15.

59. Bush to Conant, September 26, 1944, Bush-Conant file, S-1 Interim Committee Postwar folder; see also British Liaison-Special folder. For British documents, see Prem. 3/139-8A, 311 and 313–21.

60. Churchill, July 18, 1943, Prem. 3/139-8A, 479.

61. Hewlett and Anderson, *The New World*, 280. The reference is to the cross-Channel invasion vehemently opposed by Churchill.

62. FRUS, 1941, 1 (Washington, 1958), 363, 365–66.

63. Roosevelt, as quoted in "Mr. Sweetser's Notes," May 29, 1942, Sweetser mss, box 39, FDR Interview folder.

64. For Roosevelt's remarks to Molotov, see FRUS, 1942, 3 (Washington, 1961), 573; to Eichelberger, see "President's Conversation at Luncheon with G.G.T. [Grace G. Tully] and S.I.R. [Samuel I. Rosenman], Nov. 13, 1942," in Elliot Roosevelt, ed., *F.D.R., His Personal Letters, 1928–1945*, 4 (New York, 1950), 1366–7; to Stalin see FRUS, *Conference at Cairo and Teheran*, 1943 (Washington, 1961), 530–2.

65. Robert A. Divine, *Roosevelt and World War II* (Baltimore, 1970), 58. Also see Willard Range, *Franklin D. Roosevelt's World Order* (Athens, Ga., 1959), and Roland Stromberg, *Collective Security and American Foreign Policy: From the League of Nations to NATO* (New York, 1963).

CHAPTER 4

1. Bush to Conant, September 25, 1944, AEC doc. no. 280.
2. Neumann, *After Victory*, 187; see also John L. Gaddis, *The United States and the Origins of the Cold War, 1941–1947* (New York, 1972), 28, 29, 150, 156; James M. Burns, *Roosevelt: The Soldier of Freedom 1940–1945* (New York, 1970), 359, 516, 528.
3. Smith, *A Peril and a Hope*, 14–24; Hewlett and Anderson, *The New World*, 324–5.
4. Quoted in Rud Nielson, "Niels Bohr," *Physics Today*, 16 (November 1963), 29.
5. J. Robert Oppenheimer, "Niels Bohr and Atomic Weapons," *The New York Review of Books*, 3 (December 17, 1966), 7.
6. Bohr memo, May 8, 1945; Bohr to Roosevelt, July 3, 1944, Oppenheimer mss, box 34, Frankfurter-Bohr folder. An edited version of the memo to Roosevelt is printed in Bohr's *Open Letter to the United Nations* (Copenhagen, 1950). See also Frankfurter mss, box 45, Bohr folder. Frankfurter had the complete file of Bohr's wartime correspondence with Roosevelt, but gave it to Oppenheimer to use for his Pegram Lectures: "Three Lectures on Niels Bohr and His Times" (Brookhaven National Laboratory, August 1963).
7. John A. Wheeler, "Niels Bohr and Nuclear Physics," *Physics Today*, 16 (November, 1963), 37–45.
8. Bohr, *Open Letter*, 13; Nielson, "Niels Bohr," 27.
9. A. Bohr, "The War Years and the Prospects Raised by Atomic Bombs," in *Niels Bohr*, Stefan Rozental, ed. (New York, 1967), 190; Weisskopf, "Niels Bohr," *Physics Today*, 16 (October 1963), 58.
10. S. Rozental, "The Forties and Fifties," in *Niels Bohr*, Rozental, ed., 153.
11. Bohr to Roosevelt, March 24, 1945; Bohr to Roosevelt, July 3, 1944, Oppenheimer mss, box 34, Frankfurter-Bohr folder.
12. Oppenheimer, "Niels Bohr and Atomic Weapons," 8.
13. Bohr to Roosevelt, July 3, 1944, Oppenheimer mss, box 34, Frankfurter-Bohr folder.
14. *Ibid.*; Bohr, *Open Letter, passim*.
15. Bohr memo, May 8, 1945, summarizing his communications with Roosevelt, Oppenheimer mss, box 34, Frankfurter-Bohr folder.
16. Hewlett and Anderson, *The New World*, chapter 15; Margaret L. Coit, *Mr. Baruch* (Cambridge, 1957), chapter 20; Bernard M. Baruch, *Baruch: The Public Years* (New York, 1960), chapter 19; Barton J. Bernstein, "The Quest for Security: American Foreign Policy and International Control of Atomic Energy, 1942–1946," *The Journal of American History*, LX, No. 4 (March 1974), 1003–44.
17. Bohr to Roosevelt, July 3, 1944, Oppenheimer mss, box 34, Frankfurter-Bohr folder.

18. Niels Bohr, "Notes Concerning Scientific Cooperation with the USSR. Written in Connection with Memorandum of July 3, 1944," September 30, 1944, Oppenheimer mss, box 34, Frankfurter-Bohr folder.

19. The account of Bohr's activities given in the text is drawn from the correspondence and documents collected by Felix Frankfurter. See, especially, Frankfurter to Lord Halifax, April 18, 1945, Oppenheimer mss, box 34, Frankfurter-Bohr folder.

20. Regarding Groves, see Anderson to Churchill, July 26, 1943, Prem. 3/139-8A, 422–4.

21. Frankfurter to Halifax, April 18, 1945, Oppenheimer mss, box 34, Frankfurter-Bohr folder.

22. A. Bohr, "The War Years," 194.

23. Frankfurter to Halifax, April 18, 1945, Oppenheimer mss, box 34, Frankfurter-Bohr folder.

24. Stimson diaries, December 27, 1942. The British were not obligated to tell the Russians about the bomb under the terms of this agreement.

25. William H. McNeill, *America, Britain and Russia: Their Cooperation and Conflict, 1941–1946* (London, 1953), 313–37.

26. *Ibid.*, 348–75; Feis, *Churchill, Roosevelt, Stalin*, 237–79.

27. Groves and Lansdale testimony, *Oppenheimer Hearings*, 163–80, 258–81.

28. Stimson diaries, September 9, 1943; other sources documenting the Top Policy Group's knowledge that the Soviets were aware of work on the atomic bomb in the U.S. include: Groves to Bundy, February 6, 1945, MED, H-B files, box 148, folder 27; Anderson to Churchill, March 7, 1945, Prem. 3/139-11A, 831–32; Bush to Feis, February 29, 1960, Feis mss, box 11, "Correspondence about atomic bomb book" folder.

29. Burns, *Roosevelt: Soldier of Freedom*, 136.

30. Bush, "Memorandum of Conference with the President," September 22, 1944, AEC doc. no. 185. Selected portions of this memo have been reprinted in FRUS, *The Conference at Quebec*, 1944 (Washington, 1972). See especially 492 *n.*, but also see 296.

31. Stimson diaries, March 3, and May 17, April 8, May 22, and June 1, June 9, 1944.

32. Diane Shaver Clemens, *Yalta* (New York, 1970).

33. "Agreement and Declaration of Trust," June 13, 1944, DHMP, Annex No. 22a.

34. Hewlett and Anderson, *The New World*, 285–6

35. Bush, "Memoranda for Dr. Conant," February 15, 1944, Bush-Conant mss, Reports to and Conferences with the President folder.

36. A. Bohr, "The War Years," 30.

37. Nielson, "Niels Bohr," 296 (italics added).

38. Frankfurter to Halifax, April 18, 1945, Oppenheimer mss, Frankfurter-Bohr folder.

39. Anderson to Churchill, March 21 and April 27, 1944, Prem. 3/139-2, 140–3 and 126–7.

40. Cherwell to Churchill, May 10, 1944; Smuts to Churchill, June 15, 1944, Prem. 3/139-11A, 769–70 and 757–60. See also Gowing, *Britain and Atomic Energy*, 346–56.

41. Memorandum discussing Bohr's relationship to Kapitsa, June 28, 1944, is unsigned, but it is likely that Frankfurter wrote it as it is on stationery with a U.S. Government watermark. It appears with Frankfurter's other papers (as well as Bohr's) in Oppenheimer mss, box 34, Frankfurter-Bohr folder. In same file, see also "Correspondence Between Kapitsa and Bohr," May 2, 1945.

42. "Report, Written immediately after the conversation took place between Bohr and Counsellor Zinchenko at Soviet Embassy in London on April 20, 1944 at 5 p.m.," *ibid.*

43. Bohr to Roosevelt, July 3, 1944, *ibid.*

44. By February 1943 the Soviet Union had already begun work on the development of a "uranium bomb," according to I. N. Golovin in his biography of a leading Soviet scientist, *I. V. Kurchatov* (Moscow, 1967, in Russian); see review by Arnold Kramish, *Science*, 157 (August 25, 1967), 912–13.

45. Gowing, *Britain and Atomic Energy*, 355. See also Bohr to Churchill, May 22, 1944, Oppenheimer mss, box 34, Frankfurter-Bohr folder.

46. Churchill to A. Eden, March 25, 1945, Prem. 3/139-6, 243–5.

47. Bohr to Roosevelt, July 3, 1944, Oppenheimer mss, box 34, Frankfurter-Bohr folder.

48. A. Bohr, "The War Years," 197–9. Bohr sent a letter to Roosevelt on September 7, 1944, Roosevelt-OF, file 2240.

49. The complete text of the *aide-mémoire* is reprinted in Appendix C of the present work.

50. Churchill to Cherwell, September 20, 1944, Prem. 3/139-8A, 298–9.

51. Cherwell to Churchill, September 12, 1944, Prem. 3/139-8A, 309.

52. Conant to Bush, "Some thoughts concerning the correspondence between the President and the Prime Minister on S-1," March 25, 1943, Hopkins mss, A-bomb folder. See chap. 3 above.

53. Churchill to Cherwell, September 21, 1944, Prem. 3/139-8A, 305 (italics added).

54. Anderson to Churchill, March 21, 1944, Prem. 3/139-2, 140–3.

55. *Ibid.*

56. Herbert Feis mentions it in *The Atomic Bomb and the End of World War II* (Princeton, 1966), 33–4. He does not, however, draw out its full implications. See also Gaddis, *U.S. and Cold War*, 87.

57. C. K. Berryman, December 30, 1943, Washington (D.C.) *Star*; reprinted in Burns, *Roosevelt: Soldier of Freedom*, 423.

58. Roosevelt to Secretary of State, September 29, 1944, State Department Records, World War Two Conferences, Box 6, [H. Freeman] Matthews files, Germany Treatment folder.

59. Cherwell, "Memorandum of a conversation at the White House between Lord Cherwell and Mr. Harry Hopkins," October 3, 1944, Cherwell-OF, OFF 23.2, box 23.

60. Bush to Conant, September 25, 1944, AEC doc. no. 280.

CHAPTER 5

1. Bush to Conant, September 25, 1944, AEC doc. no. 280.
2. Percy W. Bridgman, *Reflections of a Physicist* (New York, 1950), 265–6.
3. Speech at Los Alamos, November 2, 1945, Rush mss, box 1, No. 10.
4. Szilard to Bush, December 13, 1943, Bush-Conant file, Szilard folder.
5. Lamont-OHT, 258.
6. Conant to Bush, ca. January 1944, Bush-Conant file, Reports to and Conferences with the President folder.
7. Bush to Conant, "Conference with Dr. Szilard, March 6, 1944," dated March 9, 1944, *ibid.*
8. Conant to Bush, July 31, 1943, *ibid.*
9. Szilard to Bush, January 14, 1944, *ibid.* (italics added.)
10. Undersigned to A. H. Compton, November 6, 1944, OSRD, S-1 file, box 13, A. H. Compton folder.
11. *Ibid.*, marginal notations by A. H. Compton.
12. See attachments to doc. no. NDN-45338, Met. Lab. files.
13. Smith, *A Peril and A Hope*, 19–23.
14. *Ibid.*, see app. A for sections I, V, VI, and VII of the Jefferies report. A copy of the entire report is located in MED, H-B files, box 151, folder 59.
15. Smith, *A Peril and a Hope*, 22–3.
16. Bush to A. Compton, August 7, 1944, Bush-Conant files, Misc. S-1 JBC Material, April–August 1944 folder. See also Bush-Conant file, S-1 Interim Committee-Postwar folder.
17. Bush to Conant, April 17, 1944, AEC doc. no. 180 (italics added).
18. Conant to Bush, April 18(?), 1944, handwritten note attached to Bush to Conant, April 17, 1944, AEC doc. no. 180 (italics added). See also Conant to Bush, "Summary of Conversation between JBC, VB, and IS [James B. Conant, Vannevar Bush, and OSRD Deputy Director Irving Stewart] on proposed legislation covering S-1," September 15, 1944, AEC doc. no. 184. There is no mention of the Soviet Union in this memorandum, either.
19. Bush, "Memorandum of Conference," September 22, 1944, AEC doc. no. 185. Their ideas had changed little since April; see Bush and Conant to Stimson, September 14, 1944, AEC doc. no. 279. To follow the evolution of their thinking, see: Bush to Conant, April 17, 1944,

AEC doc. no. 180; Conant to Bush, July 27, 1944, AEC doc. no. 297; Stewart to Bush, August 25, 1944, AEC doc. no. 299.

20. Bush, "Memorandum of Conference," September 22, 1944, AEC doc. no. 185.

21. Bush to Conant, September 23, 1944, AEC doc. no. 186.

22. Bush to A. Compton, August 7, 1944, Bush-Conant file, Misc. S-1 JBC material, April–August 1944 folder.

23. Conant to Bush, July 27, 1944, AEC doc. no. 297.

24. Bush, "Memorandum of Conference," September 22, 1944, AEC doc. no. 185.

25. Bush to Conant, September 23, 1944, AEC doc. no. 186.

26. *Ibid.*

27. Hewlett and Anderson, *The New World*, 328.

28. Stimson diaries, September 25, 1944.

29. Bush and Conant to Stimson, September 30, 1944, AEC doc. no. 281.

30. *Ibid.*; see also Hewlett and Anderson, *The New World*, 328–9.

31. *Ibid.*

32. Stimson diaries, October 9, 1944.

33. Bush to Conant, February 13, 1945, AEC docs. nos. 197 and 198, Bush-Conant file, Bush-1945 DSM folder.

34. For concern in Washington regarding Soviet policies at this time, see Feis, *Churchill, Roosevelt and Stalin*, 378–89, 434–7.

35. *Ibid.*, 434–7.

36. Stimson diaries, October 23, 1944. See also Stimson and Bundy, *On Active Service*, 606–7; Churchill describes "October in Moscow" in his *The Second World War, VI: Triumph and Tragedy* (Boston, 1953), chap. 15.

37. Stimson diaries, October 23, 1944.

38. Bush, "Memorandum of Conference," December 8, 1944 as paraphrased in Hewlett and Anderson, *The New World*, 330–1; see also Bush, "Memorandum for Dr. Conant," December 13, 1944, AEC doc. no. 284, Bush-Conant file, S-1 Interim Comm.-Postwar folder.

39. Stimson and Bundy, *On Active Service*, 643.

40. Sachs to Baruch, June 1, 1946, Baruch-AEC mss, Miscellaneous, 1946–1949 folder. A popular myth exists that Roosevelt accepted Sachs's view and would have acted upon it. See Nat S. Finney, "How FDR Planned to Use the A-bomb," *Look*, 14 (March 14, 1950), 23–7.

41. Hewlett and Anderson, *The New World*, 331–3. The details of this interesting and complicated aspect of wartime atomic energy diplomacy may be traced through the following American manuscript sources: MED, H-B, box 148, folder 26, box 149, folder 36; MED-TS, box 10, folders A, 26A, 26B, 26F, 26G, 26J, 26L; Bush-Conant files, V. Bush folder. The British side of the story can be followed through documents found in the Prem. 3/139 series, 5, 6 and 11A.

42. Stimson diaries, December 30, 1944.

43. For a recounting of the feud between Roosevelt and de Gaulle, see Milton Viorst's *Hostile Allies: FDR and Charles de Gaulle* (New York, 1965).

44. Stimson diaries, December 31, 1944.

45. See Fletcher Knebel and Charles W. Bailey II, *No High Ground* (New York, 1960), for a dramatized retelling of the story of the bombing of Hiroshima by the 509th Composite Group, USAAC.

46. For a perceptive analysis of the diplomatic strategy that lay behind Hitler's counter-attack, see John Ehrman, *Grand Strategy: History of the Second World War*, VI (London, 1956), 64–9.

47. Stimson diaries, December 31, 1944.

48. *Stalin's Correspondence with Roosevelt and Truman, 1941–1945*, (New York, 1965), nos. 255, 182. This is Volume I of two volumes of correspondence issued by the Ministry of Foreign Affairs of the USSR (hereafter cited as *Stalin's Correspondence*, I, with msg. no.).

49. Stimson diaries, December 31, 1944.

50. Bush to Conant, February 13, 1945, AEC doc. no. 197; Bush to Conant, February 13, 1945, AEC doc. no. 198; Bush to Conant, February 13, 1945, AEC doc. no. 199 in Bush-Conant file, Bush-1945 DSM folder.

51. Stimson diaries, February 13, 1945.

52. "The substance of recommendations which will be made by Major General Groves," January 20, 1945, MED-TS file, box 10, folder 26G.

53. Bundy, "Problems with Respect to the French," January 19, 1945, MED, H-B file, box 149, folder 36.

54. Churchill to A. Eden, March 25, 1945, Prem. 3/139-6, 248–50. This document is a draft. The references cited of the conversation with Roosevelt, Churchill's remarks about de Gaulle and atomic bombs, and the sentence beginning, "Even six months . . ." were removed from the memo Eden received; see Prem. 3/139-6, 243–5.

55. Sherwood, *Roosevelt and Hopkins*, 869–70; Feis, *Churchill, Roosevelt, Stalin*, 557–8; Burns, *Roosevelt*, 579.

56. Stimson diaries, February 15, 1944.

57. Hewlett and Anderson, *The New World*, 338.

58. Stimson diaries, March 5, 1945.

59. *Ibid.*, March 8, 1945.

60. *Ibid.*, March 15, 1945.

61. *Ibid.*, April 2, 1945; Forrestal diaries, April 2, 1945; see also Walter Millis, ed., *The Forrestal Diaries* (New York, 1951), 38.

62. *Ibid.*; Feis, *Churchill, Roosevelt, Stalin*, 583–95; Churchill, *Triumph and Tragedy*, 440–54; McNeill, *America, Britain, and Russia*, 569–73.

63. Stimson diaries, April 2, 1945.

64. *Ibid.*, April 3, 1945 (italics added).

65. *Ibid.*, summary entry for April 6–11, 1945.

CHAPTER 6

1. Field Marshal Wilson to Anderson, April 30, 1945, Prem. 3/139-11A, 807; Field Marshal Wilson to Stimson, June 20, 1945, MED, H-B, box 149, folder 37; see also Anderson to Churchill, July 16, 1945, Prem. 3/139-9, 652.
2. Bush to Conant, September 23, 1944, AEC doc. no. 185.
3. Hewlett and Anderson, *The New World*, 321.
4. *Oppenheimer Hearings*, 32–3.
5. Stimson diaries, April 13, 1945; see also Kenneth Glazier, Jr., "The Decision to Use Atomic Weapons Against Hiroshima and Nagasaki," *Public Policy*, 18 (Winter 1969).
6. Harry S. Truman, *Memoirs, Vol. I: Year of Decisions* (Garden City, N. Y., 1955), 1–4; see also "The White House Usher's Appointment Diary," (copy), Roosevelt-Truman mss; Alfred Steinberg, *The Man from Missouri: The Life and Times of Harry S. Truman* (New York, 1962), 228–35; Jonathan Daniels, *The Man of Independence* (Philadelphia, 1950), 256–7.
7. Truman, *Year of Decisions*, 6; Margaret Truman, *Harry S. Truman* (New York, 1973), 205.
8. Vaughan-OHT, 36; see also Smith diary, April 18, 1945.
9. Truman, *Year of Decisions*, 30–2. Mary Hedge Hinchey, "The Frustration of the New Deal Revival, 1944–1946" (unpublished doctoral dissertation, University of Missouri, 1965), 75–6. See Truman's personal appointment diary: Truman-PP, "Truman Personal, February, 1945."
10. Vaughan-OHT, 36.
11. Daniels, *Man of Independence*, 175–96; Steinberg, *Man from Missouri*, 110–21; Eugene F. Schmidtlein, "Truman the Senator" (unpublished doctoral dissertation, University of Missouri, 1962); Cabell Phillips, *The Truman Presidency: A History of a Triumphant Succession* (New York, 1966), 18–36.
12. *New York Times*, June 24, 1941, 7.
13. Quoted in Daniels, *Man of Independence*, 29.
14. *Ibid.*, 262.
15. Quoted in H. Wayne Morgan, "History and the Presidency: Harry S. Truman," *Phylon Quarterly*, 19 (July 1958), 169.
16. *Ibid.*, 165, 169.
17. Sherwood, *Roosevelt and Hopkins*, 881.
18. Truman, *Year of Decisions*, 44.
19. *Ibid.*, 19.
20. Barkley-OHT, 13, Shalett mss, box 1.
21. Truman, *Year of Decisions*, 9.
22. *Ibid.*, 10.
23. Stimson diaries, March 13, 1944; see also March 12, 1944, and June 17, 1945.

24. Elting E. Morison, *Turmoil and Tradition: A Study of the Life and Times of Henry L. Stimson* (New York, 1964), 54, 168.
25. Stimson diaries, April 23, 1945.
26. Truman, *Year of Decisions*, 15.
27. *Ibid.*, 23, 25.
28. Truman to Stalin, *Stalin's Correspondence*, I, msg. no. 293.
29. Churchill, *Triumph and Tragedy*, 486.
30. Truman, *Year of Decisions*, 37.
31. Feis, *Churchill, Roosevelt, Stalin*, 571–6.
32. Henry Kissinger, *The Necessity of Choice* (New York, 1962), 17.
33. Feis, *Churchill, Roosevelt, Stalin*, 595–6, 597–8.
34. *Ibid.*, 597–8.
35. Truman, *Year of Decisions*, 37.
36. *Ibid.*, 50.
37. *Ibid.*, 70–2.
38. *Ibid.*
39. *Ibid.* (italics added).
40. *Stalin's Correspondence*, I, Truman to Stalin, msg. no. 293.
41. Truman, *Year of Decisions*, 75–6.
42. Stimson diaries, April 23, 1945; Millis, ed., *Forrestal Diaries*, 48–51; Leahy, *I Was There*, 351.
43. Stimson diaries, April 2, 1945.
44. *Ibid.*, April 23, 1945.
45. Millis, ed., *Forrestal Diaries*, 49.
46. Leahy diaries, April 23, 1945; Leahy, *I Was There*, 352.
47. Truman, *Year of Decisions*, 80–2.
48. *Ibid.*
49. *Ibid.*, 85.
50. Truman to Stalin, April 17, 1945, *Stalin's Correspondence*, I, msg. no. 293; Truman, *Year of Decisions*, 86.
51. Leahy, *I Was There*, 349.
52. Stimson diaries, April 23 and April 2, 1945.
53. *Ibid.*, April 23, 1945.
54. Morison, *Turmoil and Tradition*, 169.
55. Truman, *Year of Decisions*, 85.
56. Stimson, "Memo Discussed with the President," April 25, 1945, MED, H-B file, box 151, folder 60.
57. Stimson diaries, April 25, 1945.
58. Hewlett and Anderson, *The New World*, 343.
59. Alperovitz, *Atomic Diplomacy*, 41–61, 270, *passim*.
60. Groves, "Report of Meeting with the President," April 25, 1945, MED-TS, Commanding General's file #24 tab D; Truman, *Year of Decisions*, 87. See also Harrison to Stimson, May 1, 1945, MED H-B, box 152, folder 69.
61. Truman, *Year of Decisions*, 87.

CHAPTER 7

1. Gaddis, *U.S. and the Cold War*, 227 n. 49, 229–30.
2. Joseph C. Grew, *Turbulent Era: A Record of Forty Years in the U.S. Diplomatic Service*, Vol. 2, ed. by Walter Johnson (London, 1953), 1444–6.
3. Thomas G. Paterson, "The Abortive American Loan to Russia and the Origins of the Cold War, 1943–1946," *Journal of American History*, 56 (June 1969), *passim*.
4. Bohr to Roosevelt, July 3, 1944, and Memo, March 25, 1945, Oppenheimer mss, box 34, Frankfurter-Bohr folder. See also Hewlett and Anderson, *The New World*, 344.
5. Hewlett and Anderson, *The New World*, 344.
6. *Ibid.*
7. Stimson diaries, May 1, 1945.
8. See MED, H-B file, box 156, folders 98 and 100 for records of the organization, administration and discussions of the Interim Committee.
9. Stimson to Conant, May 4, 1945, AEC doc. no. 286. Identical letters were sent to all nominees.
10. Stimson diaries, May 2, 1945.
11. *Ibid.* For an impressive analysis of Byrnes's role in the formulation of U.S. policy at this time, see Robert L. Messer, "The Making of a Cold Warrior: James F. Byrnes and American-Soviet Relations, 1945–1946" (unpublished doctoral dissertation, University of California, Berkeley, 1975).
12. Truman, *Year of Decisions*, 107–9.
13. Herbert Feis, *Between War and Peace: The Potsdam Conference* (Princeton, 1960), 85.
14. George F. Kennan, *Memoirs 1925–1950* (Boston, 1967), 82–4. Kennan has referred to Davies's willingness to "turn the other cheek in the face of various Soviet harassments," 83. Davies gained popular recognition as the author of *Mission to Moscow* (New York, 1941), which presented Stalin's purges in a favorable light. See also Alexander Werth, *Russia at War: 1941–1945* (New York, 1964), for a description of how the film *Mission to Moscow* was received in the Kremlin, 617.
15. Davies journals, April 23, 1945.
16. Edward Stettinius, Jr., *Roosevelt and the Russians: The Yalta Conference*, ed. by Walter Johnson (New York, 1949), 309.
17. *Stalin's Correspondence*, I, msg. nos. 299–305.
18. Entry in Davies journals of April 30, 1945, is the source for all following quotations and descriptions of this meeting unless otherwise cited.
19. For Vichy, see William L. Langer, *Our Vichy Gamble* (New York, 1947), Louis Gottschalk, "Our Vichy Fumble," *Journal of Mod-*

ern History, 20 (March 1948), 47–56; for Badoglio, see Feis, *Churchill, Roosevelt, Stalin*, 153–76; for Greece, see *ibid.*, 335, and William H. McNeill, *The Greek Dilemma: War and Aftermath* (London, 1947).

20. Davies journals, April 30, 1945.

21. For details of the loan dispute, see: Paterson, "The Abortive American Loan," 70–92.

22. Davies diaries, May 2, 1945.

23. *Stalin's Correspondence*, I, msg. no. 316.

24. Truman, *Year of Decisions*, 206.

25. Davies diaries, May 21, 1945.

26. Grew, *Turbulent Era*, II, 1485 *n*.

27. George C. Herring, Jr., *Aid to Russia, 1941–1946: Strategy, Diplomacy, the Origins of the Cold War* (New York, 1973), xiii, 196–200.

28. Feis, *Churchill, Roosevelt, Stalin*, 645–6; Thomas G. Paterson, *Soviet-American Confrontation: Postwar Reconstruction and the Origins of the Cold War* (Baltimore, 1973), 33–50.

29. As quoted in George C. Herring, Jr., "Lend-Lease to Russia and the Origins of the Cold War, 1944–1945," *Journal of American History*, 56 (June 1969), 195, *n.* 53.

30. Herring, *Aid to Russia*, 202.

31. Stettinius to Grew, May 9, 1945, FRUS, 1945, V, 998.

32. Herring, "Lend-Lease," 102–6.

33. *Ibid.*, 106; Stettinius, *Roosevelt and the Russians*, 318; Herring, *Aid to Russia*, 202–4.

34. Davies diaries, May 12, 1945.

35. *Ibid.*, May 13, 1945.

36. Davies diary and journal entries for May 13, 1945, are the sources for all following quotations and descriptions of this meeting unless otherwise cited.

37. Truman maintained a good opinion of Davies over the years—see Truman, *Year of Decisions*, 261. He personally invited Davies to Potsdam.

38. For an interpretation of the origins of the cold war based upon the consequences of this situation, see John Bagguley, "The World War and the Cold War," in David Horowitz, ed., *Containment and Revolution* (Boston, 1967), 76–124.

39. For another view, see: Adam B. Ulam, *Expansion and Coexistence: The History of Soviet Foreign Policy, 1917–1967* (New York, 1968), 334.

40. J. K. Zawodny, *Death in the Forest* (South Bend, 1962). Zawodny concludes that it was Soviet security forces that committed this atrocity in the spring of 1940. Ulam finds Zawodny's evidence on this matter convincing and accepts his conclusion.

41. On Standley's ambassadorship, see: William H. Standley and Arthur A. Ageton, *Admiral Ambassador to Russia* (Chicago, 1955).

42. As quoted in Davies journals, May 13, 1945. I was unable to locate the letter from Molotov to Davies.

43. For the view that Hopkins's mission was part of a "strategy of delayed showdown" based on the availability of the atomic bomb, see Alperovitz, *Atomic Diplomacy*, 41–61. For a detailed critique of this part of his "delayed showdown" thesis, see Martin J. Sherwin, "The Atomic Bomb, Scientists and American Diplomacy During the Second World War" (unpublished doctoral dissertation, University of California, Los Angeles, 1971), 252–69.

44. Truman, *Year of Decisions*, 257–8. In developing his "strategy of delayed showdown" argument, Alperovitz ignores Truman's initial request to Hopkins to go to Moscow; he also states that Truman was "extremely secretive about preparations," overlooking the fact that Truman checked with Hull, Byrnes, and the State Department after Hopkins agreed to go. *Atomic Diplomacy*, 70.

45. As quoted in Churchill, *Triumph and Tragedy*, 501.

46. FRUS, *Conference of Berlin*, I, 3, 10–11.

47. Leahy, *I Was There*, 367.

48. FRUS, *Conference of Berlin*, I, 12.

49. *Ibid.*, 4.

50. Hewlett and Anderson, *The New World*, 352; see also Herbert Druks, *Harry S. Truman and the Russians, 1945–1953* (New York, 1966), 40.

51. Stimson diaries, May 14, 1945.

52. *Ibid.*, May 2, 1945.

53. Stimson diaries, May 9, 1945.

54. R. Gordon Arneson, Secretary, "Notes of an Informal Meeting of the Interim Committee," May 9, 1945, MED, H-B, folder 100.

55. Stimson diaries, May 16, 1945.

56. Copy of Grew memo and Stimson's comments in Stimson diaries, May 13, 1945; see also Grew, *Turbulent Era*, II, 1455–6.

57. Stimson diaries, May 15, 1945; see also: War Department (Stimson) to Grew, May 21, 1945, in Grew, *Turbulent Era*, II, 1457–8.

58. Stimson diaries, May 15, 1945.

59. Stimson diaries, May 16, 1945.

CHAPTER 8

1. Stimson diaries, June 6, 1945; see also Davies diary, May 21, 1945.

2. *Ibid.*

3. Truman, *Year of Decisions*, 87.

4. Szilard, "Reminiscences," 126–8, and his "A Personal History of the Atomic Bomb," University of Chicago *Roundtable*, no. 601 (September 25, 1949), 14–15; Hewlett and Anderson, *The New World*, 355.

5. "The Franck Report," June 11, 1945, in Smith, *A Peril and a Hope*, app. B.

6. Stimson diaries, March 5, 1945.

7. Morison, *Turmoil and Tradition*, 167–8.

8. Bohr to Roosevelt, July 3, 1944, Oppenheimer mss, box 34, Frankfurter-Bohr folder.

9. Stimson diaries, April 6–11, 1945.

10. *Ibid.*, May 16, 1945.

11. *Ibid.*

12. *Ibid.*, dates as indicated in text (italics added).

13. William A. Williams, *The Tragedy of American Diplomacy* (New York, 1962), 248, 253–6; Alperovitz, "The Use of the Atomic Bomb," in his *Cold War Essays* (New York, 1970), 72.

14. Stimson, "The Decision to Use the Bomb," *Harper's Magazine* (February 1947), 107.

15. See page 30 of the present work.

16. Patterson, "Memo for General Styer," February 15, 1945, MED-TS, box 14, Groves misc. records folder 1.

17. Tolman to Conant, October 9, 1943, Bush-Conant files, S-1 MPC folder.

18. Truman to Stimson, March 10, 1944; see also: Patterson to Stimson, March 11, 1944, and Stimson to Truman, March 13, 1944, MED, H-B files, box 151, folder 62.

19. Byrnes to Roosevelt, March 3, 1945, MED, H-B file, box 147, folder 2.

20. Stimson to Swing, February 4, 1947, Stimson papers (italics added).

21. The details of the Spartanburg interview are from the following sources: Szilard, "Reminiscences," 122–8; Smith, *A Peril and a Hope*, 28–30 and her "Behind the Decision to Use the Atomic Bomb, Chicago 1944–1945," *Bulletin of the Atomic Scientists*, 14 (October 1958), 351–2; Szilard, "A Personal History," 14–15; James F. Byrnes, *All in One Lifetime* (New York, 1958), 284–5; see also Szilard to Byrnes, May 26, 1945, Byrnes mss, box 150, k folder (misfiled under Les Kilard, Personal 1944–1945 k).

22. Szilard, "Atomic Bombs and the Postwar Position of the United States in the World," *Bulletin of the Atomic Scientists*, 3 (December 1947), 351–2. A copy of this memo (dated April 15, 1945) without the security deletions can be found in Oppenheimer mss, box 70, Szilard folder.

23. Szilard to Roosevelt (March 25, 1945), app. II, Szilard, "Reminiscences," 146–8. Roosevelt died before Szilard could bring this memo to his attention.

24. For documents relating to Groves's investigation of the Spartanburg interview, see MED-TS box 7, folder 12, and box 14, folder 4.

25. Minutes of these meetings can be found in MED, H-B files, folder 100.

26. Stimson diaries, May 31, 1945.

27. Agenda, May 30, 1945, MED, H-B file, folder 100.

28. Stimson and Bundy, *On Active Service*, 617.

29. Unless otherwise noted, all references to the May 31 meeting are from the notes by the Interim Committee's secretary, Lt. R. Gordon Arnson, located in MED, H-B files, folder 100 (italics added).

30. Stimson diaries, May 31, 1945.

31. Lawrence to Conant, May 31, 1944, Bush-Conant files, S-1 Historical Material folder.

32. Arthur H. Compton, *Atomic Quest: A Personal Narrative* (New York, 1956), 238.

33. Lawrence to Karl Darrow, August 17, 1945; also see Darrow to Lawrence August 9, 1945, Lawrence mss, file 1015, box 1, folder 27.

34. Compton, *Atomic Quest*, 238–9.

35. Lawrence to Darrow, August 17, 1945.

36. Compton, *Atomic Quest*, 238–9.

37. Stimson diaries, May 31, 1945.

38. Szilard, "Reminiscences," 128.

39. Smith, *A Peril and a Hope*, 43–4.

40. For a copy of the report see *ibid.*, app. B, 560–72 (italics added).

41. Szilard, "Reminiscences," 129.

42. Compton, *Atomic Quest*, 236 (italics added).

43. Conant to Grenville Clark, November 8, 1945, Bush mss, box 27, Conant folder.

44. Stimson, "The Bomb and the Opportunity," *Harper's Magazine*, 192 (March 1946), 204.

45. Oppenheimer, "The Atomic Bomb as a Great Force for Peace," *The New York Times Magazine* (June 9, 1946), 60.

46. Compton, *Atomic Quest*, 239–40.

47. Quoted in Stimson, "The Decision to Use the Atomic Bomb," 101. See Appendix M for complete document.

48. *Ibid.*

49. Arneson, "Notes of the Interim Committee Meeting," June 21, 1945; see also Arneson to Harrison, June 25, 1945, MED, H-B files, folder 100.

50. Bush and Conant to Harrison, June 22, 1945, Bush-Conant files, S-1 Interim Committee-Postwar folder.

51. Arneson, "Notes of the Interim Committee Meeting," June 21, 1945, MED, H-B files, folder 100.

52. Bard, "Memorandum on Use of S-1 Bomb," June 27, 1945; see also Harrison to Stimson, June 28, 1945; Harrison to Stimson, June 26, 1945, MED, H-B files, box 154, folder 77; and Smith, *A Peril and a Hope*, 52–3.

53. Smith, "Behind the Decision to Use the Atomic Bomb," 303–5.

54. Szilard to Oppenheimer, July 10, 1945, Oppenheimer mss, box 70, Szilard folder.

55. Teller to Szilard, July 2, 1945, Oppenheimer mss, box 71, Teller folder (italics added).

CHAPTER 9

1. Pages 117–18 of the present work.
2. Stimson and Bundy, *On Active Service*, 637–8.
3. Truman, *Year of Decisions*, 421.
4. The most comprehensive published records of the conference are FRUS, *Conference of Berlin*, I and II, and The Teheran, Yalta, and Potsdam Conferences, Documents (Moscow, 1969). The British records are located among the War Cabinet files (CAB 99), Public Record Office, London. Interpretive studies include: Alperovitz, *Atomic Diplomacy*, 127–87; Winston A. Churchill, *Triumph and Tragedy, The Second World War*, 6 (New York, 1953), 630–76; Herbert Feis, *Between War and Peace: The Potsdam Conference, passim*; Gabriel Kolko, *The Politics of War: The World and United States Foreign Policy, 1943–1945*, (New York, 1968), 549–93; William H. McNeill, *America, Britain, and Russia: Their Cooperation and Conflict, 1941–1946* (London, 1953), 606–40; Rose, *After Yalta*, 52–85 and his *Dubious Victory*, 305–55; Truman, *Year of Decisions*, 343–426; C. L. Mee, *Meeting at Potsdam* (New York, 1975).
5. Truman, *Year of Decisions*, 331.
6. J.S., G.A., S.I.R. to Truman, July 6, 1945. Rosenman mss, box 2, Potsdam Conference folder.
7. Groves diaries, July 2, 1945; see also July 3 and 7, 1945; Hewlett and Anderson, *The New World*, 374–80.
8. Stimson diaries, July 17 and 18, 1945.
9. *Ibid.*, July 21, 1945.
10. Groves to Stimson, July 18, 1945, MED-TS, box 2, Trinity test folder no. 4; see also "Thoughts of E. O. Lawrence, July 16, 1945," and other attached documents, *ibid.*
11. Stimson diaries, July 21, 1945.
12. FRUS, *The Conference of Berlin*, II, 203–21.
13. *Ibid.*, 221.
14. *Ibid.*, 225.
15. As quoted in Stimson diaries, July 22, 1945.
16. *Ibid.*, July 23, 1945.
17. *Ibid.*
18. Davies diaries, July 28, 1945.
19. The most recent efforts to defend American diplomacy from the charge of having been influenced by considerations based on the atomic bomb can be found in Rose, *After Yalta*, 52–85, and his *Dubious Victory*, 305–55. These books appear to have been written as direct rebuttals to

Alperovitz's *Atomic Diplomacy*; in confronting Alperovitz head-on, however, they err on the other side of the argument. See also Herbert Feis, *The Atomic Bomb and the End of World War II* (Princeton, 1966) and his *Between War and Peace*.

20. Stimson and Bundy, *On Active Service*, 638.

21. Grew, "Appointment with the President, 12:35 pm," May 28, 1945, and "Possible inclusion in President's forthcoming speech of statement on Japan," May 29, 1945, Grew mss, MSAM 1687.3 vol. 7. See also Grew, *Turbulent Era*, 1406–42; and Grew to Stimson, Feb. 12, 1947, Stimson papers, Grew folder.

22. Feis, *Churchill, Roosevelt, Stalin*, 108–11, 153–4, 218, 220, 273, 350–8.

23. Truman, *Year of Decisions*, 322–3.

24. Davies diaries, July 14 and 15, 1945; but see also July 16.

25. Stimson diaries, July 23, 1945.

26. *Ibid.*; see also Churchill, *Triumph and Tragedy*, 640.

27. *Ibid.*, and July 24, 1945.

28. "W. B.'s Book," July 24, 1945, Byrnes mss, folder 602; see also Byrnes, *Speaking Frankly*, 208; Truman, *Year of Decisions*, 444 and Millis, ed., *The Forrestal Diaries*, 78–9; Forrestal diaries (manuscripts), July 24, 26, 29 and 30, 1945; Thomas G. Paterson, "Potsdam, the Atomic Bomb, and the Cold War: A Discussion with James F. Byrnes," *Pacific Historical Review*, vol. 41, no. 2 (May 1972), 225–30.

29. FRUS, *Conference of Berlin*, 225.

30. Truman, *Year of Decisions*, 416.

31. Bohlen to Feis, Jan. 25, 1960, Feis mss, box 14, Churchill, Roosevelt, Stalin folder. Stalin knew that Truman was referring to the atomic bomb. See G. K. Zhukov, *The Memoirs of Marshal Zhukov*, tr. APN (New York, 1971), 674–5.

32. Stimson and Bundy, *On Active Service*, 639.

33. FRUS, *Conference of Berlin*, I, 885–910.

34. Len Giovannitti and Fred Freed, *The Decision to Drop the Bomb* (New York, 1965), 202.

35. Derry and Ramsey to Groves, May 12, 1945, 6 MED-TS, box 3, Target Committee Meetings, folder 5D.2 (italics added).

36. *Ibid.*; the target selection process may be traced through documents in MED-TS, box 3, Proposed Targets, folders 5D.1 and 5D.2.

37. Quoted in Giovannitti and Freed, *The Decision to Drop the Bomb*, 41.

38. Harrison to Stimson, July 21, 1945, War 35987, MED, H-B, box 151, folder 64.

39. Stimson to Harrison, July 21, 1945, Victory 189, *ibid.*

40. Stimson diaries, July 24, 1945; see also July 21.

41. Harrison to Stimson, July 23, 1945, War 37350; Harrison to Stimson, July 23, 1945, War 36792, MED, H-B, box 151, folder 64.

42. Oppenheimer to Farrell and Parsons, July 23, 1945, MED-TS, box 14, folder 2.
43. Groves to Chief of Staff, Aug. 6, 1945, MED-TS, box 3, folder 5B.
44. *Ibid.*
45. Robert J. C. Butow, *Japan's Decision to Surrender* (Stanford, 1954), 153–4; see also John Toland, *The Rising Sun*, vol. 2 (New York, 1970), 915–1087.
46. The President was aboard the cruiser *Augusta* returning from Potsdam when he was informed about the attack on Hiroshima. His announcement had been prepared by the Interim Committee and the War Department. For complete text, see *Public Papers of the Presidents of the United States: Harry S. Truman, 1945* (Washington, 1961), 200.
47. Butow, *Japan's Decision to Surrender*, 158.
48. Ramsey to Oppenheimer (handwritten), middle to late August, 1945, Oppenheimer mss, box 60, Ramsey folder.
49. A phrase from the Nagasaki Prefectural Report as quoted by Butow, *Japan's Decision to Surrender*, 159.
50. Spaatz to Marshall, no. 1027, July 31, 1945, and Pasco to Spaatz, no. 3542, July 31, 1945, MED-TS, box 3, folder TD.3. William Craig, *The Fall of Japan* (New York, 1967), reports one American POW injured and several Allied POWs killed, 94–9. See also "Locations and Strengths of Prisoner of War Camps and Civilian Assembly Centers in Japan and Japanese-occupied Territories (July 1, 1945)," Provost Marshal General files, box 1584, "POW Camps in Japan" folder; box 2245, "Recovery Team Reports" folder. Although there is no report by the recovery teams of American POWs killed by the atomic bomb, the teams did not arrive in Nagasaki until mid-September and there is no evidence that they looked into this possibility. The discovery after thirty years that two Americans were killed by radiation poisoning in Hiroshima, and the incomplete information available on American POWs in and around Nagasaki on August 9, leaves little room for confidence in claims that no U.S. POWs were killed in the Nagasaki raid.
51. Butow, *Japan's Decision to Surrender*, 168.
52. Joseph Lawrence Marx, *Nagasaki: The Necessary Bomb?* (New York, 1971), 223; see also review by Martin J. Sherwin, *Wisconsin Magazine of History*, 56 (Spring 1973), 245–6.
53. Eugene H. Dooman to Herbert Feis, December 7, 1960, Feis mss, box 20, "Letters about Japan Subdued, 1960–1961" folder; Buchanan, *The United States and World War II*, 588; Butow, *Japan's Decision to Surrender*, 116–23.
54. Butow, *Japan's Decision to Surrender*, 130.
55. FRUS, *The Conference of Berlin*, II, 1474–6.
56. Butow, *Japan's Decision to Surrender*, 145.
57. Stimson and Bundy, *On Active Service*, 625.
58. Butow, *Japan's Decision to Surrender*, 175–6, 179.
59. Stimson and Bundy, *On Active Service*, 628. For an overview of

the debate, see Barton J. Bernstein, "The Atomic Bomb and American Foreign Policy, 1941–1945: An Historiographical Controversy," *Peace and Change*, 11, no. 1 (Spring 1974), 1–16.

60. Conant to Bush, May 18, 1945, Bush-Conant files, S-1 Interim Committee Postwar folder.

61. Gregory F. Herken, "Atomic Diplomacy Reversed and Revised: James F. Byrnes and the Russians," a paper read at the American Historical Association Convention, Chicago, Illinois (December 29, 1974); see also Herken, "American Diplomacy and the Atomic Bomb, 1945–1947" (unpublished doctoral dissertation, Princeton University, 1973), 97–146; and Robert Messer, "The Making of a Cold Warrior: James F. Byrnes and American-Soviet Relations, 1945–1946"(unpublished doctoral dissertation, University of California, Berkeley, 1975).

62. Stimson diaries, September 4, 1945.

63. Bush to Conant, November 7, 1945, Bush mss, box 27, Conant folder.

64. "So we may conclude that the dropping of the atomic bombs was not so much the last military act of the second World War, as the first major operation of the cold diplomatic war with Russia now in progress." P. M. S. Blackett, *Fear, War and the Bomb: Military and Political Consequences of Atomic Energy* (New York, 1948), 139.

A
BIBLIOGRAPHICAL
ESSAY

ON PRIMARY SOURCES IN THE FIELD:
A BIBLIOGRAPHICAL ESSAY

During the past few years the governments of the United States and Great Britain have declassified numerous documentary collections relating to many of the most secret and important diplomatic and military decisions taken during World War II. Although the process will have to continue for decades before it is completed, it is already clear to those who have worked with the recently opened collections that the diplomatic history of World War II is entering a new era of scholarship.*

The history of the atomic bomb can now be studied in detail from the documents themselves. The files of every major government agency that participated in wartime diplomatic, military, and political atomic energy decisions have been declassified. Although sections of these collections are still inaccessible, a large portion of this remaining classified material appears to contain primarily technical or personnel data. And even in these areas a considerable number of important documents have become available. In writing this book I have made extensive use of these official files and the private papers of participants. Thus I thought it more useful to prepare an essay on the primary sources rather than a conventional bibliography. With this in mind the chapter notes were designed to direct the interested reader to the most important secondary sources. (Specialists interested in a more complete list will find approximately four hundred publications listed in the bibliography of my dissertation, "The Atomic Bomb, Scientists and American Diplomacy During the Second World War" [UCLA, unpublished Ph.D. dissertation, 1971], 335–59.) Having begun my research as an inquiry into the impact of atomic energy on the political, diplomatic, and social life of the nation after the war (a study that still awaits its historian), that bibliography, like the present essay, contains references applicable to the early postwar as well as the war years.

After reviewing the secondary sources, with special attention to two excellent official histories—Richard G. Hewlett and Oscar E. Anderson, Jr., *The New World, 1939/1946: A History of the United States Atomic Energy Commission*, I (University Park, Pa., 1962), and Margaret Gowing, *Britain and Atomic Energy, 1939–1945* (London, 1964)—the historian interested in studying the atomic energy decisionmaking process at the highest level would do well to begin at the Franklin D. Roosevelt Library, Hyde Park, New York. There *Roosevelt's Map Room files* will be found—a large, diverse collection opened in 1970 documenting the diplomatic, military, and political direction of the war. It contains,

---

* What seems less clear, given the ill service that ignorance of the truth invariably performs for a democracy, is what good purpose was achieved by the arbitrary delay Americans have endured, short as it may have been compared to the policies imposed in other nations.

among other items, the voluminous wartime correspondence between Roosevelt and Churchill (opened separately in 1972) and atomic energy materials not available from any other source. Several years ago the library staff compiled a separate *atomic energy file* from documents in the *Map Room file*, the *Harry Hopkins papers*, the *President's Secretary's file*, the *Official File*, the *President's Safe file* and *Roosevelt's Confidential file*. Like the *Hopkins* and *Map Room files*, these files contain important related information and should be searched closely along with the *President's Personal file*.

The *Henry A. Wallace papers* at the University of Iowa contain surprisingly little atomic energy material and what there is of it pertains to the postwar years. However, in the Special Collections Division, Butler Library, Columbia University, there are a collection of *Wallace papers* and an *oral history memoir* due to open on November 18, 1975, which may contain some additional information on the atomic energy policies of the Roosevelt administration.

Collections that do not contain atomic energy information, but are helpful for understanding the pattern and style of Roosevelt's diplomacy, include: the papers of *Edward Stettinius* at the University of Virginia, the papers of *Samuel I. Rosenman, Henry Morgenthau,* and *Harold Smith* in the Roosevelt Library; the papers of *Cordell Hull, Frank Knox,* and *Arthur Sweetser* in the Library of Congress; and the files of the *Department of State* in the National Archives.

Two collections in the United States are most essential for the scholar writing on *any* aspect of the history of the wartime atomic bomb project: the *Office of Scientific Research and Development, Section 1 (OSRD, S-1) files* and the *Manhattan Engineer District (MED or Manhattan Project) files*, both deposited in the National Archives, Washington, D.C. The *OSRD, S-1* files were transferred to the archives of the Atomic Eenergy Commission soon after that agency was established in 1946, and they remained there until 1973, when they were transferred, in thirty-five large cartons, to the Industrial and Social Branch of the National Archives. This collection contains the atomic energy files of Vannevar Bush, first director of OSRD, and James Conant, whose special responsibilities as Bush's deputy included overseeing atomic energy work. The files contain a wealth of information, including numerous scientific reports, some recruiting data, internal MED memoranda related to the Anglo-American atomic energy partnership, and many interesting insights into the activities of individual scientists. The importance and diversity of these papers emerge from Bush's administrative responsibilities: he coordinated the civilian direction of the Manhattan Project, had direct access to Roosevelt, advised the Secretary of War and his special assistants, served on every important atomic energy policymaking body, and dealt directly with General Leslie R. Groves, the officer in charge of the Manhattan Project. The National Archives are also the depository for the records of the other sections of OSRD and its predecessor, the National

Defense Research Committee. Research in the files of OSRD, S-1 or MED could make valuable contributions to the history of the administration of weapons-development projects. Studies of these organizations would shed invaluable light on the origins of the postwar relationship between universities and government.

Historians interested in these projects would find it necessary as well to study *Vannevar Bush's papers* at the Library of Congress. *James Conant's papers* are there too, but as of this writing they remain closed to all except those granted special permission. Important insights into Bush's efforts to include scientists in military policymaking are available from the diaries of Rear Admiral *Julius A. Furer* at the Naval Historical Foundation, Washington, D.C. Other collections that illuminate the role of scientists, university-government relations, and atomic energy decisions during the war include: the papers of *Ernest O. Lawrence* in the History of Science and Technology collection at the Bancroft Library, University of California, Berkeley; and the *University of Chicago Metallurgical Project papers* at the Argonne National Laboratory archives, Argonne, Illinois. And, the availability of papers concerned with the Manhattan Project at Columbia and Princeton universities should be especially looked into by the historian of university-government relations.

Other important relationships of current significance that were given a major impetus during the war by atomic energy work include government-industry and university-industry collaboration. For such a project the atomic energy papers of the Atomic Energy Division of *E. I. du Pont de Nemours and Company*, Wilmington, Delaware, should be consulted, as well as materials at atomic energy laboratories in: Oak Ridge, Tennessee; Hanford, Washington; Sandia Base, New Mexico; and Los Alamos, New Mexico. Two helpful sources for locating atomic energy documents are the Historical Division of the Office of the Chief of Engineers, Department of the Army, Baltimore, Maryland, and the Historical Division of the Atomic Energy Commission, Washington, D.C. In correspondence with Engineering Corps historians, I learned of the existence of Corps records for MED at Suitland, Maryland, and of MED material assembled for historical purposes at AEC headquarters in Germantown, Maryland. The AEC's Historical Division was also extremely cooperative several years ago before the OSRD, S-1 and MED files were sent to the National Archives.

The *Manhattan Engineer District* files in the Modern Military Branch of the National Archives must be listed among the most valuable of atomic energy records. Through these papers one can follow the day-to-day direction of the bomb's development under General Groves. In addition to memoranda on every issue from Groves's opinion of individual scientists to his scheme for gaining postwar control for the United States of the world's thorium and uranium supplies, the collection contains a mass of reports to and from all the Project's sites: Columbia University, Princeton University, the University of Chicago, the University of California at Berkeley, Oak Ridge, Hanford, Los Alamos, and others. The records reveal a remarkably efficient administrator, but a man who 'had less to do with the formulation of policy at the highest level than he himself apparently believed. An important segment of this collection is designated "Top Secret, Special Interest to General Groves"—a group of records set aside by Groves to be used for his book, *Now It Can Be Told* (New York, 1962). Another separate and recently declassified part of the MED collection consists of Groves's diaries, which provide a record of his appointments and telephone calls; regrettably, they usually omit the substance of his conversations. The diaries have been micro-filmed and may be purchased separately. A biography of Groves could offer an interesting and useful study of military-civilian relations, especially during World War II and the early years of the AEC.

Constituting one of the most valuable sections of the MED collection are the atomic energy files of the *Office of the Secretary of War*—the *Harrison-Bundy* files, named for Stimson's two closest special assistants, George Harrison, a New York insurance company executive, and Harvey Bundy, a prominent Boston lawyer. These files contain the essential data on the atomic bomb that flowed in and out of the Secretary's office including the minutes of the Interim Committee. They must be supplemented, however, with *Stimson's personal diaries and papers*, located at the Sterling Memorial Library, Yale University, New Haven, Connecticut. This valuable collection has been microfilmed for sale to libraries and scholars. Recent declassifications now offer the prospect of a thorough study of the Office of the Secretary of War under Stimson. For such a project the papers of the *Joint Chiefs of Staff*, the *Office of Strategic Services*, and the *Office of the Secretary of War* itself, all at the National Archives, and the papers of *H. H. Arnold* and *Carl Spaatz* at the Library of Congress, would all be essential.

Some of the most important documents available to diplomatic historians of World War II are located at the Public Record Office in London, the depository for the *Cabinet*, *Foreign Office*, and *Prime Minister's* official papers. Any new researcher's starting point should be Public Record Office handbook number 15, *The Second World War: A Guide to Documents in the Public Record Office* (London, Her Majesty's Stationery Office, 1972). By far the most important collection for Anglo-American atomic energy policy is the *Prime Minister's Operational File* (*Premier 3*) which contains the most complete record available anywhere of the atomic energy discussions and agreements between Roosevelt and Churchill. In addition, the atomic energy papers (listed under the wartime code name "tube alloy," in series no. 139) contain memoranda exchanged between Churchill and his atomic energy advisers, Postmaster General Lord Cherwell (F. A. Lindemann), the Prime Minister's confidant and science adviser, and Sir John Anderson, Lord President and later Chancellor of the Exchequer, Britain's senior atomic energy administrator. Beyond the atomic energy material, the *Prem 3* collection contains many important sections documenting Churchill's general diplomatic strategy for the war and the postwar years. These records are essential to a full understanding of the diplomatic history of the Manhattan Project in particular, and Anglo-American relations in general.

The papers of the *War Cabinet* also contain material bearing directly and indirectly upon British atomic energy policy. The most important material is located in *CAB 90* (*War Cabinet Scientific Advisory Committees*), which contains reports and discussions about atomic energy from the early war years on a level just below the highest. The *Foreign Office* (*F.O.*) files are valuable for understanding the general political and diplomatic view of the world from London, and no American historian of World War II would want to miss the analyses of American politics, of President Roosevelt, and of Roosevelt's advisers preserved in *F.O. 371*. Finally, the *Prem 4* files, a collection of papers that Churchill kept at No. 10 Downing Street, contains information of interest to historians studying the wartime summit conferences. *Lord Cherwell's* papers at Nuffield College, Oxford, contain substantial material on atomic energy and other important issues that is not to be found in official government records.

To piece together the wartime atomic energy and diplomatic policies of Harry S. Truman, I used the following collections, in addition to many of those already cited: the *James F. Byrnes* and *Walter Brown* papers at Clemson University, Clemson, South Carolina; the *Joseph E. Davies*, *Robert P. Patterson*, *Herbert Feis*, and *Admiral William D. Leahy* papers at the Library of Congress; the *Department of State* files in the National Archives; the *Forrestal Diaries* at the Firestone Library, Princeton University, Princeton, New Jersey; the *Joseph C. Grew* papers at the Houghton Library, Harvard University, Cambridge, Massachusetts; *Lansing Lamont's* oral history transcripts from his book, *Day of Trinity* (New York, 1965), at the Truman Library, Independence, Missouri; and a variety of *President Truman's* official files at the Truman Library. The *Byrnes* papers proved to be easily the most important collection in this group; the others, with the exception of the *Department of State* files and the *Feis* and *Davies* papers, contain only scattered bits of information beyond what is available in published sources.

Other collections searched at the Truman Library covering the first year of Truman's presidency included papers of: *Thomas C. Blaisdell, Jr.*, *William L. Clayton, Clark Clifford, George M. Elsey, James H. Foskett, Ellen Clayton Garwood, Joseph M. Jones, J. Weldon Jones, E. A. Locke, Jr., James I. Loeb, Edward G. Miller, Frank McNaughton, William M. Rigdon, Charles G. Ross, Sidney Shalett,* and *John W. Snyder*. Although none of these papers contained any material on atomic energy policy, together they provided considerable insight into the nature of the decisionmaking process within the Truman administration. The papers of *Dean Acheson* and the collections that Truman held privately during his lifetime should shed additional light on many aspects of his atomic energy policies in the immediate postwar years. Two collections at Princeton University are also of central importance for the period immediately after the war: the papers of *Bernard Baruch*, the U.S. Ambassador to the United Nations Atomic Energy Commission, and the papers of *David Lilienthal*, the first commissioner of the U.S. AEC.

My research into the political activities of scientists associated with the Manhattan Project only scratched the surface of the numerous collections in the history of science in the twentieth century available across the country. Among the collections I found most useful were the *J. Robert Oppenheimer* papers at the Library of Congress, and the collection of his tape recordings located in the Library's Recording Division. Within the more than 250 manuscript boxes of this collection are letters to and from almost every important physicist in Europe and America. Although Oppenheimer's papers reveal little information on the pre-World War II years, they form an excellent supplement to the official files for the war period, and are important for study of the postwar years. A large segment of the collection contains material relating to Oppenheimer's AEC security hearing, and the collection also contains *Niels Bohr's* wartime memoranda, which Oppenheimer obtained from *Felix Frankfurter*, who acted as liaison between Bohr and Roosevelt. (*Frankfurter's* papers are also at the Library of Congress, and should be checked for the supplementary information they contain on atomic energy policy.) Although several fine studies of Oppenheimer have been written, they all place their strongest emphasis on his security hearing. His papers, however, are a rich resource for a historian of physics and science policy who is capable of evaluating one of the most complex minds and personalities of the twentieth century.

Leo Szilard is another scientist of central importance to the political history of the Manhattan Project. His papers are stored in the University of California, San Diego, Library, under the control of his widow, Dr. Gertrude Weiss Szilard, a resident of La Jolla, California. A great many documents written by and about Szilard during the war are available in the OSRD, S-1 and MED files. But a definitive biography of the man who in many respects was the guiding spirit for political activity among Manhattan Project scientists must await the opening of his own papers.

Several libraries across the country have begun to build up collections in the field of science and technology. Those that have important oral history and manuscript collections bearing upon the scientific, political, diplomatic, social, or military history of the atomic bomb include the Center for the History of Physics at the American Institute of Physics in New York City. Among the Center's collections are oral history transcripts of interviews with several Manhattan Project scientists, including *Hans Bethe* and *Luis Alvarez*, who was a witness to one of the atomic bomb raids aboard the attack aircraft. The *Columbia University Oral History Collection* has several transcripts covering the Manhattan Project, including interviews with *Norman Ramsey*, *Kenneth Bainbridge*,

A Bibliographical Essay

Charles Coryell, and *Harvey Bundy*. The papers of *Hans Bethe* are available at Cornell University to those granted his permission, and the papers of *Arthur H. Compton* can be studied at Washington University, St. Louis, Missouri.

Although the revolt of scientists against the U.S. government's atomic energy policies began during the war, the course of that revolt can be traced through a number of manuscript collections at the University of Chicago's Regenstein Library. In the early postwar years, Chicago served as communications and intelligence center for scientists seeking to ensure civilian control of the AEC and the international control of atomic energy. There historians will find the files of the following: the *Bulletin of the Atomic Scientists*, the *Atomic Scientists of Chicago*, the *Federation of Atomic Scientists*, the *Association of Los Alamos Scientists*, the *Association of Oak Ridge Engineers and Scientists*, the *Association of Cambridge Scientists*, and the *Emergency Committee of Atomic Scientists*. In addition to these large collections, useful information about the postwar role of scientists of various political persuasions can be obtained from the papers of *Enrico Fermi*, *Samuel Allison*, *J. H. Rush*, *Charles Merriam*, *James Franck*, *Robert Hutchins*, and others. The files of the *National Committee on Atomic Information*, which worked closely with the Federation of Atomic Scientists, are located at the Library of Congress. Historians interested in the public reaction to atomic energy legislation should investigate the files of the *Special Committee on Atomic Energy*, *79th Cong.*, at the National Archives. And finally, those interested in the response of pacifists to atomic energy issues would profit from a visit to Swarthmore College to study the papers of *A. J. Muste*.

APPENDICES:
SELECTED DOCUMENTS

A
*Resumption of Anglo-American
Atomic Energy Partnership, May 1943*

B
*Roosevelt's Postwar Plans?
September 1944*

C
*Hyde Park Aide-Mémoire,
September 18, 1944*

D
"Indefinite Collaboration"

E
*Roosevelt:
"Keep Britain from Bankruptcy"*

F
*Summary by Bush and Conant
of Their Views on Atomic Energy,
September 1944*

G
*"Problems with Respect
to the French"*

H
*Churchill Insists on Secrecy,
March 1945*

I
*Stimson: Memo Discussed
with the President, April 25, 1945*

J
*Groves: Report of Meeting
with the President, April 25, 1945*

K
*Stimson Is Urged to Organize
the Interim Committee, May 1945*

L
*Notes of the Interim Committee Meeting,
May 31, 1945*

M
*Science Panel: Recommendations
on the Immediate Use of Nuclear Weapons,
June 16, 1945*

N
*Stimson Is Informed of
Scientists' Concerns, June 26, 1945*

O
Ralph Bard's Dissent

P
*Groves: Report on
Alamogordo Atomic Bomb Test*

Q
*Byrnes Sees International Control
as Impractical for the Time Being,
August 1945*

A

Resumption of Anglo-American Atomic Energy Partnership, May 1943

<u>MOST</u> <u>SECRET</u>
From: TRIDENT
PENCIL NO. 405 (Saving)   26th May, 1943.
<u>PRIME</u> <u>MINISTER</u> <u>TO</u> <u>LORD</u> <u>PRESIDENT</u>

The President agreed that the exchange of information on Tube Alloys should be resumed and that the enterprise should be considered a joint one, to which both countries would contribute their best endeavours. I understood that his ruling would be based upon the fact that this weapon may well be developed in time for the present war and that it thus falls within the general agreement covering the interchange of research and invention secrets.
Lord Cherwell to be informed.

<u>Circulation</u>
Lord President of the Council
Lord Cherwell
Mr. Martin
Capt. Clifford

Premier 3 Records, file no. 139/8A, Public Record Office, London.

B

Roosevelt's Postwar Plans? September 1944

GREAT GEORGE STREET, S.W. 1
12 September 1944

<u>PRIME</u> <u>MINISTER</u>

<u>T.A.</u>

The London T.A. Committee hopes you will try to discover from the President in broad outline what the Americans have in mind about work on T.A. after the war ends. In Stage II there is, I believe, no question but that collaboration will continue. Do they wish, however, as we should like, to go on collaborating after Japan is defeated—and could the two countries continue to cooperate in developing such a vital weapon unless they were united in a close military alliance?
That we shall have to undertake work on T.A. in the United Kingdom

as soon as resources are available must, I think, be realised by the Americans. But the scope, scale and form clearly depends upon whether we continue to co-operate with the U.S.A. or not. As it will take at least three or four years to get any full-scale plant going, it is urgent to discover as soon as we can where we stand.

[signed]   Cherwell

Premier 3 Records, file no. 139/8A, Public Record Office, London.

C

Hyde Park Aide-Mémoire, September 18, 1944

10, Downing Street,
Whitehall

TUBE ALLOYS

Aide-mémoire of conversation between the President and the Prime Minister at Hyde Park, September 18, 1944.

1. The suggestion that the world should be informed regarding Tube Alloys, with a view to an international agreement regarding its control and use, is not accepted. The matter should continue to be regarded as of the utmost secrecy; but when a "bomb" is finally available, it might perhaps, after mature consideration, be used against the Japanese, who should be warned that this bombardment will be repeated until they surrender.

2. Full collaboration between the United States and the British Government in developing Tube Alloys for military and commercial purposes should continue after the defeat of Japan unless and until terminated by joint agreement.

3. Enquiries should be made regarding the activities of Professor Bohr and steps taken to ensure that he is responsible for no leakage of information, particularly to the Russians.

[initialed]   F.D.R.   W.C.C.
18.9

President's Map Room Papers, Naval Aide's File, box 172—General folder, Roosevelt Library, Hyde Park, New York. The following notations appear on Churchill's copy: "A copy of this aide-memóire was left with Pres. Roosevelt, Another copy was given to Adl. Leahy to hand to Lord Cherwell." Another note states that the conversation recorded by the aide-mémoire took place on the 19th: "Actually 19th." Both notes are initialed J.M.M. (J. M. Martin). Premier 3 Records, file no. 139/9, Public Record Office, London.

D

"*Indefinite Collaboration*"

EXTRACT FROM GUNFIRE 293, 21st September, 1944.

From: OCTAGON
To: ADMIRALTY

*   *   *   *   *

2. Most especially secret. You may tell the Chancellor of the Exchequer that the President and I exchanged satisfactory initialled notes about the future of T.A. on the basis of indefinite collaboration in the post-war period subject to termination by joint agreement.

*   *   *   *   *

Premier 3 Records, file no. 139/8A, Public Record Office, London.

E

Roosevelt: "*Keep Britain from Bankruptcy*"

THE WHITE HOUSE
WASHINGTON

Top Secret

PRIVATE   September 29, 1944

MEMORANDUM FOR THE SECRETARY OF STATE

I do not think that in the present stage any good purpose would be served by having the State Department or any other department sound out the British and Russian views on the treatment of German industry. Most certainly it should not be taken up with the European Advisory Commission which, in a case like this, is on a tertiary and not even a secondary level.

The real nub of the situation is to keep Britain from going into complete bankruptcy at the end of the war.

Somebody has been talking not only out of turn to the papers or on facts which are not fundamentally true.

No one wants to make Germany a wholly agricultural nation again, and yet somebody down the line has handed this out to the press. I wish we could catch and chastise him.

You know that before the war Germany was not only building up war manufacture, but was also building up enough of a foreign trade to finance re-arming sufficiently and still maintain enough international credit to keep out of international bankruptcy.

I just can not go along with the idea of seeing the British empire collapse financially, and Germany at the same time building up a potential re-armament machine to make another war possible in twenty years. Mere inspection of plants will not prevent that.

But no one wants "complete eradication of German industrial productive capacity in the Ruhr and Saar".

It is possible, however, in those two particular areas to enforce rather complete controls. Also, it must not be forgotten that outside of the Ruhr and Saar, Germany has many other areas and facilities for turning out large exports.

In regard to the Soviet government, it is true that we have no idea as yet what they have in mind, but we have to remember that in their occupied territory they will do more or less what they wish. We cannot afford to get into a position of merely recording protests on our part unless there is some chance of some of the protests being heeded.

I do not intend by this to break off or delay negotiations with the Soviet government over lend-lease either on the contract basis or on the proposed Fourth Protocol basis. This, however, does not immediately concern the German industrial future.

F.D.R.

World War Two Conferences, Box 6, [H. Freeman] Matthews files, Germany Treatment folder, Department of State Records, National Archives, Washington, D.C.

F
_____

*Summary by Bush and Conant of Their Views
on Atomic Energy, September 1944*

September 30, 1944.
Top Secret

MEMORANDUM

To: The Secretary of War
From: V. Bush and J. B. Conant
Subject: Salient Points Concerning Future International Handling of Subject of Atomic Bombs.

1. Present Military Potentialities. There is every reason to believe that before August 1, 1945, atomic bombs will have been demonstrated and that the type then in production would be the equivalent of 1,000 to

10,000 tons of high explosive in so far as general blast damage is concerned. This means that one B-29 bomber could accomplish with such a bomb the same damage against weak industrial and civilian targets as 100 to 1,000 B-29 bombers.

2. Future Military Potentialities. We are dealing with an expanding art and it is difficult to predict the future. At present we are planning atomic bombs utilizing the energy involved in the fission of the uranium atom. It is believed that such energy can be used as a detonator for setting off the energy which would be involved in the transformation of heavy hydrogen atoms into helium. If this can be done a factor of a thousand or more would be introduced into the amount of energy released. This means that one such super-super bomb would be equivalent in blast damage to 1,000 raids of 1,000 B-29 Fortresses delivering their load of high explosive on one target. One must consider the possibility of delivering either the bombs at present contemplated or the super-super bomb on an enemy target by means of a robot plane or guided missile. When one considers these possibilities we see that very great devastation could be caused immediately after the outbreak of hostilities to civilian and industrial centers by an enemy prepared with a relatively few such bombs. That such a situation presents a new challenge to the world is evident.

3. Present Advantage of United States and Great Britain Temporary. Unless it develops that Germany is much further along than is now believed it is probable that the present developments in the United States undertaken in cooperation with Great Britain put us in a temporary position of great ascendency. It would be possible, however, for any nation with good technical and scientific resources to reach our present position in three or four years. Therefore it would be the height of folly for the United States and Great Britain to assume that they will always continue to be superior in this new weapon. Once the distance between ourselves and those who have not yet developed this art is eliminated the accidents of research could give another country a temporary advantage as great as the one we now enjoy.

4. Impossibility of maintaining complete secrecy after the war is over. In order to accomplish our present gigantic technical and scientific task it has been necessary to bring a vast number of technical men into the project. Information in regard to various aspects of it is therefore widespread. Furthermore, all the basic facts were known to physicists before the development began. Some outside the project have undoubtedly guessed a great deal of what is going on. Considerable information is already in the hands of various newspaper men who are refraining from writing our stories only because of voluntary censorship. In view of this situation it is our strong recommendation that plans be laid for complete disclosure of the history of the development and all but the manufacturing and military details on the bombs as soon as the first bomb has been demonstrated. This demonstration might be over enemy territory,

Appendices

or in our own country, with subsequent notice to Japan that the materials would be used against the Japanese mainland unless surrender was forthcoming.

5. Dangers of partial secrecy and international armament race. It is our contention that it would be extremely dangerous for the United States and Great Britain to attempt to carry on in complete secrecy further developments of the military applications of this art. If this were done Russia would undoubtedly proceed in secret along the same lines and so too might certain other countries, including our defeated enemies. We do not believe that over a period of a decade the control of the supply could be counted on to prevent such secret developments in other countries. This is particularly true if the super-super bomb were developed for the supply of heavy hydrogen is essentially unlimited and the rarer materials such as uranium and thorium would be used only as detonators. If a country other than Great Britain and the United States developed the super-super bomb first we should be in a terrifying situation if hostilities should occur. The effect on public reaction of the uncertainties in regard to an unknown threat of this new nature would be very great.

6. Proposed international exchange of information. In order to meet the unique situation created by the development of this new art we would propose that free interchange of all scientific information on this subject be established under the auspices of an international office deriving its power from whatever association of nations is developed at the close of the present war. We would propose further that as soon as practical the technical staff of this office be given free access in all countries not only to the scientific laboratories where such work is contained, but to the military establishments as well. We recognize that there will be great resistance to this measure, but believe the hazards to the future of the world are sufficiently great to warrant this attempt. If accurate information were available as to the development of these atomic bombs in each country, public opinion would have true information about the status of the armament situation. Under these conditions there is reason to hope that the weapons would never be employed and indeed that the existence of these weapons might decrease the chance of another major war.

[sgd] J. B. CONANT
[sgd] V. BUSH

Manhattan Engineer District Records, Harrison-Bundy files, folder no. 69, National Archives, Washington, D.C.

G

"Problems with Respect to the French"

WAR DEPARTMENT

WASHINGTON

Top Secret

19 January 1945.

PROBLEMS WITH RESPECT TO THE FRENCH:

I.

The first problem is a political question.

Sir John Anderson reports that there is grave danger that the French, through Mr. Joliot or possibly through DeGaulle instigated by Joliot, may press for immediate participation in the T.A. Project. It is not known whether this request will include only industrial aspects or whether it will also be for military participation.

Assuming that the United States and Great Britain do not want this question raised at this time, the problem is what minimum assurance to Joliot can be given which will bring about a postponement of the issue and thereby protect against political explosion by the French with or without collaboration with the Russians, with great danger to security.

It is anticipated that in order to accomplish this result the Secretary of War will recommend to the President and Sir John Anderson recommend to the Prime Minister that a statement along the following lines be made by Sir John Anderson, if necessary even in a letter to Joliot:

"Since it is inadvisable to attempt detailed discussions as to arrangements with France in the field of nuclear sources of power until the termination of hostilities, the Government of the United Kingdom is prepared to assure the French Government that upon the termination of hostilities it will discuss further with the French any claims of the French Government relating to commercial or industrial application of nuclear sources of power."

II.

The other problem involves the best methods of best preventing disclosure of further information to the French.

First, three fairly trustworthy French scientists are employed on the Montreal Project. We do not know what temptations or pressure they might be put to disclose information to the French Government. They are under contract to stay in Montreal until July, 1945, subject, however, to an agreement with each that he can make one short trip to France for personal reasons at a time when this is feasible. One has already gone; one does not care to go at once; but one Mr. Goldschmidt does desire to make this brief trip. Dr. Chadwick thinks that his trip would be an advantage and would tend to postpone radical immediate action by the

French authorities. General Groves has his doubts about this but we are faced with a written commitment to this effect.

It is suggested that the policy should be to extend the contracts with these three Frenchmen, keep them under as close security control as possible, and let Goldschmidt go to Paris for a brief trip if this proves to be unavoidable under the commitments already made.

Second, the worst security problem involves a fourth Frenchman, Halban, who is not trusted fully by anyone and least of all by the American authorities. There are various alternative possibilities on this matter which require further discussion.

H.H.B. [Harvey H. Bundy]

Manhattan Engineer District, Harrison-Bundy files, folder no. 36, National Archives, Washington, D.C.

H
———————

Churchill Insists on Secrecy, March 1945

10 Downing Street,
Whitehall.
March 25, 1945

FOREIGN SECRETARY

1. I certainly do not agree that this secret should be imparted to the French. My agreement with President Roosevelt in writing forbids either party to reveal to anyone else the secret. I believe you underrate the lead which has been obtained by the United States, in which we participate, through their vast expenditure of money—I believe above four hundred million pounds.

2. *I was shocked at Yalta too when the President in a casual manner spoke of revealing the secret to Stalin on the grounds that de Gaulle, if he heard of it, would certainly double-cross us with Russia.*

3. In all the circumstances our policy should be to keep the matter so far as we can control it in American and British hands and leave the French and Russians to do what they can. The Chancellor said that the Frenchmen whom he had interviewed would never betray the secret to de Gaulle, and he vouched for their good behaviour. Now we are threatened that the Russians will be told. But anyhow there is all the difference between having certain paper formulae and having a mightly [sic] plant in existence, and perhaps soon in working order. Once you tell them they will ask for the very latest news, and to see the plants. This will speed them up by two years at least. You may be quite sure that any power that gets hold of the secret will try to make the article and that this touches the existence of human society.

4. I am getting rather tired of all the different kinds of things that we must do or not do lest Anglo-French relations suffer. *One thing I am sure that there is nothing that de Gaulle would like better than to have plenty of T.A. to punish Britain, and nothing he would like less than to arm Communist Russia with the secret.* This matter is out of all relation to anything else that exists in the whole world, and I could not think of participating in any disclosure to third or fourth parties at the present time. I do not believe there is anyone in the world who can possibly have reached the position now occupied by us and the United States.

5. As to questions of honour as between us and France. At that time France was represented by Vichy and de Gaulle had no status to speak for her. I have never made the slightest agreement with France or with any Frenchman. I shall certainly continue to urge the President not to make or permit the slightest disclosure to France or Russia. *Even six months will make a difference should it come to a show-down with Russia, or indeed with de Gaulle.*

[signed] w.c.c.

Churchill's draft reply to Foreign Secretary Anthony Eden's Minute of March 20. Paragraph 2 and sections of paragraphs 4 and 5 (identified here by italics) were edited out of the final draft. Premier 3 Records, file no. 139/6, Public Record Office, London.

I

Stimson: Memo Discussed with the President, April 25, 1945

1. Within four months we shall in all probability have completed the most terrible weapon ever known in human history, one bomb of which could destroy a whole city.

2. Although we have shared its development with the UK, physically the US is at present in the position of controlling the resources with which to construct and use it and no other nation could reach this position for some years.

3. Nevertheless it is practically certain that we could not remain in this position indefinitely.

a. Various segments of its discovery and production are widely known among many scientists in many countries, although few scientists are now acquainted with the whole process which we have developed.

b. Although its construction under present methods requires great scientific and industrial effort and raw materials, which are temporarily mainly within the possession and knowledge of US and UK, it is extremely probable that much easier and cheaper methods of production will be discovered by scientists in the future, together with the use of materials of much wider distribution. As a result, it is extremely probable that the future will make it possible to be constructed by smaller nations or even groups, or at least by a large nation in a much shorter time.

4. As a result, it is indicated that the future may see a time when such a weapon may be constructed in secret and used suddenly and effectively with devastating power by a wilful [sic] nation or group against an unsuspecting nation or group of much greater size and material power. With its aid even a very powerful unsuspecting nation might be conquered within a very few days by a very much smaller one, although probably the only nation which could enter into production within the next few years is Russia.

5. The world in its present state of moral advancement compared with its technical development would be eventually at the mercy of such a weapon. In other words, modern civilization might be completely destroyed.

6. To approach any world peace organization of any pattern now likely to be considered, without an appreciation by the leaders of our country of the power of this new weapon, would seem to be unrealistic. No system of control heretofore considered would be adequate to control this menace. Both inside any particular country and between the nations of the world, the control of this weapon will undoubtedly be a matter of the greatest difficulty and would involve such thorough-going rights of inspection and internal controls as we have never heretofore contemplated.

7. Furthermore, in the light of our present position with reference to this weapon, the question of sharing it with other nations and, if so shared, upon what terms, becomes a primary question of our foreign relations. Also our leadership in the war and in the development of this weapon has placed a certain moral responsibility upon us which we cannot shirk without very serious responsibility for any disaster to civilization which it would further.

8. On the other hand, if the problem of the proper use of this weapon can be solved, we would have the opportunity to bring the world into a pattern in which the peace of the world and our civilization can be saved.

9. As stated in General Groves' report, steps are under way looking towards the establishment of a select committee of particular qualifications for recommending action to the Executive and legislative branches of our government when secrecy is no longer in full effect. The committee would also recommend the actions to be taken by the War Department prior to that time in anticipation of the postwar problems. All recommendations would of course be first submitted to the President.

Manhattan Engineer District Records, Harrison-Bundy files, folder no. 60, National Archives, Washington, D.C. Also in Henry L. Stimson diaries, April 25, 1945, Sterling Memorial Library, Yale University, New Haven, Connecticut.

J

Groves: Report of Meeting with the President, April 25, 1945

MEMO TO FILES: TOP SECRET

SUBJECT: Report of Meeting with The President
April 25, 1945.

The desirability of the Secretary of War being accompanied by General Marshall and General Groves at his conference with the President at which he was to disclose to the President all of the facts with respect to the Manhattan Engineer District was discussed between the Secretary of War and General Marshall. General Marshall felt it would be unwise for him to attend on account of the close news watch being kept on the White House. Also as a result of this discussion General Groves didn't go to the White House with the Secretary but entered through the back door and was brought into the President's office from the back door about 5 or 10 minutes after the conference started.

During this period the Secretary had presented his short opening statement and had initiated the discussion emphasizing the importance from the standpoint of the San Francisco conference of the problem.

Prior to going over to the White House I read the statement of the Secretary and expressed my concurrence in it with the exception that I pointed out the dangers of over-emphasizing the power of a single bomb.

After General Groves entered[,] his memorandum to the Secretary of War dated April 23rd was read by the President and the President asked questions concerning various items. A great many of these questions were answered by the Secretary with little or no amplification by General Groves. The answers to the remainder of the questions were either considerably amplified by General Groves or were answered in their entirety by him.

The President did not keep the report as he felt it was not advisable. A great deal of emphasis was placed on foreign relations and particularly on the Russian situation. The President did not show any concern over the amount of funds being spent but made it very definite that he was in entire agreement with the necessity for the project.

The President approved our ideas about taking a few members of the Congress to Tennessee and concurred in the advisability of leaving the choice to the Speaker for the House and to Senator Barkley for the Senate.

The Secretary and myself both emphasized to the President that our present interest was purely military, that while there was unquestionably great prospects for future commercial developments our immediate prospects were military only and it was towards that field that our entire effort was devoted. The steps taken by us to secure control of raw materials were discussed at considerable length and the reasons why I had been first opposed to and later in favor of bringing the British into the project (i.e., the securing of the Belgian Congo ore) was brought out distinctly.

The Secretary stated that the entire work was under the charge of General Groves and expressed his entire confidence in him. The President replied that he had known General Groves for a number of years and had the highest regard for him.

[signed] L. R. GROVES
Major General, USA.

Manhattan Engineer District Records, Commanding General's file no. 24, tab. D, National Archives, Washington, D.C.

K

Stimson Is Urged to Organize the Interim Committee, May 1945

WAR DEPARTMENT

WASHINGTON

1 May 1945

MEMORANDUM FOR THE SECRETARY OF WAR.

SUBJECT: Interim Committee on S-1.

Last week you presented to President Truman a fairly complete memorandum on the S-1 project, outlining its genesis, its present state of development and in general its availability for military usage. Your presentation was acompanied by a brief memo which you prepared relative to the broader political and international implications of the problem and the need for post war controls, both national and international. You had in mind the advisability of setting up a committee of particular qualifications for recommending action to the executive and legislative branches of the government when secrecy is no longer fully required. The committee would also be expected to recommend actions to be taken by the War Department in anticipation of the post war problems.

In view of the possibly short time available before actual military use and the relaxation of secrecy, it seems to me,—and as you know both Dr. Conant and Dr. Bush agree—that it is becoming more and more important to organize such a committee as promptly as possible. This committee should, I think, be a relatively small committee which should be prepared to serve temporarily or until Congress might appoint a permanent Post War Commission to supervise, regulate and control the use of the product.

Certain things, however, must be done now before use if we are to avoid the risk of grave repercussions on the public in general and on

Congress in particular. For instance, the committee will need to prepare appropriate announcements to be available for issue (a) by the President and (b) by the War Department as soon as the first bomb is used. These announcements or later publicity would presumably give some of the history of the project, its importance from a military standpoint, its scientific background, and some of its dangers. Most importantly as soon as possible after use some assurance must be given of the steps to be taken to provide the essential controls over post war use and development, both at home and abroad. With that in mind it will be necessary as soon as possible after use to make recommendations for the necessary Congressional legislation covering patents, use, controls, etc.

All of these and many other factors will have to be studied by the committee with the understanding that all recommendations must be for your own approval and for submission to the President for his approval.

It seems clear that some machinery is essential now to provide the way for continuous and effective controls and to insure or provide for the necessary and persistent research and development of the possibilities of atomic energy in which the United States now leads the way. If properly controlled by the peace loving nations of the world this energy should insure the peace of the world for generations. If misused it may lead to the complete destruction of civilization.

In the circumstances I suggest that a committee of six or seven be set up at once to study and report on the whole problem of temporary war controls and publicity, and to survey and make recommendation on post war research, development and controls, and the legislation necessary to effectuate them.

The members of this committee should be appointed by you as Secretary of War subject to the approval of the President. When appointed the committee will need promptly to organize appropriate panels to aid in its work—panels of specially qualified scientists, Army and Navy personnel, Congressional advisers, legislative draftsmen and others.

[signed] GEORGE L. HARRISON

Manhattan Engineer District Records, Harrison-Bundy files, folder no. 69, National Archives, Washington, D.C.

L

Notes of the Interim Committee Meeting, May 31, 1945
10:00 A.M. to 1:15 P.M. - 2:15 P.M. to 4:15 P.M.

PRESENT:

Members of the Committee
Secretary Henry L. Stimson, Chairman
Hon. Ralph A. Bard
Dr. Vannevar Bush

Hon. James F. Byrnes
Hon. William L. Clayton
Dr. Karl T. Compton
Dr. James B. Conant
Mr. George L. Harrison

Invited Scientists
Dr. J. Robert Oppenheimer
Dr. Enrico Fermi
Dr. Arthur H. Compton
Dr. E. O. Lawrence

By Invitation
General George C. Marshall
Major Gen. Leslie R. Groves
Mr. Harvey H. Bundy
Mr. Arthur Page

I. OPENING STATEMENT OF THE CHAIRMAN:

Secretary Stimson explained that the Interim Committee had been appointed by him, with the approval of the President, to make recommendations on temporary war-time controls, public announcement, legislation and post-war organization. The Secretary gave high praise to the brilliant and effective assistance rendered to the project by the scientists of the country and expressed great appreciation to the four scientists present for their great contributions to the work and their willingness to advise on the many complex problems that the Interim Committee had to face. He expressed the hope that the scientists would feel completely free to express their views on any phase of the subject.

The Committee had been termed an "Interim Committee" because it was expected that when the project became more widely known a permanent organization established by Congressional action or by treaty arrangements would be necessary.

The Secretary explained that General Marshall shared responsibility with him for making recommendations to the President on this project with particular reference to its military aspects; therefore, it was considered highly desirable that General Marshall be present at this meeting to secure at first hand the views of the scientists.

The Secretary expressed the view, a view shared by General Marshall, that this project should not be considered simply in terms of military weapons, but as a new relationship of man to the universe. This discovery might be compared to the discoveries of the Copernican theory and of the laws of gravity, but far more important than these in its effect on the lives of men. While the advances in the field to date had been fostered by the needs of war, it was important to realize that the implications of the project went far beyond the needs of the present war. It must be controlled if possible to make it an assurance of future peace rather than a menace to civilization.

The Secretary suggested that he hoped to have the following questions discussed during the course of the meeting:

1. Future military weapons.
2. Future international competition.
3. Future research.
4. Future controls.
5. Future developments, particularly non-military.

II. STAGES OF DEVELOPMENT:

As a technical background for the discussions, Dr. A. H. Compton explained the various stages of development. The first stage involved the separation of uranium 235. The second stage involved the use of "breeder" piles to produce enriched materials from which plutonium or new types of uranium could be obtained. The first stage was being used to produce material for the present bomb while the second stage would produce atomic bombs with a tremendous increase in explosive power over those now in production. Production of enriched materials was now on the order of pounds or hundreds of pounds and it was contemplated that the scale of operations could be expanded sufficiently to produce many tons. While bombs produced from the products of the second stage had not yet been proven in actual operation, such bombs were considered a scientific certainty. It was estimated that from January 1946 it would take one and one-half years to prove [sic] this second stage in view of certain technical and metallurgical difficulties; that it would take three years to get plutonium in volume, and that it would take perhaps six years for any competitor to catch up with us.

Dr. Fermi estimated that approximately twenty pounds of enriched material would be needed to carry on research in current engineering problems and that a supply of one-half to one ton would be needed for research on the second stage.

In response to the Secretary's question, Dr. A. H. Compton stated that the second stage was dependent upon vigorous exploitation of the first stage and would in no way vitiate the expenditure already made on the present plant.

Dr. Conant mentioned a so-called "third stage" of development in which the products of the "second stage" would be used simply as a detonator for heavy water. He asked Dr. Oppenheimer for an estimate of the time factor involved in developing this phase. Dr. Oppenheimer stated that this was a far more difficult development than the previous stages and estimated that a minimum of three years would be required to reach production. He pointed out that heavy water (hydrogen) was much cheaper to produce than the other materials and could eventually be obtained in far greater quantity.

Dr. Oppenheimer reviewed the scale of explosive force involved in these several stages. One bomb produced in the first stage was estimated to have the explosive force of 2,000 - 20,000 tons of TNT. The actual blast effect would be accurately measured when the test was made. In the second stage the explosive force was estimated to be equal to 50,000 - 100,000 tons of TNT. It was considered possible that a bomb developed from the third stage might produce an explosive force equal to 10,000,000 - 100,000,000 tons of TNT.

III. DOMESTIC PROGRAM:

Dr. Lawrence expressed his great appreciation for the fact that the leaders of the Government had been willing to take the chances inherent in the development of this program. He expressed a view that if the United States were to stay ahead in this field it was imperative that we knew more and did more than any other country. He felt that research had to go on unceasingly. There were many unexplored possibilities in terms of new methods and new materials beyond thorium and uranium. In fact, all heavy elements held potentialities for exploitation in this field. He thought it might be possible one day to secure our energy from terrestrial sources rather than from the sun. Dr. Lawrence pointed out that there was no real doubt about the soundness of the program. Any failures that had occurred or would occur in the future were nothing more than temporary setbacks and there was every reason to believe that such setbacks would be quickly overcome.

Dr. Lawrence recommended that a program of plant expansion be vigorously pursued and at the same time a sizable stock pile of bombs and material should be built up. For security reasons plants that were built should be widely scattered throughout the country. Every effort should be made to encourage industrial application and development. Only by vigorously pursuing the necessary plant expansion and fundamental research, and by securing adequate government support could this nation stay out in front. With this view Dr. A. H. Compton expressed complete agreement.

Dr. Karl T. Compton, summarizing the views expressed above, suggested the following program:

1. Expand production under the first stage to produce bombs for stock pile and to furnish material for research.
2. Intensify "second stage" research.
3. Build necessary "second stage" pilot plants.
4. Produce the new product.

Dr. Oppenheimer pointed out that one of the difficult problems involved in guiding a future domestic program would be the allocation of materials as between different uses. Dr. Karl T. Compton added further that every effort should be made to encourage industrial progress in order that our fundamental research program would be strengthened.

The Secretary summarized the views of the group concerning our domestic program as follows:

1. Keep our industrial plant intact.

2. Build up sizable stock piles of material for military use and for industrial and technical use.

3. Open the door to industrial development.

IV. FUNDAMENTAL RESEARCH:

Dr. Oppenheimer felt that the work now being done under war pressure was simply a process of plucking the fruits of earlier research. In order to exploit more fully the potentialities of this field, it was felt that a more leisurely and a more normal research situation should be established. Dr. Oppenheimer strongly urged that numbers of the present staff should be released to go back to their universities and research laboratories in order to explore the many ramifications of this field, to avoid the sterility of the present orientation to specific problems only, and to develop cheaper and simpler methods of production. Dr. Bush expressed the view that while it was imperative in war time to concentrate on specific problems such a narrowing of the field in peace time was completely wrong. He agreed with Dr. Oppenheimer that only a nucleus of the present staff should be retained and that as many as possible should be released for broader and freer inquiry. Drs. A. H. Compton and Fermi reenforced this view by emphasizing that we could never be sure of the tremendous possibilities in this field until thorough fundamental research could be brought to bear.

V. PROBLEMS OF CONTROL AND INSPECTION:

The Secretary inquired what other potentialities beyond purely military uses might be exploited. In reply Dr. Oppenheimer pointed out that the immediate concern had been to shorten the war. The research that had led to this development had only opened the door to future discoveries. Fundamental knowledge of this subject was so wide spread throughout the world that early steps should be taken to make our developments known to the world. He thought it might be wise for the United States to offer to the world free interchange of information with particular emphasis on the development of peace-time uses. The basic goal of all endeavors in the field should be the enlargement of human welfare. If we were to offer to exchange information before the bomb was actually used, our moral position would be greatly strengthened.

The Secretary stated that an understanding of the non-military potentialities was a necessary background to the consideration of the question of interchange of information and international co-operation. He referred to the Bush-Conant memorandum which had stressed the role of science in securing a policy of self-restraint. This memorandum had recommended that in any international organization which might be established complete scientific freedom should be provided for and the right of inspection should be given to an international control body. The Secretary asked what kind of inspection might be effective and what would be the position of democratic governments as against totalitarian regimes under such a program of international control coupled with scientific freedom. The Secretary said that it was his own feeling that the democratic countries had fared pretty well in this war. <u>Dr. Bush</u> indorsed this view vigorously, pointing out that our advantage over totalitarian states had been tremendous. Evidence just in from Germany revealed that she was far behind us in the technology of this field and in other scientific fields. He said that our tremendous advantage stemmed in large measure from our system of team work and free interchange of information by which we had won out and would continue to win out in any competitive scientific and technological race. He expressed some doubt, however, of our ability to remain ahead permanently if we were to turn over completely to the Russians the results of our research under free competition with no reciprocal exchange. <u>Dr. Karl T. Compton</u> felt that we would hold our advantage at least to the extent of the construction lag, but, in any event, he felt that secrets of this nature could not be successfully kept for any period of time and that we could safely share our knowledge and still remain ahead.

<u>Dr. A. H. Compton</u> stated that the destructive applications of these discoveries were perhaps easier to control than the constructive ones. He referred to the nucleonics prospectus prepared some time ago in which were indicated certain other potential uses in such fields as naval propulsion, health, chemistry, and industrial development. He pointed out that Faraday's hopes and predictions in the field of electro-dynamics were realized by Edison only after the lapse of several decades. Such a lag in this field with as yet uncharted possibilities seemed likely. He stressed the impossibility of keeping technological advances secret, as witness the experience of industry. The fundamental knowledge in this field was known in many countries and a policy of restraint, of the nationalization of scientific ideas[,] could not work. Unless scientists were able to keep abreast of advances in the field throughout the world they would probably lose out on many developments.

<u>Dr. Conant</u> felt that international control in this field would require the power of inspection and that international arrangements among scientists would be by a means of strengthening this power. <u>Dr. Oppenheimer</u> expressed doubts concerning the possibility of knowing what was going on in this field in Russia, but expressed the hope that the fraternity of interest among scientists would aid in the solution.

<u>General Marshall</u> cautioned against putting too much faith in the effectiveness of the inspection proposal. Mr. Clayton also expressed considerable doubt on this point.

VI. <u>RUSSIA</u>:

In considering the problem of controls and international collaboration the question of paramount concern was the attitude of Russia. <u>Dr. Oppenheimer</u> pointed out that Russia had always been very friendly to science and suggested that we might open up this subject with them in a tentative fashion and in the most general terms without giving them any details of our productive effort. He thought we might say that a great national effort had been put into this project and express a hope for cooperation with them in this field. He felt strongly that we should not prejudge the Russian attitude in this matter.

At this point <u>General Marshall</u> discussed at some length the story of charges and counter-charges that have been typical of our relations with the Russians, pointing out that most of these allegations have proven unfounded. The seemingly uncooperative attitude of Russia in military matters stemmed from the necessity of maintaining security. He said that he had accepted this reason for their attitiude in his dealings with the Russians and had acted accordingly. As to the post-war situation and in matters other than purely military, he felt that he was in no position to express a view. With regard to this field he was inclined to favor the building up of a combination among like-minded powers, thereby forcing Russia to fall in line by the very force of this coalition. General Marshall was certain that we need have no fear that the Russians, if they had knowledge of our project, would disclose this information to the Japanese. He raised the question whether it might be desirable to invite two prominent Russian scientists to witness the test.

<u>Mr. Byrnes</u> expressed a fear that if information were given to the Russians, even in general terms, Stalin would ask to be brought into the partnership. He felt this to be particularly likely in view of our commitments and pledges of cooperation with the British. In this connection <u>Dr. Bush</u> pointed out that even the British do not have any of our blue prints on plants. <u>Mr. Byrnes</u> expressed the view, <u>which was generally agreed to by all present</u>, that the most desirable program would be to push ahead as fast as possible in production and research to make certain that we stay ahead and at the same time make every effort to better our political relations with Russia.

VII. INTERNATIONAL PROGRAM:

<u>Dr. A. H. Compton</u> stressed very strongly the need for maintaining ourselves in a position of superiority while at the same time working toward adequate political agreements. He favored freedom of competition and freedom of research activity to as great an extent as possible consistent with security and the international situation. To maintain rigid security over this project would result in a certain sterility of research and a very real competitive disadvantage to the nation. He felt that within the larger field of freedom for research it would still be possible to maintain close security of the military aspects of the field. We could maintain our technical advantage over other nations only by drawing on the free interchange of scientific investigation and curiosity. He urged the view, expressed earlier by General Marshall, that we should secure agreements for cooperation with other like-minded nations and at the same time work toward solidifying our relations with the Russians.

<u>Dr. A. H. Compton</u> recommended that roughly the following program should be adopted for at least a decade:

Appendices

1. Freedom of research be developed to the utmost consistent with national security and military necessity.
2. A combination of democratic powers be established for cooperation in this field.
3. A cooperative understanding be reached with Russia.

The meeting adjourned for luncheon at 1:15 P.M. and resumed at 2:15 P.M. All who attended the morning session were present with the exception of General Marshall.

VIII. EFFECT OF THE BOMBING ON THE JAPANESE AND THEIR WILL TO FIGHT:

It was pointed out that one atomic bomb on an arsenal would not be much different from the effect caused by any Air Corps strike of present dimensions. However, Dr. Oppenheimer stated that the visual effect of an atomic bombing would be tremendous. It would be accompanied by a brilliant luminescence which would rise to a height of 10,000 to 20,000 feet. The neutron effect of the explosion would be dangerous to life for a radius of at least two-thirds of a mile.

After much discussion concerning various types of targets and the effects to be produced, the Secretary expressed the conclusion, on which there was general agreement, that we could not give the Japanese any warning; that we could not concentrate on a civilian area; but that we should seek to make a profound psychological impression on as many of the inhabitants as possible. At the suggestion of Dr. Conant the Secretary agreed that the most desirable target would be a vital war plant employing a large number of workers and closely surrounded by workers' houses.

There was some discussion of the desirability of attempting several strikes at the same time. Dr. Oppenheimer's judgment was that several strikes would be feasible. General Groves, however, expressed doubt about this proposal and pointed out the following objections: (1) We would lose the advantage of gaining additional knowledge concerning the weapon at each successive bombing; (2) such a program would require a rush job on the part of those assembling the bombs and might, therefore, be ineffective; (3) the effect would not be sufficiently distinct from our regular Air Force bombing program.

IX. HANDLING OF UNDESIRABLE SCIENTISTS:

General Groves stated that the program has been plagued since its inception by the presence of certain scientists of doubtful discretion and uncertain loyalty. It was agreed that nothing could be done about dismissing these men until after the bomb has actually been used or, at best, until after the test has been made. After some publicity concerning the weapon was out, steps should be taken to sever these scientists from the program and to proceed with a general weeding out of personnel no longer needed.

x. CHICAGO GROUPS:

Dr. A. H. Compton outlined briefly the nature and size of the Chicago program. In line with directives from General Groves it was intended to limit the operations at Chicago to those useful in the prosecution of this war. Its activities fell into the following categories:

1. Aid to the Hanford project on plutonium development.
2. Aid to the Santa Fe group.
3. Research on a thorium-using pile.
4. Preliminary investigations of the extension of uranium piles.
5. Studies of the health of personnel working with these materials.

It was pointed out that programs 3 and 4 above did not bear directly on current war use, but that they comprised only about 20 per cent of the work being carried on in Chicago and that it was considered desirable in terms of future development to continue this work.

It was the consensus of the meeting that the Committee should lean on the recommendations of Drs. Conant and Bush as to what should be done with the Chicago group. Dr. Bush, as seconded by Dr. Conant, recommended that the present programs, including Chicago, should be continued at their present levels until the end of the war. It was agreed that this recommendation should be transmitted to the Secretary of War.

XI. POSITION OF THE SCIENTIFIC PANEL:

Mr. Harrison stated that the Scientific Panel had been called in at the suggestion of Drs. Bush and Conant and with the heartiest approval of all members of the Committee. It was considered a continuing Panel which was free to present its views to the Committee at any time. The Committee was particularly anxious to secure from the scientists their ideas of just what sort of organization should be established to direct and control this field. The Committee requested the Panel to prepare as speedily as possible a draft of their views on this subject. In this connection Dr. Bush pointed out that there would be no need at this time in drawing up a draft of an organization in this field to consider relationships with the Research Board for National Security. Dr. Karl T. Compton suggested that the organization could be tied in later to the Research Board for National Security through its section on nuclear physics.

The question was raised as to what the scientists might tell their people about the Interim Committee and their having been called before it. It was agreed that the four scientists should feel free to tell their people that an Interim Committee appointed by the Secretary of War and with the Secretary of War as Chairman had been established to deal specifically with the problems of control, organization, legislation, and publicity. The identity of the members of the Committee should not be divulged. The scientists should be permitted to explain that they had met with this Committee and had been given complete freedom to present their views on any phase of the subject. The impression should definitely be left with their people that the Government was taking a most active interest in this project.

XII. NEXT MEETING:

The next meeting of the Committee was scheduled for Friday, 1 June 1945, at 11:00 A.M. in the office of the Secretary of War. The purpose of this meeting was to secure the views of four representatives from industry.

The meeting adjourned at 4:15 P.M.

[signed]   R. GORDON ARNESON
2nd Lieutenant, A.U.S
Secretary

Manhattan Engineer District Records, Harrison-Bundy files, folder no. 100, National Archives, Washington, D.C.

M

*Science Panel: Recommendations
on the Immediate Use of Nuclear Weapons, June 16, 1945*

TOP SECRET

RECOMMENDATIONS ON THE IMMEDIATE USE OF NUCLEAR WEAPONS

June 16, 1945

You have asked us to comment on the initial use of the new weapon. This use, in our opinion, should be such as to promote a satisfactory adjustment of our international relations. At the same time, we recognize our obligation to our nation to use the weapons to help save American lives in the Japanese war.

(1) To accomplish these ends we recommend that before the weapons are used not only Britain, but also Russia, France, and China be advised that we have made considerable progress in our work on atomic weapons, that these may be ready to use during the present war, and that we would welcome suggestions as to how we can cooperate in making this development contribute to improved international relations.

(2) The opinions of our scientific colleagues on the initial use of these weapons are not unanimous: they range from the proposal of a purely technical demonstration to that of the military application best designed to induce surrender. Those who advocate a purely technical demonstration would wish to outlaw the use of atomic weapons, and have feared that if we use the weapons now our position in future negotiations will be prejudiced. Others emphasize the opportunity of saving American lives by immediate military use, and believe that such use will improve the international prospects, in that they are more concerned with the prevention of war than with the elimination of this specific weapon. We find

ourselves closer to these latter views; we can propose no technical demonstration likely to bring an end to the war; we see no acceptable
alternative to direct military use.

(3) With regard to these general aspects of the use of atomic energy,
it is clear that we, as scientific men, have no proprietary rights. It is true
that we are among the few citizens who have had occasion to give
thoughtful consideration to these problems during the past few years. We
have, however, no claim to special competence in solving the political,
social, and military problems which are presented by the advent of
atomic power.

A. H. Compton
E. O. Lawrence
J. R. Oppenheimer
E. Fermi
[signed] J. R. Oppenheimer
For the Panel

*Manhattan Engineer District Records, Harrison-Bundy files, folder no. 76,
National Archives, Washington, D.C.*

N
_____

Stimson Is Informed of Scientists' Concerns, June 26, 1945

WAR DEPARTMENT
WASHINGTON

26 June 1945
TOP SECRET

MEMORANDUM FOR THE SECRETARY OF WAR:

Many of the scientists who have been working on S-1 have expressed
considerable concern about the future dangers of the development of
atomic power. Some are fearful that no safe system of international control can be established. They, therefore, envisage the possibility of an
armament race that may threaten civilization.

One group of scientists, working in the Chicago Laboratories, urges
that we should not make use of the bomb, so nearly completed, against
any enemy country at this time. They feel that to do so might sacrifice
our whole moral position and thus make it more difficult for us to be
the leaders in proposing or enforcing any system of international control
designed to make this tremendous force an influence towards the mainte-
nance of world peace rather than an uncontrollable weapon of war.

This anonymous statement of the Chicago scientists was submitted for
comment to the Panel of Scientists appointed by the Interim Committee.
Their answer was that they saw no acceptable alternative to direct mili-

tary use since they believe that such use would be an obvious means of saving American lives and shortening the war.

It is interesting that practically all of the scientists, including those on the panel, feel great concern for the future if atomic power is not controlled through some effective international mechanism. Accordingly, most of them believe that one of the effective steps in establishing such a control is the assurance that, after this war is over, there shall be a free interchange of scientific opinion throughout the world supplemented, if possible, by some system of inspection. This they admit is a problem of the future. In the meantime, however, they feel that we must, even before actual use, briefly advise the Russians of our progress.

This matter of notice to the Russians was made a subject of thorough discussion at the last meeting of the Interim Committee on June 21. It was unanimously agreed that in view of the importance of securing an effective future control, and in view of the fact that most of the story, other than production secrets, will become known in _____ [sic] in any event, there would be considerable advantage, if a suitable opportunity arises at the "Big Three" meeting, in having the President advise the Russians simply that we are working intensely on this weapon and that, if we succeed as we think we will, we plan to use it against the enemy. Such a statement might well be supplemented by the statement that in the future, after the war, we would expect to discuss the matter further with a view to insuring that this means of warfare will become a substantial aid in preserving the peace of the world rather than a weapon of terror and destruction.

It was felt by the Committee that if the Russians should ask for more details now rather than later or if they should raise questions as to time-tables, methods of production, etc., they should be told that we are not yet ready to discuss the subject beyond the simple statement suggested above. Our purpose is merely to let them know that we did not wish to proceed with actual use without giving them prior information that we intend to do so. Not to give them this prior information at the time of the "Big Three" Conference and within a few weeks thereafter to use the weapon and to make fairly complete statements to the world about its history and development, might well make it impossible ever to enlist Russian cooperation in the set-up of future international controls over this new power.

It was agreed by the Committee that in view of the provisions of the Quebec Agreement it would be desirable to discuss this whole aspect of the question with the Prime Minister in advance of the "Big Three" Conference.

[signed] GEORGE L. HARRISON

Manhattan Engineer District Records, Harrison-Bundy files, folder no. 77, National Archives, Washington, D.C.

O
————————

Ralph Bard's Dissent

WAR DEPARTMENT

WASHINGTON

28 June 1945

TOP SECRET

MEMORANDUM FOR THE SECRETARY OF WAR:

In the last few days I have had several talks with Ralph Bard about the use of S-1. He has just sent me a memorandum which he explained on the telephone is merely an effort to think out loud and not to make any specific recommendations. In view of the fact, however, that the Interim Committee has previously voted to use the bomb as soon as possible and without notice, I thought it only fair to let you know that Mr. Bard himself is now thinking along the line of the memorandum which is enclosed.

[signed] GEORGE L. HARRISON

Bard's memorandum follows:

TOP SECRET

MEMORANDUM ON THE USE OF S-1 BOMB:

Ever since I have been in touch with this program I have had a feeling that before the bomb is actually used against Japan that Japan should have some preliminary warning for say two or three days in advance of use. The position of the United States as a great humanitarian nation and the fair play attitude of our people generally is responsible in the main for this feeling.

During recent weeks I have also had the feeling very definitely that the Japanese government may be searching for some opportunity which they could use as a medium of surrender. Following the three-power conference emissaries from this country could contact representatives from Japan somewhere on the China Coast and make representations with regard to Russia's position and at the same time give them some information regarding the proposed use of atomic power, together with whatever assurances the President might care to make with regard to the Emperor of Japan and the treatment of the Japanese nation following unconditional surrender. It seems quite possible to me that this presents the opportunity which the Japanese are looking for.

I don't see that we have anything in particular to lose in following such a program. The stakes are so tremendous that it is my opinion very real consideration should be given to some plan of this kind. I do not believe under present circumstances existing that there is anyone in this country whose evaluation of the chances of the success of such a program is worth a great deal. The only way to find out is to try it out.

[signed] RALPH A. BARD

27 June 1945

Manhattan Engineer District Records, Harrison-Bundy files, folder no. 77, National Archives, Washington, D.C.

P

Groves: Report on Alamogordo Atomic Bomb Test

18 July 1945

TOP SECRET

MEMORANDUM FOR THE SECRETARY OF WAR.

SUBJECT: The Test.

1. This is not a concise, formal military report but an attempt to recite what I would have told you if you had been here on my return from New Mexico.

2. At 0530, 16 July 1945, in a remote section of the Alamogordo Air Base, New Mexico, the first full scale test was made of the implosion type atomic fission bomb. For the first time in history there was a nuclear explosion. And what an explosion! It resulted from the atomic fission of about 13-½ pounds of plutonium which was compressed by the detonation of a surrounding sphere of some 5000 pounds of high explosives. The bomb was not dropped from an airplane but was exploded on a platform on top of a 100-foot high steel tower.

3. The test was successful beyond the most optimistic expectations of anyone. Based on the data which it has been possible to work up to date, I estimate the energy generated to be in excess of the equivalent of 15,000 to 20,000 tons of TNT; and this is a conservative estimate. Data based on measurements which we have not yet been able to reconcile would make the energy release several times the conservative figure. There were tremendous blast effects. For a brief period there was a lighting effect within a radius of 20 miles equal to several suns in midday; a huge ball of fire was formed which lasted for several seconds. This ball mushroomed and rose to a height of over ten thousand feet before it dimmed. The light from the explosion was seen clearly at Albuquerque, Santa Fe, Silver City, El Paso and other points generally to about 180 miles away. The sound was heard to the same distance in a few instances but generally to about 100 miles. Only a few windows were broken although one was some 125 miles away. A massive cloud was formed which surged

and billowed upward with tremendous power, reaching the substratosphere at an elevation of 41,000 feet, 36,000 feet above the ground, in about five minutes, breaking without interruption through a temperature inversion at 17,000 feet which most of the scientists thought would stop it. Two supplementary explosions occurred in the cloud shortly after the main explosion. The cloud contained several thousand tons of dust picked up from the ground and a considerable amount of iron in the gaseous form. Our present thought is that this iron ignited when it mixed with the oxygen in the air to cause these supplementary explosions. Huge concentrations of highly radioactive materials resulted from the fission and were contained in this cloud.

4. A crater from which all vegetation had vanished, with a diameter of 1200 feet and a slight slope toward the center, was formed. In the center was a shallow bowl 130 feet in diameter and 6 feet in depth. The material within the crater was deeply pulverized dirt. The material within the outer circle is greenish and can be distinctly seen from as much as 5 miles away. The steel from the tower was evaporated. 1500 feet away there was a four-inch iron pipe 16 feet high set in concrete and strongly guyed. It disappeared completely.

5. One-half mile from the explosion there was a massive steel test cylinder weighing 220 tons. The base of the cylinder was solidly encased in concrete. Surrounding the cylinder was a strong steel tower 70 feet high, firmly anchored to concrete foundations. This tower is comparable to a steel building bay that would be found in typical 15 or 20 story skyscraper or in warehouse construction. Forty tons of steel were used to fabricate the tower which was 70 feet high, the height of a six story building. The cross bracing was much stronger than that normally used in ordinary steel construction. The absence of the solid walls of a building gave the blast a much less effective surface to push against. The blast tore the tower from its foundations, twisted it, ripped it apart and left it flat on the ground. The effects on the tower indicate that, at that distance, unshielded permanent steel and masonry buildings would have been destroyed. I no longer consider the Pentagon a safe shelter from such a bomb. Enclosed are a sketch showing the tower before the explosion and a telephotograph showing what it looked like afterwards. None of us had expected it to be damaged.

6. The cloud traveled to a great height first in the form of a ball, then mushroomed, then changed into a long trailing chimney-shaped column and finally was sent in several directions by the variable winds at the different elevations. It deposited its dust and radioactive materials over a wide area. It was followed and monitored by medical doctors and scientists with instruments to check its radioactive effects. While here and there the activity on the ground was fairly high, at no place did it reach a concentration which required evacuation of the population. Radioactive material in small quantities was located as much as 120 miles away. The measurements are being continued in order to have adequate

data with which to protect the Government's interests in case of future claims. For a few hours I was none too comfortable about the situation.

7. For distances as much as 200 miles away, observers were stationed to check on blast effects, property damage, radioactivity and reactions of the population. While complete reports have not yet been received, I now know that no persons were injured nor was there any real property damage outside our Government area. As soon as all the voluminous data can be checked and correlated, full technical studies will be possible.

8. Our long range weather predictions had indicated that we could expect weather favorable for our tests beginning on the morning of the 17th and continuing for four days. This was almost a certainty if we were to believe our long range forecasters. The prediction for the morning of the 16th was not so certain but there was about an 80% chance of the conditions being suitable. During the night there were thunder storms with lightning flashes all over the area. The test had been originally set for 0400 hours and all the night through, because of the bad weather, there were urgings from many of the scientists to postpone the test. Such a delay might well have had crippling results due to mechanical difficulties in our complicated test set-up. Fortunately, we disregarded the urgings. We held firm and waited the night through hoping for suitable weather. We had to delay an hour and a half, to 0530, before we could fire. This was 30 minutes before sunrise.

9. Because of bad weather, our two B-29 observation airplanes were unable to take off as scheduled from Kirtland Field at Albuquerque and when they finally did get off, they found it impossible to get over the target because of the heavy clouds and the thunder storms. Certain desired observations could not be made and while the people in the airplanes saw the explosion from a distance, they were not as close as they will be in action. We still have no reason to anticipate the loss of our plane in an actual operation although we cannot guarantee safety.

10. Just before 1100 the news stories from all over the state started to flow into the Albuquerque Associated Press. I then directed the issuance by the Commanding Officer, Alamogordo Air Base of a news release as shown on the inclosure. With the assistance of the Office of Censorship we were able to limit the news stories to the approved release supplemented in the local papers by brief stories from the many eyewitnesses not connected with our project. One of these was a blind woman who saw the light.

11. Brigadier General Thomas F. Farrell was at the control shelter located 10,000 yards south of the point of explosion. His impressions are given below:

"The scene inside the shelter was dramatic beyond words. In and around the shelter were some twenty-odd people concerned with last minute arrangements prior to firing the shot. Included were: Dr. Oppenheimer, the Director who had borne the great scientific burden of developing the weapon from the raw materials made in Tennessee and

Washington and a dozen of his key scientists—Dr. Kistiakowsky, who developed the highly special explosives; Dr. Bainbridge, who supervised all the detailed arrangements for the test; Dr. Hubbard, the weather expert, and several others. Besides these, there were a handful of soldiers, two or three Army officers and one Naval officer. The shelter was cluttered with a great variety of instruments and radios.

"For some hectic two hours preceding the blast, General Groves stayed with the Director, walking with him and steadying his tense excitement. Every time the Director would be about to explode because of some untoward happening, General Groves would take him off and walk with him in the rain, counselling with him and reassuring him that everything would be all right. At twenty minutes before zero hour, General Groves left for his station at the base camp, first because it provided a better observation point and second, because of our rule that he and I must not be together in situations where there is an element of danger, which existed at both points.

"Just after General Groves left, announcements began to be broadcast of the interval remaining before the blast. They were sent by radio to the other groups participating in and observing the test. As the time interval grew smaller and changed from minutes to seconds, the tension increased by leaps and bounds. Everyone in that room knew the awful potentialities of the thing that they thought was about to happen. The scientists felt that their figuring must be right and that the bomb had to go off but there was in everyone's mind a strong measure of doubt. The feeling of many could be expressed by "Lord, I believe; help Thou mine unbelief." We were reaching into the unknown and we did not know what might come of it. It can be safely said that most of those present— Christian, Jew and Atheist—were praying and praying harder than they had ever prayed before. If the shot were successful, it was a justification of the several years of intensive effort of tens of thousands of people— statesmen, scientists, engineers, manufacturers, soldiers, and many others in every walk of life.

"In that brief instant in the remote New Mexico desert the tremendous effort of the brains and brawn of all these people came suddenly and startlingly to the fullest fruition. Dr. Oppenheimer, on whom had rested a very heavy burden, grew tenser as the last seconds ticked off. He scarcely breathed. He held on to a post to steady himself. For the last few seconds, he stared directly ahead and then when the announcer shouted "Now!" and there came this tremendous burst of light followed shortly thereafter by the deep growling roar of the explosion, his face relaxed into an expression of tremendous relief. Several of the observers standing back of the shelter to watch the lighting effects were knocked flat by the blast.

"The tension in the room let up and all started congratulating each other. Everyone sensed "This is it!" No matter what might happen now all knew that the impossible scientific job had been done. Atomic fission would no longer be hidden in the cloisters of the theoretical physicists' dreams. It was almost full grown at birth. It was a great new force to be used for good or for evil. There was a feeling in that shelter that those concerned with its nativity should dedicate their lives to the mission that it would always be used for good and never for evil.

"Dr. Kistiakowsky, the impulsive Russian, threw his arms around Dr. Oppenheimer and embraced him with shouts of glee. Others were equally enthusiastic. All the pent-up emotions were released in those few minutes and all seemed to sense immediately that the explosion had far exceeded the most optimistic expectations and wildest hopes of the scientists. All seemed to feel that they had been present at the birth of a new age— The Age of Atomic Energy—and felt their profound responsibility to help in guiding into right channels the tremendous forces which had been unlocked for the first time in history.

"As to the present war, there was a feeling that no matter what else might happen, we now had the means to insure its speedy conclusion and save thousands of American lives. As to the future, there had been brought into being something big and something new that would prove to be immeasurably more important than the discovery of electricity or any of the other great discoveries which have so affected our existence.

"The effects could well be called unprecedented, magnificent, beautiful, stupendous and terrifying. No man-made phenomenon of such tremendous power had ever occurred before. The lighting effects beggared description. The whole country was lighted by a searing light with the intensity many times that of the midday sun. It was golden, purple, violet, gray and blue. It lighted every peak, crevasse and ridge of the nearby mountain range with a clarity and beauty that cannot be described but must be seen to be imagined. It was that beauty the great poets dream about but describe most poorly and inadequately. Thirty seconds after the explosion came first, the air blast pressing hard against the people and things, to be followed almost immediately by the strong, sustained, awesome roar which warned of doomsday and made us feel that we puny things were blasphemous to dare tamper with the forces heretofore reserved to The Almighty. Words are inadequate tools for the job of acquainting those not present with the physical, mental and psychological effects. It had to be witnessed to be realized."

12. My impressions of the night's high points follow:

After about an hours sleep I got up at 0100 and from that time on until about five I was with Dr. Oppenheimer constantly. Naturally he was nervous, although his mind was working at its usual extraordinary efficiency. I devoted my entire attention to shielding him from the excited and generally faulty advice of his assistants who were more than disturbed by their excitement and the uncertain weather conditions. By 0330 we decided that we could probably fire at 0530. By 0400 the rain had stopped but the sky was heavily overcast. Our decision became firmer as time went on. During most of those hours the two of us journeyed from the control house out into the darkness to look at the stars and to assure each other that the one or two visible stars were becoming brighter. At 0510 I left Dr. Oppenheimer and returned to the main observation point which was 17,000 yards from the point of explosion. In accordance with our orders I found all personnel not otherwise occupied massed on a bit of high ground.

At about two minutes of the scheduled firing time all persons lay face down with their feet pointing towards the explosion. As the remaining time was called from the loud speaker from the 10,000 yard control station there was complete silence. Dr. Conant said he had never imagined seconds could be so long. Most of the individuals in accordance with orders shielded their eyes in one way or another. There was then this burst of light of a brilliance beyond any comparison. We all rolled over and looked through dark glasses at the ball of fire. About forty seconds later came the shock wave followed by the sound, neither of which seemed startling after our complete astonishment at the extraordinary lighting intensity. Dr. Conant reached over and we shook hands in mutual congratulations. Dr. Bush, who was on the other side of me, did likewise. The feeling of the entire assembly was similar to that described by General Farrell, with even the uninitiated feeling profound awe. Drs. Conant and Bush and myself were struck by an even stronger feeling that the faith of those who had been responsible for the initiation and the carrying on of this herculean project had been justified. I personally thought of Blondin crossing Niagara Falls on his tight rope, only to me this tight rope had lasted for almost three years[,] and of my repeated confident-appearing assurances that such a thing was possible and that we would do it.

13. A large group of observers were stationed at a point about 27 miles north of the point of explosion. Attached is a memorandum written shortly after the explosion by Dr. E. O. Lawrence which may be of interest.

14. While General Farrell was waiting about midnight for a commercial airplane to Washington at Albuquerque—120 miles away from the site—he overheard several airport employees discussing their reaction to the blast. One said that he was out on the parking apron; it was quite dark; then the whole southern sky was lighted as though by a bright sun; the light lasted several seconds. Another remarked that if a few exploding bombs could have such an effect, it must be terrible to have them drop on a city.

15. My liaison officer at the Alamogordo Air Base, 60 miles away, made the following report:

"There was a blinding flash of light that lighted the entire northwestern sky. In the center of the flash, there appeared to be a huge billow of smoke. The original flash lasted approximately 10 to 15 seconds. As the first flash died down, there arose in the approximate center of where the original flash had occurred an enormous ball of what appeared to be fire and closely resembled a rising sun that was three-fourths above a mountain. The ball of fire lasted approximately 15 seconds, then died down and the sky resumed an almost normal appearance.

"Almost immediately, a third, but much smaller, flash and billow of smoke of a whiteish-orange color appeared in the sky, again lighting the sky for approximately 4 seconds. At the time of the original flash, the field was lighted well enough so that a newspaper could easily have been read. The second and third flashes were of much lesser intensity.

"We were in a glass-enclosed control tower some 70 feet above the ground and felt no concussion or air compression. There was no noticeable earth tremor although reports overheard at the Field during the following 24 hours indicated that some believed that they had both heard the explosion and felt some earth tremor."

16. I have not written a separate report for General Marshall as I feel you will want to show this to him. I have informed the necessary people here of our results. Lord Halifax after discussion with Mr. Harrison and myself stated that he was not sending a full report to his government at this time. I informed him that I was sending this to you and that you might wish to show it to the proper British representatives.

17. We are all fully conscious that our real goal is still before us. The battle test is what counts in the war with Japan.

18. May I express my deep personal appreciation for your congratulatory cable to us and for the support and confidence which I have received from you ever since I have had this work under my charge.

19. I know that Colonel Kyle will guard these papers with his customary extraordinary care.

L. R. GROVES,
Major General, USA.

4 Inclosures:
   Sketch
   Picture
   News Release
   Statement by E. O. Lawrence

Manhattan Engineer District Records, Top Secret of Special Interest to General Groves files, folder no. 4, Trinity Test, National Archives, Washington, D.C.

Q
——————

*Byrnes Sees International Control
as Impractical for the Time Being, August 1945*

18 August 1945

MEMORANDUM FOR THE RECORD:

I showed the attached letter* and memorandum to Secretary Byrnes

* Oppenheimer, 17 August. [handwritten]

and emphasized that the subject matter in Paragraph 1B was a matter which would probably require early consideration and decision by the Administration, especially in view of the Oppenheimer letter addressed to Secretary Stimson and dated August ly [sic] which he read. He was so interested in it that he asked me to leave a copy with him; this I did. Secretary Byrnes was definitely of the opinion that it would be difficult to do anything on the international level at the present time and that in his opinion we should continue the Manhattan Project with full force, at least until Congress has acted on the proposed Bill. He also said that we should continue our efforts and negotiations in behalf of the Combined Development Trust. In his opinion the whole situation justifies and requires a continuation of all our efforts on all fronts to keep ahead of the race. For that reason, he said that he would ask the President to sign a memorandum which Mr. Marbury and General Groves are to prepare requesting Mr. Snyder, Director of Mobilization, formally to approve a continuation of all necessary expenditures by the Manhattan District or by the Combined Development Trust.

Secretary Byrnes felt so strongly about all of this that he requested me to tell Dr. Oppenheimer for the time being his proposal about an international agreement was not practical and that he and the rest of the gang should pursue their work full force. I told Secretary Byrnes that I understood from Dr. Oppenheimer the scientists prefer not to do that (superbomb) unless ordered or directed to do so by the Government on the grounds of national policy. I thought, however, work in the Manhattan District could proceed the way he wants in improving present techniques without raising the question of the "super" at least until after Congress has acted on our proposed Bill.

GEORGE L. HARRISON

Manhattan Engineer District Records, Harrison-Bundy files, folder no. 98, National Archives, Washington, D.C.

INDEX

Abelson, Philip, 14
Acheson, Dean, 229
Adams, Henry, 238
Agreement and Declaration of
   Trust (Anglo-American), 104–5
aide-mémoire (Roosevelt-Chur-
   chill), 109–11, 112, 144
Alamogordo (N.M.), 206, 222–3,
   225, 231
Allison, Samuel K., 50, 118 n.
Alvarez, L., 55
Anderson, Sir John, 70, 87 n., 98,
   106, 132, 134; quoted, 76, 77, 82,
   83, 84, 111, 216
Anglo-American atomic partnership, 7, 68–88, 106, 112, 135, 138;
   new policy in, 71–6; postwar extension of, 38, 90, 111, 113, 124,
   126
Anglo-American international police force, 88
Anglo-Soviet exchange of scientific
   information, 100, 101 n.
anti-aircraft, anti-submarine weapons, 40, 45
anti-Soviet feelings, 7, 62, 63, 82–3,
   104, 147, 173, 180, 182, 226
Argentina, 182
Association for Scientific Collaboration, 21 n.
Atlantic Conference, 88
atomic arms race, 6, 90, 94, 95, 105,
   107, 112, 125, 127, 162, 195, 201,
   202, 211, 227–8
atomic bomb: administration of
   program to make, 42–6; Americans killed by, 232 n., 234; as bargaining agent, 5, 7, 112, 166–7,
   187, 193; case against surprise attack with, 211; costs of develop-

ing, 42, 138, 202; domestic reactions to the use of, 199–200;
dropped on Japan, 229–37; effect
of, on moral leadership, 131; as
essential part of war effort, 5; explosive force of, 208, 231–2; impact of, on diplomacy, 4, 5, 6,
188, 190, 191–2; and moral questions, 40, 195, 197, 218 n.; overall
effect of, 237–8; and personnel
employed, 42, 53–5; postwar significance of, 116, 161–4; pressure
of speed in developing, 41, 44, 47,
48, 52, 70; problem of informing
allies about, 100, 101, 102, 104,
131, 132–3, 135–6, 214–15, 227;
problem of revealing to public,
118–19; psychological effect of,
212; question of use of, against
Japan, 111, 123, 128, 144, 194, 195,
196–7, 198, 199, 200, 202–9, 210–
16; reasons for use against Japan
rather than Germany, 209 n.;
testing of, 186, 189, 191, 206, 222–
3, 225, 231; time schedule for
producing and using, 71, 76, 133,
145, 231–2, 233–4; use of, to assure
abolition of war, 200; and weapons technology, 126–7, 200, 205;
and world peace, 168, 201; see
also international control; Manhattan Project; nuclear research;
nuclear weapons technology
atomic diplomacy, 3, 4, 8, 89, 90,
92–8, 193–4, 195–202, 207, 220,
230, 237–8; defined, 191 n.
Atomic Energy Authority (British), 34
Atomic Energy Commission, 33, 58
Atomic Energy Planning Board, 43

atomic energy policy, 4, 5, 6, 7, 115,
195; and benefit to humanity, 92,
213; criteria of, 72, 83–4, 216;
and larger policy issues, 67; and
opposition to international control, 9; postwar, 63, 67, 76–84,
104, 206
atomic war, danger of, 162

Bacher, R. F., 55, 56 n.
Badoglio government (Italy), 173
Bard, Ralph A., 169, 217
Barkley, Alben, 149
Bartky, Walter, 118 n., 200
Baruch Plan, 97
Battle of the Bulge, 133
Baxter, James P., 40
Becquerel, Henri, 14
Bethe, Hans, 48, 49, 50, 57
Bohlen, Charles E., 154, 157, 158;
quoted, 172 n., 227
Bohr, Aage, 93, 99, 100, 105
Bohr, Niels, 17, 103, 105, 112, 122,
127, 130, 135, 214; and Bush, 167–
8; and Churchill, 6, 7, 106, 107–8,
110, 111; and the diplomatic
problem, 121, 195, 196, 216; and
Frankfurter, 99, 108; and interna-
tional control of atomic energy,
6, 7, 90, 91–2, 94–8, 102; invited to
join Manhattan Project, 199; nuclear theory of, 15; quoted, 18,
91, 92, 93, 94, 97–8, 109 n., 195;
and Roosevelt, 6, 7, 96 n., 98 n.,
99, 108–9
Brest-Litovsk, 181
Bridgman, P. W., 115–16
Briggs, Lyman C., 28, 30, 32, 35, 43
Briggs Committee, 28, 29, 30, 32, 33,
37, 59, 199
Brissette (Navy flier), 232 n.
Britain: atomic energy research in,
34, 35, 36; future position of, 111,
113; and question of allowing
French access to restricted data,

133 n.; relations with Soviet Union, 100, 101 n., 182; see also
Agreement and Declaration of
Trust; aide-mémoire; Anglo-
American atomic partnership
Brown, Constantine, 173 n.
Brown, Walter, 227
Bundy, Harvey, 43, 87 n., 130, 137,
144 n., 150, 161, 167, 168, 170, 204
Bush, Vannevar, 30–2, 33, 39, 48, 50,
53, 56–7, 67, 69, 70, 74, 83, 88, 116,
163, 169, 207, 237; and Bohr, 167–
8; as director of OSRD, 31, 37,
42–6; and international control,
136–7; and postwar policy, 38, 84,
85, 91, 115, 121–3, 125, 127–8,
129–30; and question of use of
atomic bomb, 144–5, 195; quoted,
36, 44, 45, 47, 70, 71, 75–6, 81, 82,
87, 90, 113, 123, 124, 125, 128, 238;
and restricted-interchange policy, 78, 79, 80, 81, 82; and Soviet-
American relations, 124, 126; and
Szilard, 117
Byrnes, James F., 138, 169–70, 184,
187, 188 n., 206–7, 210, 211, 220,
224, 225, 226, 229; quoted, 194,
200, 202, 209, 238; and Szilard,
200, 201–2

California, University of, 71, 102–3
Canada: French scientists in,
133 n., 134, 135; heavy-water
work in, 74–5; uranium from, 75
Chadwick, James, 16, 81 n.
chain reaction, 20, 21–4, 35, 36, 51
Cherwell, Lord, 82, 106, 107, 112,
122, 124; quoted, 61, 83, 87, 111
Chiang Kai-shek, 189
Chicago, University of, 47, 49, 52–3,
116, 118, 210
China, 189
Churchill, Winston: and Anglo-
American atomic partnership, 7,
38, 68, 69, 73, 78–85 passim, 90,

91, 135; anti-Soviet attitude of, 7, 82–3, 104, 180; and atomic diplomacy, use of, 68; and Big Three meeting, 184–5, 223, 227; and Bohr, 106–11 *passim*; on Far Eastern war, 191; at Hyde Park conference, 109–11, 112; and military use of atomic bomb, 123; quoted, 73, 83, 84, 108, 110, 111, 135–6, 152, 184–5, 224, 227; and Roosevelt, 68, 69, 78, 79, 84, 85, 86–7, 88, 104–5, 109–11, 112, 123, 124, 136, 144; and Stalin, 129, 170; and Truman, 152
Clayton, William L., 169, 178
cold war, 4, 8, 237–8
Columbia University, 21 *n.*, 23, 24 *n.*, 25, 29, 30, 33
Combined (U.S.-British-Canadian) Policy Committee, 43
commercial interests, postwar, 72, 79
Committee for the Scientific Survey of Air Warfare (British), 35
Communist cell (at Radiation Laboratory), 102–3
Communist Poles, *see* Lublin Poles
compartmentalization, 59–61, 116–17
Compton, Arthur H., 43, 47, 50, 52, 121, 169, 204, 205, 210; quoted, 119, 207, 213, 214
Compton, Karl T., 31, 32, 169
Conant, James B., 46, 47, 50, 67, 77, 79, 116, 169, 195, 200, 209, 213, 220, 237; and Anglo-American partnership, 70, 73, 81, 84, 88, 111, 115; and NDRC, 31, 32, 42; and OSRD, 37, 43, 44; and postwar policy, 121, 122, 124, 125, 126, 127–8, 129; quoted, 51, 54, 71, 72, 74, 75, 80, 81 *n.*, 117, 122, 213; and restricted-interchange policy, 78, 80; and scientists, 56, 57; and security regulations, 53, 55
Connelly, Matt, 200

Copenhagen, 93
Council for National Defense (World War I), 31
counterespionage, 60, 61, 62
Creutz, Edward, 48–9
Crowley, Leo, 177

Dale, Sir Henry, 106
Daniels, Farrington, 118 *n.*
Danish Committee for the Support of Fugitive Intellectuals and Scientists, 93
Davies, Joseph E., 134 *n.*, 165, 184, 224–5; quoted, 172, 173–4, 181, 182, 183, 224, 226; and Soviet-American relations, 171, 172–5, 178, 179–83
Deane, John R., 133, 134 *n.*
de Gaulle, Charles, 135, 136
Dempster, A. J., 118 *n.*
Dennison, Dr., 229 *n.*
Derry, J., 229 *n.*
de Silva, Peer, 63 *n.*
Divine, Robert A., 88, 89
Dumbarton Oaks Conference, 128
Dunn, James C., 135, 157, 158
du Pont Company, 51, 103

Early, Steve, 149
Eastman, E. D., 118 *n.*
economic leverage in diplomacy, 166, 173, 176, 187
Eden, Anthony, 180, 184, 185
Eichelberger, Clark, 88
Einstein, Albert, 15, 20, 26, 201; letter to Roosevelt by, 13, 27–8; quoted, 27, 29
emperor, institution of (Japan), 228–9, 235–7
England, *see* Britain

Far Eastern policy, 188, 189–90
Farrell, Thomas, 229 *n.*, 231

Fermi, Enrico, 14, 16, 17, 18, 22, 23, 24, 25, 29–30, 32, 33, 49, 51, 119, 169, 204, 213

fission, nuclear, 13, 14–15, 16, 127 *n.*, 205; and chain reaction, 24; fast-neutron, 51; military potential of, 13, 14–15, 16, 18, 20; plutonium and, 74

Forrestal, James, 139, 157, 158, 161

France, 132–3, 135–6

Franck, James, 49, 118 *n.*, 119, 121, 210, 212, 218

Franck Committee and Report, 210–13, 214–15

Frankfurter, Felix, 99, 103, 106, 108, 109 *n.*; 179–9; quoted, 99, 100, 195

Frisch, Otto, 16, 34, 69

Furer, Julius A., 45

fusion, nuclear, 15, 127 *n.*

gamma rays, 16

General Electric Company, 119

Germany: and Battle of the Bulge, 133; nuclear fission discovered in, 13, 14; and nuclear research, 18 *n.*, 32; question of atomic progress in, 19, 23, 26, 27, 37, 38, 47, 50, 69, 76; Soviet pact with, 183; surrender of, 165, 166, 175, 193

Gowing, Margaret, 87 *n.*, 101 *n.*

Great Britain, *see* Britain

Grew, Joseph C., 154, 166, 177, 185, 189, 225, 228; quoted, 176

Groves, Leslie R., 44, 46, 63, 105, 150, 161, 162, 237; and administration of Manhattan Project, 48, 58–63, 199; anti-Soviet attitude of, 62, 63; and bomb, testing and use, 145, 222, 230; at Interim Committee meetings, 204, 207, 208; quoted, 59, 60, 61, 62, 87, 223; and scientists, 60; security system of, 53, 55, 56, 57–8, 59,

132; and Szilard, 117, 210; in Top Policy Group, 42, 43, 133 *n.*

Hahn, Otto, 14, 16, 18

Halban, Hans von, Jr., 20 *n.*, 24 *n.*, 74, 135

Hanford (Wash.), 52

Harriman, Averell, 129, 153–8 *passim*, 166, 176, 177, 178, 184, 185 and *n.*, 187, 188, 224, 226

Harrison, George L., 43, 150, 161, 167, 169, 170, 213–14, 230

Harrison, Richard A., 113 *n.*

heavy water, 74–5

Heisenberg, Werner, 50

Hilberry, N., 118 *n.*

Hill, A. V., 35

Hirohito, Emperor, 235, 236–7

Hiroshima, 3, 62, 209, 232–3 and *n.*, 237, 238

Hogness, Thorfin R., 118 *n.*, 119

Hopkins, Harry, 78, 80, 113, 166, 171, 184, 186

Hull, Cordell, 184, 229

Hungary, 129

Hyde Park conference, 109–11, 112, 144

hydrogen bomb, 127, 200, 205

industrial development of atomic energy, 51, 52, 61, 116, 206

industrial scientists, 49

intelligence gathering, 50

Interim Committee, 169–70, 187, 188, 189, 202–9, 215–16

international control of atomic energy, 7, 74, 90, 91–8, 102, 103–4, 107, 108, 121–31, 136, 137, 138, 162, 163–4, 168, 200, 206, 210, 212, 216, 227–8

international inspection, 94, 138, 201

Irving, David, 18 *n.*
isolationism (U.S.), 19, 91
Italy, 173

Jackson, Andrew, 148
Jacobson, L. O., 118 *n.*
Japan: atomic bombing of, 229–37;
  democratization of, 228–9; proposed invasion of, 188; question
  of use of atomic bomb on, 111,
  123, 128, 144, 194–200 *passim*,
  202–9, 210–16; scientists' attempts
  to prevent bombing of, 53, 202;
  Soviet declaration of war on,
  233, 237; *see also* Hiroshima;
  Nagasaki
Jefferies, Zay (Jefferies Report),
  119–21
Jewett, Frank B., 31, 32
Johnson, Warren C., 118 *n.*
Joliot, Frédéric, 14, 22, 24, 25, 29,
  32, 132, 135

Kapitsa, Peter, 106, 110
Katyn Forest massacre, 181
Kellex (engineering firm), 61 and
  n.
King, Ernest J., 45, 157
King, Mackenzie, 83
Kissinger, Henry, 153
Knox, Frank, 45
Korea, 189, 226
Kowarski, L., 24 *n.*
Kuriles, 189
Kwantung army (Japanese), 233
Kyoto, 230, 231

Lansdale, John, Jr., 62
Latimer, Wendell M., 118 *n.*
Laurence, William L., 202–3
Lauritsen, C., 229 *n.*
Lawrence, Ernest O., 43, 63, 169,
  204, 206, 207, 213; quoted, 14,
  20 *n.*, 205

Leahy, William D., 157, 185, 226;
  quoted, 125 *n.*, 160
LeMay, Curtis E., 232
lend-lease, 176–8
Levine, Stanley, 232 *n.*
London Poles, 152, 181
Los Alamos (N.M.), 18 *n.*, 48, 52,
  57, 116; civilian and military
  phases at, 55; recruiting staff for,
  53–5
Lowen, Irving S., 117
Lublin Poles, 133, 154, 156, 157

MacLeish, Archibald, 229
Makins, Roger, 144 *n.*
Manchuria, 189, 226, 227, 233
Manhattan Project: administrative
  structure of, 42–6; costs of, 42,
  138, 202; directed by Groves, 48,
  58–63, 199; postwar implications
  of, 91; scientists and, 40, 41, 42,
  44–5, 46, 47; shift in orientation
  of, 51; and Soviet espionage, 62,
  90, 102–3, 106, 107, 112; *see also*
  atomic bomb
Marshall, George C., 37, 42, 43,
  87 *n.*, 137–8, 139, 140, 157, 158,
  169, 198, 204, 206, 226, 232
Massachusetts Institute of Technology (M.I.T.), 18 *n.*, 53
MAUD Committee (British), 35,
  36, 69
McCloy, John J., 130, 161, 189
McMillan, E. M., 55
Meitner, Lise, 16
Military Policy Committee (MPC),
  43, 44, 46, 72–6 *passim*
Molotov, V. M., 153, 156–9, 171,
  172, 181, 182, 183, 238
morale problems (of scientists), 52,
  54–5
moral issues (of bomb's development), 40, 131, 195, 197, 218 *n.*,
  231 *n.*
Morrison, Philip, 50, 52

Mulliken, Robert S., 118 *n.*, 119, 121
Munnecke, W. C., 118 *n.*
Murphree, E. V., 43

Nagasaki, 3, 62, 209, 233–4, 235, 237, 238
National Advisory Committee for Aeronautics, 31
National Defense Research Committee (NDRC), 30–7 *passim*, 42
national security, effect of atomic bomb on concept of, 96, 116, 127, 200–1
Navy Department (U.S.), 45, 46
neutrons, 16, 23, 24
Nielson, Bud, 106
Noddack, I., 15
nuclear raw materials, 201, 206
nuclear reaction, *see* chain reaction; fission; fusion
nuclear research, 13, 14, 17–20; consequences of, for America, 19–20; military potential of, 26, 27, 28; *see also* atomic energy policy
nuclear weapons technology, development of, 126–7, 200, 205; *see also* atomic bomb
Nye, Gerald P., 173 *n.*

Oak Ridge (Tenn.), 48, 52, 61
Office of Scientific Research and Development (OSRD), 31, 37, 42, 43
Oppenheimer, J. Robert, 9, 62, 169, 204–8 *passim*, 212, 213, 214, 217, 220, 222, 229 *n.*, 231; at Los Alamos, 47, 48, 53, 54–5, 61; quoted, 6, 54, 56, 61, 92, 116, 145, 213; security clearance of, 63
Oumansky, Constantine, 171 *n.*, 182

Page, Arthur W., 204
Parsons, William S., 229 *n.*, 231
Patterson, Robert P., 199
Pauley, Edwin, 226
peace: atomic bomb and, 168, 200, 201, 218; "police" approach to, 88–9; through international science, 93, 116, 167; through military power, 114
Pegram, G. B., 25
Peierls, Rudolph, 34, 69, 81 *n.*
Penny, W., 229 *n.*
plutonium, 36, 74
plutonium bomb, 231, 232
police force, international, 88–9
Polish question, 133, 139, 151–60, 161, 170, 171, 173, 181
Potsdam Conference, 167, 184–5, 186–7, 191, 193, 220, 221–8
Potsdam Declaration, 236, 237 *n.*
"Prospectus on Nucleonics, The" (Jefferies Report), 119–21
proximity fuse, 128
Purnell, W. R., 46

quantum theory, 92
Quebec Conference and Agreement, 68, 85–8, 133 *n.*, 215; second, 109

Rabi, I. I., 25, 55, 56 and *n.*, 58
Rabinowitch, Eugene, 120–1
radar research, 18 *n.*, 53, 68
radioactivity, 16, 34, 232, 233
Ramsey, Norman F., 18 *n.*, 229 *n.*, 233–4
Rome, 14–15
Roosevelt, Franklin D., 13, 171, 181, 182; and Anglo-American partnership, 38, 68, 69, 90, 124; and atomic advisers, 28, 73, 78, 87, 103, 115, 125, 126, 144; atomic energy policies of, 4, 5, 6, 7, 28, 32, 37, 39, 44, 46, 67–8, 73, 74, 76, 90, 115,

122–3; and Bohr, 108–9; caution
of, in moving toward war, 19;
and Churchill, 68, 69, 78, 79, 84–
8 *passim*, 104–5, 109–11, 112, 123,
124, 136, 144; concern of, for secrecy, 37–8, 57, 104, 132, 138–9;
and continuing support for Britain, 113; and criticism of compartmentalization, 117; death of,
8, 140, 143, 146; Einstein's letter
to, 13, 27–8; and Frankfurter,
100; and international control, 90,
100, 102, 103–4; and the isolationists, 91; mobilization of scientists
by, 30, 31; personal diplomacy of,
174; and the Polish question, 133;
and postwar plans, 89, 96, 101,
122–3; and question of telling
Russians about bomb, 100, 101,
102, 104; and question of using
bomb against Japan, 123, 128;
quoted, 31, 38, 39, 69–70, 78, 85,
133, 153 *n.*; and relations with Soviet Union, 8, 63, 96, 104, 112,
136; and Stalin, 139; at Yalta, 135
Root, Elihu, 150, 162
Royal Navy Air Force, 90–1
Rutherford, Ernest, 15, 16

Sachs, Alexander, 26–7, 32, 38, 131
San Francisco Conference, 149, 153,
157, 167, 170, 175, 182
Sato, Naotake, 233, 235
science: alliance between government and, 40; for all mankind,
109 *n.*, 115; automony in, 54, 55,
56, 57; and foundation for peace,
93, 116, 167; international collaboration in, 98, 137, 138, mobilization of, for war, 30, 31; role of, in
the world, 92–3; values of, 94, 97
Scientific Panel, 169, 204, 205, 213–
15
scientists: attempts of, to block
atomic bombing of Japan, 53,

202; émigré, 13, 18–25 *passim*, 29–
30, 34, 49, 93–4; freedoms of, 22;
industrial and university, 49; and
military restrictions, 41, 42, 47,
48–9, 52–3, 54–7, 58, 59–60, 115–
17; and policymaking, 17, 41–7
passim, 91, 116, 194, 210–11; postwar implications of work of, 115–
16, 117–21; protest of, at military
use of atomic weapons, 210; repercussions of Manhattan Project
among, 40, 41; responsibility of,
23, 48, 53, 92, 93, 95; and secrecy,
22, 94
scientists' movement, 58–60
second front (in Europe), 180, 181
secrecy, 5, 7, 22, 23–5, 37–8, 57, 68,
102, 104, 110, 118, 119, 135, 138,
145; national, and nuclear threat,
97; and question of Soviet cooperation, 130, 131; scientists' distrust of, 94
security, *see* national security
security system (Manhattan Project), 41, 44, 48, 55, 56–8, 62–3,
72, 132; compartmentalization in,
59–61; and policymaking, 63
Seeman, Col., 229 *n.*
Segrè, Emilio, 14, 15, 16
Sherwood, Robert E., 148
Smuts, Jan Christian, 106, 180
Smyth, Henry D., 118 *n.*, 122 *n.*
Social and Political Implications
Committee (Franck Committee),
210–13, 214–15
Soong, T. V., 191
Soviet-Polish treaty, 156
Soviet Union: American relations
with, 8, 124–31 *passim*, 134, 139,
140, 143, 151, 154, 156–60, 165,
170, 179, 180, 206–7, 238; Anglo-
Soviet scientific pact, 100, 101 *n.*;
atomic capability of, 237–8;
and atomic diplomacy, 5, 7, 68,
166, 216; Churchill's hostility to,
7, 82–3, 104, 180; Davies's anal-

Soviet Union (*cont'd*)
ysis of policy of, 180–3; espionage by, 62, 90, 102–3, 106, 107, 112; and international atomic energy control, 212, 215; lend-lease to, 176–8; as member of Grand Alliance, 7; nature of society in, 129, 130, 228; need for cooperation of, 116, 140, 163–4, 171, 174, 179, 184, 191; objectives of, 166, 193, 226; pact between Germany and, 183; and Polish question, 128, 139, 151–60 *passim*, 170, 173, 181; in postwar world, 79, 81, 91, 92, 96–7, 98, 112, 128, 135, 136; and Potsdam Conference, 224–8; and question of entry into war with Japan, 158, 165, 225–7; Roosevelt's attitude toward, 8, 63, 96, 104, 112, 136; and Roosevelt's death, 153; secret of atomic bomb withheld from, 131, 215, 227; and treatment of neighboring states, 155; Truman and, 170, 171, 172, 174; use of secret police by, 129; use of U.S. security system against, 41, 63; at war with Japan, 233, 237; *see also* anti-Soviet feelings

Spartanburg interview (Szilard-Byrnes), 200–2

Spedding, F. H., 118 *n.*

Stalin, Joseph, 109, 116, 135, 172 *n.*, 180, 182, 183, 184, 196, 221; and atomic diplomacy, 207; and Churchill, 129, 170; and international control, 227; and lend-lease, 176; and Polish question, 133, 151–60 *passim*, 170, 181; and Potsdam Conference, 186, 187; quoted, 153 *n.*, 227; and Roosevelt, 101, 102, 139, 143; and Truman, 8, 166, 172, 174, 183, 184, 187, 227

Standley, William, 181

State Department (U.S.), 130, 157, 173, 226

Stearns, J. C., 118 *n.*, 229 *n.*

Stern, Isaac, 63

Stettinius, Edward R., Jr., 133, 139, 151, 157, 158, 161, 170, 176, 178; quoted, 151, 154

Stimson, Henry L., 5, 37, 42–3, 67, 83, 87, 96, 97, 100, 115, 128, 130–1, 136, 139, 157, 158, 167, 168; and atomic diplomacy, 188–90, 191, 193, 194, 195, 196–9, 200; and atomic problems, 137–8, 140, 212, 220; and Bush, 45; and cooperation with Soviet Union, 143; and French scientists, 132, 133, 134; and Interim Committee, 169–70, 203–9 *passim*; and international control, 97, 125–6, 135, 228; and Japanese policy, 228–9, 230–1, 236–7; Kyoto rejected by, as bomb target, 230–1; and postwar problems, 161–4; quoted, 3, 4, 6, 72, 78, 101, 103, 126, 129, 130, 133–4, 136, 137, 140, 144 *n.*, 150, 161, 162–3, 169, 170, 187, 188 and *n.*, 190, 191, 197–8, 200, 213 and *n.*, 220, 223–4, 226, 228, 230–1, 236; and Truman, 150, 160–4

Stolper, Gustav, 26

Stone, Robert S., 118 *n.*, 119

Strassmann, Friedrich, 14, 16

Styer, W. D., 46

Suzuki, Kantaro, 236–7

Sweetser, Arthur, 88

Swing, Raymond, 200

Szilard, Leo, 14, 20–3, 24–30 *passim*, 32, 38, 47, 49, 50, 59, 210, 212, 220; and attempt to block military use of atomic bomb, 202; criticism by, 116–17; and international control, 117–18; protest petition of, 217–18 and *n.*; quoted, 20, 23, 24–5, 116, 117–18, 201, 202, 217; and Spartanburg interview with Byrnes, 200–2

Taft, Robert A., 177
Target Committee, 229–30
Teheran Conference, 88, 101, 182
Teller, Edward, 21, 24, 33, 48, 49, 217–19, 220; quoted, 217–18 and *n*.
Thomas, Charles A., 119
Thomson, G. P., 34, 35
Tito, Marshal, 180
Togo, Shigenori, 235
Tokyo fire raids, 208, 229
Tolman, Richard, 199, 229 *n*.
Top Policy Group, 42, 43, 72, 74, 76, 102, 145, 194
Trail Heavy Water Plant (Canada), 74–5
Trident conference, 84
Truman, Harry S., 6, 140, 143, 144, 212, 217, 220; and American-Soviet relations, 8, 154–6, 159–60, 165–6, 170, 171, 172, 174, 179–83; anti-Soviet bias of, 147; and atomic diplomacy, 193, 194; atomic legacy of, 145–6; character of, 147–8, 175, 176; Davies and, 179–83; delegation of authority by, 175, 177; first days as President, 8, 148–50, 153; and Japan, 231; and lend-lease policy, 176–8; and Molotov, 156–9, 182; and Polish question, 151–2, 154, 156, 157; at Potsdam, 167, 186–7, 221–8; quoted, 147, 148, 149, 152, 153, 155, 156, 159, 160, 170, 175, 199, 221, 222, 226, 227, 233; and Stalin, 8, 166, 172, 174, 183, 184, 187; and Stimson, 160–4
"trustee question," 139
Turkey, 226

unconditional surrender, 203, 225, 229, 233, 235, 236, 237
United Nations Charter, 137
United Nations Organization, 128, 139, 149, 159, 162, 170, 175, 182
uranium: chain reaction in, 21–4;

fission of, 14, 16, 34, 35, 36, 48, 51; sources of, 26, 38, 75, 105
uranium bomb, 36, 231, 232
Uranium (Briggs) Committee, 28, 29, 30, 32, 33, 37, 59, 199
Urey, Harold C., 30, 43, 74, 200

Vichy government (France), 173
Von Neumann, J., 229 *n*.

Waggoner, Walter H., 177
Wallace, Henry A., 37, 42, 43
war: atomic bomb an essential part of effort in, 5; cold, 4, 8, 237, 238; necessity of abolishing, 200; nuclear, danger of, 162; organizing scientists for, 44, 45
War Department (U.S.), 37, 38, 39, 42, 45, 47, 48–9, 52–3, 67, 71
Warner, J. C., 118 *n*.
Warsaw Provisional Government, 152, 154
Washington, George, 19
Watson, William W., 118 *n*.
Weisskopf, Victor, 24, 93
Wheeler, Burton K., 173 *n*.
Whitaker, M. D., 118 *n*.
Wigner, Eugene, 21, 24, 26, 30, 33, 118 *n*., 218; quoted, 25, 49
Wilmington (Del.), 51
Wilson, Sir Henry, 144 *n*.
Wilson, R. R., 229 *n*.
Winant, John G., 101

Yalta Conference and agreements, 104, 133, 135, 151–2, 153–4, 156, 158, 159, 174, 189
Yugoslavia, 160

Zinchenko, Counselor, 106
Zinn, Walter H., 23, 118 *n*.

A NOTE ABOUT THE AUTHOR

Martin Sherwin is a historian at Princeton University. He was born and raised in Brooklyn, received a B.A. from Dartmouth College, and a Ph.D. from the University of California, Los Angeles. After four years of teaching American history at the University of California, Berkeley, he joined the faculties of both the Peace Studies and Science, Technology and Society programs at Cornell University. In 1973 he went to Princeton, where he now resides with his wife and two children.

This book was set on the Linotype in Janson, a re-cutting made direct from type cast from matrices long thought to have been made by the Dutchman Anton Janson, who was a practicing type founder in Leipzig during the years 1668–87. However, it has been conclusively demonstrated that these types are actually the work of Nicholas Kis (1650–1702), a Hungarian, who most probably learned his trade from the master Dutch type founder Dirk Voskens. The type is an excellent example of the influential and sturdy Dutch types that prevailed in England up to the time William Caslon developed his own in-comparable designs from them.

The book was composed, printed, and bound
by American Book-Stratford Press, Inc.,
Saddle Brook, New Jersey.
Typography and binding design
by Camilla Filancia.